Biblical counseling should be a natural and vital component of discipleship within the covenant community that the Bible calls the body of Christ. It should also be a means of reaching out beyond the community to minister redemptive grace to the nations. This book, written by thirty-four committed biblical counselors, will equip a church to do both. I am happy to commend its widest reading and use.

Daniel L. Akin, President, Southeastern Baptist
Theological Seminary, Wake Forest, NC

In an age when too much of the care and cure of souls takes place outside the church, this book offers a clarion call to embed counseling ministry within local congregations. It provides not only the biblical-theological rationale for this interpersonal ministry of the Word, but it also draws upon the multi-faceted experiences of many authors to describe specifically what counseling looks like in the trenches of church life. Whether you are a pastor tasked with the shepherding of God's flock or a layperson who takes seriously the one-another passages of Scripture, you will be further motivated and equipped to be a conduit of God's care.

Michael R. Emlet, MDiv, MD, Faculty and Counselor,
the Christian Counseling and Educational
Foundation (CCEF); author of *CrossTalk*

To say there is a lot of trouble in the world today would be to state the obvious. Trouble is everywhere … but it's not just in the world "out there"; it's in the church "in here." The question facing every pastor is, "How can I possibly help all the people whose lives are overflowing with troubles, conflicts, emotional problems of every kind, and relational breakups?" This book will help provide you with answers. The Lord of the church has gifted us with all we need to minister to those within our walls who are suffering. The authors are seasoned, wise counselors, committed to the local church and to the sufficiency of the Word of the church's Lord. I highly recommend it.

Elyse Fitzpatrick, author of *Counsel from the Cross*

Biblical Counseling and the Church is packed with the wisdom of today's leaders in biblical counseling. This book will greatly assist in moving the care of souls out of the exclusive realm of the counseling office and into small groups and every aspect of church life! I am excited to watch as this book revolutionizes how we connect counseling and the church!

Julie Ganschow, Director of Reigning Grace Counseling Center;
author of *Seeing Depression Through the Eyes of Grace*

Since my first counseling class in seminary, I've aspired to preach like a counselor. Jesus preached as a counselor, and those who heard him felt like he knew everything about them. To apply the gospel—full of grace and truth—to the multifaceted brokenness in people's lives is the essence of Christian ministry. The authors of *Biblical Counseling and the Church* demonstrate that gospel-centric counseling is not just for a select few, but the responsibility of every believer. If you want to help people progress in the gospel in meaningful ways, you need to read this book.

J. D. Greear, PhD, Pastor, The Summit Church;
author of *Gaining by Losing* and *Jesus Continued*

How can biblical counseling shape the week-by-week work of ministry? What effect should our approach to counseling have on small groups, church discipline, evangelism, and more? Throughout this book, seasoned ministry practitioners articulate clearly and practically the impact of biblical counseling in every area of the local church's life and work. A much-needed resource for church staff!

Timothy Paul Jones, C. Edwin Gheens Professor of Christian Family
Ministry at the Southern Baptist Theological Seminary; author of *PROOF*

This is the Biblical Counseling Coalition's best and most compelling book to date. The authors are pastors and counselors who know their craft. They have developed a thriving culture of biblical counselors and formal counseling ministries that not only help but also "equip the saints for the work of ministry" (Ephesians 4:12). If you believe the church should set the standard for compassionate, life-giving counsel and that making disciple-makers is part of the Great Commission, this book will both inspire and equip you to do it better.

Dr. James MacDonald, Senior Pastor of Harvest Bible Chapel;
author of *Act Like Men* and *Vertical Church*; JamesMacdonald.org

It is rare for me to read a book and have it be all that I hoped it would be. I wanted a big, bold vision for biblical counseling in the church. That is what I got. This book is a treasure trove because time and time again my heart soared as the authors held up the Bible as the Book above every book for the church of Jesus Christ.

Jason C. Meyer, Pastor for Preaching and Vision,
Bethlehem Baptist Church

Treacherous, painful, and *lengthy* are words and moments I'd typically rather avoid. Counseling can be an emotionally devastating work for the faithful and feeling elder. But counseling in the church isn't optional. In fact, counseling is a gift to us who live under the curse of sin and a means of grace to bring growth and health to the church. This collection of authors take God's Word out of the abstract and into the concrete for God's people. Ministry practice without sound doctrine is a disaster. Buy this book and wear it out for the love and care of the church.

Daniel Montgomery, Lead Pastor of Sojourn Community
Church, Louisville; Founder of the Sojourn Network;
author of *Faithmapping* and *PROOF*

The church is a place of real-life change. Central to that vision and hope is the specific connection between what the Bible teaches and how to help people change. I'm grateful for *Biblical Counseling and the Church*—a powerful resource that identifies how any local church can become a culture of life change through biblical counseling in all aspects of the ministry. This book is practical, needed, and important.

Mark Vroegop, Lead Pastor, College Park Church,
Indianapolis, Indiana

A BIBLICAL COUNSELING COALITION BOOK

BIBLICAL COUNSELING
AND THE
CHURCH

GOD'S CARE THROUGH GOD'S PEOPLE

BOB KELLEMEN, GENERAL EDITOR

KEVIN CARSON, MANAGING EDITOR

FOREWORD BY PAUL TRIPP

http://biblicalcc.org

Promoting Personal Change Centered on the Person of Christ
through the Personal Ministry of the Word

ZONDERVAN

Biblical Counseling and the Church
Copyright © 2015 by the Biblical Counseling Coalition

This title is also available as a Zondervan ebook. Visit www.zondervan.com/ebooks.

Requests for information should be addressed to:

Zondervan, 3900 *Sparks Dr. SE, Grand Rapids, Michigan 49546*

Library of Congress Cataloging-in-Publication Data
      Biblical counseling and the church : God's care through God's people / Bob Kellemen, general
editor; Kevin Carson, managing editor.
      pages cm
      "A Biblical Counseling Coalition book."
      Includes bibliographical references and index.
      ISBN 978-0-310-52062-7 (hardcover)
      1. Counseling—Religious aspects—Christianity. I. Kellemen, Robert W., editor.
BR115.C69B53 2015
253.5—dc23   2015018730

Scripture quotations marked NIV are taken from The Holy Bible, *New International Version*®, NIV®. Copyright © 1973, 1978, 1984, 2011 by Biblica, Inc.® Used by permission. All rights reserved worldwide.

Scripture quotations marked KJV are taken from the King James Version of the Bible.

Scripture quotations marked NKJV are taken from the New King James Version. Copyright © 1982 by Thomas Nelson, Inc. Used by permission. All rights reserved.

Scripture quotations marked ESV are taken from *The Holy Bible, English Standard Version*. Copyright © 2001 by Crossway Bibles, a division of Good News Publishers. Used by permission. All rights reserved.

Scripture quotations marked NASB are taken from the *New American Standard Bible*. Copyright © 1960, 1962, 1963, 1968, 1971, 1972, 1973, 1975, 1977, 1995 by The Lockman Foundation. Used by permission.

Scripture quotations marked NLT are taken from the *Holy Bible, New Living Translation*. Copyright © 1996, 2004, 2007 by Tyndale House Foundation. Used by permission of Tyndale House Publishers, Inc., Carol Stream, Illinois 60188. All rights reserved.

Scripture quotations marked RSV are taken from the *Revised Standard Version of the Bible*. Copyright © 1946, 1952, 1971 by the Division of Christian Education of the National Council of Churches of Christ in the USA. Used by permission.

The personal identities and situations of the individuals described in this book have been disguised in order to protect their privacy.

Any Internet addresses (websites, blogs, etc.) and telephone numbers in this book are offered as a resource. They are not intended in any way to be or imply an endorsement by Zondervan, nor does Zondervan vouch for the content of these sites and numbers for the life of this book.

Published in association with the literary agency of Wolgemuth & Associates, Inc.

Cover design: LUCAS Art and Design
Cover photography: Lightstock
Interior design: Matthew Van Zomeren

Printed in the United States of America

---

15 16 17 18 19 20 21 22 23 24 25 /DCI/ 20 19 18 17 16 15 14 13 12 11 10 9 8 7 6 5 4 3 2 1

CONTENTS

ACKNOWLEDGMENTS

It is the mission of the Biblical Counseling Coalition (BCC) to advance the ministry of the biblical counseling movement through *collaborative relationships* and *robust resources*. *Biblical Counseling and the Church* clearly matches this mission. We're thankful for the servant leadership of the BCC's Board of Directors: Nicolas Ellen, John Henderson, Garrett Higbee, Bob Kellemen, Randy Patten, David Powlison, Deepak Reju, and Steve Viars. It is because of their vision and commitment that *Biblical Counseling and the Church* came to fruition.

We are also thankful for all the coauthors of *Biblical Counseling and the Church*. Each man and woman contributed their chapter in the midst of a heavy load as pastors, counselors, professors, and ministry leaders. And each coauthor donated all payments back to the BCC to further advance our mission. Thank you!

We would like to express a special thanks to Ryan Pazdur of Zondervan for his vision for this book and for his commitment to it. Thank you, Ryan, for the work you and your team have done to shape *Biblical Counseling and the Church*.

Our agent, Andrew Wolgemuth, of Wolgemuth & Associates, Inc., has a rare blend of a sharp mind, business acumen, and a loving heart. He understands biblical counseling and is passionate about advancing the ministry of the BCC. Thank you, Andrew.

FOREWORD

PAUL TRIPP

Why invest your time and energy in reading *Biblical Counseling and the Church*? There is only one answer to that question: because every author of every line of every chapter in this book shares a single thought-shaping, heart-engaging, ministry-guiding, and word-selecting commitment. What is that commitment? *To let the Bible shape everything they think.* To shape what they think about themselves, about life, about identity, meaning and purpose, about relationships, about human emotions and human problems, about solutions and change, about the past, present, and future, and about how we can be instruments in the hands of the God of the Bible, agents of grace and change in the lives of people we counsel.

Because the authors of this book are committed to looking at all of life through the lens of the Word of God, they have a particular perspective on people and on change. This is more than telling people to "take two verses and call me in the morning." No, here you find expansive and practical wisdom that works where the rubber meets the road in everyday life in this fallen world. This wisdom flows from two central perspectives: in how a biblical thinker views *people* and how a biblical thinker views *change*.

TWO ESSENTIAL QUESTIONS, TWO GUIDING ANSWERS

This may sound arrogant and mystical, but I believe it really is possible to know the answers before you've heard the questions. No, I am not talking about the contextual counsel that you would give a potential counselee. I'm simply noting the fact that if you take the Bible seriously you always have two answers to two questions that form the basis for what you will say to every counselee.

What are these questions? What are the two essential questions that every counselor will ask and that each of the authors of this book addresses in a distinctively biblical way?

Question One: Who are people, anyway?

The way that you answer this question will shape and direct everything you do. The Bible gives four deeply specific and helpful answers to this question; people are *creatures, sinners, sufferers* and *saints*. Now, these aren't four separate identities, but the collected identity that makes each person who and what they are. Everyone carries three of these identities and many people all four.

You simply cannot offer people the help they need unless you understand that you are looking into the face of a *creature* of God. No counselee is an independent being with a right and ability to achieve happiness however they see fit. No, every person is the creation of God; made for His purpose, made dependent of Him for life and made morally responsible to Him.

But the authors know something else as well. It is the mournful reality that every person is not only a creature; they are *sinners* as well. They have rebelled against God and are, therefore, separate from him but are also broken inside. Their hearts don't function the way that the Creator intended, so they will insert themselves in the center of their world and they will look for life where it cannot be found. They will attempt to live independently and to get others to serve their kingdom. In so doing, they will suffer their own insanity while laying the blame on the people and circumstances around them. In counseling you have to recognize that you're always dealing with the sinfulness of sin.

Creatures, yes, and sinners, yes, but there is more. These writers know that everyone they counsel is also a *sufferer*. Between the "already" of their birth and the "not yet" of God drawing his world to an end, suffering is the universal experience of every human being. From the pains of childbirth to the physical ravages of old age, from being picked on by your friends to gross racism, from family violence to murder, from political corruption to global war, from physical sickness to mental dysfunction, from being rejected to never knowing true love—nothing in this broken world operates as God intended, and we all suffer the results.

But there is a fourth identity, one not shared by all. By grace many human beings are not just creatures, sinners, and sufferers, they are also *saints*: people who have been forgiven by God, restored to relationship with him, and have God's life now bubbling up inside of them. By grace they have new eyes to see and a new heart to receive and understand all that God has given them. By grace they know that the thing they need to be rescued from most of all is themselves.

The book you're about to read is trustworthy because every writer takes seriously these four identities; *creature, sinner, sufferer* and *saint*. But there's a second, equally foundational question to be asked and answered.

Question Two: What in the world does change look like?

The work of counseling *is* change, and submission to the Word of God drives you to a unique perspective on personal change. Only someone committed to biblical thinking would ever hold to the idea that *the hope of change is a person and His name is Jesus*. The authors of this book offer you something very different. They haven't put the hope of their counseling work in a system. Everything that is written in this book flows out of a deeply held belief that lasting personal change requires a person, a Redeemer. Here's why this is true.

The humbling bottom line of the work of counseling is that the thing we most need to be rescued from is ourselves! Our basic problem is deeper than history, biology, or our relationships. What's *inside* of us is far more dangerous to us than what's *outside* of us. You can live beyond your history, you can run from a bad situation, you can escape a destructive relationship, but you simply cannot run away from yourself.

God sent His Son to provide the rescue we could not provide for ourselves. And we don't just need that rescue once, we need it again and again and again until all is finally restored and made new.

So I commend this book to you, not because of my confidence in the authors, but because of the confidence the authors have in the liberating truths of the Word of God. With this unwavering confidence, they can know things about you and me and Jesus that make counselors and churches powerful tools of transforming grace in the hands of our Redeemer, who came to make lasting change possible for everyone who humbly seeks it. Read, reread, and absorb this book. It will not only help you as you serve others as an agent of God's grace, it will change you as well.

Dr. Paul David Tripp, author and
President of Paul Tripp Ministries

SPEAKING CHRIST'S TRUTH IN LOVE

KEVIN CARSON AND BOB KELLEMEN

The saying in small group ministry has been, "We don't want to be a church *with* small groups; we want to be a church *of* small groups." In other words, the small group ministry mindset should saturate every aspect of the church.

We are communicating a similar message in *Biblical Counseling and the Church: God's Care through God's People*. We don't want to promote a vision simply of churches *with* a biblical counselor or even *with* a biblical counseling ministry. We are casting a vision focused on churches *of* biblical counseling where speaking the truth in love saturates every aspect of church life. It's more than counseling; we have a vision to see every Christian equipped to relate Christ's gospel of grace to people's lives so we all mature in Christ—God's care through God's people.

GOD'S VISION FOR HIS PEOPLE

Sometimes we perceive counseling as a "side ministry" in the church, reserved for people who are especially troubled in some way. But that professional model of the personal ministry of the Word is *not* the mindset the apostle Paul develops in Ephesians 4:11–16. Instead, Paul casts a vision that calls upon every shepherd/teacher "to equip the saints for the work of ministry, for building up the body of Christ" (Eph. 4:12 RSV). Those sixteen words serve as the pastor/equipper mission statement from God.

After casting this pastoral vision, Paul moves into a parenthetical statement in Ephesians 4:13 – 14, where he develops what it does and does not look like to build up the body of Christ. Then, in 4:15, Paul provides a succinct vision, a clear definition, of the work of ministry: "Speaking the truth in love, we are to grow up in every way into him who is the head, into Christ" (RSV). Those twenty-one words capture Christ's calling for His people. And what ministry is *every* pastor to equip *every* Christian to perform? The ministry of biblical counseling: speaking and embodying gospel truth in love so we all grow up in Christ.

We are writing *Biblical Counseling and the Church* to assist every pastor and every Christian to fulfill God's call on their life and ministry. It is the Biblical Counseling Coalition's passion to equip all of God's people to *promote personal change centered on the Person of Christ through the personal ministry of the Word.*

To those of you who are pastors or leaders in churches, we want you to know that we understand the challenges you face and the concerns you have. Most of our thirty-four coauthors have been trained in Bible colleges and seminaries as pastors and have served local churches as pastors. We know from experience that most evangelical pastors receive a solid biblical education in the pulpit ministry of the Word—preaching and teaching God's Word. Unfortunately, we also know by experience that few evangelical pastors receive anything more than one general course in the personal ministry of the Word—pastoral counseling. And typically pastors take zero courses in equipping their congregations for the personal ministry of the Word—biblical counseling. If you are a pastor, we've penned *Biblical Counseling and the Church* to equip you to fulfill your Ephesians 4:11 – 16 calling to prepare your people for the personal ministry of the Word. We want to help you shepherd your church toward being a church *of* biblical counseling where every member speaks God's truth in love.

And for those of you who are active lay leaders in your church, we want you to know that this book is for you as well. Our thirty-four coauthors have given their lives to empowering people just like you. We've written *Biblical Counseling and the Church* so that you can fulfill your Ephesians 4:15 – 16 calling to speak the truth in love. Our culture has professionalized the ministry of helping people to walk through their suffering and overcome their besetting sins. God's Word tells us that every Christian — believers just like you — can and should be equipped to competently counsel one another (Rom. 15:14; Phil. 1:9 – 11; 1 Thess. 2:8). We want to help you to become a part of a congregation *of* biblical counselors — where every member promotes personal change centered on the Person of Christ through the personal ministry of the Word.

AN INVITATION TO JOIN US ON AN EQUIPPING JOURNEY: SIX PATHS

We invite you to join us on this equipping journey. Along the way, you will encounter twenty-three chapters penned by thirty-four leading biblical counselors. These men and women, educators, pastors, and counselors, will be your guides along six paths. In the first path or part, Brad Bigney, Steve Viars, Deepak Reju, Garrett Higbee, Kevin Carson, and Paul Tautges will develop the vision of "More Than Counseling: A Vision for the Entire Church." On this path, you'll receive a taste of what it's like for one-another ministry to become a natural part of the daily life of your congregation.

Next, in the second part, Brad Bigney, Ken Long, Abe Meysenburg, Mike Wilkerson, Garrett Higbee, Lee Lewis, and Michael Snetzer equip you to integrate your small group ministry with your biblical counseling ministry. These pastors have found that one of the greatest ways to embed the personal ministry of the Word into the daily life of the church is to train small group leaders and members to speak the truth in love to one another. In this section, you'll learn four different but overlapping approaches to uniting biblical counseling and small group ministry.

In part 3, Robert Cheong, Robert Jones, and Judy Dabler address the relationship between biblical counseling and conflict resolution. These experienced biblical counselors/conciliators demonstrate how the competent biblical counselor can and should be a competent peacemaker — both in personal conflict and in organizational conflict.

In part 4, eleven experienced equippers—Ron Allchin, Tim Allchin, Greg Cook, Jack Delk, Jim Newheiser, Rod Mays, Randy Patten, Nicolas Ellen, Charles Ware, Wayne Vanderwier, and Bob Kellemen—provide the "nuts and bolts" of equipping biblical counselors in the local church. In this section, you'll discover practical principles for launching and leading a church *of* biblical counseling—whether your church is "larger," "midsize," "smaller," multicultural, or international. These chapters will be surrounded by bookends that provide universal principles for equipping counselors as well as relevant ethical and legal principles related to counseling in the church.

Since the first four parts of the book focus primarily on ministry *within* the church, in part 5 we look at the topic of outreach, beyond the walls of the church. Increasingly, churches are finding that biblical counseling provides a tremendous and often untapped arena for outreach. Kevin Carson and Randy Patten equip you to use biblical counseling as a means of bringing the lost to Christ. Rob Green and Steve Viars depict unique and powerful ways that your church can impact your community through biblical counseling. Then Heath Lambert, David Powlison, Lilly Park, Jeremy Pierre, Ed Welch, and Sam Williams suggest ways that biblical counseling can impact our world as they present a case for the sufficiency of Christ to address human concerns.

Finally, in part 6, Howard Eyrich and Jonathan Holmes will put the modern biblical counseling movement in historical perspective. Ernie Baker will cast a final vision for the power of biblical counseling to impact the church and our world for Christ.

EVERY BELIEVER A BIBLICAL COUNSELOR

By now we're sure that you are picking up the idea that we don't see biblical counseling as a ministry staffed *by a few for the few*. Instead, it is our conviction that God calls *all of us* to be biblical counselors. He calls every believer to know how to relate His Word to one another's lives so that every believer in every congregation grows more like Christ. It is our prayer that *Biblical Counseling and the Church: God's Care through God's People* will spark a one-another revolution in your life and in your church.

PART 1

MORE THAN COUNSELING: A VISION FOR THE ENTIRE CHURCH

CHAPTER 1

A CHURCH *OF* BIBLICAL COUNSELING

BRAD BIGNEY AND STEVE VIARS

Followers of Jesus Christ love the word *church* and everything it entails. Do you remember in Matthew 16, when Peter makes that marvelous declaration that Jesus is the Messiah and Son of the living God? Immediately after that, what does Jesus promise to him? Jesus says that He will build His church and the gates of hell will not prevail against it (Matt. 16:18).

Of all the topics Jesus could have chosen to discuss at that pivotal moment, He emphasized the birth and development of His church. The word He chose to use there, *ecclesia*, literally means "called out ones." This is how Jesus describes His church, the body He would create and develop after His death, burial, and resurrection. The church was of critical importance to the Lord and, for that reason, it is of critical importance to us as well.

LOVING THE CHURCH

As the New Testament unfolds, we see that the church plays the central role in all that happens. When the resurrected Christ promises His followers that something tremendous is going to happen a few days after His ascension, shortly thereafter the church is miraculously born. Thousands of people from many nations place their faith in Jesus Christ and become transformed proof of Jesus' promise. This new entity is so Spirit-filled that some detractors accuse these early believers of turning the world upside down with their teaching (Acts 17:6 KJV). The apostle Paul goes so far as to call this new community "the household of God, which is the church of the living God, a pillar and buttress of the truth" (1 Tim. 3:15 ESV). We love the church because our Lord is mediating His work through this unique group of people.

Many of us also love the church because some of our most wonderful experiences occur among God's people. We love gathering together and worshiping our Savior with our brothers and sisters in Christ, and we have powerful memories of doing so over the years. We think back to all the times the Word of God was proclaimed in a way that resulted in encouragement, conviction, comfort, and dramatic life change. We have developed deep and abiding friendships as we have served shoulder to shoulder. The church is not a perfect institution. After all, it is made up of imperfect people like you and me. But it is a community that many of us hold near and dear.

We (Brad and Steve) love that we have been called to pastor two of Jesus' churches. We would not trade this adventure for anything the world has to offer. But we don't just want to serve Jesus—we want to serve Him well. We want our churches to fit the biblical pattern and accomplish the goals articulated for us in the Word of God. One passage that has been especially helpful is Ephesians 4:12–16. After spending three chapters unpacking and explaining the gospel indicatives—who we are in Christ—the apostle directs our attention in the second half of the book to the gospel imperatives. He shows us *how* we are to live in the power and strength of our resurrected Savior.

In chapter 4 of his letter to the Ephesians, Paul includes a delightful passage describing the local church. The theme is spiritual growth, or what we theologically refer to as the doctrine of progressive sanctification. Paul is clear that this growth is not just the growth of individuals, but the growth of the entire local church. This suggests that soul care is not just something limited to a few people to do; it is something the entire church is called to do. This "soul care" includes counseling and discipleship, and these must permeate every facet of ministry. They should be part of the church's DNA. This is what God wants us to develop in our congregations — not just churches that have counseling centers, but churches that *are* counseling centers.

WHERE SHEPHERDS/TEACHERS EMBRACE THEIR ROLE AS EQUIPPERS SEVEN DAYS A WEEK

If you want to see Ephesians 4:11 – 16 at work in your local church, as a pastor you need to understand that your role is bigger than just preaching and teaching every week. Ephesians 4:11 says that Christ gave the church some to be *shepherds* as well as teachers. Sadly, most seminaries focus almost exclusively on homiletics and exegesis, essential teaching functions, but they neglect the tasks of shepherding and equipping others in counseling or soul care. Too often the training for the shepherd/equipper is reduced to a single class titled "Practical Theology," where they learn to marry and bury people. But where is the practical training in how to shepherd people through the various struggles of life?

For the past twenty years, I've (Brad) invested my life in training godly disciples who can handle life effectively by handling God's Word accurately. That is a broader and, I think, more biblical goal than just saying, "I want to preach and teach faithfully through the Bible so that I can feed my people the right spiritual food." Preaching is important and necessary. But it's not the total package of ministry that Paul writes about in Ephesians 4:11 – 16.

The ministry that a pastor does from Monday through Saturday is just as important as what he does each Sunday in preaching. And if a pastor or leader is gripped by Ephesians 4:11 – 16, they will value the time they have counseling one-on-one with people throughout the week, spending time with other church leaders, equipping them and showing them how to actually use God's Word to help a real person with a real problem. These are pastors who look for every opportunity to take a regular "business" meeting with staff, deacons, elders, trustees, or board members and to infuse it with an element of showing leaders how to help real people with real problems, using God's Word.

In America, a pastor is typically viewed as the lead vision-caster—a biblically glorified CEO of a corporation with a mission. But Ephesians 4:11–16 calls us to fight against the pressures of this world and the expectations of the "corporate" American church that try to squeeze us into the mold of CEO, holding us captive to the pulpit. Standing behind the pulpit is important, but there are many times when we do our most effective ministry seated at a kitchen table or sitting in the living room with our people.

John Piper reflects the tension we feel to specialize as simply professional preaching "machines" when he says:

> We pastors are being killed by the professionalizing of the pastoral ministry. The mentality of the professional is not the mentality of the prophet. It is not the mentality of the slave of Christ. Professionalism has nothing to do with the essence and heart of the Christian ministry. The more professional we long to be, the more spiritual death we will leave in our wake.[1]

He goes on to say, "The world sets the agenda of the professional man; God sets the agenda of the spiritual man."[2] And that agenda can be seen clearly in Ephesians 4:11–16. May God give us a revival of those who seek to live out "shepherd" as well as "teacher" to the glory of God!

WHERE CHURCH MEMBERS LOVE BEING EQUIPPED FOR THE WORK OF SERVICE

The word "equip" in Ephesians 4:12 (NIV) is a Greek word that connotes making something fit or preparing something fully through training and discipline. It also communicates the idea of mending or restoring. Many of the people who come into the church are crushed by the struggles and pains of life and the effects of sin, and they will need mending and restoring, but that's not the end game. Ephesians 4:12 calls us to go further and equip those who have been mended to do ministry! Pastors should know that we're not looking for spectators, people to fill the pews. We don't need fans, and the church is not a Christian cruise ship, focused on how comfortable we can make our people. Ephesians 4:12 calls us to equip people to do ministry because the church is a battleship, on a mission, engaged in a spiritual war. Bill Hull recognizes this problem when he writes:

> The evangelical church has become weak, flabby, and too dependent on artificial means that can only simulate real spiritual power. Churches are too little like training centers to shape up the saints.... The average Christian resides in the comfort zone of "I pay the pastor to preach, administrate, and counsel.... I am the consumer, he is the retailer.... I have the needs, he meets them ... that's what I pay for."[3]

Ephesians 4:12 flies in the face of this consumer Christianity. There's a marvelous chain of events spelled out in 4:12 (ESV), with three prepositions that unpack God's plan for what church ministry should look like. And it all begins with the little word "to." Paul calls pastors "to equip the saints."

A shepherd/teacher is called not only to *do* ministry but to help others *learn* how to do it! This is why whenever I counsel someone, I have someone else who sits in with me to observe and learn how to do it. It's why I have an apprentice in the small group I lead so that I can eventually birth my group to him. It's why I meet with "young eagles" in our church who show interest in full-time ministry. It's why I trained eight godly couples to do all of our premarital counseling — instead of doing it myself. It's why I started a men's and women's leadership development ministry, where we select men and women to spend a year reading good books, memorizing Scripture, and discussing theology and practical ministry concerns, so that they can go to the next level in their ability to do ministry.

Pastors and leaders in the church are called to equip God's people "for the work of the ministry" (Eph. 4:12 ESV). Notice here, who is supposed to actually do the work of ministry? Ephesians 4:12 tells us the answer—"the saints." Paul doesn't say anything here about Bible college training or special calling or giftedness. There are no diplomas mentioned in Ephesians 4:12. Ministry is the work of the church, the everyday saints, and not just those with a special calling or professional training.

And what's the end result of doing things this way? Paul says that this ministry is for "building up the body of Christ" (Eph. 4:12 ESV). The church grows strong as people engage in ministry. It grows healthy and matures and it stops looking so anemic and sickly. Some of God's people, sitting in Bible-believing churches, have been *objects* of God's mercy and love for years. Maybe it's time for them to become an *instrument* of God's love in the lives of others around them! But they cannot do it alone. They will need pastors/teachers who are committed to showing them *how*.

WHERE THE BODY OF CHRIST IS BEING BUILT UP

Churches that are biblical counseling centers are constantly looking for ways to comfort those who are suffering and to confront and correct those who are sinning. Consider the way many churches deal with suffering. Somewhere along the line, the American church bought into the notion that Christians shouldn't be real and honest about their feelings. We've been told that we should tape plastic smiles over our broken hearts. We've bought into the lie that big boys don't cry and that followers of Jesus Christ should not be authentic about how and why we are hurting. Is it any wonder that some people say that they feel more comfortable pouring out their problems at a bar than at a church?

The Scripture paints a markedly different picture of the church for us. The only way a Christian will get serious about growing and maturing as a follower of Christ is by being honest and speaking the truth. We need to tell people when we are knocked down, when we fall apart, when sin captures our heart. And the most natural place in the entire world for this to occur is at the church. Imagine the power unleashed if fellow sufferers lock arms and go to the throne of grace together. Our focus is on our perfect Savior, not the painted false perfection we show to others. God's grace, experienced alongside others, enables us to be authentic about our hurts.

This affects every facet of local church ministry. Small groups and adult Bible fellowships should be places where men and women can suffer together. The body of Christ is built up because the men and women in a church family openly acknowledge their pain, hurts, and struggles. There is mutual edification. This is biblical counseling!

The same is true during those times when we struggle with sin. In moments of honesty, we must admit our need and our struggle. There needs to be a willingness to be vulnerable about where we are failing. Friendships in the church family include being honest about the ways we still need to grow.

My (Steve) mentor Bill Goode taught me that this level of authenticity needs to be modeled at the level of the top leadership. Bill would say to our pastors and deacons, "Men, if we want the members of our church to grow spiritually, we have to grow spiritually." One of the qualifying questions we ask potential leaders is how they would respond if they thought one of our pastors was sinning in some way. Would they contact that pastor and talk with him? If the answer is no, we cannot consider them for a position of leadership in our church.

In our pastors' and deacons' meetings, we regularly split up into accountability groups and talk about specific ways we need to change. During these times we are counseling one another as church leaders. Such conversations over time become a natural part of what we do in our meetings.

We believe that this type of counseling should extend to every person in our church family. Each church member is assigned to a deacon's care group, and that deacon in turn contacts the men and women in his care group. A significant percentage of our leaders have received biblical counseling training, and their conversations with the people in their care groups often have the feel of an informal counseling session. For situations that are more intense, more formal biblical counseling ministry is also available. But even when that is necessary, it does not feel awkward or out of place because there is a sense in which *every* person in our church is being counseled in some way. Counseling is normal and natural, embedded in the culture of our church.

WHERE THE FOCUS IS MATURITY IN CHRIST

One of the biggest mistakes people make with biblical counseling is to boil it down to nothing more than naming a sin and sharing a Bible verse that commands you to stop what you are doing. Biblical counseling is more than simplistic answers. Biblical counseling is not person-centered or problem-centered, but Christ-centered.

Ephesians 4:13 tells us the goal of counseling: "Until we all attain to the unity of the faith and of the knowledge of the Son of God, to a mature manhood, to the measure of the stature of the fullness of Christ" (ESV). Good biblical counselors understand that we're doing more than just fixing a problem; we're making a disciple. A problem may have brought the counselee in, but the scope of counseling is bigger than just fixing a problem. We want to see the counselee become more like Christ — thinking more like Christ, following harder after Christ, and making choices that please Christ.

Ed Welch points out the danger, and captures the focus well, when he says:

> When principles or steps wander from Christ himself, they become self-serving guidelines. They make our marriages, families, friendships, and work go better, but the goal is our own betterment more than the glory of God ... "Be good" and "Do right" are fine messages, but when they stand alone they have more in common with the Boy Scouts' Handbook than Scripture.[4]

It's a vital growing relationship with Jesus Christ that keeps the counseling process from being sheer drudgery filled with accountability or just listening compassionately but never helping the counselee to move forward. A growing love for Christ, with increasing spiritual maturity, is what helps people go places they never thought they could go in their life. And it's possible because the counseling process is focused on the Person of Jesus Christ rather than just a system or model of change.

Intimacy with Christ is a powerful engine for change; otherwise, drudgery sets in and people lose heart. As Sam Storms says:

> It is a dreary holiness indeed that is merely resisting sin. The joy of holiness is found in having heard a sweeter song.... Grace is the work of the Holy Spirit in transforming our desires so that knowing Jesus becomes sweeter than illicit sex, sweeter than money and what it can buy, sweeter than every fruitless joy. Grace is God satisfying our souls with his Son so that we're ruined for anything else![5]

Counseling is far more than just "fixing" a problem; it's also an opportunity to lead someone closer to Christ, helping them to taste and see how good He is (Ps. 34:8) so that their appetite is ruined for anything else! Leslie Vernick concurs:

> Rules won't change us, but a growing relationship with Christ will. Change or maturity for a Christian comes about through deepening our intimacy with Jesus, not by following certain rules or doctrines. When we begin to grasp his love for us, our hearts respond with love for him. He tells us if we love him, we will keep his commandments (John 14:15). Our love for him is what begins to move our hearts toward obedience. We cease when we come to love something else more than ourselves or our sin.[6]

What a joy to step into the sin and suffering of people's lives and lead them not to a system, but a Savior, Jesus Christ!

WHERE THERE IS A THIRST FOR AND DELIGHT IN SOUND DOCTRINE

Woven right into this passage about believers growing up into maturity is Paul's statement in Ephesians 4:14 that we are "no longer to be children, tossed here and there by waves and carried about by every wind of doctrine, by the trickery of men, by craftiness in deceitful scheming" (NASB). While an emphasis on doctrine is sometimes dismissed in favor of a simple and pure devotion to Christ, simple and pure devotion to Christ, Paul never took that approach. He was certainly concerned that believers not wander from a pure and simple devotion to Christ (2 Cor. 11:3), but he didn't think the solution was to avoid doctrine altogether.

In fact, through his letters, Paul shows that believers need to understand doctrine. That's why his letters to the church are structured the way they are. Paul usually spends the first part reviewing and laying a solid foundation of doctrine before he ever touches on any area of concern. His letters are front-loaded with indicatives long before he ever backs up the truck of imperatives and starts telling believers what to do and not do. This is a grammatical distinction worth noting as you read your Bible. Indicatives are verbs that simply state facts, while imperatives are verbs that require action and are often urgent in nature.

The book of Ephesians is a perfect example of this, as chapters 1–3 are full of doctrine (indicatives) regarding who we are and what God has done for us. Strikingly, chapter 1 is nothing more than a run-on sentence of glorious indicatives, all strung together, as to who we are now in Christ: chosen, forgiven, predestined, redeemed, adopted, ransomed, sealed with the Holy Spirit, seated in the heavenlies with Christ, and blessed with every spiritual blessing. It's only after Paul has gushed on and on about all that God has done *for* us that he even thinks about telling us what to *do* (imperatives). Not until chapter 4 does he change gears from indicatives to imperatives when he says, "I, therefore ... urge you to walk in a manner worthy of the calling to which you have been called" (Eph. 4:1 ESV).

And even though Paul was counted among those Christians who had some amazing personal experiences (2 Cor. 12:1–4), he didn't make those experiences the basis of his Christian life, and he certainly didn't exhort other believers to seek after the same. He knew all too well that experiences come and go, but a growing foundation of solid doctrine will keep you alive and growing for a lifetime.

John Piper gives the same warning when he writes:

> Large spiritual passion with small doctrinal understanding is large sails and tall masts on a tiny boat in high winds. It will dart wildly over the surface for a hundred yards. Then one wave, or one crosswind, will bring it all crashing into the unforgiving sea. Give as much attention to enlarging the depth of your ballast as you do to the height of your sails.[7]

In Hosea 4:6 God tells us, "My people are destroyed from lack of knowledge." He doesn't say they're destroyed for lack of a certain kind of experience. Experiences come and go, but the unchanging truth of God's Word is what we desperately need to know. If we want to see the church of Jesus Christ rise up in power, with ability to persevere through suffering as well as persecution, then we'll need pastors who are committed to feeding the church with solid doctrine from God's Word—all of it—just like Paul, who said to the elders of Ephesus, "I have not shunned to declare to you the whole counsel of God" (Acts 20:27 NKJV).

WHERE THERE IS AUTHENTIC COMMUNICATION CENTERED ON SPIRITUAL GROWTH

Paul says spiritual growth occurs by "speaking the truth in love" (Eph. 4:15 NASB). Churches that are biblical counseling centers find ways to move relationships from surface level communication to appropriate levels of depth. This is achieved, in part, by laying out clear expectations. Church members *expect* their deacons to ask how things are going spiritually. Small group and adult Bible fellowship participants *expect* their leaders and fellow members to ask hard questions. Teenagers *expect* questions on accountability from their youth leaders. It should seem like everyone is talking about spiritual growth on all sorts of levels and in all sorts of ways.

Paul explains that this involves a willingness on the part of God's people to speak the truth. This is seldom easy for either the speaker or the recipient. But if change and growth need to occur, what more appropriate venue for that kind of truth-telling than the church of the living God. Truth-speakers must be willing to risk the possibility of being rejected or criticized in some way. Truth-recipients must truly believe that "faithful are the wounds of a friend" (Prov. 27:6 NASB).

Such words must always be spoken in the context of Christian love. Some of the most life-giving conversations we have been involved in at our churches were times when hard challenges were honestly faced in a context of Christlike love. Thankfully, the person confronted is often grateful and expresses a sincere desire to find tools and accountability to bring about lasting change.

One of my (Steve) earliest recollections of ministry at Faith was speaking with a young couple about a serious conflict within their family. I was shaking in my ministerial boots as I contemplated the meeting, fearing all the possible bad responses I might encounter. But I prayed, planned, and then spoke to the man and his wife. I'll never forget their response when our meeting was over: "Thank you for loving us enough to come and talk to us about this concern." That experience developed a conviction in my heart that biblical counseling, when it is done in a truthful and loving manner, can lead to marvelous results.

WHERE EVERYONE IS PART OF A GROWING TEAM

I (Steve) have always believed that Ephesians 4:16 is a pastor's dream. Paul describes a church where the members are growing spiritually as "the whole body, joined and held together by every joint with which it is equipped, when each part is working properly, makes the body grow so that it builds itself up in love" (Eph. 4:16 ESV). Notice that this passage ends with everyone involved. Paul speaks about "the whole body," "held together by every joint," and what happens when "each part is working properly."

When every person in the church family is growing spiritually in a church that embraces the ministry of biblical counseling, everyone can identify their spiritual gifts, be equipped to use those gifts well, and be deployed in meaningful ministry in the body of Christ. Our mantra at Faith is, "Everyone growing in Christ—everyone serving Christ—everyone glorifying Christ."

This is not a church where 90 percent of the work is done by 10 percent of the people. The average church on Sunday morning is far too much like a college football game on Saturday afternoon: 66,000 people badly in need of exercise watching twenty-two young men badly in need of rest.

Often this dynamic occurs because men and women in the church feel guilty about their own lack of spiritual growth. Why serve in the church if you aren't healthy? Who wants to spread their spiritual measles to others? Conversely, when someone is experiencing genuine life change, that person wants to serve. When you provide the counseling and training resources to equip the entire church family to serve in these ways, powerful things will occur to the glory of God.

BECAUSE GOD'S WAY WORKS

When the body of Christ is growing the way God designed, it is a beautiful thing. But that should not surprise us, because Jesus is a beautiful Savior. The more His people grow, the more we will reflect the beauty that is ours in Christ.

The broad philosophy of ministry we have articulated in this chapter is hard work. It amounts to pastoring seven days a week, not just one or two. But the results are worth it, because we are cooperating with the work of Jesus Christ Himself. Always remember that the Lord is the One who promised to build His church. When we seek to bring the principles and resources He gives us for spiritual growth to every facet of local church ministry, we can be assured that Jesus Himself will bless our endeavors.

The church members will rejoice along with their Savior. There is something powerful about being part of a family where problems are being solved and lives are being changed for the glory of God. It is refreshing to see a group of people united under and around this sanctifying goal.

CHAPTER 2

DEAR PASTOR: SHEPHERD GOD'S FLOCK

DEEPAK REJU

I can't stand it anymore."
"I don't think I can make it through another day."
"I don't think God loves me."
"I'm stressed and depressed."
"Why am I going through this?"

As a pastor, you've heard these expressions and many others—Christians struggling with the difficulties of sin and suffering in a fallen world. They are cries of hurting sheep needing the help of a shepherd.

The work of caring for God's people is not easy. I've often heard pastors say, "Counseling hurting members is the *hardest* part of the job." And why should that surprise us? Consider this:

- Most pastors come into the pastorate to be preachers, not counselors. They want to teach the Bible because they love God's Word and have full confidence it will change lives.
- As mentioned in chapter 1, seminary doesn't prepare pastors to be counselors. The typical seminary curriculum has just one counseling class in a 100-credit-hour master of divinity degree.

Seminary does very little to prepare pastors for the *private* ministry of the Word. The focus is on the *public* ministry — preaching and teaching God's Word.

- Pastors have to deal with church members who make consistent demands on their time. They expect their pastor to shepherd them through the nitty-gritty details of life, to get down into the weeds of life and sort it out with them.
- Pastors can be impatient. There is no guarantee that your pastor is a good listener just because he earned a professional divinity degree.
- Many pastors don't know how to ask heart-piercing questions to get a person to open up, or how to apply the Word wisely to very hard situations like suicide, cocaine addiction, or rape.

Is it any wonder that pastors struggle with shepherding their members? No one has prepared them, and in their first few years of pastoring, they are forced into the crucible of other people's problems and left to find ways to help. It's essentially trial by fire; under the heat and pressure of pastoral ministry, you have to figure this out basically on your own.

So here is our goal: to look to Scripture to determine the calling of a pastor to shepherd God's flock. Pastor, you might not have signed up for this. I get that. It surprised you in your first few years of pastoring just *how much* counseling you are expected to do. So let's see if we can realign your motivations and let Scripture inform your mind and heart of the noble and worthy task of shepherding God's people. In the end, what I hope you'll see is that preaching and shepherding are *both* essential to the task of a pastor. We'll look at three texts — 1 Peter 5:1 – 4; Ezekiel 34; and John 10 — to examine the shepherding motif developed in Scripture as *inspiration* for modern-day pastors. If the Bible makes clear that task of shepherding God's people, then how can pastors avoid it? Do these texts *compel* and even *motivate* busy pastors to take on this shepherding role?

Just a word to those who are not pastors: I hope our study of 1 Peter 5, Ezekiel 34, and John 10 will be useful for you too. While the Bible's metaphor of shepherd applies primarily to those who have been called to serve as pastors in a local church, it also has lessons for all of us who instruct, exhort, love, and care for struggling sheep. Counselors who daily help hurting Christians, lay leaders who disciple men and women in their congregation, fathers and mothers who instruct their children—what do these texts teach you about how to care for others?

BE SHEPHERDS OF GOD'S FLOCK: 1 PETER 5:1 – 4

The apostle Peter writes:

> So I exhort the elders among you, as a fellow elder and a witness of the sufferings of Christ, as well as a partaker in the glory that is going to be revealed: shepherd the flock of God that is among you, exercising oversight, not under compulsion, but willingly, as God would have you; not for shameful gain, but eagerly; not domineering over those in your charge, but being examples to the flock. And when the chief Shepherd appears, you will receive the unfading crown of glory.   1 Peter 5:1 – 4 ESV

Peter is writing to Christians who are enduring suffering (1 Peter 1:6 – 7; 2:3, 9, 13 – 17, 18 – 20; 4:1 – 4, 12 – 19; 5:9) and are fighting for faith. He has written "encouraging" the believers and "testifying that this is the true grace of God. Stand fast in it" (1 Peter 5:12). In the midst of their difficulties, he is urging them to entrust themselves to their creator God and to continue to do good (1 Peter 4:19). Don't give up on the truth. Rather, persevere. Stand fast in it.

Peter Appeals to Elders

In 1 Peter 5, Peter makes an appeal to the elders in the churches in Pontus, Galatia, Cappadocia, Asia, and Bithynia (see 1 Peter 1:1 and 5:1). It is interesting that he doesn't use his credentials as an apostle, but he appeals to them as a fellow elder (1 Peter 5:1a). "I'm an elder just like you," he says. "This is how we—*as shepherds*—carry ourselves and care for others" (paraphrased, emphasis added). Yet, he is not too far from reminding them that he is also an apostle—as a "witness of the sufferings of Christ" (1 Peter 5:1b, NASB). He was there when Christ was crucified. "The very One that we are all going to see one day, *I* have seen crucified."

Peter will also share in the glory to be revealed (5:1c). Suffering precedes glory. Both suffering and glory are paired together and run throughout 1 Peter as a major theme (1:6–7, 11, 21; 2:4, 7, 19–20; 3:13–14, 18; 4:6, 13; 5:4, 6, 10). Peter held out this "suffering, then glory" theme to these Christians as hope that their suffering will not end in futility. To Peter this wasn't an abstract idea; he himself held on to this hope—that he would personally experience the glory that comes after suffering.

On the basis of these three things—an appeal as a fellow elder, a personal witness of Christ's sufferings, and one who will share in the glory to be revealed—he makes his main point: "Shepherd the flock of God that is among you" (5:2 ESV). His primary goal is to encourage pastors *to be shepherds.* As you read this, don't think of the little statues that are found as trinkets in Christian bookstores or on greeting cards. Shepherding is dirty, smelly, manly work. It might require the shepherd on occasion to kill a bear or a lion to protect the sheep (1 Sam. 17:34–36).[8]

Notice the elders are called to shepherd "the flock of God." They are undershepherds entrusted with God's sheep. The sheep do not belong to the undershepherd, but to the chief Shepherd (1 Peter 5:2–4). So the undershepherd carries the privilege and weighty responsibility of caring for God's own. He works on behalf of God and cares for what is God's.

The participle—"exercising oversight"—qualifies the verb "shepherd." Shepherding—a life devoted to deliberate care of God's sheep—involves exercising oversight. Someone has to watch over the sheep—tending, protecting, guiding, feeding, and encouraging. Shepherding and oversight are two basic *functions* of the pastor/elder.[9] This is part of what a pastor is expected to do.

In light of the preceding section, 1 Peter 4:12–19, Peter is making an appeal to the elders to consider the great suffering of the believers who are "among you" (1 Peter 5:2 ESV). These people need the pastor's help. *His job is to shepherd these Christians through their suffering,* reminding them of truth and encouraging them to cling to it.[10]

Peter explains further what it means to be a shepherd and overseer with three contrasts (1 Peter 5:2b–3). With each contrast, on one side stands a ditch (don't fall in!), and on the other side an aspirational goal. He says three times, "Not this, but that." He starts with elders who work "not under compulsion, but willingly, as God would have you" (5:2b ESV). Elders should not shepherd their members out of a sense of obligation ("compulsion"), but they shepherd because they have chosen to pursue this work. A pastor freely and willingly gives his life to pastor God's flock because this is what God wants of him.

Peter adds a second phrase: "not for shameful gain, but eagerly" (5:2c ESV). Peter's warning: Be careful of your motivation for being a pastor. Don't use this ministry role for dishonest gain, greed, or self-interest. Rather, Peter encourages the elders to shepherd "with eagerness" (NASB). It's not just that you should be *willing*, but you should *desire* to do this. The NIV translators appropriately add the words "to serve" to draw out this contrast. The pastor's motivation is not self-gain, but an earnest eagerness to serve God's people.

The third phrase is "not domineering over those in your charge, but being examples to the flock" (5:3 ESV). In any position of authority, there is a danger of the pastor abusing those under his care. The term "domineering" implies a style of leadership that is harsh, excessively restrictive, or flaunting power. Instead of "domineering," Peter talks about church members looking at the life of an elder and following his example. Throughout Scripture, the apostles call on believers to imitate their way of life and their faith (1 Cor. 4:16; Phil. 3:17; 4:9; 2 Thess. 3:7–9; 1 Tim. 4:12; Titus 2:7–8). For pastors, living a life worthy of imitation is not optional—it's a fundamental part of the job.[11] As one author put it: "Elders are not to enter the ministry so they can boss others around but so they can exemplify the character of Christ to those under their charge."[12]

Calvin sums up these phrases by warning against "three vices which are found to prevail much"—sloth, desire for gain, and lust for power.[13] And on the other hand we see the elder's three aspirational goals—serving willingly, eagerly, and as an example.

Peter ends by pointing elders to the "chief Shepherd," Jesus (cf. Heb. 13:20; Matt. 26:31; John 10:11–16). When the chief Shepherd "appears," the elders will receive an "unfading crown of glory" (1 Peter 5:4 ESV). His appearing is a reference to Christ's final return. The crown harks back to first-century competitions or battles. Crowns were given to victorious athletes or soldiers in order to honor them and publicly recognize their work.[14] This is a fitting ending for this section. After Peter has taken time to describe the vices and aspirational goals for the pastorate, he says to elders, "This is what you get in the end if you are faithful to your calling." This "unfading crown of glory" is not an earthly reward, but something that comes after death.

Heart Checks for Pastors Today

Consider a few lessons that pastors can take away from this text, starting with the fact that *the pastorate is more than just preaching*. To be a pastor means to do more than just stand in a pulpit on Sunday mornings; it means shepherding God's flock. That's the unavoidable reality of this text—to be a pastor and to be a shepherd is synonymous in Peter's mind, and so also it must be in the mind of every pastor.

I remember in seminary that there was a culture of exalting preaching ministry as glorious, and so students talked about it often, but people rarely talked about shepherding. Is it any surprise that pastors grow strong desires for preaching, but end up astonished at how much counseling is required of them?

If you are a pastor, look at the contrasts in 1 Peter 5:2–3 and check your heart. Pastor: *Do you serve out of a sense of obligation?* If so, you are in a dangerous place. Obligation is a kind of earthly motivation that won't last. The pastorate is a high calling. To handle God's Word and shepherd God's people are very serious tasks for which there is a stricter judgment (Heb. 13:17; James 3:1). Those who enter into the pastorate should do it because they feel called by God, because they have been affirmed by their church as someone who has the maturity and giftedness that it takes to be a pastor, and because they desire to do this work. It's at this cross-section of calling, affirmation, and desire that most pastors enter into the ministry. And it is this cross-section that helps to sustain the pastor. It's a good thing, too, because when things get hard and church members are demanding or mean or bitter or frustrated with you, when you feel stressed out because you've got too much on your plate, when you feel like you are doing a poor job of balancing life and ministry, when your wife is struggling with feeling neglected because you pour so much into your work, when you feel like you need a break from the chaos or the constant complaints — obligation just won't be enough. A pastor must never shepherd because he *must*, but because he is *willing*. A pastor freely chooses to pursue this noble calling.

Again, Pastor, check your heart: *Do you do your job because of what you can get from it?* Pastors are sinners. They are not above greed, self-interest, or shameful gain. For most pastors, ministry is not a wealth-generating endeavor. Many pastors are earnestly seeking to provide for their families, yet meeting their needs is a struggle. Some pastors, while toiling away, at some point dream of the promised land of a bigger salary, bigger church, nicer home, happier family, book contracts, and nice vacations. Greed and gain can take on many forms for the shepherd.

In our evangelical culture, the popularity of celebrity pastors creates yearning in some pastors for something more than being content in their own local church ministry. What creates a celebrity pastor? Books that influence many; podcasts that are listened to by thousands; conference speaking which influences large crowds. None of this is bad if done with the right motives, but a lack of humility, and a temptation (embedded in all of our hearts) to self-exaltation, makes the pastorate just another means of making much of ourselves, when the real goal is to make much of God. Do you use your ministry as a means to your own success? If so, remember that Peter's exhortation is not to pursue *shameful gain*, but to learn to *eagerly serve* God's people.

Once again, Pastor, check your heart: *Do you ever misuse your pastoral authority?* Do any of these descriptors fit you, even in the faintest sense: Do you have a tendency to boss people around? Are you ever harsh in your tone when you address your church members? Are you domineering—that is, do you bulldoze over others in order to get your agenda done and remove anyone who is in your way? Do you flaunt your authority, pulling out the trump card of pastoral authority rather than humbly listening and being teachable? Are you excessively restrictive in how you teach your members to live the Christian life and what you as a pastor expect of them? If you are not sure about these things, ask your wife or another godly man who knows you well. And be humble in your response, because you might not like what they say about this.

A misuse of pastoral authority is especially dreadful because the pastor represents God to his members. The pastor's character reflects, albeit imperfectly, the character of God to his people. If church members see the pastor abuse the sheep, they will begin to think poorly of God because of His undershepherd. So be warned: Don't give in to *a lust for power and authority*; rather, live *a Christlike, humble life that is exemplary* to all those around you.

One final heart check. Pastor: *Can you hold out for your reward?* Peter ends by pointing elders to their eschatological motivation (1 Peter 5:4). If a pastor's aim in counseling and caring is just to help people, that won't be enough motivation to be a shepherd. Peter understands that this work is hard and that pastors need more. Pastors need to not work for earthly rewards (as many pastors do!), but for the rewards that come beyond this life. Jesus' return is a reminder to pastors that their work is temporary and that one day their labors will be done. If they are found faithful (1 Peter 5:2–3), there is a kind of honor that comes later on. Unlike earthly crowns that eventually rust or lose their luster, the pastor's reward is a crown with unfading glory.

THE LORD WILL BE ISRAEL'S SHEPHERD: EZEKIEL 34

The prophet Ezekiel prophesied these words to the leaders of Israel:

> The word of the LORD came to me: "Son of man, prophesy against the shepherds of Israel; prophesy, and say to them, even to the shepherds, Thus says the Lord GOD: Ah, shepherds of Israel who have been feeding yourselves! Should not shepherds feed the sheep? You eat the fat, you clothe yourselves with the wool, you slaughter the fat ones, but you do not feed the sheep. The weak you have not strengthened, the sick you have not healed, the injured you have not bound up, the strayed you have not brought back, the lost you have not sought, and with force and harshness you have ruled them. So they were scattered, because there was no shepherd, and they became food for all the wild beasts. My sheep were scattered; they wandered over all the mountains and on every high hill. My sheep were scattered over all the face of the earth, with none to search or seek for them." Ezekiel 34:1–6 ESV

At the time of this prophecy, Ezekiel was likely a young man who was preaching to the exiles in Babylonia, trying to provide hope to the prisoners of war who had been removed from the southern kingdom of Judah.[15] Like other prophets, he was given a "word of the LORD" (Ezek. 34:1, 7, 9) — a word directly from God for him to speak to "the shepherds of Israel" (Ezek. 34:2). God is giving a harsh warning to the leaders of Israel; hence, Ezekiel is to "prophesy *against* the shepherds of Israel" (Ezek. 34:2, emphasis added).

The Great Shepherd Warns His Undershepherds

In verse 2, the blunt statement ("Ah, shepherds of Israel who have been feeding yourselves!" ESV) and the question that immediately follows ("Should not shepherds feed the sheep?" ESV) both make clear the main problem — the leaders are only concerned to feed themselves and do not care for God's flock. The shepherds' self-concern is spelled out in verse 3 — they eat the fat, clothe themselves with wool, and slaughter the choice animals. Their neglect of the sheep is explained further in verse 4 — they don't care for the weak, sick, or injured; they don't search for the lost or bring back the strays; and they rule God's people with force and harshness. In 34:5–6, Ezekiel traces out the consequences of this bad leadership. "Because there was no shepherd" (34:5 ESV) to protect them, the sheep were scattered over the whole earth, wandering throughout the mountains, and became food for wild beasts.

In 34:1–6, the Lord is addressing Ezekiel and telling him to speak to the shepherds of Israel. In 34:7–10, the Lord is now addressing the shepherds directly ("Therefore, you shepherds, hear the word of the LORD"), and in 34:7–8 we find a summary of what has been said to Ezekiel. In 34:9–10, we find the most chilling words in the whole chapter— *God declares that He is against the shepherds and will hold them accountable.* Because of their failure to care for His sheep, God removes the leaders of Israel, and in their stead He will rescue His flock and no longer let them be food for the bad shepherds or wild animals.

God as Israel's Shepherd

What follows in Ezekiel 34:11–16 is a beautiful portrayal of God as Israel's shepherd. In stark contrast to the corrupt shepherds, God will *personally* care for His sheep. What's most striking is the proliferation of "I will …" statements in these six verses.[16] Fourteen times God states how He will rescue Israel: "I myself will search … so will I seek out my sheep, and I will rescue them … I will bring them out from the peoples … [I] will bring them into their own land … I will feed them on the mountains …, by the ravines … I will feed them with good pasture … I myself will be the shepherd of my sheep … I will seek the lost … I will bring back the strayed … I will bind up the injured … I will strengthen the weak … the fat and the strong I will destroy … I will feed them in justice" (Ezek. 34:11–16 ESV).

In Ezekiel 34:17–31, God shifts focus from the external threat of bad shepherds to mediating justice within God's flock between the strong and the weak sheep. Two things are important to note from this section. In 34:23–24, Ezekiel points to a Davidic shepherd who will be the human agent God uses to care for His flock in the place of the corrupt leaders of Israel. The pairing described in these two verses is *both* God as the rescuer and a human Davidic shepherd who will tend to His sheep. This is a time when Israel's leaders, especially her kings, were consistently corrupt. No surprise, then, that Ezekiel stresses a human Davidic "prince" (34:24 ESV) working under God, the true shepherd-King.[17]

The other focus to note is found in the final verses in the chapter (Eze. 34:30–31) where, in the context of talking about a covenant of peace (34:25), God reaffirms His personal relationship with Israel and uses the covenant language that is consistent throughout the Bible of "I am your God" and "you are My people" (cf. Lev. 26:11–12; Ezek. 37:27–28; Rev. 21:3).

Lessons for Pastors Today

Consider some of the lessons that pastors can learn from this text. First, *self-interest, irresponsibility, or harshness of bad shepherds can cause harm to God's sheep.* Just like the concern in 1 Peter 5:2–3 against elders pursuing "shameful gain" or being "domineering" over God's people, Ezekiel prophesies in 34:3–4 against Israel's leaders because they are consumed with care for themselves, and they are negligent, harsh, and brutal to God's sheep. But what I want to stress at this point are *the consequences* of bad shepherding on the sheep. The word "so" in 34:5 marks a transition from the corrupt attitudes and actions of the shepherds to the bad effects that poor shepherding has on God's sheep. Because of bad shepherding, God's flocks are scattered throughout the world. They wander on every mountain, and they become prey for wild animals.

So also it is in our pastoral ministries. If a pastor lets self-interest, irresponsibility, or harshness slip into his work, it is costly for the sheep. God's people need your help. Pastor, they need your time and attention. Your laziness, comfort-seeking, or being consumed with your own agenda might be a sign that you don't care enough about how God's sheep are affected by your *selfishness*. Or maybe you have been having a hard time with some of your church members, so you either subtly or willfully avoid them.

Have you, Pastor, ever been in the position of needing to have a hard conversation with someone? But because of your fear or your tendency to avoid conflict or because you just didn't want to do the hard work, you put off the conversation? If that is true, then God's flock is affected by your *irresponsibility*. Or maybe your tone tends toward harshness or contempt or disdain when you are frustrated with your church members. Or maybe it's not just when you are frustrated, and it is a common problem for you. Pastors are sinners, so as shepherds they make mistakes. But that's not what we're talking about. Pastors as *selfish, irresponsible, or harsh* sinners will let their sin ruin their pastoral ministry and hurt the sheep. In any sense, does this describe you? In all of these cases, if a pastor is unwilling to deal with his own sin, the lives of the sheep are made worse, not better. With the responsibility of leadership come greater consequences for sin, not only because the pastor's sin affects him, but because it also affects those God has entrusted to his care. There are consequences for God's people when a pastor is unwilling to face up to his own sin.

Think about *how seriously God takes this task of shepherding*. This entire passage is cloaked in a warning to the corrupt shepherds. The chilling statement in Ezekiel 34:10 ("Behold, I am against the shepherds" [esv]) should send shivers up a pastor's spine. God cares about shepherding so much that He would declare Himself an enemy of corrupt shepherds. This is the exact opposite of God's declaration: "Well done good and faithful servant" (Matt. 25:21, 23). Pastor, if you find yourself not wanting to shepherd God's flock, the fear of God being against you should be enough motivation for you to fulfill this work. Woe to anyone who finds the God of the universe against them!

The shepherding of His flock matters so much to God that *God Himself* will take the place of bad shepherds and rescue His sheep. Everything that corrupt shepherds did not do, we find that God personally will take on as a shepherd. If the corrupt shepherds did not strengthen the weak or heal the sick, God will. If they did not take care of the flock, God will tend the sheep. If they scattered the sheep, God will bring them back to a promised land. If they let the sheep wander, God will search for and rescue the lost. This is God's shepherding heart. We want to be pastors who line up with God's heart. We don't want to slip into getting fat off of the sheep.

God is so committed to rescuing His sheep that He will use a human agent to accomplish His purposes (Ezek. 34:23 – 24). This Davidic shepherd points to someone else who will come to be God's replacement for the bad shepherds in Israel. It's a perfect foreshadowing of Christ as the true shepherd of God's flock.

JESUS AS THE GOOD SHEPHERD OF GOD'S SHEEP: JOHN 10

The apostle John writes in John 10 about Jesus' conversation with the Pharisees:

> "Truly, truly, I say to you, he who does not enter the sheepfold by the door but climbs in by another way, that man is a thief and a robber. But he who enters by the door is the shepherd of the sheep. To him the gatekeeper opens. The sheep hear his voice, and he calls his own sheep by name and leads them out. When he has brought out all his own, he goes before them, and the sheep follow him, for they know his voice. A stranger they will not follow, but they will flee from him, for they do not know the voice of strangers." This figure of speech Jesus used with them, but they did not understand what he was saying to them.
>
> So Jesus again said to them, "Truly, truly, I say to you, I am the door of the sheep. All who came before me are thieves and robbers, but the sheep did not listen to them. I am the door. If anyone enters by me, he will be saved and will go in and out and find pasture. The thief comes only to steal and kill and destroy. I came that they may have life and have it abundantly.
>
> "I am the good shepherd. The good shepherd lays down his life for the sheep. He who is a hired hand and not a shepherd, who does not own the sheep, sees the wolf coming and leaves the sheep and flees, and the wolf snatches them and scatters them. He flees because he is a hired hand and cares nothing for the sheep.
>
> "I am the good shepherd. I know my own and my own know me, just as the Father knows me and I know the Father; and I lay down my life for the sheep. And I have other sheep that are not of this fold. I must bring them

also, and they will listen to my voice. So there will be one flock, one shepherd." John 10:1–16 ESV

In John 9, the blind man has been poorly treated by the religious authorities of the day. Jesus gives sight to the blind so that they can see who He really is (9:35–38), but the Pharisees, who refuse to believe in Jesus, remain spiritually blind (9:39–41). With this backdrop, Jesus in John 10 addresses the Pharisees again, using the shepherd imagery to create contrasts between Himself and the Pharisees. Because they are *blind* shepherds, they are also *bogus* shepherds.[18] They stand in stark contrast to Jesus, the one, true shepherd for God's sheep.

The True Shepherd and the False Shepherds

In John 10:1–6, the first contrast is between the true shepherd (Jesus) who enters by the door and calls his own sheep by name, and the thief and robber (the Pharisees) who enter by another way.[19] These verses focus on the voice of the shepherd, which prompts the sheep to leave the pen and to follow him because "they know his voice" (John 10:4).

In Jesus' day, the sheep from several neighbors usually were packed into one large fenced pen. The shepherd stood at a spot outside the enclosure and, using peculiar sounds, called out his own sheep, who responded by coming out of the pen and gathering around him.[20] Eastern shepherds are known to name their sheep, so the text describes the shepherd calling each sheep by name.[21] This differs from the thief or robber, who is a "stranger" to the sheep. The sheep "will not follow" the stranger, but will "flee from him, for they do not know the voice of strangers" (John 10:5–6 ESV).

Because the Pharisees don't understand this figure of speech (John 10:6), Jesus uses the same kind of imagery, but switches His focus to the door for the sheep (10:7–10) and the good shepherd laying down his life (10:11–16).

In John 10:7–10, Jesus uses the door imagery to explain that salvation comes through Him. He says, "I am the door" (10:7, 9 ESV). While this might sound strange to modern ears, Jesus often used physical images (water, bread, light, and now a door) to help the listener to think about what it means to believe in Him (John 4:10 – 14; 6:35, 47 – 48, 50 – 51, 53 – 56; 7:37 – 38; 8:12; 12:35 – 36). Salvation comes solely through Christ, as Jesus illustrates by describing safety for the sheep as them entering through Him (10:9). He adds that those who follow Him will "have life and have it abundantly" (10:10 ESV). Jesus will lead His sheep to the best of all pastures, where they will find a much richer life. In contrast to Jesus, the thieves and the robbers "steal and kill and destroy" (10:10 ESV), and the sheep do not listen to them (10:8).

In 10:11 – 16, Jesus twice describes Himself as "the good shepherd" who "lays down his life for the sheep" (10:11, 14 – 15 ESV). The term "good" conveys the idea of a noble or worthy shepherd.[22] The gospel motif presented here is the noble shepherd's willingness to die for his own sheep. In real life, this wouldn't make sense because the death of a shepherd would only make his flock more vulnerable. But this metaphor is meant to point to Christ, who according to the Father's will (John 10:17 – 18), would give His life on the cross for His sheep. As one author put it: "Far from being accidental, Jesus' death is precisely what qualifies him to be the good shepherd ... by his death, far from exposing his flock to further ravages, he draws them to himself."[23] The contrast in this section is with the hired hand who is oriented around his own deep self-interest. When danger comes, he runs away and leaves the sheep exposed because the hired hand "cares nothing for the sheep" (John 10:13 ESV).

Two other aspects of this good shepherd are important to note. First, the shepherd's knowledge of his sheep and the sheep's knowledge of their shepherd are so strong that the only adequate analogy is to compare them to the Father's relationship with His Son (John 10:14 – 15). Second, the shepherd has "other sheep that are not of this fold" (John 10:16 ESV) that he plans to bring into the fold. This is most certainly a reference to the Gentiles and the gospel message being proclaimed not only to the Jews but also to the Gentiles.

Lessons for Shepherds Today

Consider some of the lessons we get from this third text, starting with *marveling at Jesus as the good shepherd*. The prophecy of Ezekiel 34, which spoke of God as the greater rescuer and of a (human) Davidic shepherd being used by God to care for His flock, comes to full fruition in the life of Jesus. In this, we see the Incarnation. Christ did what no pastor can do — He atoned for the sins of God's sheep.

So the first lesson from this text is to adore Christ for giving over His life for His sheep. Praise God the Father that He sent a good shepherd to die for the sins of His people, including the religious leaders (like you and me). Jesus is the chief Shepherd (1 Peter 5:4), and His death on the cross is the crucial point in this shepherding motif.

A secondary application of this text is pastors laying down their lives by being servant-hearted and dying to self in the pastorate (Mark 8:34 – 35; Phil. 2:1 – 4). But this is at best a secondary application because the primary point of John 10 is that Jesus as the good shepherd gave over His life to atone for the sins of His sheep.

It is also important to consider *how much a pastor knows his own church members*. There is no such thing as a pristine, clean shepherd. The shepherd smells like his sheep because his life is intimately tied with theirs. The shepherd knows each sheep so personally, he is able to call them out by name (John 10:3). The mutual knowledge of shepherd and sheep is so strong that Jesus compares it to the closest relationship in the entire universe, that of the Father and His Son (cf. John 17:21 – 22).

Pastor, do you know your sheep? What I'm referring to is not a *casual* knowledge of your church members, but an *intimate* knowledge of their joys, hates, struggles, and sorrows. What's presumed here is both that the sheep view their pastor as approachable and that the pastor deliberately affords time in his schedule to get down into the weeds of life and walk alongside the sheep. To be a shepherd cannot mean viewing the sheep casually from a distance or only preaching to them, but shepherding them. That means walking with and sometimes even carrying them through the difficulties and many plights of this fallen world, pointing them to truth along the way and reminding them of their hope in Christ. God wants pastors to take the time to know their church members just as He knows and loves His very own Son.

SHEPHERDING IS MUCH MORE

My boss, Pastor Mark Dever, tells a story of his lunch with an Episcopal priest. Among many things, they talked about faith, and to Mark's surprise, the priest said he did not believe in God.

Mark asked, "Why are you working as a priest if you don't believe in God?"

The priest replied, "Because I need a job."

Shepherding is much more than just a job. It's a noble calling of pastors to shepherd God's flock. It's work done on behalf of God. It's the chance to live a Christlike example, to serve, to teach and instruct, to counsel, to pray, to bear burdens and joys and sorrows. It's the opportunity to hold Christ up as you walk alongside the sheep, to show Christ as the beginning and end of all things.

Pastor, remember these three texts — 1 Peter 5, Ezekiel 34, and John 10 — and let them serve as a backdrop to your ministry and motivation for you to pursue your sheep. As you think of your work today, pray that the Lord will help you to think of the pastorate as much more than just a job or just a preaching ministry. Ask the Lord to help you think and live as a worthy shepherd of God's flock.

CHAPTER 3

BIBLICAL COUNSELING AND SOUL CARE IN THE CHURCH

GARRETT HIGBEE

Do you remember this car commercial popular several years ago: "This is not your father's Oldsmobile"? The idea behind the slogan was to stir those watching to give the new line of Oldsmobiles a second look, to suggest that they weren't just the same old cars driven by your dad. I'd like to borrow that slogan in this chapter on biblical counseling. The biblical counseling movement today is *not* your father's biblical counseling. Biblical counseling today has made significant advances in understanding how to help people grow and change. I hope this book and others like it will help to combat stereotypes and give us pause to take another look at biblical counseling. Contemporary biblical counseling has a relatively short, but somewhat colorful, history, and it has changed in significant ways over the last forty years.

What is the first thing you think of when you hear the term "biblical counseling"? This might depend on how much you know about the movement, if you know it by personal experience or if, like many, you have drawn a caricature from secondhand information. As someone formally trained in psychology who joined the movement in the early 1990s, I have seen the best and worst of the movement over the last twenty years. And I can tell you that most biblical counselors are great people with good intentions. Perhaps you've heard that biblical counselors are too harsh or they only have one tool in their tool belt: "If you only have a hammer, everything looks like a nail." While some of this, unfortunately, may be true, most biblical counselors today are equipped with many tools (1 Thess. 5:14) and have a far more nuanced perspective of care.

In this chapter, we'll focus on the way biblical counseling has matured as a discipline and why it should be an essential part of every healthy local church. We will start by taking a brief look at the history of counsel and care in the local church, and then I will compare and contrast what I see as two outcomes of a relatively recent return to the Scriptures in counseling. On the one hand, those who specialize in biblical counseling have come a long way in promoting and practicing the sufficiency of God's Word in helping people. Yet on the other hand, we have a long way to go to restore the ministry of soul care to every believer in the church. In the pages that follow, I will outline two approaches to biblical counseling in the local church: the traditional biblical counseling (BC) approach and what we will call the "Counseling In Community" (CIC) approach. I believe these two approaches are both built on the doctrine of the sufficiency of Scripture, but have differences in philosophy and methods of training and care. While they are not altogether separate from each other, by comparing and contrasting them in method and manner, we can see how to harness the strengths of both. Finally, I want to propose that by combining and complementing the strengths of these two models, we can increase our influence, impact, and efficacy as a biblical counseling movement.

Let's look back to learn, and let's look forward with an appreciation for where we have come. I think the lessons from the past need to extend far beyond the last forty years to consider the rich history of soul care of the early church, the Puritans, and pastoral care in the local church. A brief look back at the longer history of the cure of souls will help us to avoid a myopic or reactive analysis of the biblical counseling model of discipleship and care.

CULTURAL TRENDS THAT SHAPED COUNSELING IN THE CHURCH

In the last 2,000 years of pastoral care in the church, there have been many variations on how to cure souls. From a top-down clergy model to giving laymen specific roles and authority over those seeking care to emphasizing the priesthood of believers, counseling or caring for souls in and through the church has seen a lot of changes.[24] In the last two hundred years, psychology, modernism, and the medical model have clearly shaped counseling in the church. In the last fifty years there has been a growing commitment to bring back the authority and sufficiency of the Bible in church-based counseling. I believe there are truths we still need to learn from each epoch. While we are all indebted to those who fought to bring God's Word front and center in the counseling of believers, I believe we must look past a few pioneer voices or para-church movements to a rich historical perspective of soul care in the local church. The first place we must look is to Scripture itself. Scripture gives us not only great content for biblical counseling but also the context in which it is to be ministered.

God's Word has outlined a compelling and clear method and manner for wise counsel in and among the body of Christ (cf. ch. 7 in this book as well as the larger volume *Scripture and Counseling*[25]). To really see this, you would have to look not only for the word "counsel" in Scripture, but also see words like "discipline," "admonish," "encourage," "rebuke," "train," and "equip" as often synonymous with it (2 Tim. 3:16–17). In our church we have replaced the phrase "biblical counseling" with the term "biblical soul care." This was largely because biblical counseling has come to mean something so different from discipleship (later in this chapter you will see that these are not all that different). The "care of souls," as John McNeil calls it, has a longer and richer history than "biblical counseling."[26] The scope of this is beyond the focus of this chapter, but I would encourage you to do your own study of the cure of souls. It's a practice that can be traced back to the early church. We continue to learn from the past by taking a closer look at early church practices and the writings of the Puritans and of those who have written on the history of the pastoral care movement.

A Common Heritage

With the privatizing and professionalization of psychology in the last century, we have seen a departure from historic models of pastoral care toward pragmatism, from a priesthood of believers to more of a top-down medical model. I believe these are trends that have, over time, led the church to abdicate responsibility to care for its own. Integration of psychology in our practice is one challenge, but we also need to address the secularization of not only the message but the method of our care, ultimately influencing our approach to discipleship as well.

The idea of counseling and caring for one another is as old as the church. For centuries, the local church was at the center of what today are the disciplines of social science and social work. While the church did not immediately embrace secular practices of counseling, the church did, sadly, adapt to these over the centuries. Eventually the mainline churches and seminaries even allowed psychology to be the predominant theory and practice in the private ministry of counseling.[27]

In times past, pastors and priests were seen as *the* persons to turn to for wisdom, counsel, and confession. The church was a place for the widow or the fatherless to receive help both financially and emotionally. Clergymen visited homes, knew their people well, and provided guidance on a multitude of matters. Privacy was not valued over community, and soul care was not the exclusive privilege or obligation of the pastor.[28] In fact, it was the habit of those in the early church to eat together, share materials things, and pray for each other regularly (Acts 2:42–48). Many Reformers (like Luther and Calvin) as well as the Puritans, the Methodist Church, and other Protestant movements and denominations had a strong focus on the doctrine of the priesthood of believers.[29] This care for strangers and brothers alike is close to God's heart and in line with His Word. It is commanded in imperatives like "love one another," "encourage one another," and "bear one another's burdens," among many others.

A Changing Culture

Unfortunately, the rise of humanistic thinking in culture and in life-style led to changes in pastoral care and counseling. By the start of the twentieth century, the church was no longer seen as the epicenter for counsel and care. Psychology and psychiatry were growing in popularity and influence, and the church had all but lost its voice in helping those needing counsel and care.[30] Heath Lambert describes this well in *The Biblical Counseling Movement after Adams* when he says:

> As the church was focusing on revivalistic effort at soul winning and a defense of the fundamentals for the faith, secular psychologists were gaining ascendency employing the scientific method with cutting-edge work in understanding people in their relationships with others. As it turns out, this was information that a changing American culture found useful, while the church sat on the sidelines.[31]

The perceived need for a trained professional became the norm. The church was marginalized, having little authority to speak into what the world now called "mental illness." Since habitual sin and ongoing suffering were now classified as diseases, the proposed answer to these problems was a medical model of treatment. Issues of faith were still the business of the church, but what did that have to do with problems originating from complex physiological or environmental factors? People went to school to receive specialized training to treat these things. The idea of coming to the church for something more than pre-marital counseling or common wisdom for decisions of life was mocked by many professionals.[32]

And what became of counseling in the church? It was something to defer to others in the church who were specially trained or to refer out to professionals. Unfortunately, but understandably, pastors felt ill-equipped to handle anything beyond everyday concerns. In fact, this was acceptable and even taught, as most seminaries would typically offer just one or two classes on pastoral care to prepare those going into full-time ministry.

In the 1970s, Jay Adams published his groundbreaking book *Competent to Counsel*. David Powlison, writing about Adams, notes, "Adams, like many other observers before and since, noted that secular psychologies had largely replaced the church as the culture-wide authority in the personal problems domain."[33] Adams called the church back to care for its own people, elevating the authority and sufficiency of God's Word as useful for counseling believers. Lambert explains Adams' impact:

> Adams sought to alert Christians to their failures in the area of counseling and began pointing the way to the resources laid out in Scripture for helping people. It was the role of Adams to begin to restore to the church an understanding that … counseling was in the realm of the church, every bit as much as its counterpart in public ministry, preaching.[34]

This was the start of a small but growing movement called "nouthetic" or "biblical counseling," one that is still growing today. The focus was on teaching and admonishing those in sin and struggles to turn to God and His Word for answers, rather than turning to philosophies and therapies offered by the world. Slowly, a number of conservative churches sought training to equip both clergy and laity to counsel from God's Word.

THE MATURING OF THE BIBLICAL COUNSELING MOVEMENT

This initial model of biblical counseling is what I now refer to as the "traditional" model. It was developed in a time that Jerry Bridges has called a "crisis of caring"[35] in the church. Fellowship was shallow and people were not receiving biblical counsel, being referred to secular care instead. Few churches had even a basic understanding of how to begin a biblical counseling ministry in their church, and fears of liability, credibility, and a lack of competence were real.[36] Resources were limited, pastors ill-equipped, and a syncretistic mindset in the congregation made starting such a ministry an uphill battle. The pendulum swing was often an all-or-nothing proposition: "Either you are with us or you are not." This traditional biblical counseling model, as Health Lambert describes, was like "building an airplane while it was flying in the air."[37] There was a strong emphasis on efficiency, pragmatism, and departmentalism as small silos of biblical counseling, separated from other church ministries, began to take root in many churches. It was rocky soil, and planting seeds and silos of biblical counselors in the church was a good start.

In the almost fifty years since Adams heralded a call back to Scripture in counseling, the discipline of biblical counseling has changed and grown. Solid resources for addressing issues like anger, depression, addictions, and fear are now readily available. Never has the church been more ready to competently care for their people instead of referring and deferring to mental health professionals. Agencies like the Association of Certified Biblical Counselors (ACBC), the Christian Counseling and Educational Foundation (CCEF), the Association of Biblical Counselors (ABC), and the International Association of Biblical Counselors (IABC), among others, have created rigorous biblical training and resources for counselors who want to handle problems with competence and provide biblically grounded care. And the Biblical Counseling Coalition (BCC) has helped to unify and advance the movement in a more coordinated way that is impacting biblical counseling efforts globally.

The "traditional" biblical counseling model has matured. And yet, similar to the season between the period of the early church and the Reformation, the care of souls in the church has become so specialized that the average layperson does not understand how to speak the truth in love. I believe this has created an inadvertent gap between discipleship and counseling, one that has grown as we have emphasized certification and training, both in doctrine and in counseling methods and techniques.

A False Dichotomy

So while I agree that there is a need for rigorous training for those engaged in formal counseling, this has created a false dichotomy between the counsel of God's Word and ongoing discipleship, similar to what we find in preaching and teaching. I don't want to create an either/or mentality here. The traditional biblical counseling approach is a gift to the church, one of the best things that has happened in the local church in our lifetime. But I believe there is a complementary approach that can enhance its impact, what we referred to earlier as the "Counseling In Community" (CIC) approach. Simply stated, CIC is the care of souls from intentional to intensive discipleship. It is an every-believer ministry. CIC describes a combination of informal and formal counsel where discipleship and biblical counseling are on the *same* continuum. The CIC approach, with its rich community context and focus, differs in some methodologies from the traditional BC approach. It intentionally tries to avoid structuring biblical counseling as a silo ministry, separate from other ministries, and instead is working in partnership with each discipleship avenue in the local church. Second, it includes advocacy in formal counseling.[38] And third, in the CIC approach, there is more focus on prevention as well as the power of the "one-anothers" as we live out the priesthood of all believers. Let me try to unpack each of these points.

In a church with a traditional BC model, there is a tendency for the average church member to see counseling as beyond their reach. Members believe they must have extensive, specialized training before they can engage in counseling others (as shown in figure 1). In addition, some who have been formally trained are guilty of neglecting some of the basics of good discipleship and have become too problem-focused, more like an expert consultant than a walk-alongside discipler. In figure 2 you see the continuum where good discipleship includes elements of biblical counsel *and* good counsel includes elements of discipleship. The nature and role of the person who is training or helping changes as you move across the continuum. Every believer needs to find himself or herself somewhere on this continuum. Every believer needs to get equipped.

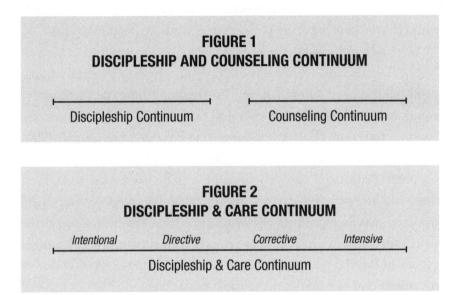

FIGURE 1
DISCIPLESHIP AND COUNSELING CONTINUUM

Discipleship Continuum   Counseling Continuum

FIGURE 2
DISCIPLESHIP & CARE CONTINUUM

Intentional   Directive   Corrective   Intensive

Discipleship & Care Continuum

A Seamless Unity

In figure 2, we see a continuity of care and seamless delivery of discipleship, which sound great in theory but have been criticized as a bit ambitious in practice. The truth is that involving community in counseling is harder and less convenient in many ways. That said, it is well worth the effort and something that we have tried and tested in our church. If it was easy, everyone would be doing it. Only in the last decade have we seen more churches aggressively equipping their people, breaking down walls between professional ministry and the average church member so that the church is not a church *with* a counseling department (or referral process), but a church *of* biblical counselors. While there is an acknowledgment in theory, the number of churches practicing a "counseling in community" model of discipleship and care is still small.

How many churches do you know that involve every believer in the ministry of soul care, from the janitor to the senior pastor? This is more of a shift in philosophy and execution of discipleship and care than a change in counseling content or theological convictions. My goal is to provoke thought on how you can include everyone in your church in the privilege of speaking the truth in love and how this will increase your effectiveness in caring for souls and winning people to Christ.

In our church we choose to practice a CIC approach that we call "Biblical Soul Care." While it is certainly not the only model for doing good biblical counseling, I have seen firsthand how the inclusion of community and a focus on prevention can result in a radically positive effect on the entire church. It is our goal to be uncompromisingly biblical in both the content and context of our counseling. I am aware that the phrase "soul care" can sometimes be used by secular counselors and those who integrate psychology and the Bible. We in no way purposely integrate psychology in theory or practice (that is why we added the term "biblical"). We have full doctrinal alignment with the traditional model, but we have expanded what we do to embrace the doctrine of the priesthood of believer and discipleship as well.

I'll be the first to admit that the CIC approach is riddled with challenges. Breaking down walls and building bridges is harder than staying behind established boundaries. Bringing advocates into the counseling room is a logistical nightmare at times. But we believe the CIC approach models more of the context and manner of early church community and leverages the strengths of the Puritan way of life. In particular, we see the power of intentional, deep fellowship and "radical hospitality."[39] It has been our hope to further develop and refine this into the "third generation" of biblical counseling.[40] First-generation BC was helpful in bringing the sufficiency of God's Word back to counseling, and the second-generation leaders helped us to find a balance in caring for the sufferer as well, but it is time to embrace the power of community in counseling. Hopefully, you will see how this translates into action in the next chapter.

While many in the BC movement agree in principle that everyone should be equipped, less has been done on creating levels of training for laypeople below BC certification. However, there are those who are attempting to disciple by equipping the saints for the work of ministry. The fulcrum of biblical counseling is beginning to shift to more prevention at the small group level and more intentional "spiritual friendship."[41] That shift leverages the power of detection and prevention of problems so that they can be addressed earlier. This has broad implications for both the methods and manner by which we train for and practice biblical counseling.

COMPARING CARE AND PRACTICE

The CIC approach elevates the unique position of the local church as a community of helping, healing, and hope for a broken world.[42] In sharing this approach, my goal is not to diminish the contribution of the traditional biblical counseling approach, but to complement it. In the last fifty years this model has been very helpful in establishing a new standard of practice. There are policies and procedures for formal biblical counseling that have decreased liability and increased ethical standards and effectiveness in the counseling room. The counselors' understanding of God's Word, their concern for the person in front of them, and the professional manner by which they serve are all to be commended. We need certified and educated counselors. My point in presenting this complementary approach is that trained staff and certified counselors will never meet *all* of the needs of the body of Christ.

In the table below you can see an overview of some of the contextual/methodological differences between the two approaches as well as the secular approach. This table highlights where we overlap with other models, including the medical model of care. While this table is helpful to illustrate key differences, the key point is to show that there is no significant difference in doctrine between the traditional and CIC approach.

TABLE 1
KEY DIFFERENCES IN COUNSELING METHODS

	Secular (Medical) Model	Traditional Biblical Counseling	Counseling in Community
50 minute sessions	✓	✓	Usually Longer
One-on-one	✓	✓	Rarely
Trained "expert" practitioner	✓	✓	Sometimes**
Formal setting	✓	✓	Sometimes**
Biblical authority	n/a	✓	✓
Biblical sufficiency	n/a	✓	✓
Advocates/godly friend involved	n/a	*	✓
Relational 360-degree assessment	n/a	*	✓
Emphasis on small group/community	n/a	*	✓
Local church based care	n/a	*	✓
Apprentices in counseling sessions	Sometimes	*	✓

* Some para-church counseling ministries and conventional BC departments in churches are increasingly moving toward adopting these in their counseling approaches.
** CIC includes both informal and formal counseling. In the higher levels of care, our BSC ministry, for example, uses trained counselors in more formal office settings.[43]

The first several categories on the chart show how the modern biblical counseling movement was a product of its time. As a psychologist who practiced in a clinical setting, I was taught to put a premium on getting people in and out quickly, doing a quick diagnostic so I could get to the counseling, guarding privacy, and promising absolute confidentiality. When I transferred to the biblical counseling model, I found the formal counseling training and practices very similar. I was taught how to do a fifty- to fifty-five-minute session, to treat people as an "expert relating to a counselee" rather than as "a person coming alongside another hurting person." No one else in the person's life seemed to know what we did in the counseling room. Again, some of this was understandably driven by a need to look more professional and legitimate. Unfortunately, it limited our cultural impact and biblical effectiveness.[44]

Today, more than ever before, we see the importance of healthy community and body-life. A growing number of leaders and churches focus on prevention and intervention. Jay Adams and others have always had an appreciation for an every-believer ministry, but we have not developed our training to accomplish that end. As a movement, we are finally developing training and resources so that every believer can effectively participate in the health and welfare of their brother and sister in Christ (cf. Gal. 6:1 – 2; Col. 2:8; Heb. 3:12 – 13). I believe you will see the biblical counseling movement becoming more proactive in establishing biblical norms for healthy church leadership, healthy church community, and healthy church members.

So how does this change the way we train for and practice biblical counseling? This is the question now being addressed by many "second- and third-generation" BC leaders. It was the topic of a recent Biblical Counseling Coalition retreat as well. As we take back the responsibility to care for our people rather than to defer or refer, we also need to establish a model of care that is uniquely formed in the context of the local church. We have the ability to see and intervene, to deal with issues in the context of community, and to use testimony to give hope and help to others.

Let me illustrate this with the practice of data gathering. Biblical counselors will often say, "Start with good data gathering." But when you're sitting in your living room after small group, you're not thinking, "I have to get data on this couple." What you really want to do is "get to know them." You are not going to whip out a personal data inventory or self-report questionnaire over coffee. So we need to train our people to ask the right questions and to get to know folks well enough to be able to help them. We also want to take advantage of every perspective in the room. As a small group leader, you may want your spouse's perspective if it's a couple you're caring for. We train our small group leaders to ask each spouse being counseled to describe the other. The leaders watch, ask questions, listen carefully, and evaluate what they need. Those being counseled will be better served if we don't presume or just have one angle on how they got where they are (Prov. 18:13, 17; 20:5). All of this is more like a relational 360-degree assessment as opposed to a formal or one-on-one clinical interview (Prov. 11:14).

So while it is helpful in some contexts of biblical counseling to have a more structured, even clinical, approach, I believe the church needs to move toward greater flexibility. Small group leaders can be taught assessment skills to allow the church to grow in caring deeply, not only at the corrective/intervention level but at the directive/prevention level.

Another example would be the trend of having professional distance. A CIC approach changes the way we talk to and about our people. There is less sterile distance and more relational richness. We don't fear the past, but see it as important in shaping the heart. We see it as influential but not determinative. We conduct a life-story interview that allows us to know the counselee(s) on a more personal basis rather than with a problem focus. We invite others into the room who know the counselee well, people we refer to as "advocates." These individuals walk alongside and encourage the person in the formal counseling process.

These changes revolutionized the long-term gains and leveraged relationship at a whole new level. One might think the counselee would be less likely to disclose if we include others in the counseling process, but we have actually found that to rarely be the case. Not only do counselees share deeply, but the person in the room who has history with them can bring context and nuances that provide added insights and information that would otherwise be difficult, if not impossible, to get. We teach a relational discretion that comes with being confidants with zero tolerance for gossip, but we don't put privacy over community. Again, I'm not saying that traditional biblical counseling is cold and uncaring; I'm saying we can be even more pastoral and effective in our care and equipping of the saints.

Figure 3 is an attempt to simply illustrate the focus I am highlighting. It portrays the primacy of the Word of God (emphasized by Adams) and pictures the importance of progressive sanctification and caring for the sufferer (the work of Powlison, Welch, Tripp, and others). However, the third side of the triangle is where I am suggesting the traditional model and even second-generation biblical counseling have been lacking. It points out the need to emphasize the priesthood of believers and community—the very means by which the world is supposed to know that we love one another.[45] It's essential to have the sufficiency of Scripture as our doctrinal foundation for counseling. And we need the hope that is given through solid teaching on progressive sanctification. But I believe that the value of teaching our people to speak the truth in love to one another at every level in the body of believers is the missing ingredient today. It is not emphasized, taught, and lived out in many churches, which may be part of why our young people are growing disenfranchised with the church today. I'm thankful for the example of Paul Tripp, Jerry Bridges, Brad Bigney, Steve Viars, Bob Kellemen, Jonathan Holmes, and many others, who are encouraging a growing inclusion of deep fellowship and community in counseling.

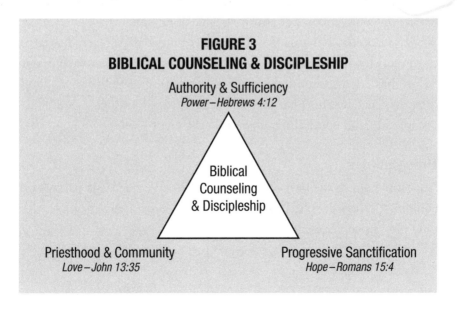

FIGURE 3
BIBLICAL COUNSELING & DISCIPLESHIP
Authority & Sufficiency
Power—Hebrews 4:12

Biblical Counseling & Discipleship

Priesthood & Community
Love—John 13:35

Progressive Sanctification
Hope—Romans 15:4

REDEFINING COMPETENCE TO COUNSEL

There is one final question I would like to address: Just who is qualified to do discipleship and care?[46] As I have said, the doctrine of the priesthood of believers does not negate the need for excellence in training and care; it just expands it to a wider audience. In the conventional biblical counseling approach, the average small group member and even small group leader can get away with saying, "I'm not a biblical counselor." My usual response is, "Really? Then what kind of counselor are you? You counsel yourself, your family, and your friends all the time." We need to teach people that they are counselors, that we all bear the responsibility and the privilege of offering counsel to others in the body of Christ.

At the same time, we wrongly give people the sense that they don't need to be better equipped when we tell them, "We have people who do that." Certainly some training agencies would love to equip more people but, understandably, in the culture we live in, many still want credentials and not just "training." So we need to redefine what we mean by *competent* to counsel. Competence is a tricky thing. Imagine if you had to pass a competency test to be a spouse or a parent. Marriage and parenting are more "learn as you go" and "know when you are in over your head" than something you can train and prepare for. Scripture would encourage maturity of character and knowledge of the Word as criteria, but this is not exclusive to certified or credentialed counselors by any means. It is not by certifying others that we fail; our failure has been more in the neglect of training at the informal and directive level of care. That may be because we still train and equip like discipleship and counseling are on two different planes.

Equipping

As pointed out in the first chapter, Ephesians 4 is the classic passage on equipping God's people. In a classic New Testament passage on equipping God's people, we read:

> And he gave the apostles, the prophets, the evangelists, the shepherds and teachers, to equip the saints for the work of ministry.
>
> Ephesians 4:11–12 ESV

This passage points to the fact that we need to wake up the whole body of Christ. Christ's hands and feet seem to have fallen asleep from inactivity.[47] It's time to equip all the saints to do the work of ministry in the local church. But what would that look like? Let me draw you a picture of someone trained in the traditional model of BC versus a CIC model of care. I will purposely use extremes to illustrate the differences. However, I would argue that these examples are not all that far-fetched. They are more common in our churches than we might like to admit.

The Practical Impact of Two Approaches to Training

First, imagine being trained and sent back to your church as their official counselor. You find yourself isolated in a room with a line of people waiting for help. There is no plan to multiply the ministry and no one to truly help or hold you accountable. You need help from the body of Christ, but your church doesn't understand this, and on top of that you have not been trained to counsel in community. You are soon overwhelmed and under-supported. You really can't talk about the sessions due to confidentiality, and you can't explain the burden you are feeling. You live for the next biblical counseling conference or a chance to talk with a pastor who might understand because you feel so out on a limb. You love what you do, but you are not sure how long you can sustain this pace or carry these burdens. It is a heavy feeling, and it can lead to fatigue and moments of wanting to call it quits. Again, not everyone trained in biblical counseling is in this position, but some are, and part of the reason is because we have mimicked the medical model of training, creating sole-practitioner experts who have little accountability and little support.

Now imagine what it would be like if you were trained with a group of peers. Most of the equipping happened in your local church, and when outside training was needed, others were sent along with you. You interacted both personally and in depth about your own struggles and your growing understanding of heart change. You sharpened each other and went into the practicum with trusted leaders at your side. In the counseling room, you were often not the only apprentice, and there were always advocates learning as well. You saw the power of multiple perspectives and manifold gifts. You weren't just an observer, but an active participant as you prayed out loud, did the homework, and connected with the person in need of help to answer questions the best you could. You debriefed and discreetly talked about what you saw and heard after sessions. You were taught to pray and leave the burdens at the foot of the cross and knew others would be praying with and for you. You sensed that you would never be alone in bearing burdens or if you got stuck in the process. It gave you confidence and helped you to see a sustainable future in the biblical counseling ministry of your church.

I have seen both examples and believe part of growing a healthy church is making sure we model care and community with our counselors as well.

Important Care Structures in the Local Church

One obvious implication of the CIC approach is that it is dependent on, and can only really function in, a church context. If the goal were simply to train competent counselors, this model would fall short. However, in the local church this model thrives because only the local church can potentially provide the ecclesiastical support of a biblical and healthy supervision hierarchy. God designed it that way. We have pastors, elders, and lay leaders to guide the flock. We would benefit as a movement to think about how to interact with that structure and figure out where formal counseling fits in, not to compensate for, but to complement both those who minister above and below the counselors. Specifically, training counselors to work with elders and pastors in the church and the small group leaders would be helpful. If you are currently the "expert in counseling" at your church, how do the elders or your pastor really help develop you or hold you accountable? What do you do to involve elders in discipline, especially if they don't understand biblical counseling principles? How do you help small group leaders to receive a counselee back into group in a way that maximizes the gains made in counseling? If you involve advocates, how do you train and equip them to come alongside people in need? What about apprentices?

The traditional biblical counseling model has its strengths and works well in a small church and for crisis situations. Sometimes people need immediate care and need to be seen quickly. This makes the coordination of schedules next to impossible to get several people in the room the same day for both advocacy and apprentice training. Other times a person, perhaps in deep shame, is barely ready to share with the counselor, let alone any others. This is where the traditional biblical counseling model has more flexibility in speed and privacy that makes it more helpful in crisis care. Ideally, however, both options should be available in the local church. I would suggest that as someone is de-escalated from crisis care, the community should begin to be more involved.

There is also the issue of capacity and time. If resources are limited and your church has only a few leaders, the traditional model is a great place to start. The structure of one hour with a trained counselor who can get people helped while you are building a small group ministry is very helpful. The management of multiple people—advocates, apprentices, and small group leaders—in the care plan takes time and maturity. Realistically, that needs to be built over months. While changes do take time, there needs to be some training available at each level.[48] Getting proper supervision in place in the local church is crucial. Parachurch training agencies often have fellows who can do supervision for you. The tests and practicum training for these agencies are standardized and rigorous. Again, this is a good starting point for some churches, especially since not all churches want to or can develop their own training in this area.

We Are Better Together

What would it look like to have a full-orbed, healthy discipleship and care culture in your church? Churches should encourage or offer certification (or its equivalent) for formal counselors. At the same time, we need to take more advanced training and adapt it for small group leaders and advocates. The more equipped counselors in your church should teach and supervise those at the front lines of soul care. We need to develop standards for confidentiality and communication between group leaders and counselors. We need to glean the advantages from the various approaches to training as we work together as a coalition. And we need to learn from the para-church ministry that uses volunteers and often adapts training more readily. We can and will get stronger by combining our strengths and learning together from our failures.

I will admit that there is a tension in striving for strong competence while not excluding everyday believers from being equipped. There is an increasing need for equipping and experience as you move from intentional discipleship to intensive crisis counseling. But I hope we stop sacrificing pastoral care for a sense of professionalism. I love what John Piper has said: "The more professional we long to be, the more spiritual death we will leave in our wake. For there is no professional childlikeness (Matt. 18:3); there is no professional tenderheartedness (Eph. 4:32); there is no professional panting after God (Ps. 42:1)."[49] The bottom line is that we need the competence of highly trained formal counselors, but not at the expense of de-motivating the less trained but highly effective preventive arm of soul care at the ground level.

CONCLUSION

I will leave you to ponder the following questions in hopes you will live in the tension of both a biblical context and content for counseling in the local church:

- How do we help the church to see biblical counseling as a vital part of all discipleship training and help trained counselors to see the need to involve the community in the care of souls?
- How do we combine rigorous training and uncompromising biblical standards while not training people to hang a shingle or do counseling in isolation?

- How do we provide ongoing training and peer review, but help pastors and local church leaders stay connected with the biblical counseling staff and leaders in the church?
- How do we train biblical counseling leaders to multiply the ministry by taking the lead in a team of counselors, advocates, and small group leaders, not allowing counseling in a vacuum where the right hand doesn't know what the left hand is doing?
- How do we keep the baton moving forward with a seamless continuum of care as we return the person to a small group after formal counseling?
- How do we set up formal counseling times and have clear expectations for that time, but take the time needed to unpack a life story, give counsel, and heart-targeting homework?

We are God's chosen people for discipleship and care. Nowhere else on earth has God put together the Word of God, the Spirit of God, and the people of God in a culture able to speak the truth in love at every level of relationship. It's this power that God entrusted to the local church that gives us a platform to help a broken world see who Christ is and how He redeemed us, set us apart, and called us to be known by our love. I hope you will be part of this exciting time in our history as we strive for counseling in the context of the local church community and the unity of the movement going forward (John 17:20–23).

CHAPTER 4

UNITING THE PUBLIC
MINISTRY OF THE WORD
AND THE PRIVATE
MINISTRY OF THE WORD

KEVIN CARSON AND PAUL TAUTGES

Our passionate longing as biblical counselors is to see the flock under our care brought to maturity in Christ. "Maturity" for all is the goal (Eph. 4:13). Therefore, the ministry of the Word is all about applying the truth of the believer's union with Christ to a life lived in loving relationship with God and others. Helping others to experience this "measure of the stature which belongs to the fullness of Christ" (Eph. 4:13 NASB) is the focus of counseling in the church.

Not a single leading figure in the New Testament comes close to the apostle Paul when it comes to modeling his ministerial life after the Lord Jesus Christ—the Perfect Man, Perfect Shepherd, and Perfect Gospel Minister. Consider Paul's testimony to the Ephesian elders as he left them in charge of the church that God had used him to plant; sense his ministerial heartbeat.

> From Miletus he sent to Ephesus and called to him the elders of the church. And when they had come to him, he said to them,

"You yourselves know, from the first day that I set foot in Asia, how I was with you the whole time, serving the Lord with all humility and with tears and with trials which came upon me through the plots of the Jews; how I did not shrink from declaring to you anything that was profitable, and teaching you publicly and from house to house, solemnly testifying to both Jews and Greeks of repentance toward God and faith in our Lord Jesus Christ. And now, behold, bound by the Spirit, I am on my way to Jerusalem, not knowing what will happen to me there, except that the Holy Spirit solemnly testifies to me in every city, saying that bonds and afflictions await me. But I do not consider my life of any account as dear to myself, so that I may finish my course and the ministry which I received from the Lord Jesus, to testify solemnly of the gospel of the grace of God.

"And now, behold, I know that all of you, among whom I went about preaching the kingdom, will no longer see my face. Therefore, I testify to you this day that I am innocent of the blood of all men. For I did not shrink from declaring to you the whole purpose of God. Be on guard for yourselves and for all the flock, among which the Holy Spirit has made you overseers, to shepherd the church of God which He purchased with His own blood. I know that after my departure savage wolves will come in among you, not sparing the flock; and from among your own selves men will arise, speaking perverse things, to draw away the disciples after them. Therefore be on the alert, remembering that night and day for a period of three years I did not cease to admonish each one with tears. And now I commend you to God and to the word of His grace, which is able to build *you* up and to give *you* the inheritance among all those who are sanctified."   Acts 20:17–32 NASB

Paul's challenge to these elders suggests three helpful observations for the ministry of the Word: (1) Paul's teaching ministry included both the public and private proclamation of the Word; (2) he explained his goal as teaching the gospel of the grace of God; and (3) he described his teaching ministry as that which carefully taught the whole counsel of God and challenged the elders to care for the church of God. These church shepherds were to provide protection and care through an ongoing teaching ministry. Paul's public and private ministry of the Word complemented each other and worked toward the fulfillment of Jesus' great command to make disciples (Matt. 28:18–20).

The public and the private ministry of the Word provide the skeletal structure and muscular system for biblical discipleship, respectively. In this light, we'll consider the relationship of teaching to discipleship, the importance of both the public and private ministry of the Word, and some practical steps we can take to make sure these complement each other, functionally, in the life of the church.

THE RELATIONSHIP OF TEACHING TO DISCIPLESHIP

Teaching is an integral part of the process of discipleship — the movement of a believer toward the goal of becoming an obedient follower and reflection of Jesus. Both the public and private ministry of the Word is essential to a faithful teaching ministry.

Teaching Is a Necessary Part of Fulfilling the Great Commission

The goal of teaching is to help others obey God as we all learn to walk by faith, empowered by the indwelling Spirit, thus living in the presence of Christ who said He would be with us until the end of the age (Matt. 28:20). The heart of discipleship is developing passionate followers of Christ who die to self by loving God and others daily. In order to obey Christ, it is necessary to be taught the content of the Bible. This includes the general teaching of the Bible — the whole purpose of God — with special consideration to what Jesus taught (Matt. 28:20).

Teaching Is a Necessary Part of the Pastor's Role

Paul not only provides us with an example of teaching in his own personal ministry; he also emphasizes the importance of teaching to the overall growth of the church (Eph. 4:11 – 16). He explains the specific purpose of the pastor-teacher: to equip the body of Christ. An equipped member of the body is capable of doing the work of the ministry; that is, doing his or her part to edify the body. The goal of this equipping ministry is to see that the body grows in unity of the faith and knowledge of the Son of God until the church becomes mature in Christlikeness.

The desire of the biblical minister is to see the church move from spiritual gullibility to mature discernment as believers speak truth to the other (Eph. 4:14–15). As truth-speaking takes place, in love, among the members of the congregation, the whole body grows together in Christ.

Understanding this emphasis should lead to two convictions. First, the life of the church *must include* both a consistent emphasis on the meaning and impact of living out faith in Christ (the vertical dimension), as well as the reality of living in authentic relationship with others in the body (the horizontal dimension). This is the manifestation of mature love. Second, teaching the Word verbally and by example is *central* to the pastor's role. It is his most vital work in the church. It is through consistent biblical teaching that the church is equipped, grows in the unity of the faith and knowledge of the Son of God, and becomes mature in Him.

Paul is not alone in emphasizing the teaching priority of the pastor. The writer of Hebrews exhorts his readers to remember what their leaders had taught them, how their leaders lived, and urged them to make life joyful for their pastors since they watch over their souls (Heb. 13:1–19). Leaders play a role in the life of the believer and will ultimately give an account for what impact they make on the believer's life. Furthermore, Peter emphasizes teaching in his epistles (2 Peter 1:12–15). Peter describes the teaching process as worth his best effort—constantly reminding people of the truth, stirring people in the truth of Christ. Peter strives for them to understand their union in Christ (2 Peter 1:2–4) and how to live out that union in the day-by-day pursuits of life (2 Peter 1:5–11).

Teaching Is a Necessary Part of Maturity in Christ

Paul describes the focus of his ministry as making Christ fully known so that he may present believers to God as mature, Christlike worshipers (Col. 1:24–29). He rightly viewed his ministry as a stewardship of truth. Paul willingly labored diligently in the strength of Christ to help those he taught to grow in Christlikeness.

Teaching Is a Necessary Part of the Transference of Truth

Paul helped Timothy to understand the disciple-making process by describing it as a spiritual relay race, so to speak, whereby the runners pass off what they learn to one who follows. He exhorted Timothy to "follow the pattern of the sound words that you have heard from me, in the faith and love that are in Christ Jesus" (2 Tim. 1:13 ESV), and added, "What you have heard from me in the presence of many witnesses entrust to faithful men who will be able to teach others also" (2 Tim. 2:2 ESV). Essentially, the faithful transfer of truth is a four-generation model which, in this text, includes Paul to Timothy, Timothy to faithful men, faithful men to others, and others who will then teach others—and on and on. Successful transfer of truth from one generation to the next depends upon the ongoing faithful teaching of the Word.

THE PUBLIC MINISTRY OF THE WORD

The public ministry of the Word involves the proclamation of truth in the corporate setting. Public ministry includes anything that involves proclamation to a group, such as corporate preaching, classroom teaching, small groups in homes, and media outlets (e.g., blogs). Of course, these are just a handful of examples.

The Concern of Public Ministry

The burden of public ministry is to speak God's words accurately with appropriate application to God's children who need to hear it in order to grow and change. Just as a human father cares for his own children, how much more, then, does God care what His children hear and how they are treated. God's children were bought at the highest price—the blood of His Son, Jesus Christ. In order to be a good minister of Jesus Christ, it is necessary to speak truth that builds people in the faith (1 Tim. 4:6–16; Heb. 13:7), to communicate as one who responsibly cares for God's children (1 Peter 5:2; Heb. 13:17), and to convey words that God wants His children to hear (1 Peter 4:11).

The Responsibility of Public Ministry

Along with the privilege of talking on behalf of God to His children comes great responsibility. What we say and how we say it matters. An example of this is seen in early biblical narrative, in the book of Job. When Job's friends verbalized their perspective of God as it related to Job's misery, they spoke inaccurately about God. Their erroneous theology came through loud and clear. Even though Job at times also spoke inaccurately concerning God, it was for Job's friends that God reserved His anger and stern words. God said to them, "My anger burns against you and against your two friends, for you have not spoken of me what is right" (Job 42:7 ESV). Thus, in the process of dealing with Job, God forgave Job and was not angry; in contrast, though, God held Job's friends accountable for their bad counsel.

Similarly, in the book of James, the pastor of the church of Jerusalem wrote, "Not many of you should become teachers, my brothers, for you know that we who teach will be judged with greater strictness" (James 3:1 ESV). What a solemn warning to those of us who teach God's Word!

The Importance of Public Ministry

Paul, in his final challenge to the Philippians, referred to the importance of teaching as he urged them to live a life that honored Christ. He exhorted, "What you have learned and received and heard and seen in me — practice these things, and the God of peace will be with you" (Phil. 4:9 ESV). Notice that in order for another person to learn, receive, hear, and see, it is necessary for a public speaker to teach, give, say, and do. Public ministry provides the foundation from which a person wisely lives through all the complexities of life. Biblical truth is the benchmark against which the followers of Christ measure their response to life's various circumstances.

The Content of Public Ministry

The task of public ministry is to teach truth and apply it generally through implications for living and consistent illustrations that enlighten the listener. When the teacher communicates God's Word in a loving manner, the listener is helped to understand and apply gospel implications to daily situations and relationships. Through the careful exposition of the text, the listener learns Christ (Eph. 4:17 – 24). Key areas of content are especially helpful as people easily forget their union with Christ and forget how their identity in Christ impacts their daily living (2 Peter 1:2 – 11).

KEY CONTENT THAT HELPS TO GROUND BELIEVERS "IN CHRIST"

As the teaching ministry develops in a particular local church, key content should be reviewed regularly. Teaching may be divided into five general categories: (1) the big picture, (2) theology, (3) personal sanctification, (4) the Gospel, and (5) Christ.

First, followers of Christ need to see the *big picture* — the story line of the Bible, which includes Creation, Fall, Promise, Redemption, and Consummation. This big picture reorients life for believers in terms of God's greater plan as they learn to trust the character of God by seeing it manifested in human lives they can relate to.

Second, followers of Christ must understand *theology*. Public ministry helps tie the teachings of the Bible together into helpful categories of thought. The basic nine are the doctrines of the Bible, God, Christ, the Holy Spirit, man, sin, salvation, the church, and the end times. In each of these general categories of doctrine there are primary components to review, such as the authority, relevancy, richness, inerrancy, and sufficiency of the Scriptures, or, in relationship to God the Father, issues such as His trustworthiness, sovereign control, and immutability.

Additionally, followers of Christ must grasp what the Bible teaches regarding *personal sanctification*. Key issues include God's goodness in common grace, the problem of sin, the context of suffering, personal faith, and the goal of loving God and one's neighbor. The teacher seeks to connect the various joys and sorrows, delights and distresses, ups and downs, along with the pleasures and displeasures of life within the context of God's plan and purposes for personal growth and change in Christ.

The fourth category is the *Gospel*. Here the teacher provides the good news of the life, death, burial, and resurrection of Jesus, along with the value of the believer's union in Christ. Living in a God-honoring way demands that the follower of Christ understand how life in Christ motivates (2 Cor. 5:14), empowers (Eph. 3:14–21), reorients (Col. 3:1–17), comforts (Rom. 8:1–11), and challenges (Titus 2:11–15).

The fifth category of teaching content is *Christ*. Paul refers to salvation, which includes sanctification, as learning Christ (Eph. 4:20–21). Christ is the living Word of God whom we come to know experientially as believers through the written Word of God. Ministers of the gospel preach Christ to others so that they may know Him — not merely intellectually in terms of content, but know Him in vibrant, growing relationship.

Preparing for the Public Ministry of the Word

Preparing for the public ministry of the Word ultimately revolves around two primary questions: (1) What does the biblical text mean? and (2) How does God expect us to apply it? (1 Tim. 4:13).

WHAT DOES THE BIBLICAL TEXT MEAN?

The first step in preparing for public ministry of the Word is to determine what the biblical text means. This process involves asking many questions: What is the context of the book? Who was it written to? When was it written in relation to the development of the Bible? Why was it written? What is the primary purpose of the writer? How does the book break down into various paragraphs? How does each paragraph relate to the purpose of the book and the author's development of his thought? At this level, the goal is to understand the context, or the big picture.

The paragraph level aims to understand how the pieces in the paragraph work together to teach its fundamental truth. The fundamental truth of the paragraph is the key idea that the author, under the inspiration of the Spirit, desired to communicate to his audience. What was the author's intended goal in writing these words, in this order, in this part of the overall discussion of the book? What did he want his original readers to understand? What truth stretches across all generations for all time? Answering these questions requires careful study of the vocabulary, the parts of speech, how the phrases and clauses in the sentence connect with one another, and how the sentences connect with each other in the paragraph. The objective of this process is to understand what the text means and determine how best to communicate it to others.

HOW DOES GOD EXPECT US TO APPLY IT?

The second element of preparing for the public teaching of the Word is to answer the question, How do you apply the meaning of this text to these people? Since we have determined the meaning of the text, we must then consider what connects this meaning to our audience, to their life. What is the significance of this text to these individuals facing their particular circumstances? How does this fundamental truth speak to the pressures, hurts, hardships, sorrows, troubles, and various forms of suffering and sin here and now? How does it call on them to respond?

In order to answer these questions carefully, it may be necessary to consider some general questions as we consider our audience. What do we learn in this text about God, Christ, the Spirit, or the Bible? What do we learn about people generally? What do we learn about living in a broken world? Given the fundamental truth of this passage and what we know about people generally and our heart specifically, what are potential temptations as a response to this teaching? How are you tempted to react? What may be their struggles to honor God? Are there areas of anger, irritation, anxiety, temptations, escapes? How could this truth be used to motivate living for the glory of God? Where can this passage support honesty, candor, authenticity, courage, gratitude, joy, or love? How can I use this to help an individual consider love for Christ (vertically) and love for neighbor (horizontally) versus love of self (internally)? Your goal is to make a connection generally between what you know about your audience and how the intended meaning of a text speaks God's redemptive truth into the life of the listener as a saint or one who needs to become saved and as both a sinner and a struggler.

Benefits of Public Ministry of the Word

Many benefits result from the faithful public ministry of the Word. As a pastor diligently studies the meaning of the biblical text and seeks to apply what is taught in wisdom and love, God provides a number of blessings to the hearer.

LEARN AND APPLY THE BIBLE

Week after week, as the pastor faithfully handles the biblical text, the hearer learns how to study Scripture (2 Tim. 2:15). As the pastor-teacher explains the meaning of the text as he systematically moves through the text, the listener begins to identify what is of special importance. The wise pastor aids the learning process by asking and answering key questions related to understanding the meaning of the text he preaches. Likewise, the listener grows in the ability to apply the text to personal life circumstances. Again, the wise pastor-teacher desires to equip the hearer to make appropriate application in the contexts of living. Thus, in the actual public ministry of the Word, the pastor teaches a process, by example, and answers key questions about how to move from understanding the biblical text to applying it to "street life," so to speak. Just as the Bible was written by people living within the context of the complexities of real life, we must communicate the Bible in a present-day context, connecting its truths to the life situations of our listeners.

TEACHING BIBLICAL TRUTH ENABLES MEMBERS' GROWTH AND STABILITY

As church members receive long-term public ministry of the Word, they learn and grow (Eph. 4:13; 2 Tim. 2:15–17). The content learned corporately and individually provides a greater understanding of God's perspective for all matters of living.

A BIBLICAL VALUE SYSTEM

The individual grows in thinking as God thinks, which brings stability to life. The person develops a biblical value system or worldview. It is through this lens that the listener may then engage life biblically. Through meditation on the truth (Phil. 4:8), the individual receives God's help to respond to life's difficulties and pressures in a God-pleasing manner.

A NETWORK OF SHARED WISDOM

As we participate in these conversations with one another—especially as we discuss the meaning and significance of the public ministry of the Word—we both share and receive wisdom for myriad issues. Together, then, the church family grows in its ability to face the difficulties of life in God-honoring ways as we share life together in Christ. Essentially, the public ministry of the Word helps build relationships where people worship, bear burdens, love, serve, enjoy grace, forgive, forbear, and evangelize—together. This public ministry creates a community of wise counselors who together receive and share the content (meaning), wisdom (significance), and encouragement (implications) of the Bible (1 Thess. 5:14; Eph. 4:17–32; Col. 3:12–17).

THE PRIVATE MINISTRY OF THE WORD

Alongside faithful preaching of the Word there must be a consistent and more personal kind of ministry. This often takes place in a one-to-one setting ideally involving every member of the body as they live the Christian life in community with other believers.

Private Ministry Defined

Private ministry of the Word includes the one-to-one, face-to-face ministry conversations that take the Word of God and apply it to a specific person's life context. It is talking about, and through, matters of eternal significance. This is what we might call the "house-to-house" part of ministry. This ministry is *shaped* by what is learned from the public ministry of the Word (the truth spoken in love) and *shared* in love with one another. This ministry takes place everywhere in the church. It is one member of the body talking with another member of the body — informally and formally. It combines the experiences of life in a fallen world with our life in Christ as a child of God. We focus on loving Christ and each other. We strive to be wise. We work through issues of sin and suffering; we live life, together. Here we have personal, prayerful, change-oriented, and Christ-focused conversations with one another as we speak truth, provide accountability, and pray with one another (Matt. 7:5; Rom. 15:14; 2 Cor. 1:4; Eph. 4:15, 29 – 32; 1 Thess. 5:14; Heb. 3:13, 10:24; 1 Peter 4:7 – 11).

How Does Private Ministry Differ from Public Ministry?

Private ministry of the Word, in contrast with corporate ministry, has a person's name attached to it, an address, a specific situation, a particular set of pressures, a real concern within a real situation. Whereas preaching is planned and controlled by the teacher, one-to-one ministry calls for a readiness to apply wisdom "on the fly." Public ministry of the Word, when applied accurately and creatively, speaks generally into life in a broken world; private ministry of the Word speaks specifically into *this* life, into *this* part of the fallen world. Private ministry is the specific voice of the broader public ministry. Private ministry is grace, mercy, kindness, wisdom, discernment, and the gospel pinpointed to *this* person, here and now, in word and deed. It is personal.

Benefits of Private Ministry of the Word

Good private ministry of the Word makes the public ministry ring true to real life. It keeps public ministry grounded to where we live. It makes the process of sanctification described in the pulpit practical because private ministry hears the connections — or lack of them — to a typical message or series. Good private ministry of the Word benefits the pastor by keeping sermons from soaring to the highest levels of exegesis and theology, keeping the message closer to the treetops of daily living. It helps the teacher develop the implications of a message in a way that is helpful, insightful, and broad. It also possibly influences preaching calendars and church emphases. The teacher can bring truth down to the private conversation level so members of the body can take what is said publicly and immediately employ those words, concepts, and instructions in ministry conversations over lunch, playing softball, or sharing in a small group.

HELPFUL STEPS TO TAKE IN UNITING THE MINISTRY OF THE WORD

Public and private ministries of the Word complement one another and benefit the body of Christ. Specifically, public ministry of the Word has incredible potential to develop, heighten, and extend the positive impact private ministry of the Word has on the local church. The private ministry of the Word may impact the quality, clarity, and practicality of public ministry. But how does this happen?

General Expository Preaching

Over the long haul of faithful ministry in the church, the consistent proclamation of the text through verse-by-verse study benefits private ministry the most. In a sermon, the pastor takes the timeless truth and applies it to the private ministry of the Word. He must make it personal and connect it to real-life concerns, pressures, and events. The pastor who preaches toward life change asks himself how the expounded text might impact the hearer in terms of obeying the two greatest commandments, to love God and others (Matt. 22:36 – 40).

Specific Series and Topics

Depending on what a pastor hears and sees in his private ministry (spoken words and body language), observes in his local community and the world, and recognizes in the life of his local church, there will be times when he will need to teach on specific topics. These topics help to inform the private ministry and discussions taking place all week long between members of the church. You might consider the following series and topics: one-another passages, biblical friendship and fellowship, Christ-honoring communication, and wisdom.

ONE-ANOTHER PASSAGES

Based on the specific needs of the congregation, consider teaching a series on the one-another passages in the Scriptures. There are approximately fifty "one-another exhortations" in the New Testament, commands related to unity, love, humility, and service. Possibly complement your teaching on the one-anothers with video vignettes. Remember to give very practical steps to achieve the biblical command. Consider what the application of these might look like in person-to-person fellowship.

BIBLICAL FRIENDSHIP AND FELLOWSHIP

Preach on biblical friendship and fellowship. Explain it by using key passages like Psalm 119:63 and biblical examples such as David and Jonathan. Help church members understand the biblical priority of fellowship among the members of the body (1 John 1) and corresponding passion for authentic relationships that provide mutual benefit (Gal. 6). Biblical fellowship is a conduit for spiritual growth and change which then are promoted in the private ministries of the Word.

CHRIST-HONORING COMMUNICATION

Preach on Christ-honoring communication in everyday living by emphasizing passages such as Ephesians 4:25–32 and James 3:1–12. Scripture passages such as these help church members to learn the importance of every word that comes out of the mouth — as well as the motive behind them. Like the apostles did in their writings, we must make application within the context of daily relationships such as the husband/wife, parents/children, brothers/sisters, employer/employee, fellow employees, fellow church members, neighbors in the community, and strangers.

WISDOM

Preach on the beauty and importance of wisdom. Wisdom flows from the fear of the Lord and prepares the believer to live the kind of life that honors Christ (Prov. 1:7; James 3:13–18). As the public ministry of the Word imparts wisdom, the wise person hears God's Word and obeys (Matt. 7:24–27; James 1:21–27). The believer learns to ask God for wisdom (James 1:2–12) and ask each other for help along the journey (James 5:13–20). Encourage all to seek help while in the midst of struggles, when they have questions, when gripped by fear, and when facing obstacles, and to be thankful as they receive God's many blessings in life.

Celebrate God's Work in People

You may use public ministry to celebrate what God is doing through private ministry. There are many ways of sharing what is going on in the greater body. For example, personal testimony from those experiencing God's transforming grace impacts the body in profound ways. Depending on the circumstance and your resources, you may use public testimonies and interviews (prerecorded or live) that make the point for you. Celebrate together as a body what you want to see duplicated in the lives of others. As you share how God is working in His people, you want to make sure there are no man-made boundaries, real or implied, that keep people from taking the next step in their own personal growth.

Celebrate God's Work in You

As you teach, you may want to refer to your own small group and how living the Christian life together impacts your walk with Christ. Give personal stories of how your spouse or a friend or another person has helped you grow in discernment or has given you the tools to grow and change. Publicly thank members of the congregation who have reproved you, exhorted you, encouraged you, or loved you through speaking the truth in love. You may tell about personal sacrifices you have made to attend, prioritize, and pursue biblical friendships through small group and in other ways. Furthermore, you may mention how your private ministry challenges you, personally, and gives you opportunities to counsel yourself with the Scriptures. Your public ministry provides the opportunity for others to hear how private ministry benefits you and furthers God's work within you.

Provide Resources and Next Steps

There are many practical ways you may help further the teaching process at home, in specific contexts in which the church members live. Provide the sermon outline and notes for them to study later in the week; leave them with leading questions or a suggested list of next steps; offer them "For Further Study" sheets. You may use "connection cards" to advance the dialogue. Possibly you can help them with prayer starters or creative family activities that help them continue to learn as a family. For small groups you may supply suggested conversation starters or ministry ideas that relate to your day's message or series. With the permission of publishers, you may duplicate journal articles and other reading material. If your church has a bookstore or resource center, you may also highlight materials that will be of help. Your blog entries and other social media communication can further the discussion through key links and sermon podcasts. In other words, there is no limit to the creative ways you may spread biblical instruction.

Invitation

The ways that teachers close public ministry teaching vary. No matter how you conclude, do not neglect to invite people to participate in further private ministry conversations and deeper relationships within the body. The process of discipleship was designed by God to not work effectively in isolation from other people. Every member needs a mentor, a student, and a manner of accountability. Invite your listeners to continue the conversation. Make them aware of people to whom they may talk. Point out the necessity of mentors (leaders, shepherds, etc.) in small groups, Sunday school, or adult Bible fellowships. Invite them to be a participant. Help them to see the structure you have in place to benefit their personal growth. Depending on the size of the church, possibly have ministry booths set up for people to visit. Regardless of size, become aware of the process through which your members and attendees can become involved.

MAXIMIZE YOUR EFFORTS IN THE MINISTRY OF THE WORD

God's children need us to do everything we can to maximize our efforts as we minister the Word. Good public ministry of the Word takes time, effort, creativity, diligence, and hard work. So also does the private ministry of the Word. Thankfully, done well, our diligence in each realm will not merely complement the other but will enhance our overall ministry of the Word. The synergy provided by both is important because God's children are important. What an incredible privilege God entrusts to us as we minister His Word to His children! As we faithfully carry out the teaching of God's Word for the sake of God's church, we commend believers to God and to the word of His grace, which is able to build them up and give them the inheritance of all those who are being sanctified.

PART 2

BIBLICAL COUNSELING AND SMALL GROUP MINISTRY

CHAPTER 5

TOOLS TO GROW YOUR CHURCH: UNITING BIBLICAL COUNSELING AND SMALL GROUPS

BRAD BIGNEY AND KEN LONG

The title of our chapter might be a bit misleading. Some of you may see the phrase "grow your church" and assume that this is a chapter about numbers. You know—bodies, buildings, and bucks! And to some degree, who doesn't want to see their church grow? We love to see the hand of Jesus move as He builds His church—drawing men and women into the grace and light of the gospel, fulfilling His promise when He said, "I will build my church, and the gates of hell shall not prevail against it" (Matt. 16:18 ESV). We long to see God do this in our midst.

However, when we use the word "grow," we're talking about growing to become more like Christ—in what we think, how we act, and what we prize and pursue most. The growth we're talking about is what John the Baptist reflects in John 3:30 when he says, "He must increase, but I must decrease" (ESV). We long to see the fruit and Spirit of Christ at work in our people's lives. In Galatians 5, Paul says, "But the fruit of the Spirit is love, joy, peace, patience, kindness, goodness, faithfulness, gentleness, self-control; against such things there is no law" (Gal. 5:22–23 ESV). The sweet aroma of the knowledge of Christ (2 Cor. 2:14) and people looking and living more like Him stir us far more than packed worship services that are focused on numbers.

The two of us serve together at Grace Fellowship Church, GFC, in northern Kentucky, just across the Ohio River from Cincinnati. Brad is the Senior Pastor and the first pastor called to the church in January of 1996. Ken serves as the Executive Pastor, involved in the day-to-day ministries of the church. We're so thankful that God has grown our body and is still at work among us. Yes, there have been people added to the numbers, but more importantly we believe that God has spiritually grown our people in Christlikeness. Are we perfect? Far from it! We'd simply like to share with you some of the tools we've used that we think have provided fertile ground for the Spirit to work in a local body of Christ. To this end we hope to serve you by sharing ideas, practices, and guidelines that have been part of how we have intentionally sought to promote spiritual growth. Unifying small groups and biblical counseling together has been a tool God has used to transform our people. But doing this holds no power apart from the moving of God's Spirit in and through these ministries. So even though we speak highly of small groups and biblical counseling, remember that they are never ends in themselves.

Finally, before you dive in, we'd like to say a quick word about the format of the chapter. We've chosen to follow a question-and-answer format, highlighting key questions. Our hope is that this will be helpful for you as you learn from our experience. Let's get started!

WHAT IS THE PURPOSE AND FUNCTION OF YOUR SMALL GROUP MINISTRY?

There are many reasons why small groups should exist in a church — none of them necessarily bad, but a lot of them unclear and peripheral to what's going on in the heart and soul of the church. Often the name attached to a ministry gives us a clue to the reason for its existence. For example, we call a ministry a care group, or a men's Bible study, or a ladies' group, or a growth group. Many churches looking for a way to meet the personal and physical needs of their people in a loving, decentralized manner will establish care groups. Others want their men to dig into the Bible so they have men's Bible studies. Still others want to emphasize growth in numbers for the kingdom, so they have growth groups modeled after the principles contained in Carl George's book *Prepare Your Church for the Future.*

Careful and prayerful thought should be given to the purpose of the small group ministry of any church, because small groups cannot do *everything*, but they can do a few things really well. Don't just put some chairs in a circle and invite people over. A small group ministry should directly align with the larger ministry of the church. This means that you'll need to back up and answer the question, "What is the primary ministry of the church?" We believe the answer to this can be found in Ephesians 4, a passage that has been referenced in earlier chapters:

> Now these are the gifts Christ gave to the church: the apostles, the prophets, the evangelists, and the pastors and teachers. Their responsibility is to equip God's people to do his work and build up the church, the body of Christ. This will continue until we all come to such unity in our faith and knowledge of God's Son that we will be mature in the Lord, measuring up to the full and complete standard of Christ.
>
> Then we will no longer be immature like children. We won't be tossed and blown about by every wind of new teaching. We will not be influenced when people try to trick us with lies so clever they sound like the truth. Instead, we will speak the truth in love, growing in every way more and more like Christ, who is the head of his body, the church.
>
> Ephesians 4:11–15 NLT

Ephesians 4 drives home the fact that God has given Spirit-gifted people, "pastors and teachers ... to equip God's people ... to ... build up the church, the body of Christ" (4:11–12 NLT). What is meant by building the church is further explained: having all of God's people "be mature in the Lord, measuring up to the full and complete standard of Christ" (4:13 NLT). Or stated another way in Scripture, "growing in every way more and more like Christ, who is the head of his body, the church" (4:15 NLT). One of the primary purposes of the church is for the whole church to participate with the Spirit (2 Cor. 3:18) in the transformation of God's people to be more like Christ.

Let's say it in just two words—spiritual formation! If spiritual formation is the purpose of the church, then *personal* transformation in community with other believers is the purpose of small group ministry. Bible study is great. Fellowship is wonderful. Evangelism is essential. But changing and growing to be more like Christ is the purpose of a small group ministry. People do not drift naturally toward transformation; they retreat toward information. That's why you can attend a Bible study and still not experience transformation. Retaining information is "safe"—less intrusive and not as messy.

WHAT HAPPENS IN YOUR SMALL GROUPS?

We have seen God use small group ministry to transform His people as the group spends time applying the Word of God to each member's life. Sometimes this can also be a theological book based on the Scriptures. Some of you might say, "But aren't most churches and small groups focused on this already?"

We don't think so. Most Bible studies are really focused on acquiring knowledge with limited, and often private, application. The bulk of the time together is dominated by a mini-lecture from the small group leader, while participants dutifully "fill in the blanks" in their study guide or workbook. Occasionally the leader will ask some inductive questions about the text, but even then, the questions are often focused on facts rather than life application.

To be clear, Bible knowledge is never irrelevant. It's just not enough. Small groups are the place to push past Bible knowledge and on to life application, so that transformation more and more into the image of Christ can be seen in our churches. A transformational small group focuses on everyone giving and receiving hope and help from God's Word so as to spiritually mature in Christ (Heb. 10:24–25).

So a transformational group is focused on asking questions with spiritual formation in mind. Take, for instance, a small group discussion of the first chapter in the book of James. The text should prompt the leader to press each member of the group, perhaps to consider a personal trial in their own life and to humbly share that with the others. The goal is to spark a spiritual discussion that moves below the surface of "Hey, how ya' doin'?" The leader might ask their group, "Looking at verse 2, what difficulty or trial are you personally facing right now in your own life?" After listening to people share, a follow-up question might be, "On a scale of one to ten, with ten being the highest, what is your joy quotient right now as you persevere through this God-given trial?"

The small group leader, through a series of questions, is providing fertile ground for each person to examine their own attitude of submission to God's Word in their life, which is indicated by their current level of joy in the midst of the trial. One desired result of this kind of transformational discussion is that it would naturally lead into a meaningful time of prayer for each other. Too often prayer times are focused on minor surgeries and the problems of other people outside of the group that they have never met. Prayer for one another should be asking for the Spirit to help us "put on the new self, created to be like God in true righteousness and holiness" (Eph. 4:24 NIV).

Helping each member of the group move toward greater submission to God during a trial is the transformational result for which the small group leader is aiming. God has commanded us to be joyful in our trials (James 1:2). So how are we doing? We're not joyful that we have cancer. But we can be joyful that in this horrendous trial our Father's steadfast love, which endures forever (Ps. 100:5), will use even this circumstance for His glory and our good. For God's good work to be made complete in us, we have to "count it all joy" when we "meet trials of various kinds" (James 1:2 ESV). In other words, the passage is teaching us to not waste our trials, but to be good stewards of them. Our people need more than just help in understanding this. They need help doing it and living it out. And that's where the small group ministry should focus.

In a small group setting, others can see areas where we need wisdom and prayer (James 1:5). So the small group becomes a greenhouse or incubator for spiritual growth, as we spur one another on to love and good deeds (Heb. 10:24–25), giving hope and help to keep moving forward, by God's grace. But this is all hinged upon allowing others to speak into our lives.

HOW DO YOU LINK YOUR SMALL GROUP MINISTRY TO YOUR BIBLICAL COUNSELING MINISTRY—PHILOSOPHICALLY, ORGANIZATIONALLY, AND PRACTICALLY?

As you can imagine, significant personal issues will arise in transformational small groups. Typically small group leaders will be able to handle some of the soul care issues that arise in their group, but not all of them. Since they are providing "personal discipleship" for the eight to fifteen people in their group, those who need long-term "personal intensive discipleship," or what is commonly referred to as "biblical counseling," may need to be cared for by others. For many small group leaders, there simply isn't enough time available to also do long-term biblical counseling.

Fortunately, there is a way to handle this. Those who need long-term "personal intensive discipleship" are referred to the church's counseling center. Typically, these are life-dominating sins that manifest themselves as adultery, alcohol or drug abuse, pornography, persistent unbelief, sexual abuse, crippling fear, etc. (Heb. 12:1). The difference between issues that can be handled in the group and those that might require more one-on-one counseling can be illustrated by a story told by Steve Viars, Senior Pastor of Faith Church, in Lafayette, Indiana. Steve tells the story of a person in a boat that is going down the river and gets trapped in an eddy, which keeps on bumping into the shore. He is no longer making any progress down the river. Discipleship is represented by the progress down the river (growth in Christlikeness.) The eddy represents a life-dominating sin that impedes spiritual growth. Until the person is freed from that eddy, the life-dominating sin, they won't be able to progress spiritually. To get out of the eddy, someone must enter the boat to help them see their problem and begin moving down the river again. Biblical counseling is "getting into the boat," helping through loving confrontation and instruction from the Scriptures. Hopefully, repentance will take place and the boat will get unstuck and start floating down the river again.

This means that a transformational small group ministry is dependent upon a biblical counseling ministry to care for the people requiring long-term "personal, intensive discipleship." If long-term biblical counseling is not available, then a well-intended transformational small group ministry will eventually shift focus. For those who are ensnared in their sin, talking about continual change and growth will become frustrating and even foolish over time. People with problems who want to change will lose hope when there is no one who is spiritual and able to come alongside them (Gal. 6:1–2). A group that started out with the purpose of transformation will shift to a Bible study or to a care group, focusing on acquiring more Bible information or on changing the circumstances. The leaders of the church need to ask themselves, "Is this most pleasing to God for our people?" (see 2 Cor. 5:9).

We have talked with churches that want to have a transformational small group ministry but, for one reason or another, have not developed a biblical counseling ministry. Eventually, they get bogged down and deteriorate. Either the pastoral staff is swamped with counseling requests or the small group ministry becomes less focused on sanctification. Conversely, we've seen problems in churches that have a counseling center but no small group ministry. These churches tend to have an inordinately large number of biblical counseling cases. People are hungry to change, and for help they turn to the biblical counseling ministry, yet many of these people could be effectively cared for in a transformational small group ministry. Additionally, once they have been helped through biblical counseling, where do they turn for ongoing personal discipleship if transformational small groups do not exist?

What we're advocating here is not complicated. We believe that a transformational church should have an interdependent biblical counseling and small group ministry. The two should be paired together. We've seen this model work for both small and large churches. In 1996, as a church plant, Grace Fellowship adopted this model with only eighty people attending on a Sunday morning. Today, with an attendance of over 1,500, the emphasis on growing in Christlikeness remains unchanged. In fact, the interconnectedness of the two ministries is even more necessary today. A major concern for larger churches is how to spiritually care for all the people that God brings through the doors. Pastors equip the saints for the work of ministry, but they cannot do it all. And works of ministry for laypeople should be more than just keeping the nursery staffed; it should include caring for the souls of others (Gal. 6:1 – 2; Rom. 15:14). The integration of small group and biblical counseling ministries fosters Ephesians 4:11 – 12 involvement with everyone in the church. Each small group leader is effectively caring for eight to fifteen people.

Under this model, our pastors don't spend the bulk of their time directly caring for everyone; they spend their time assisting and caring for the small group leaders who shepherd the people in our church family. Another pastor leads the counseling ministry, which primarily utilizes trained lay counselors. Since 1996 the counseling ministry has grown from a single certified ACBC (Association of Certified Biblical Counselors) counselor to a team of over 50 counselors, with 23 of them certified. This illustrates the God-given mandate that pastor-teachers should equip their people to be involved in ministry to their level of giftedness (Rom. 12:4 – 8; 1 Cor. 12:7). We're thrilled that after eighteen years of equipping, now lay counselors are doing a majority of the counseling cases — about 60 percent.

DO YOU REQUIRE, RECOMMEND, OR ENCOURAGE COUNSELEES TO BECOME A PART OF A SMALL GROUP?

The short answer is, "Yes, all our counselees are required to be part of a small group." All who call GFC their home church are asked to participate in a small group. So a person will normally be in a small group before they request biblical counseling. If the person requesting counseling is not part of a small group, they are asked to join a group before their counseling begins, though we waive this requirement in crisis situations.

For those seeking counseling who are not part of our church family, they are asked to participate with a small group and attend GFC Sunday services *during the season of their counseling*. This is so they hear truth in small group and during the worship service, which serves to reinforce the teachings they receive during the counseling sessions. When the counseling ends, they are already plugged into a small group where they continue their "personal discipleship." This interconnectedness helps to till the soil of the heart for spiritual growth and change toward Christlikeness.

In short, small groups are the heart of a transformational church. The goal is to not just be a church *with* small groups, but a church *of* small groups. This is where people are personally made disciples and are cared for. The elders realize that by God and under God, they are responsible for the spiritual care of the people Christ has given them, but the shepherding of the elders is done through the small group leaders caring for the people in their group. This is why everyone is expected to be active in a small group.

HOW DO YOU TRAIN YOUR SMALL GROUP LEADERS? TO WHAT EXTENT ARE THEY TRAINED IN BIBLICAL COUNSELING?

Hopefully, you are excited by the idea of integrating your biblical counseling and small group ministries, but you're also thinking, "Where am

I going to get the leaders who will lead small groups that are more than 'Yak 'n' Snack' (you know, a group that likes to chat about sports and eat desserts together but not much else) and are focused on transformation?"

At first this will be a challenge, but that can be overcome if the church leadership makes this one of their top priorities — and it should. For a small group ministry to be focused on transformation, you *must* make selecting and training your small group leaders a top priority. Your church leadership should be praying and funneling potential small group leaders into an intentional equipping process — constantly identifying and raising up new leaders and apprentices. Why? Because not just anyone can do this. You are looking for more than just an outgoing personality and a spiritual pulse!

The small group leader needs to be equipped to carry out the vision of personal life transformation. He or she must have "a growing relationship with God and a heart for the people of God in the group."[50] Guidelines for being a small group leader should contain milestones that demonstrate theological understanding and personal spiritual maturity. Clearly defined expectations for the leader will promote a unified and effective ministry for both the participants of every small group and the small group leaders.

There are a number of ways churches train up their leaders. Here for your consideration is the way we do it. The GFC guidelines for becoming a small group leader are as follows:

1. Are members of Grace Fellowship Church: 1 Peter 5:2 – 7.
2. Have served as an apprentice for a GFC small group and have been recommended by their small group leader: 2 Timothy 2:2.
3. Have completed Fundamentals of Biblical Counseling: Romans 15:14; 2 Timothy 2:15.
4. Have participated in Joshua's Men (JM) or Women of the Word (WOW) leadership training: 1 Timothy 4:16.
5. Are demonstrating being "spiritual" and being used by God to "restore [others] in a spirit of gentleness" in the transformational process: Galatians 6:1 – 2 ESV.

Everyone who becomes a small group leader first serves in an already established small group as an apprentice (guideline 2). They are discipled as a potential leader both spiritually and in the ways of shepherding brothers and sisters in a small group. The leader will continue to give his or her apprentice increasing opportunities to oversee responsibilities relating to the transformation of the other participants.

Another component of apprentice training is completing the Fundamentals of Biblical Counseling training (guideline 3). This is thirty hours of biblical counseling training based on the Association of Certified Biblical Counselors (ACBC) model. Having this biblical counseling background has been invaluable for our small group leaders. When a soul care issue comes up in small group, the leader has confidence that the Scriptures have the hope and help needed. By the Spirit's power, the leader will be able to give hope and even some initial help from God's Word.

Furthermore, in preparation for leading a small group, both husband and wife are asked to complete our leadership training (guideline 4). Our men go through the Joshua's Men (JM) program, and their wives go through Women of the Word (WOW). These experiences train leaders in biblical theology and its practical everyday application to one's life. For two years, participants meet separately once a month for three hours to discuss the reading assignment by sharing their written answers to the provided questions. In addition, one year is devoted to working through the majority of *Systematic Theology* by Wayne Grudem. For the men, the second year is devoted to reading nine theological books: *Knowing God* by J. I. Packer, *Trusting God* by Jerry Bridges, *The Discipline of Grace* by Jerry Bridges, *Seven Reasons Why You Can Trust the Bible* by Erwin Lutzer, *Why Small Groups* by C. J. Mahaney, *The Heart of Anger* by Lou Priolo, *Disciplines of a Godly Man* by R. Kent Hughes, *The Complete Husband* by Lou Priolo, and *Spiritual Leadership* by J. Oswald Sanders. The women have a similar reading list for their second year. This is an intense time of training and an incredible season of growth. The men and women also memorize over fifty verses related to their readings during this time. It's such a joy to see men and women becoming "like great oaks that the LORD has planted for his own glory" (Isa. 61:3 NLT).

After becoming small group leaders, they are asked to attend an advanced level of Counseling and Discipleship Training each year. Our main concern here is that the leaders continue to receive encouragement and catch the vision of helping people become more like Christ.

WHAT INFORMATION SHOULD THE COUNSELOR SHARE WITH THE SMALL GROUP LEADER?

Since people are directly cared for by their small group leader, the leader is the one who should know the counselee better than any other leader in the church. Even if one of his people is being counseled, the small group leader is still responsible for the counselee's growth in Christlikeness. A counselor may be necessary, but is best seen as a temporary assistant to the leader.

It's very beneficial for the leader and counselor to be free to speak to each other about the counselee. And while we want to bring as much grace as possible to the counseling process, we certainly don't want the small group leader and counselor to sin in the way they speak about the counselee, so there is no place for gossip or slander. With that in mind, their communication can happen in a number of different ways. Sometimes the leader and counselor just speak periodically to one another during the counseling process. During these times, they compare notes on how the counselee is growing and what would be best to keep that process going. At other times, the small group leader is actually present during the counseling session.

This understanding between the small group leader and the counselor should be part of the counseling agreement from the start. The counselee should have a clear picture of who is responsible for his care. At our center, this agreement is titled "Consent to Counsel" and outlines, in a single page, the purpose and practice of biblical counseling. Before counseling begins, those being counseled sign this document, and there is a paragraph regarding confidentiality that delineates who the counselor, as well as the counselee, may speak to about any of the issues that come up in the counseling process. The small group leader is listed here along with the pastors and elders.

HOW DO YOU HELP EVERY PERSON IN THE CONGREGATION TO UNDERSTAND THEIR CALLING TO MINISTER TRUTH-IN-LOVE TO ONE ANOTHER?

We try to help every person in the congregation understand their calling to minister truth-in-love to one another. Regular training equips them for this kind of ministry. Each year we host a Counseling and Discipleship Training conference at our church. This training includes a Fundamentals Track for first-timers and an Advanced Track for those wanting to continue to grow. In an effort to draw as many new people into the training as possible, we offer a scholarship worth 50 percent of the registration fee for anyone attending Fundamentals for the first time. This makes a big statement to our church family about the value of this training.

Another way people understand their calling to help one another by ministering truth-in-love is through testimony on Sundays and at public baptisms. There are four of these services throughout the year. During these times, people share their testimonies of coming to faith in Christ through counseling or of how they've grown spiritually through counseling or being plugged into a small group. Most often the person that God used to help them was not even one of the pastors. It's in these moments our church family realizes, "Wow, you mean regular people sitting right around me could help me through a really difficult trial or suffering?" The effect of these testimonies, year after year, continues to break down the professional ministry mindset.

The pastors also preach every Sunday with a "transformational result" (TR) in mind. These TRs are not just about each of us changing to be more like Christ, but include the responsibility that each of us has in helping *one another* change and grow. We have a ministry model of pastors stepping forward to teach and equip, as well as pastors stepping back to let others do real ministry. Almost every time a pastor counsels, there are observers present in the room learning how they can be used by God. And when pastors step back from doing all the ministry themselves, it concretely demonstrates that we're all responsible to minister truth-in-love to one another.

In conclusion, equipping people to lead small groups and counsel (intensely disciple) one another unleashes the church to really be the church! While we're still sinners and riddled with the effects of sin, we're amazed and in awe at what God has done through this model of ministry. We gratefully concur with Ephesians 3:20 (NKJV) that praises, "Now to Him who is able to do exceedingly abundantly above all that we ask or think, according to the power that works in us." May the glory be to God for the work He has done.

CHAPTER 6

BIBLICAL COUNSELING
AND REDEMPTION
GROUPS

ABE MEYSENBURG AND MIKE WILKERSON

Pain is God's megaphone, as C. S. Lewis has taught us.[51] It gets our attention. A moment of captured attention is an opportunity to reorient: to help us see God, ourselves, our relationships, and the world differently. The pain that grabs our attention could be any form of sin or suffering: a besetting sin about which we've grown discouraged and feel unable to change, a broken relationship, financial turmoil, or wounds from past hurts.

Such painful times are prime opportunities to gain a new understanding or a fresh experience of God's redeeming and transforming love. Redemption Groups™ seize that opportunity by inviting participants to go deep into God's story, deep into the work of Christ, deep into their own hearts, and deep into redemptive relationships with brothers and sisters in Christ.[52] The overall impact of this process extends well beyond the participant's own life, spilling over into the life of the local churches where these Redemption Groups take place. Thus the rhythm of Redemption Groups within a local church becomes like a heartbeat, circulating redemptive vitality throughout the whole church.

Our objective in this chapter is to describe how this happens. We'll consider the message, the process of a group, the training of group leaders, the structure, and the strategy of a Redemption Groups ministry within a local church.[53]

THE MESSAGE OF REDEMPTION GROUPS

What is the message of Redemption Groups? In a word: redemption.

Redemption in the Bible is about movement from slavery to freedom; it's about the cost of purchasing that freedom; and it's about the renewal and flourishing that freedom makes possible (Col. 1:13; Eph. 1:7 – 10; 1 Peter 1:18 – 19). God in His abounding steadfast love keeps His promises and frees His children to enjoy their rest in Him.

God's story is a redemption story. It moves "from creation to new creation by way of *redemption*, which is, in effect, the renewing of creation."[54] If the *breadth* of redemption spans God's story, then its *center* is the death and resurrection of Jesus Christ. Says Gerhard O. Forde:

> The cross makes us part of its story. The cross becomes our story. That is what it means to say, as Luther did, "The cross alone is our theology." … It is vital to realize that a proper theology of the cross does not isolate attention just on the cross event. To speak of the "cross story" is a shorthand way of intending the entire story culminating in cross and resurrection. The cross is the key to unlocking the entire story.[55]

If the cross is the key to unlocking the entire story, then the *pattern* of that entire story is the exodus. According to Christopher J. H. Wright:

> If you had asked a devout Israelite in the Old Testament period "Are you redeemed?" the answer would have been a most definite yes. And if you had asked "How do you know?" you would be taken aside to sit down somewhere while your friend recounted a long and exciting story — the story of the exodus. For indeed it is the exodus that provided the primary model of God's idea of redemption, not just in the Old Testament but even in the New, where it is used as one of the keys to understanding the meaning of the cross of Christ.[56]

What is the *relevance* of all this? The message of the cross, though simple, has profound implications for every person in every possible situation. That is because the cross is at the very center of God's story, which is also the story of the world, and therefore the cross is at the center of every person's story, whether they know it yet or not. My own personal suffering is part of the suffering that plagues this whole world; therefore the story of this world's suffering is also *my* story. My own fight with sin is part of the whole world's sin problem; therefore, the story of the world's sin is also *my* story. So the redemption of the world's sin and suffering is also *my* redemption from sin and suffering.

We all are interpreters, always making sense of life and living life out of the sense we make. In other words, we live out of stories. But a story does more than *make sense*, in terms of mere cognitive reorientation. A story captivates us; it draws us into its world. And stories that make sense of our whole lives therefore have the power to change our whole lives.

A Redemption Group experience is one of "re-storying" a person's life, re-centering his story around the cross, within God's grand story of redemption. Our interpretations inform how we *feel*, what we *long* for (whether or not we are aware of those longings), and how we respond in tangible *actions*. Having your whole heart captivated by a story doesn't just change the way you think about some things — it changes your whole life.

That may sound like some kind of radical conversion. Indeed, you may have had a conversion experience that sounds like this, or you may have heard stories of people coming to a saving faith in Christ and experiencing a radical whole-life change. That is similar to some of the testimonials that we hear coming out of Redemption Groups, even (and primarily!) from those who have already professed faith in Christ.

It's not a different message from the one that we accept when we first professed Christ. It's another experience of that same message, pressed into the deepest places of the human heart. But some of the deepest places of the heart are best accessed in the midst of our most desperate needs for rescue amidst sin and suffering. So Redemption Groups tend to be pivotal experiences for people. Same gospel, new depth, changed life — again and again.

Redemption Groups use for their content the book *Redemption: Freed by Jesus from Idols We Worship and the Wounds We Carry* by Mike Wilkerson.[57] This sets the cross, by which Christ accomplished our redemption, within the context of the biblical backstory of redemption — the exodus. It also shows some of the profound implications of this redemption for various situations in which sinners and sufferers in need of God's help find themselves, such as histories of abuse, broken relationships, addictions, and sexual brokenness.

For example, in chapter 3, we discuss the plagues and the Passover and how they point forward to the substitutionary death of Jesus. We recognize that just as the Israelites were spared the wrath of God because the lamb's blood was shed, we too have been spared because Jesus' blood was shed. We then discuss some of the implications of this for our lives. In particular, the Passover shows the costliness and grace of forgiveness. We address the importance of receiving God's forgiveness and consider any distortions in our interpretations of God, ourselves, or our stories that keep us from fully receiving and enjoying the freedom of God's forgiveness. We also consider that God's gift of forgiveness to us is something He means for us to pass on as we extend forgiveness to others. In groups, participants may be encouraged to consider how they might forgive.

In chapter 4, we discuss God's miraculous parting of the Red Sea, despite His people's fear and repeated accusations that He was actually trying to kill them. This moment provided a sort of death and resurrection for Israel, as they were no longer defined by their past enslavement to their previous master. Rather, they were profoundly identified as the people of God, freed to serve their benevolent new master. This Red Sea moment points forward to the death and resurrection we have experienced as followers of Jesus, as those who "have passed out of death into life" (1 John 3:14 ESV). We are no longer defined by our past enslavement to sin and Satan, but by our relationship to the Father because of Jesus. We then discuss how our new identity as children of God liberates us to live in an entirely new way, free from guilt *and* shame.

THE STRUCTURE OF A REDEMPTION GROUP

A single Redemption Group has, ideally, five participants, two coleaders, and one apprentice. That's a total of eight people in the room, with a supervisor visiting occasionally, making nine. This collection of group members will remain fixed over the course of about twelve sessions.

That one group will normally contain participants all of the same gender but with various stories, concerns, and challenges. One is experiencing marital strife following adultery, another is battling an addiction, another longs for healing from lifelong wounds from childhood, and another may have all of those concerns at the same time. Sometimes people enter a group focused on a presenting issue and find that it is merely the tip of an iceberg. Another participant enters the group as part of a healing process in her marriage while her husband is in another group. She may think she's there for him to be "fixed" in that other group but comes to find out just how much help she herself needs too. The combinations are endless. In any case, a Redemption Group does not focus on a specific presenting issue, but helps participants understand potentially a variety of issues in their lives in light of God's story and to experience His love.

The leaders are normally volunteers. They probably came to a group as a participant at some time in the past and returned to serve as an apprentice before ultimately being approved to lead. Coleadership allows them to be paired in ways that complement one another's varying strengths and levels of experience. Placing an apprentice in the group ensures that new leaders are continually developing as the group process cycles from quarter to quarter.

Typically, Redemption Groups run on a quarterly programming

cycle of ten or twelve weeks. In a given quarter, groups will run on, say, Wednesday evenings at 7:00 p.m. in a church facility.

Weekly Rhythm

Suppose First Church has six groups running this quarter: three groups of men and three of women. Suppose that Pastor Joe is the site leader who is responsible for running Redemption Groups at First Church, including overseeing the administration of the program, the teaching, leading some of the leaders' meetings, and supervising men's groups. Suppose that Deacon Jane supervises the women's groups and leads some of the leaders' meetings. That's about fifty people showing up each Wednesday night (eight people per group, plus Joe and Jane).

Leaders and apprentices arrive early at 5:30 p.m. to have dinner together, catch up on the week, pray together, and finalize preparations for their group that evening. Joe and Jane, as the groups' supervisors, may connect with those leaders during this time for coaching or shepherding. At some point, Joe or Jane may gather the leaders' attention for a time of training, coaching, prayer—whatever seems most helpful to the leadership team that evening. This meeting is an important weekly leadership development opportunity and is utilized in lots of different ways to maximize the leadership team's effectiveness, to provide care and shepherding to them as they lead, and to continually deepen their skills and knowledge.

At 7:00 p.m., it's time for everyone from all six groups to gather for the main session, which primarily consists of teaching for about thirty minutes. Sometimes a musician will lead the gathering in song before or after the teaching time. This could be taught by Joe or by anyone to whom he delegates teaching responsibilities. After the main session, everyone is dismissed for group time, with each group meeting in its own separate space for about ninety minutes. Following the group session, leaders and apprentices normally stick around for another thirty minutes to debrief together, sometimes with their supervisors. These debrief sessions may include any or all of the following: observe key discoveries or breakthroughs in the lives of the participants, celebrate God's grace and faithfulness to the group, care for one another, talk through how challenging situations were handled, sharpen one another's skills, plan for the next meeting.

Quarterly Rhythm

This rhythm usually happens just like this for at least eight weeks in a row, depending on whether First Church utilizes the "weekend intensive" concept to launch each new quarter of groups. The weekend intensive is a great way to kick off a new quarter of ministry. It begins with a Friday evening and continues all-day Saturday. The weekend time includes the first three group sessions, with the possible addition of some extra training on storytelling for the participants. Three group sessions on the weekend intensive, followed by eight weekly sessions on Wednesday nights, comes to eleven group sessions. The twelfth and final session — usually one last Wednesday night — is a celebration service where everyone from all six groups gathers to sing, share testimonies, Communion, and anything that seems good to commemorate and celebrate. These celebrations are great opportunities to invite the rest of the church, families, friends, or future group participants.

Following this plan, including the weekend intensive, all twelve sessions are complete after about nine calendar weeks. A church with a vibrant Redemption Groups ministry will run this cycle two to four times per year. First Church runs groups in the fall (starting September or October), winter (starting January), and spring (starting March or April), taking a break for the summer.

THE PROCESS OF A REDEMPTION GROUP

How do groups form and develop over time? Well, after the initial meeting where leaders lay out some ground rules and make agreements about how to relate to one another in the group, Redemption Group members take turns telling a short version of their story, beginning with the group's leaders.[58] This initial brief storytelling allows each group member to invite the rest of the group into his journey, but is not intended to be comprehensive or exhaustive. Enough story is shared to answer questions like: "What brings me here?" "What do I think might be some shaping influences in my life, such as relationships or experiences?"

The first two or three group sessions focus on this storytelling, with the group making some initial responses to one another's stories. The group's tone during this phase is normally characterized by compassion, listening, and identifying with suffering. Relationships and trust are being established.

We have often heard group participants give feedback at this point in the process to the effect that "I didn't know we were going *there*, in *church*, until my group leaders told their own stories and gave the rest of us permission to be so open and honest." Storytelling is typically candid, vulnerable, and messy.

After the initial round of storytelling, the agenda of each group session becomes a blend of several activities, including:

- Discussing key ideas from the *Redemption* book reading and main session teaching.
- Focusing attention on individual group members, drawing out a person's story further, asking questions, and speaking love or truth into his or her life.
- Addressing the process of the group itself, such as talking about how the group is functioning or working through conflict that may arise.
- Sharing and responding to "personal psalms."

To elaborate on that last item, group members participate in a psalm-writing exercise where they consider the ways that the biblical psalmists express their deep fear, anger, confusion, hope, sorrow, and joy to the God who listens, and then they write their own psalms. These often amount to written poetic prayers. The form is almost irrelevant; what's important is for group members to engage in the activity wholeheart-edly. We find that this exercise often helps participants to tap into deep places of the heart, and by sharing, allows the group to engage more deeply with one another.

In the third or fourth group session, the group's coleaders assign the writing of this "personal psalm" as homework for each participant to complete and to bring back to read to the group at some point before the end of the last group session. Again, the leaders go first, reading a psalm they each have written. When each psalm is read, the group has another opportunity to respond to that reader and to focus attention to pursue that person as appropriate. Each group session for the remainder of the quarter typically includes one or two group members sharing a psalm.

As the group engages in all of these activities, it does so as a whole group. When someone shares a story or a psalm, the group responds. When attention is focused for a time on one group member, it's the group that focuses attention together, engaging in that pursuit, and the group then has the opportunity to reflect on the pursuit. We encourage all group members to engage with one another and to contribute to helping one another, not to leave it up to the group's coleaders.

The coleaders guide the group to maintain integrity with its agreements to treat one another with respect, they guide the group in a productive process, and they strive to ensure that what is learned in the group is faithful to the message of the cross. We encourage group leaders not to see the group as merely a collection of individuals, as if the group process were a series of individual biblical counseling sessions with observers. It's much more organic and synergistic. The whole of the group is greater than the sum of its parts.

Some key milestones that we hope to guide group members through include:

- Experiencing God's love and compassion amidst their suffering.
- Identifying roots and fruits of sin, thus promoting genuine confession and repentance.

- Receiving God's forgiveness for their sin, experiencing His grace and mercy.
- Extending forgiveness toward others.

Various chapters in the *Redemption* book set the table especially well for each of these conversations, but the way each group member reaches these personal milestones tends to be nonlinear and organic.

The final task for each group member is to develop a "Wilderness Travel Plan." This simple tool is inspired by Paul Tripp's teaching in *Instruments in the Redeemer's Hands*:

> Most of us are tempted to think that change has taken place before it actually has. We confuse growth in knowledge and insight with genuine life change. But insight is not change and knowledge should not be confused with practical, active, biblical wisdom.... In short, we must not confuse insight and change. Insight is a beginning, a part of a whole, but it is not the whole.[59]

In the Wilderness Travel Plan, a participant considers the following three areas:

1. *Pillars:* Based on the idea of the pillars of cloud and fire by which God led His people through the wilderness in the exodus story, we ask: "What is God calling you toward?" "What specific commitments will you make or actions will you take as you follow Him?" This might include going to a specific person to confess sin and seek that person's forgiveness, or inviting some specific accountability measures, or committing to ongoing forgiveness toward someone and possibly going to that person to communicate forgiveness. It could be almost anything, but it should be *specific*. We normally recommend that participants identify three to five of these points.

2. *Provision:* Based on the idea that God lavished grace, mercy, and practical provisions on His people in the exodus and gave them all that they needed for the journey, we ask: "How has God graced you and empowered you?" This is essential, because the Christian life is not about trying harder to do the right thing;

it is about responding in faithful worship to a gracious God. To concentrate only on *what I must do* (the "pillars") without enjoying *what God has done to free me* (the "provision") would be to return to a new form of merciless slavery. Long-term change requires long-term soaking in the abundant grace of God. Like the "pillars," we encourage participants to identify a few of these points of "provision" as *specifically* as possible. Think of them like the Ebenezer, or "Stone of Help," that Samuel set up as a monument to commemorate God's provision of victory in battle, sung in the hymn "Come Thou Fount": "Here I raise my Ebenezer; Hither by Thy help I'm come" (see 1 Sam. 7:12).[60]

3. *People:* Change happens in community. Here we ask participants: "With whom will you walk this journey of change?" Yet again, we encourage *specific* responses, the names of specific people. It is crucial that the conversation that has been taking place inside the Redemption Group continues outside the group, in the ongoing relationships that the participant has with other people. Ideally, the participant would continue in relationship with these people — friends, family members, or members of a small group community — sharing his or her Wilderness Travel Plan as if to say, "Here is where I think God is leading me to grow and change. Here is how He has graced me. I'll need help to press on, and I'll need help to be continually reminded of God's grace to me. Will you help me?"

As I (Mike) have observed the outcomes of Redemption Groups over the years, I have concluded that the groups are especially good at increasing one's *insight*, opening blind eyes, but, as Paul Tripp says, this insight only *begins* the change process. Redemption Groups are designed to be short-term, not ongoing experiences. The hope is that a Redemption Group experience will equip each participant — and over time, the whole church — for the long and challenging journey of life as a Christian. The Wilderness Travel Plan is a way of promoting that ongoing growth and change after the group ends. It guides participants to clarify what they intend to do to change, it reminds them of God's grace toward them, and it asks them to decide who can help them in their ongoing journey. But the plan is only a tool. It relies on community for its effectiveness.

What seems to maximize a person's likelihood of experiencing lasting change — whether or not they work out a Wilderness Travel Plan — is to find themselves enfolded in a redemptive community that continually enacts the sort of "one-another" care in the local church that the Wilderness Travel Plan invites. And this brings us to the strategy of Redemption Groups in the local church.

THE STRATEGY OF REDEMPTION GROUPS WITHIN A LOCAL CHURCH

Redemption Groups are designed to be part of an "ecosystem" of redemptive community in a local church. Rather than being a siloed ministry in the church — separated, for "those" people — we imagine it more like a heartbeat, continuously circulating nutrients throughout the body. Each quarter as participants complete the process, they continue in mainstream community rhythms in the church (such as small group communities), carrying with them fresh doses of God's grace and a vision for personal change.[61] This alone has a refreshing impact on their communities. But also, they come out of the group process better equipped to listen to and extend loving concern for their friends.

Churches who run Redemption Groups quarter after quarter have noticed that over time the ethos of their communities change. Eventually, a "tipping point" is reached where it becomes normal for people in such a church to experience redemptive relationships where deep hurts and sins can be addressed, whether or not they themselves attend a Redemption Group. People in such communities learn how to deal with the deep issues of life, and to do so in a Christ-centered way.

As good as that may sound, *we do not believe Redemption Groups should be the primary vehicle for discipleship and community in the local church.* Small group communities are better suited for that. Allow me to use a metaphor to illustrate this.

In high school chemistry you may have learned that a catalyst is a substance that speeds up a chemical reaction. The chemical reaction is the goal, and the catalyst supports this and helps to make it happen. We see Redemption Groups as a catalyst for the progressive sanctification that is the goal of small groups, but this doesn't require turning every small group into a Redemption Group. Hypothetically, if Redemption Groups did their job well, they would eventually no longer be needed.

Yet while Redemption Groups in and of themselves are not the goal, they are still powerful. A typical Redemption Groups ministry will be much smaller in size than the small groups ministry it catalyzes, yet it can exert a powerful positive influence on the culture of the entire church.

THE TRAINING OF REDEMPTION GROUP LEADERS

One of the surprising strengths of Redemption Groups is their effectiveness at training volunteers for effective personal ministry by way of immersive experience. To train to become a Redemption Group leader is to start, from day one, as a participant in a group in need of God's mercy for yourself. Toward the end of each quarter, group leaders identify participants whom they'd recommend as apprentices. These recommendations are made primarily based on demonstrated character traits in the candidate that have been observed in the group interactions. After interviewing these candidates, they are invited to serve as apprentices where they begin practicing leadership. The group's coleaders and supervisor recommend at the end of the apprenticeship whether the apprentice is ready to be approved as a group leader. An overseeing pastor or ministry director ultimately determines when and whether it's time for that person to lead.

Along the way, a Redemption Group leader is also expected to go through a training course in biblical counseling to gain conceptual knowledge of basic biblical counseling. Ministry sites that run Redemption Groups are expected to provide for their leader trainees a basic biblical counseling training program using an existing biblical counseling curriculum or to develop one of their own.

While the conceptual knowledge gained through such a curriculum is essential, the trainee's experience in the group and demonstrated growth in Christlike character remain first and foremost in the training and assessment of leaders. I (Mike) am persuaded that the most important indicator of whether a candidate is ready to lead is the *demonstrated* condition of his heart: whether he shows a tenderness to receive God's mercy amidst his own sins and sufferings, and whether he loves other people amidst theirs. Not whether he can *describe* the concept of God's mercy, but whether he *demonstrates* a need for it. And not whether he can *talk* about how to love other people, but whether he *demonstrates* love for people in hard places by actual, observed word and deed in live relationships. Because Redemption Groups are a robust relational environment where sin and suffering are deeply addressed, they provide an opportunity for supervisors to observe when a candidate may be ready to move toward leadership.

Redemption Groups have often been effective at developing ministry leaders for the local church. They offer a very powerful relational and experiential learning environment, not only for developing each successive generation of Redemption Group leaders but also for training those who will go on to practice biblical counseling in a one-on-one setting, or even for those small group leaders whose shepherding capabilities are awakened and enhanced by their experiences in Redemption Groups. In some cases, pastoral candidates have been known to go through these groups as part of their preparation for pastoral ministry.

SHOULD OUR CHURCH START REDEMPTION GROUPS?

We are often asked by church leaders about starting Redemption Groups. The question usually sounds something like this: "We have heard about how helpful Redemption Groups are in providing care for people within the context of the local church. How can we begin?"

We usually begin answering that question by issuing a caution, one that we regularly reissue to our own leaders. Redemption Groups are not a cure-all for every struggling person in your church. In fact, for leaders whose own lives have been deeply impacted by Redemption Groups, a temptation anytime they meet another believer who has experienced significant sin and suffering may be to think, "She needs Redemption Group!" The reality is that she needs *the Holy Spirit* to accomplish the ongoing work of progressive sanctification. She needs *the gospel*, and all of its implications, to work itself out in her life. A Redemption Group is only one way that might happen, and maybe not the best way for everyone.

A risk of implementing Redemption Groups in your church is that it can be viewed merely as a programmatic way to meet the needs of some of the most hurting and broken. They *are* helpful in meeting those needs. Yet we hope to maintain the vision for the local church, shared by others in this book, that every believer would be equipped to care for others, to live out the "one-anothers" in profound and meaningful ways, even with those whose needs are great (John 13:34–35; Rom. 12:10–16; 1 Peter 4:8–10). Redemption Groups properly implemented promote and catalyze that vision of the whole church "one-anothering."

So, before recommending that a church begin Redemption Groups, we'll often ask about the current health and strength of a few other facets of their ministry.

Preaching: A church's pulpit ministry should significantly advance the cause of progressive sanctification in the lives of people, as well as provide some level of equipping in the areas of shepherding and care. Simply put, preaching that exalts Christ invites repentance and renewed faith in the gospel, which is ultimately our only hope for transformation.

Small Group Leaders' Training: As mentioned above, we believe that small groups, if properly equipped, can serve as the primary vehicle for pastoral care. But equipping the small group leaders to serve in this manner is imperative. Several years ago, I (Abe) pointed out to our elders that while we were depending on our groups to provide the majority of the pastoral care (a good thing), we had provided our group leaders with very little training on how to shepherd and care for people (clearly not a good thing!). In response, we developed and implemented a training process for our leaders to be equipped in pastoral care. The results have been incredible. Nearly all of our leaders are excited about helping people walk through a variety of serious issues, ranging from adultery to divorce, from dysfunctional parenting to financial turmoil. The majority of issues that would have required input from more trained professionals (paid pastoral staff or professional counselors) are now being handled by group leaders. Thankfully, there are a number of great resources available to help churches equip group leaders for shepherding and care. To get started, you can visit *www.biblicalcounselingcoalition.org* for more information.

One-to-One or Triads: Many churches are emphasizing micro-groups of two to five as a key to growth as a disciple. This context is the perfect environment to learn and practice the very skills used by Redemption Group leaders to care for people's hearts. If properly resourced and equipped, these groups can have an exponential impact on a local church, helping normalize shepherding and care as everyday practices for all believers to engage in rather than the highly specialized disciplines of a few select specialists. Again, there are a number of great resources available for these micro-groups, but *Gospel-Centered Discipleship* by Jonathan Dodson and *The Gospel-Centered Life* by Bob Thune are both outstanding.[62]

CONCLUSION

Hopefully, this gives you an introduction to the content, format, and structure of a Redemption Group. If you'd like to learn more about launching Redemption Groups, please visit *www.redemptiongroups.com.*

As we said earlier, Redemption Groups are just one approach to biblical counseling in the local church. They aren't trying to do anything ultimately different from what other biblical counseling ministries are trying to do, nor are they pursuing different objectives in progressive sanctification from what most small group ministries are trying to do. However, we have found them to be a powerful, scalable, and catalytic enhancement to a church's discipleship strategy that enriches redemptive community.

CHAPTER 7

BIBLICAL COUNSELING AND UNCOMMON COMMUNITY

GARRETT HIGBEE

Imagine with me for a moment ... What difference would it make in your church if every pastor, lay leader, and person of influence was trained in biblical counseling? In our church, teaching everyone who will listen how to speak the truth in love with compassion and skill has created what we call "uncommon community." How might that enhance the impact of discipleship and care? While I'm not the first to suggest this, I believe in this vision. And I'm convinced that the biblical counseling movement has yet to tap into the full potential of the body of Christ to better care for itself. I often say to our leaders, "Would you rather have guardrails at the top of the cliff to keep those you are caring for from going over or build a trauma hospital at the bottom of the cliff for those that careened down the cliff, wheels spinning, on fire, and landing in your lap?" Training our ministry leaders to disciple and care more intentionally would go a long way toward decreasing the need for formal biblical counseling.

I know this is true because I've seen it happen at our church, Harvest Bible Chapel. Within a year of training our small group leaders in basic biblical counseling skills and giving them solid tools to use, the referrals to our soul care counseling ministry dropped almost 50 percent. We believe this is because our small group leaders, coaches, and family pastors are now catching the small concerns and intentionally speaking the truth in love on a regular basis. They have gained more confidence in God's Word and in their ability to speak life-giving counsel. They moved into areas they had avoided before and were quicker to pull someone aside to ask heart-revealing questions (Prov. 20:5). Small groups have become more transparent and, when needed, small group leaders or members have felt comfortable asking those with formal counseling training for help. It has been encouraging to see the people of our church accept the challenge and responsibility to join together in this vision.

So how did we get all of these leaders trained? We started by developing two core courses and made them required classes for every leader of any kind in our church. We call the courses Uncommon Leadership 101 and 201. They are not just about becoming a counselor; they share how a person can be a well-rounded disciple-maker. We define a leader as someone who has godly character, growing competence, and a genuine commitment to the mission of the church. We teach them that they have specific roles as a leader. We want them to be guided by Scriptures like Jeremiah 3:15. Our end goal is a teacher who disciples by applied instruction, a shepherd who counsels biblically, and a leader who influences by example.

With this in mind, I invite you to think about your own leadership context. How might you use biblical counseling to develop your leaders? It might help to think of biblical leadership as a three-legged stool. You ought to be able to teach, lead, and care for your people. You need all three legs to have a solid platform of leadership at any level in the church. Of course, some people are more inclined or gifted in one of those roles, but all of them must be practiced. Otherwise you would not have small groups modeled after a healthy and balanced community of Christ. Our discipleship pastors recognized this and pointed out that we were weak on the third leg of the stool. We had leaders who could teach, but they were not well equipped to shepherd when the sheep would get stuck or stray. We also saw a need for more mutual ministry between believers in the small groups, which meant teaching them how to speak the truth in love at a very basic but very profound and personal level.

We define our small groups as "uncommon communities applying God's truth in everyday life." We understand some churches don't even have small groups as their model of discipleship. But we see the goal of small groups through the lens of Scriptures like Acts 2:42 where the emphasis is on the apostles' teaching, fellowship, communion, and prayer. Small groups are not just Bible studies or support groups; yet, neither are they just another social gathering. I hope this chapter will challenge you to think about equipping and caring differently, regardless of the present discipleship model of your church. I'll start by sharing a story of a typical small group member's experience. This was a common story at our church just a few years ago. At that time, we took a survey and, of hundreds of respondents, many told us that they would *not* turn to their small group leader for help in a time of need. This was a wakeup call! The rest of this chapter is about what we did to correct that problem.

A COMMON SCENARIO

Bob and Sharon had been in their small group for almost three years. They loved the friends they had made in the group and loved to study the Bible together. They attended group meetings faithfully. John and Sherri, the leaders, were wonderful Bible teachers. Over eighteen months, John took them through the book of Acts, and now they were in the book of James. They often spent a few minutes praying before they opened the Word, and they would end with some chitchat and light refreshments. It was a great time.

Then, in the third year of meeting, Sharon caught Bob looking at porn. Bob was ashamed and Sharon was hurt. They knew they needed help.

Neither Bob nor Sharon considered talking about this with their small group. This was not something they wanted John and Sherri to know. They had never shared about intimate things in their small group. It really was more of a Bible study. Besides that, John and Sherri were not "counselors." So they decided to go to their senior pastor for help. Their pastor was sympathetic and prayed with them. He told them he was glad they came and that this was a very serious but private matter. He encouraged them to contact the biblical counseling department that had just been established in the church. He promised to continue to pray periodically for their marriage and suggested a book on purity for Bob. Bob did not follow through with any of this until his wife caught him again. This time it was clear, and both admitted that they needed more help. So they went to counseling, where a trained lay leader helped them. The counsel they received was biblical and, over time, things improved. Bob put filters on the computers, set up periodic check-ins, and Sharon read a book about trusting God. They continued to go to small group, but Sharon grew more and more discouraged that she had no one to talk to after their time in counseling. On top of that, Bob had no real long-term accountability, so his struggle became a constant topic of discussion between the two of them. They began to wonder if they would need yet another round of counseling in the near future.

AN UNCOMMON SOLUTION

Sadly, this story and others like it are very common in churches across our nation. In chapter 3, I made a case for a more fully orbed counseling model in the local church, one where biblical counseling trickles down into every ministry of the church. In that chapter, I proposed a marriage of sorts between discipleship and counseling and exposed the false dichotomy that creates "silos," disconnected from other church ministries and with a disconnected continuum of care. In this chapter, I want to illustrate how small group leaders and members can be equipped to practice soul care. The differences are there, but at the informal level of counseling, they are more like shades of gray than black and white. While I might "disciple" someone with less of a well-developed diagnostic, I certainly want to know them well. I also might "counsel" someone in a topical way related to their issue, but in our time together I certainly want to touch on the gospel, their personal relationship with Christ, and core doctrines. The overlap is significant enough that our pastors overseeing discipleship and our pastors overseeing soul care are now cross-trained.

When we look to hire pastors, we want them to oversee *both* our counseling and discipleship. This is also true for our church plants all around the world. Consider what might happen if those trained in master's programs would see discipleship and counseling on the same ministry continuum and practice accordingly. Training leaders in this way would address the "overspecialization" that has left many graduates without a job. That's not to say that advanced training in biblical counseling is not needed or that these pastors shouldn't be able to counsel the most complex problems. It is to say that we need to equip everyone, from new believers to small group leaders, how to self-counsel biblically and to care for each other at a basic level.

Adjusting the Fulcrum of Biblical Counseling

How has our small group ministry changed? Small groups were always an important part of our church, but for many years our small group training was lean on biblical counseling skills and tools. We realized that our small group leaders wanted to help their people, but they felt inadequately equipped. That meant taking basics in biblical counseling and adapting the basics to the small group context. To assist the small group leaders, we developed a field manual that included tools, diagrams, and tips for them. We then trained them and gave them the written materials to use as a reference.

We also trained the small group leaders' supervising coaches to be of help to them as they ran into problems that exceeded their skill or experience. This meant refining the training materials for each level of influence, competence, and care. Now counseling skills and tools are a part of every leader's training. Small groups have become such an important part of our biblical soul care ministry at Harvest Bible Chapel that every formal counselor has to go through the small group leader training as well.

We have not fully arrived, but we are endeavoring to create a unified discipleship and care model, and it starts by making sure we have missional alignment. We want to make disciples and disciple-makers who follow and live out the teaching of Christ, and the goal of small groups at our church is to teach our people to apply God's truth in everyday life. If leaders are going to be trained to be undershepherds who care for "their" people, teachers who equip "their" people biblically, and leaders who model and influence "their" people toward Christ, it can't be the crumbs sprinkled on top of the "discipleship pie"; it has to be the main ingredient!

Expect some resistance if you think you can just march into your pastor's office and say it is time for discipleship and biblical counseling to get married! Even though we saw this need in our church, we ran into the "silo," or isolated, ministry problem that is common at every church. We saw how hard this was going to be, and we knew we needed to talk less and pray more. All good ministry starts with prayer. Then we had to gain buy-in from senior leadership and create top-down communication of the vision. This meant a lot more prayer and, frankly, two years of knocking heads. It meant seeding the idea that counseling is really just intensive discipleship, which was a paradigm shift for many in leadership. To the average senior pastor and elder, the word "counseling" often elicits fears about liability, competency, and capacity. We had to discuss these concerns and explain that this was really more about a quality of discipleship at the informal counseling level.

We not only had to build bridges; we had to slowly break down the false dichotomy where people see biblical counseling on a whole different plane from discipleship.[63] We did this by explaining that soul care training was an enhancement to discipleship, not a replacement for it. We were fortunate that our senior pastor got on board and saw this, but that was not the case with all the senior leaders. We had to assure our senior staff that we were not going to have small group leaders calling themselves formal counselors. We also made very clear distinctions for each level of training and care. No one who was not well-trained in theology and advanced biblical counseling skills would be doing "formal" counseling. We also began developing and providing ongoing leadership training for the Uncommon Leadership 101 through 601 courses. Finally, we committed to a mentality that everyone in the church should be equipped, leader or not, to know how to minister to one another mutually by turning together to the one-another commands in Scripture. Had we not done this work and had God not given us a few strategic open doors, we would still be doing biblical soul care ministry in a silo — separate from the other ministries of the church.

We took the next step of developing clear expectations that no one should be considered a "consumer" in a small group. We had each member sign a "contract" focusing on the commitment to come prepared and ready to participate. We also had a social covenant that teaches intentional "living out" of the biblical one-anothers. We handpick those who show godly character, a growing competence, and a genuine commitment to the mission and vision of the church, and we train leaders with increased skills. We provide them with tools while being mindful of ascending levels of competence and care based on position, function, and influence (from the janitor to the senior pastor). There are no civilians in this war, and no one is exempt from bearing other people's burdens or serving others within their capacity, which should always be growing.

Closing the Gap between Informal and Formal Counsel

But how, practically, do you break down biblical soul care training for each level of competence and care? What does a member need to know to be intentional in their care? When do they need to look up for more help from the leaders above them? What does a small group leader need to know to be more directive in their care? What does a small group coach need to be better at early corrective care and consulting? Finally, what do the pastors and elders as well as gifted lay leaders need regarding advanced counseling skills to really lead, care for, and help the church effectively? My focus for the rest of this chapter is on defining what equipping and caring in each leadership context looks like. We begin by sharing how small groups fit in the bigger picture of the church.

Remember, missional alignment is important. So we view the main purpose of our small group ministry as the advancement of the mission of our church, which is rooted in Matthew 28:19: "Go therefore and make disciples" (ESV). The two main nonnegotiable functions of our small group ministry are:

1. *Mutual Ministry:* Strong emphasis on applying God's truth and love in everyday life, living out the one-anothers, and equipping the saints for ministry.
2. *Multiplication of Leadership:* Where we discern, develop, and deploy the future lay leaders of our church.

Organizationally we strive to have a seamless discipleship and care continuum. The best way to explain this is to visualize a house with five levels representing different levels of leadership training. (See figure 4.) There is a ground floor that includes training for every believer. Intentional discipleship that we commonly call "one-anothering" happens on the ground floor. This involves every member of a small group. Small group leaders are on the first floor and are the first responders when problems arise. Small group coaches are on the second floor and help small group leaders if things escalate. Pastoral staff is on the third floor, and formal counselors (both staff and lay) are on the last two levels, or fourth and fifth floors. At any level of discipleship and care we try to assure that no balls are dropped and no one is left behind.

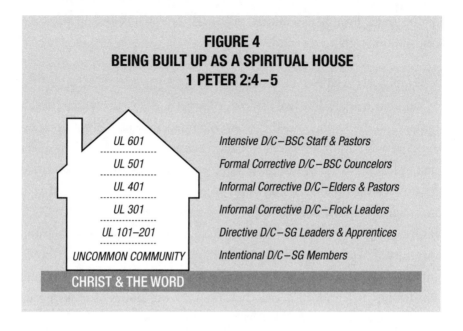

FIGURE 4
BEING BUILT UP AS A SPIRITUAL HOUSE
1 PETER 2:4–5

UL 601	Intensive D/C – BSC Staff & Pastors
UL 501	Formal Corrective D/C – BSC Councelors
UL 401	Informal Corrective D/C – Elders & Pastors
UL 301	Informal Corrective D/C – Flock Leaders
UL 101–201	Directive D/C – SG Leaders & Apprentices
UNCOMMON COMMUNITY	Intentional D/C – SG Members

CHRIST & THE WORD

It took a miracle of God, lots of humility, and a new mindset to bring the pastors together on this. This was more than "linking" our counseling ministry with our small groups; it was breaking down the artificial (and isolating) silos and redefining discipleship as a "continuum from intentional to intensive." Today we see soul care practiced in small groups as part of effective discipleship and the front lines of biblical counseling. If a small group leader is caring for someone in their group, they are already functioning preventively as a "directive counselor." More formal levels of biblical soul care are still very much needed because issues are more complex or corrective in nature. And the folks on the front lines still need supervision, consultation, and support.

START WITH A HEALTHY FOUNDATION

Because we believe in the doctrine of the priesthood of believers, soul care training happens as soon as you become a small group member. On that ground floor level, all our members go through a practical study of six specific one-another passages in Scripture in a small group study developed by our campus pastors. The end result is every member of the small group sees mutual ministry as a privilege and personal responsibility going forward.

RAISING HEALTHY LEADERS

When selecting leaders, we use the "3D method" of discerning, developing, and deploying existing group members in leadership. Our leaders start as small group members and become small group apprentices before leading a small group. When someone is hurting in the small group, a group member may serve as an advocate[64] for biblical soul care, which, by the way, gives us great candidates for formal counseling training. All leaders must demonstrate compassion, wisdom, and humility. They must grasp the basics of our care model and are trained initially for a minimum of twelve hours of class time (Uncommon Leadership 101 and 201) and then hundreds of hours of experiential time in these practices. In this leader training, they are taught the basics on how to be good listeners, how to ask heart-revealing questions, and how to "triage" care by discerning severity, ownership, and support around the person in need. We complement their counseling skills by reviewing basic doctrines such as the sufficiency of Scripture and progressive sanctification. Furthermore, we teach that if needed, they can consult or "refer up" in the discipleship and care structure. We train coaches overseeing small group leaders more extensively so as to further strengthen prevention and early correction on this end of the discipleship continuum.

In addition, everyone who attends the church is eventually funneled into small groups that are our "discipleship highway." We have created different "on/off" ramps to this highway. For example, we have specialized small groups called Biblical Soul Care small groups. They would be a part of the early corrective soul care on the second or third floor. These groups function in two ways: (1) they are a front door into the church or an "on ramp" to the discipleship highway,[65] and (2) they are like a "rest stop" for those suffering from a debilitating issue or those caught in a stronghold. The curriculum for those groups is more focused on the heart, and the small group leaders are all trained in corrective counseling. These groups are time-limited, and the goal is always to get back into our "regular" uncommon community (UC) small groups.

Counseling with the small group leader or flock leaders is an example of "routine maintenance"; a visit with a pastor or a formal biblical soul care counselor would be like a "major tune-up"; and, in rare cases, an intensive two- or three-day intervention led by biblical soul care staff would be like "pulling a seized engine," i.e., a radical overhaul of the heart. Our continuity of care is streamlined, and we endeavor to create strong connections both in the referral process to and re-assimilation from formal counseling.

MAKING HEALTHY CONNECTIONS

Still, you may be wondering, "What if someone is not connected in your church? How do they get help?" We always recommend that a person join a small group before receiving formal care, but we still see nonmembers for a formal counseling assessment even if they are not in a group. If they are in a small group, we check to see if they have asked their small group leader for help—and we lovingly push back if someone tries to go around these pathways for appropriate care. Regardless of how things begin, we require a person to be in a small group by the time the counseling ends, so "getting involved in a group" is a required homework assignment early on in the counseling. Additionally, finding an advocate to walk through the process of formal counseling with them is an important element of long-term success.[66] We are convinced by Scripture that the primary place for sustained growth through discipleship and care is the small group context.

Further, it is our conviction from studying God's Word that people do not really grow outside of community.[67] If someone is disconnected, we make it their homework from the start to get connected, and then we help them find the right group. We want them to "own" that process as much as possible. A referral to our family pastors will mean that this person will be personally walked through the process. However, they must still take initiative to get into a small group within three sessions of formal counseling or be open to having us place them in one.

ESTABLISHING HEALTHY GUIDELINES

At this point, you might have questions about confidentiality. In our church, we prioritize the protection and provision of biblical community over *absolute* confidentially. We see the Bible warning against isolation (Prov. 18:1), keeping secrets, and making unholy alliances. We see the graduated steps of accountability and disclosure outlined in Scriptures like Matthew 18:15 – 20. To be clear, we take great pains to be discreet in our communication with a zero tolerance policy for gossip or slander, and we practice informed consent. This means that we tell people that we will communicate with only those who can help us develop or support a solid care plan. The rule is to share only with those who need to know and share only what they need to know to help. That usually means consulting with a supervising leader or sharing with an advocate who is already in the care process. Again, the rule of thumb is informed consent — let the counselee know and ask if it is okay, unless it is a high-risk situation where time does not allow.[68]

COMING FULL CIRCLE

I hope what we have outlined has helped you to see that it is important and possible to integrate biblical counseling in such a way that it permeates all levels of ministry. If this were to happen in your church, how might the opening story with Bob and Sharon have gone differently? Perhaps a bit like this ...

Bob and Sharon Revisited

Bob and Sharon had been a part of their small group for three years. Recently their group multiplied, but they stayed with the leaders, John and Sherri, to continue to grow because John felt continuity in their situation would be good. John had taken an active interest in Bob's life early on, especially when they broke for accountability during small group — men with men, women with women. John discovered Bob struggled with lust. John knew this was a very common issue and had done some reading to develop a plan for his own purity. Others in the group admitted to struggles as well, but it was clear Bob was farther into the sin than the others. So John asked Bob to spend some time talking with him one on one. Both Bob and Sharon were invited to the leader's home one evening so Bob could confess his sin. This time Bob was more honest and transparent and had put some things in place to stop the cycle. He confessed to his wife and asked for her forgiveness. After a tearful and humbling time, he committed to close accountability and counseling if needed. Sharon was hurt, but deeply grateful for the support. She forgave her husband, but was at a loss on how to move forward. Bob gave her permission to talk with John's wife about the hurt and trust issues. John tried to get a read on how this would go and if they would need formal counseling. He mentioned to them both that this might be needed, and they were both open.

Sharon confided in John's wife that she thought biblical counseling would be good for her. She was hurt and angry. She felt deceived, but she did not want to grow distant or bitter. John and Sherri asked Bob and Sharon to go for dinner and suggested they go to see the counselor at the church, offering to go along as their advocates. It was humbling, and Bob was hesitant. Sharon shared her fear and her desire to work through this to avoid shutting down. Bob was moved by her honesty and the weight this had put on her, so he agreed to go. He admitted that he wanted to be free from the temptation of lust and indicated that the temptation was still strong. They set up a time to consult with their flock leader to make sure this was an appropriate referral, but at this point it was more of a formality.

The counseling was very helpful for them, not only because it was biblically sound but because John and Sherri walked through the whole process with them. They did the homework together, they prayed regularly together, and they were amazing sounding boards, helping Bob and Sharon not to divert to past patterns. They even helped them to discreetly share things gained in counseling with the entire small group. As a matter of fact, because of Bob's and Sharon's authentic and vulnerable sharing, the whole group grew in transparency and bonded around the power of God's Word to help in times of need.

You can see that this scenario was a bit different. It's the same couple and the same problems, but a very different result. Not only was the formal counseling more effective; the care before and after was much more intentional. I'm grateful to say that I have heard this type of testimony over and over again in the last two years.

And not only did things go differently for Bob and Sharon, but the whole small group benefited. Not only can intentional, careful discipleship and care change people's lives, but it can be done in a context of community that makes change easier and more long lasting.

Moving toward Leveraging the Whole Body of Christ

Imagine how this could help the church as a whole. The small group ministry is now the preventive arm of soul care and the best place for deep discipleship and care. We see fewer people in biblical counseling because many of them just needed to be discipled with wisdom. We also have fewer crisis situations because people lean on each other long before coming to us. There was a time when it seemed like referrals to our formal soul care (counseling) were like burning fireballs catapulted over a high wall. We'd douse the flames and another would hit. Now we get a call from a family pastor or a small group coach instead. Referrals are screened and people are prepared when they come for formal soul care. They often have advocates, have already done some initial biblical counseling homework, and they know their small group leader is behind them.

This significantly helps the effectiveness of formal counseling in our church. We are constantly training experientially: small group leaders, flock leaders (or coaches), advocates, and counseling apprentices. We are a teaching hospital. And the stigma around counseling is slowly dying out.

Training informal counselors and disciple-makers has not replaced the need for trained, certified counselors, but it has built a support around them that has proven invaluable. This is not a fad. We would never go back to an approach that is disconnected or top-heavy. It is more sustainable and, frankly, more enjoyable ministry.

What about your church? What is the culture of caring in your church today? Where might it benefit from some honest evaluation and a commitment to a partnership between discipleship and counseling? It may take a few years to shift the mindset and practice of leadership and your people, but I hope you will consider getting started.

CHAPTER 8

BIBLICAL COUNSELING
AND SMALL GROUPS:
COUNSELING IN
THE CONTEXT OF
COMMUNITY

LEE LEWIS AND MICHAEL SNETZER

As bi-vocational ministers, we serve as full-time pastors, yet we also each have a part-time, private counseling practice. This gives us a unique vantage point where we have seen firsthand how the church interacts with those in the counseling profession. Over the years, a statement made by one of our former supervisors has remained with us, influencing how we approach our dual roles in both the local church and in private practice:

There is no substitute for the body of Christ.

This statement has been a constant reminder to us that even though the work we do in our practice is helpful and necessary, it is never a replacement for the ministry of the local church. As a consequence of this, in our private practice we do our best to involve the church. We seek to *equip* the church so that whatever supplemental benefit comes from the counseling office for a fee might be found within the church for free. We encourage people to look toward the church, which provides opportunities to cultivate gospel-rich communities under local church authority. This means that we are constantly working ourselves out of a job (though, admittedly, there is no lack of people needing help). We also *encourage accountability* within the church by getting consent to disclose information or, at the very least, encouraging our clients to take whatever the Lord is showing them in counseling each week and fleshing that out within their respective communities. In all of this, our goal is to avoid replacing the community found in the local church with the pseudo-community of a private practice counseling office.

As pastors in the church, this means that we do our best to *counsel within the context of community*. At The Village Church, we do this in groups. We don't involve ourselves in a lot of one-on-one counseling. We equip the saints for ministry and point people to groups, which provide venues for one-another ministry to take place. Having ministries within the church along with qualified leaders helps us to keep from falling into the trap of trying to do it all ourselves. On those occasions when we do meet with an individual or couple, we typically invite the leaders of their groups to be involved. This provides accountability and can help to clarify issues while reinforcing any advice or direction given in the meeting.

In the pages that follow, we'd like to further unpack this small-group-focused, church-based approach to counseling. And to understand it better, we'll begin by looking at the theology and philosophy of ministry. We'll close by taking a look at the nuts and bolts of ministry practice.

THE VILLAGE CHURCH MISSION STATEMENT

At The Village Church our mission statement is this:

> We bring glory to God by making disciples through gospel-centered worship, gospel-centered community, gospel-centered service, and gospel-centered multiplication.

Gospel-centered worship provides the fuel for discipleship, gospel-centered community provides the context for discipleship, gospel-centered service is the overflow of discipleship, and gospel-centered multiplication is the result of gospel-centered discipleship. This provides both a picture of and a process for a maturing believer in Christ.

Because gospel-centered community is the context for discipleship, we have two primary types of groups that provide opportunities for people to connect in community, what we call Home Groups and Recovery Groups. Though it may be overused, a hospital analogy is a good way to understand how these two types of groups relate to each other. Home Groups are where we provide long-term care. Home Groups provide a consistent avenue for men and women in the congregation to engage on a deeper level. They do this by walking faithfully in a covenant community. Home Groups have a consistent tie into the life and happenings of the church. Our group leaders have to understand the goal and vision of how group life transcends into the spiritual growth of a believer. Recovery Groups offer specialized care. Recovery Groups are a continual open door to the community throughout the year, meeting weekly at the church. These groups are intended to provide individuals, couples, and families with biblical counseling within a redemptive community.

While both Home Groups and Recovery Groups provide venues for organic discipleship, they have available to them a more robust and structured discipleship process called STEPS. It is required that those who enter STEPS have a relational basis in either Home Groups or Recovery Groups. STEPS is a 13-week intensive discipleship program that explores the foundation and implications of the gospel in everyday living. The content of STEPS is basic enough for the skeptic who is curious about the gospel and rich enough to help a struggling believer through a difficult season.

History of Care and Counseling

When I (Michael) first arrived at the church, there were a couple of women's groups meeting off the radar to cope with their husbands' addictions.

I approached our lead pastor, Matt Chandler, to see if the church might want to expand their group ministry, and he was completely on board. We initially launched a grassroots recovery ministry that relied heavily on the work of Saddleback Church and the Celebrate Recovery program. This was primarily a repentance ministry for those struggling with their own sin. Very early in this ministry, God began to give us further direction, and we began writing our own lessons and developing our own materials.

My colleague, Lee, had arrived in the aftermath of Hurricane Katrina, with a seminary counseling degree, but he had not been trained as a biblical counselor. He joined me as we pursued biblical counseling professionally at a local counseling center, and he was later hired as the Care Pastor responsible for our recovery and care ministries. I was Lee's first hire with the title of Recovery and Reconciliation Pastor. I was responsible not only for the recovery ministry but for development of a reconciliation ministry. We realized that the model we had been using for our repentance ministry would also work in reconciliation. As hearts are aligned with God's heart through repentance, what follows is unity within the body of Christ. So, early on, our counseling focused on these dual ministries of repentance and reconciliation.

After our initial launch, we bolstered and streamlined our Groups ministry. Other care ministries were enfolded into what we called Recovery Groups, putting everything under one umbrella. More recently, we moved our STEPS ministry out from the Recovery Groups to further clarify the place for structured discipleship within our Groups ministry. (See figure 5.)

Recovery Groups

What is a Recovery Group? Our Recovery Groups ministry exists to *make disciples*. In the introduction to Mark Driscoll's book *Radical Reformission*, he writes that the mission of the church must include the church, the culture, and the gospel. Moving away from any of these three will lead to para-church ministry, fundamentalism, or liberalism. But none of these are an option for a local church. The mission of the local church must include a focus on all three, and that is why our philosophy of ministry is *the church engaging culture with the gospel.*

A local church needs to be informed both about the gospel (gospel reform) and the culture (gospel mission). This is so that the church can engage the culture in a way that speaks redemptively into the culture. In understanding the gospel, the church has confidence that the message they have been given is more powerful than anything the world can offer. The gospel is where people find true freedom from addiction and all other forms of sin and suffering.

This means we must lovingly engage the ideologies of our culture in this context of how our culture speaks to the topic of "recovery." We interact with traditional 12-step ministries as well as secular psychology, but we do this following the model Paul demonstrated when he engaged the vague pluralistic deism of Athens in the first century (Acts 17:16–34). Our goal is to begin by deconstructing what the culture is saying. Then we acknowledge any truth that might be there, ascribe that truth to God, and orient that truth within a gospel context.

While much can be said about this, we believe that the following distinctives speak directly to the recovery culture that surrounds us today. In engaging these ideas, we hope to lead people away from the answers our culture gives to the fullness of what the gospel offers.

- *Programs Don't Heal People:* So much of what we hear in the culture today is about the program. We don't want to exalt a program; we want to exalt a Person: the person and work of Jesus Christ.
- *Recovery Is Not Just for Addicts:* True recovery is for *anyone* seeking redemption in Christ for *any* enslaving interaction with sin and suffering.
- *You Can't Reduce Recovery to a Program:* To say that those in a program are "in recovery" and those who aren't in a program aren't in recovery is to suggest that God works only within a program. But the truth is that God is working redemptively in programs and outside of programs, as we are all ultimately either in Christ or we are enslaved to sin.

- *Sobriety Is a By-Product:* Sobriety is not the goal; it is a by-product of a reconciled heart to God.
- *Ministry of Movement:* We do not want people to spend the rest of their lives in our recovery ministry. We want them to experience the healing power of the gospel and live lives on mission to the glory of God.
- *It Is Dangerous to Reduce Your Relationship with God to a Single Issue:* When we do this, we tend to think we are good with God when we aren't engaged in a certain behavior and we aren't okay with Him when we are. Our basis of acceptance and love becomes our performance rather than the gospel. Abstinence is not the way to God—Jesus is!

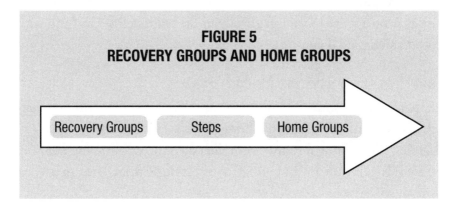

FIGURE 5
RECOVERY GROUPS AND HOME GROUPS

Recovery Groups   Steps   Home Groups

In addition to clarifying these distinctives, we try to establish a clear path of care for those who enter the church broken and seeking help. Jesus tells us that we are to receive and not mislead the weak, the wounded, the marginalized, the abused, and the addicted who are sincere in seeking help. Jesus says that when we receive them, we receive Him. Is it any wonder that many churches have become dead religious institutions when they tell broken people they need to go elsewhere for help.

As people enter into Recovery Groups, they bring the chaos of their lives and they encounter something solid on which to build. The myriad of false beliefs in our culture collide with the gospel, and it can make for some very interesting evenings! We find there is no shortage of need when you welcome broken people. And *anyone* is welcome, even skeptics who come with honest questions. The leaders of our Recovery Groups are trained and must be well equipped to navigate potential land mines. They also need to know how to speak to a variety of situations and personalities. These are places where organic discipleship happens and where we offer specialized care for specific issues.

As an outworking of our philosophy of ministry, our Recovery Groups focus on specific issues. In doing this, we hope to engage people as they understand their problem while, in turn, accomplishing four things. First, we want people to connect with people relationally. Second, we want to redefine their problems biblically. Third, we want to apply the gospel specifically. And finally, we want to offer accountability as people strive to walk faithfully in the truth before God and with others alongside them.

SPECIALIZED RECOVERY GROUPS

Specialized Recovery Groups help those who are walking through particular seasons of difficulty. They generally fall into one of three categories: (1) suffering resulting from their own sin, (2) suffering resulting from sin against them, and (3) suffering resulting from living in a fallen world. They include:

Abuse Groups:
 These gender-specific groups meet weekly to provide care, accountability, and direction for those who have been affected by various forms of abuse (physical, sexual, spiritual, ritual, mental, and emotional). The aim of these groups is to help the abused find healing from the effects of the sin of another through victory in Christ.

Addictions Groups:
 These gender-specific groups meet weekly to provide care, accountability, and direction for those who are wrestling with various forms of addiction (sexual, chemical, relational, gambling, shopping, gaming,

etc.). The aim is to help addicts discover the freedom from their sin that the gospel offers through our Redeemer, Jesus Christ.

Assorted Struggles Groups:

These gender-specific groups meet weekly to provide care, accountability, and direction for those who have struggles that might not fit well within the categories of abuse or addiction. Some of the specific struggles addressed through these groups are anxiety, anger, fear, depression, codependency, relationship struggles, etc.

We also have mixed-gender groups that meet weekly to provide support to those who are suffering as the indirect result of living in a fallen world. This would include those who are grieving the death of a loved one, facing chronic illness and pain, walking through significant loss, facing seemingly insurmountable challenges, and those who have experienced traumatic situations.

RECONCILIATION GROUPS

In addition to groups that specialize in suffering or struggles, we have reconciliation groups for couples as well as several that are gender specific. Our married couples groups meet weekly to provide an entry point of care, accountability, and direction for those who are trying to position themselves for reconciliation as they try to heal and find hope after adultery and other forms of betrayal in the covenant that is marriage. Our men's and women's reconciliation groups meet weekly to provide care, accountability, and direction for those who are trying to position themselves for reconciliation when the spouse or former spouse is not present or when it is best for the couple not to be in the same group due to the toxicity in the relationship.

In some cases, it is most helpful to have an entire family meet together. Our family groups, like the other groups we've mentioned, meet weekly to provide an entry point of care, accountability, and direction. These include families facing the difficulties of a child who has gone wayward. They provide support and encouragement to help parents to be faithful to their responsibilities as parents and to act in accordance with God's love for His children. Because the struggles of the teenage years can require even more specialized attention, we also have gender-specific groups for high school students that meet weekly to address difficulties due to rebellion (against God, law, parents, etc.), difficulties due to harm caused by another, or any other crisis or loss a student may be facing. The leaders of these groups are connected to the student ministries at the church.

Our goal is not to have a group for every possible issue that might arise. Though the types and number of groups vary from campus to campus, the categories mentioned tend to be the most common and form the basic structure of our ministry. This is not a comprehensive list, as there are groups that meet in coffee shops and homes around other issues, ranging from post-abortion groups to men coming out of AA. The church encourages these "organic" groups and does not hinder them, even though they are not an "official" program of the church.

SUPPORT: PRAYER, RESOURCES, AND TRAINING

To support our groups, we have several additional ministries that enable and equip the ministry of the group leaders. One of the most important supports is our growing prayer team. This team prays before, during, and after our weekly Recovery Groups meet. The prayer ministers pray with individuals and they pray for the ministry as a whole, including time in prayer for those who will teach or share their testimony. They are available and they are faithful. If they are not huddled in groups around the building, you will find them praying for or engaging those who may feel distressed.

We also try to provide gospel-rich resources that address the various issues discussed in our groups. We provide these on display each week for purchase, and these resources provide opportunities for learning and reflecting outside of group as well as content for discussion within the group.

Finally, we have what we call "Large Group." These large group gatherings precede our specialized group meetings and provide a time to gather together as a larger community to worship through song and prayer. Usually, there is a heart-focused, gospel-rich message or a testimony of a life changed by the gospel. At times, we also offer stones to those who are experiencing a significant "milestone" and who want to remember how God has demonstrated His faithfulness to them.

GUIDELINES AND GROUP DYNAMICS

Since it is our hope to foster biblical community within our groups, we try to avoid imposing guidelines that make the relationships feel artificial or therapeutic. We tend to shy away from blanket statements like "What is said here stays here" and "No cross talk" to give a more robust biblically accurate way of relating to one another. Though we do not betray confidences, we do not offer confidentiality in the traditional therapeutic sense. We believe there are times when it is biblically necessary for the conversation to move beyond the walls of a particular group. Additionally, while a policy prohibiting cross talk (talk among group members) might seem helpful, we do not believe this is what Christ intends for His community. He does have instructions for our communication with one another; however, we believe those are better reflected in the following group guidelines.

We know that leaders need guidelines. Some leaders have a tendency to talk too much while others let their groups go unrestrained into chaos. To seek to avoid the extremes of group life, we have established a few biblically rooted principles:

- Let leaders lead.
- No gossip.
- All counsel needs to be biblically rooted.
- Do not monopolize the group.
- Expect to be confronted with truth in love.
- Though we are interested in your circumstances, our desire is that you would learn to talk about your own heart before the Lord amidst your circumstances.

- If you have a "burning desire" (something that you believe the Spirit of God is impressing upon you to share), leaders are to leave five minutes toward the end to allow for an encouraging "word," a Scripture, or perhaps something someone feels burdened to share.
- The group is opened and closed with leaders leading in prayer.

As you can see, we intentionally keep the guidelines simple. And we don't think the weekly meeting is the goal or the end of our life together as a community. This is why we also encourage group members to find ways to connect outside of the weekly meeting. Groups are like vehicles. I can drive my car for a few hours from our church outside Dallas to Austin with several others in the car, but the fact that we are together in the same vehicle does not mean we will connect deeply. That car is a vehicle and, like a small group, it provides a means, an opportunity, for connection. But making a connection isn't automatic. Cultivating relationships takes work.

Leaders' Roles

In each group, we make sure there is a leader who has been trained. These leaders are responsible for more that facilitating a group; they are *shepherds*. Ideally, these are people who have demonstrated the ability to lead others in a way that is natural. People want to follow them! Within our Recovery Groups we know that the leader role is critical for the safety and care of those who come seeking help. Leaders must be able to navigate the wide range of personalities, beliefs, and expectations that enter the ministry. And in addition to shepherding a group, we want our leaders to be actively raising up other shepherds. *Apprentice leaders* sit under the direction of a group leader while they are being vetted for leadership. This is how we multiply our leaders.

To relationally support our group leaders, we have *coaches* who "lead the leaders." These people have demonstrated proficiency not only in biblical counseling, conflict resolution, love and care for the body, but also in understanding how groups work. When the church becomes involved in a discipline case, coaches often are the case managers.

Finally, although they are not always at the group meeting every week, we also have special leaders we call *connectors*. These are trusted leaders in the church who come into Recovery Groups to support the group leaders in connecting relationally with people in the group and outside the group. Some of these may be home group leaders themselves, while others are looking for the chance to disciple broken people. This is the newest of the leader roles we have developed within our Recovery Groups, and it was formed to address the problem of people slipping out the back door because they don't connect with others. Connectors provide a link to our organic group life that is outside of the formal programs offered in our recovery ministry.

Groups and Lay Biblical Counseling

We've spent a large part of this chapter focusing on our groups. You might wonder: Is there a lay counseling ministry at The Village Church? Yes, we have a lay biblical counseling ministry at the church, but because we believe that sanctification occurs best within the context of biblical community, our counseling ministry is structured so that it inevitably leads people into community. If someone enters the church through a Recovery Group due to a crisis in their life and they are either not prepared to enter directly into a group or their situation might otherwise necessitate more attention than what could be practically offered in a group, we might recommend that they spend a few weeks with a lay counselor.

Prior to entering the lay biblical counseling ministry, we have participants sign an informed consent form. This is not the same form you would use in professional counseling. It explains the temporary nature of the counseling relationship and indicates that in this setting the goal is to move a person from counseling sessions into a group after approximately five or six sessions. To help facilitate this transition, we bring a leader from whatever group they will be attending into the last counseling session and transition their care so the leader is up to speed on the specific issues this person is dealing with.

STEPS

Earlier, we mentioned that in addition to our Recovery Groups we have Home Groups and our STEPS ministry. You may have been left wondering: What is this "STEPS" ministry? We describe STEPS as an intense discipleship experience. STEPS is a comprehensive, structured discipleship program with daily Bible study and reflection, one-on-one meetings with a mentor, a small group component, and a large group teaching time. We offer STEPS seasonally for thirteen weeks. As someone transitions from a Recovery Group to the STEPS program, they move from being grouped primarily by issue and gender (if appropriate) to being grouped by gender and then geography. We do this to foster community closer to where they actually live.

STEPS began within our Recovery Groups ministry, and it follows the same philosophy of speaking redemptively into the culture. Instead of viewing STEPS as an attempt to climb a staircase to God through a religious system, we learn to be disciples who take steps of obedience in faithful response to what the gospel has accomplished and promised us. The language of "steps" is familiar to those who have engaged in a traditional twelve-step program, but our goal is not to legitimize the twelve steps. Instead, we deconstruct each step and reconstruct the truth we find there within a gospel context. Taking "steps" toward recovery apart from the gospel is a dead religious activity, but this approach provides a way of looking at the gospel through a familiar, culturally relevant form.

The truth is that many in our culture claim to be Christians, but they have never heard a comprehensive gospel message. So we begin by laying the foundation of what Jesus accomplished on the cross for those who believe (gospel indicatives) and then show them what it means to follow Christ (gospel imperatives). Part of the process involves examining our hearts before the Lord. We refer to this as an "assessment." The assessment process involves prayer and confession of the fruit of our lives and its roots. We bring all of this before the Lord so that He might uproot our sinful patterns and heal our hearts, freeing us to act faithfully for His kingdom.

Each participant in STEPS is required to have a mentor. Qualified mentors should have some experience in walking through STEPS and can serve as guides through the process. Following STEPS, participants are encouraged to plug into a Home Group, further explore their spiritual gifts, go on a mission trip, take a missions class, serve in the broader church, serve as a mentor or apprentice or connector, or pursue further equipping in biblical counseling.

HOME GROUPS

The final area of ministry we want to cover is our Home Group ministry. As our Home Groups have continued to grow, there has been an increased need for us to train leaders in gospel-centered biblical counseling. Equally important has been the need to make sure our Home Group leaders and coaches are aware of the tools and resources that are available to them as they walk with people through times of suffering and difficulty. STEPS has been one way of doing this, providing a focused, structured discipleship process regardless of whether a person is deeply connected in community and needing some extra care or simply looking to get connected to a community-based ministry that addresses the issues of the heart. We've seen a constant flow of people from our Recovery Groups into the STEPS program and then into our Home Groups.

When we first shifted our care and counseling ministry into our Groups model (both Recovery and Home Groups), the challenge was to provide thorough training for our leaders. Historically, many of these care concerns had been dealt with through specialized counseling. And while we saw this as a challenge, we also saw it as an opportunity for our church body to grow and mature. The shift to group-based care has placed the responsibility for caring and ministering to God's people on the congregation and its members and not on a single individual or ministry in the church. Resourcing and equipping our group leaders will always be something we need to do, but we've found that the Lord continues to equip His saints for the work of ministry.

One of the main resources we used to help in this was the curriculum *Equipped to Counsel* by John Henderson.[69] This is a comprehensive equipping curriculum, and we used it for our Home Group leader and coach training. Specific sections from *Equipped to Counsel* have been used to develop a new leader orientation as well as additional focused trainings in various areas of care and counsel. Several years into this shift to group care, we now have all of our group leaders in both the Recovery and Home Group ministries exposed to the why and how of biblical counseling in group life. We've identified several additional resources they can use for gospel ministry as well. We point our people toward several trusted biblical counselors and biblical counseling centers we partner with in the Dallas/Fort Worth metroplex. We also expose them to organizations like ABC (Association of Biblical Counselors), CCEF (Christian Counseling Educational Foundation), ACBC (Association of Certified Biblical Counselors), and the BCC (Biblical Counseling Coalition). Making our leaders aware of these organizations and resources has created additional momentum for biblical counseling ministry at The Village Church.

This past year, with the assistance of Lifeway, we were able to produce a resource called *Recovering Redemption*,[70] which includes a sermon series and small group study introducing the entire church to a flyover of the gospel truths we teach in the STEPS program. This was developed to take some of the mystery out of the recovery process. The curriculum exposes people to the power of the gospel, and we wanted people to see that the message is the same whether you are in a Home Group, a Recovery Group, or involved in the STEPS program.

CONCLUSION

We pray this has given you some insight into the mission, philosophy, and practice of how counseling is integrated into our small group model of gospel-based community. We believe that the church, when operating as Christ intended it to be, is the greatest treatment center on earth. We are delighted to bear witness to the countless lives changed by the gospel of Jesus Christ. We certainly don't believe that this is the only or even the best way to do ministry. It is, however, where the Lord has us, and we are grateful for the ongoing journey.

We have had an opportunity to see God move in powerful ways through the efforts of infusing a heart-focused, gospel-centered paradigm. Biblical counseling belongs not just in the church but throughout the entirety of the church. This is a mighty undertaking, but God desires to see His church walk in truth and maturity, so this is our call.

PART 3

BIBLICAL COUNSELING AND CONFLICT RESOLUTION

CHAPTER 9

BIBLICAL COUNSELING, THE CHURCH, AND CHURCH DISCIPLINE

ROBERT CHEONG AND ROBERT JONES

Mike and Susan have come to you in a last-ditch effort to save their marriage. They both talked about their inability to "fix" their broken relationship and their desperate desire for God to redeem their marriage. But as you listen intently to their story and seek to understand the deep desires within each of their hearts, you begin to wonder about Susan's commitment to the marriage. You also notice a shift in her demeanor over the weeks. She has become increasingly defensive and condescending toward Mike.

Hearing this, you sit back, stunned. You definitely didn't see this coming. What do you do now?

Whether you are a counselor, deacon, small group leader, or pastor, I want to start by saying thank you for stepping into difficult situations like this one with Mike and Susan. Regardless of your specific role, we want to invite you to journey with us as we step back and consider the role of "church discipline," looking at these difficult situations from God's perspective. We especially want to draw near to the pastor who is feeling overwhelmed by the relentless demands of ministry. We pray that as you read this chapter, you will be overwhelmed by the beauty of God's story of redemption, experience a renewed vision for the church, and be strengthened by the Spirit of God as you persevere in the ministry to which He has called you.

GOD'S GLORIOUS LOVE STORY

The gospel is the best love story ever written. With the wisdom and creativity of a master storyteller, God unfolds a beautiful story of redemption that starts with the first marriage in the Garden of Eden and ends with the final and ultimate wedding between Jesus Christ and His holy bride, the church.

In the beginning God created the first man and woman in His image, not only to reflect His glory but that they might dwell in and enjoy the eternal love between Father, Son, and Holy Spirit. Yet it didn't take long before Adam and Eve willfully chose to pursue intimacy with the Evil One while forsaking their intimacy with Love Himself. Unfortunately, this first act of unfaithfulness didn't end in the garden, but continues to this very day.

Thankfully, God is not blinded by His love for His people. God knew that the prognosis of His people's sinful condition was incurable (cf. Jer. 30:12–17). God knew that, left on their own, they would default to doing what was right in their own eyes (Judg. 21:25). God knew they would try to live, at worst, as if He didn't exist and, at best, as if He existed to serve them. Despite such ongoing rejection and disobedience, God never abandons His relationship with us. As we watch God's story unfold throughout the pages of Scripture and even in our own lives, we are reminded repeatedly of God's faithfulness.

God knew that His people needed rescue and, because of His great love, He would stop at nothing to redeem His bride from the deforming and destructive grip of sin. In a plot twist that defies logic, God did the unimaginable. Instead of pronouncing judgment and death upon us in the face of our rebellion, God sacrificed His own Son to satisfy His holy justice and to absorb His righteous wrath. By the blood of Jesus Christ, God established a new and everlasting covenant with us that depends solely on the faithfulness and perfect obedience of our Redeemer, Jesus Christ.

What makes this story unlike any other is God's redeeming love and glory. Such undeserved love overwhelms and stirs our affections so that we begin to live for Him and not for ourselves (2 Cor. 5:14–15). Such incomparable glory makes us more and more beautiful like Jesus as we behold Him with eyes of faith (2 Cor. 3:18). Given the details of this love story, we must realize that we, as the church, are unquestionably an unlikely bride for our holy God.

But what does God's story have to do with the topic of church discipline? Everything! To understand church discipline, we need to start with knowing that God is relentlessly pursuing, preparing, and protecting us as His bride in our ongoing struggles with sin as we journey toward heaven. If we don't understand church discipline within the movement of God's story, we will carry out church discipline in ways that will neither reflect His gospel nor accomplish His mission in the church and world. If we don't see our life with God within this redemptive story line, we can overlook church discipline out of a lack of understanding or dismiss it out of fear or out of a wrong and hurtful experience.

Not only must we understand church discipline through the lens of God's redemptive story, but we also have to see it under the broader umbrella of God's discipline. In other words, we must view church discipline as God's discipline carried out in and through His church. Let's unpack God's discipline a bit more.

GOD'S LOVING DISCIPLINE

A good story always has good character development, where the main characters grow and change over time, most often struggling with adversity while experiencing the joy and pleasures of love. Similarly, God is continually developing us in His story, transforming us more and more into the image of our Redeemer in everyday life. God uses our circumstances and relationships as a crucible to strip away everything that hinders us from running the race of faith and that distracts us from looking to Jesus for hope and life. In the midst of suffering, whether it is from our personal sin or from others sinning against us, we are tempted to grow weary and lose heart (Heb. 12:1–4). If this isn't bad enough, when we are entangled with sin, regardless of the reason, we tend to question God's love for us while being blinded to His glorious presence, promises, and power. As a result, our life with God seems meaningless and feels lonely. Reflecting and enjoying God's glory and love is not even a conscious thought.

Fortunately, the passage in Hebrews 12 continues, revealing that God sees and responds to our struggles with sin. He loves His children too much to allow them to live distracted and distorted lives that keep us from fully experiencing life with Him (12:5–9). Therefore, like a father who disciplines His children, God disciplines us as His true sons and daughters so that we may share in His holiness, knowing that He created us to live in His presence while enjoying and growing in His glory and love (12:10). God's loving discipline may seem unpleasant at the time but produces righteousness and peace through our intimate union with Jesus (12:11).

Think about those times when God made His grace more amazing and His power more evident as He pursued you in a season when your heart was apathetic, even rebellious. His Spirit stirred godly sorrow in your soul while inviting you to come back to enjoy life with Him. Reflect on how God used suffering and uncertainties to help you realize that He is your everything and His love is deeper, wider, higher, and broader than you ever imagined. One of the beautiful realities of God's love relationship with us is that He disciplines us in ongoing ways so that we will grow more and more in love with Him and reflect His glory more fully (cf. Col. 1:28).

Now that we have seen how God relentlessly pursues His people throughout His gospel story and how He disciplines His bride to prepare her for the consummation of their marriage in the new heaven and earth, we can look more specifically at how He carries out His discipline in and through His church.

GOD'S DISCIPLINE IN THE CHURCH

Why would God want the church to participate in carrying out His discipline? God can accomplish every bit of His transforming work of grace in our lives solely in His one-on-one relationship with each of us through His Spirit. But in His amazing wisdom, God invites us to join Him in every aspect of His glorious mission. God calls His church to participate in His loving discipline because He created us to grow—not just alone with Him, but also through our relationships with one another as the church. God created us to live, not alone, but in community where we can encourage one another in our life with God. God graciously invites us to join Him in building up His church in love and advancing His kingdom in this world, which includes carrying out His discipline. So given all that has been said, we can now offer a definition of "church discipline."

Church discipline can be understood as *God's ongoing, redeeming work through His living Word and people as they fight the good fight of faith together to exalt Christ and protect the purity of His bride.* This definition not only encompasses God's vision for how we are to live life together as a community of believers through the "one-another commands" but also includes the more specific passages that expand and escalate His discipline through the church in times when members refuse to listen to those pursuing and calling them back to Jesus.[71]

God calls the church to expand His discipline by involving more and more people in the redemptive pursuit as long as those in rebellion refuse to repent and submit to Jesus and His Word. According to Matthew 18, God's discipline begins by confronting one-on-one and, if they refuse to listen, then involving one or two others, to include those who know them best and who can participate in the redemptive efforts for however long it takes. Those in redemptive pursuit should inform the church leaders if those in rebellion refuse to listen to their loving pleas to trust and obey Jesus.

God's discipline continues to expand and escalate as the church leaders join those already involved and issue a series of necessary warnings. If those in rebellion refuse to respond to the warnings, then the church leaders will tell the church so that the entire body of Christ can pursue and pray for those who once professed faith in Christ but have since turned their backs on God in refusing to live according to His ways. If there is no expressed desire to turn back and submit to Jesus after a final warning and waiting period, the church will then remove those in rebellion from the covenant fellowship since the church can no longer affirm their profession of faith.

But the removal from membership is not the end, nor the goal of God's discipline. The church will continue to pray for and pursue those removed, trusting that God will bring them to repentance. If and when those removed return and seek to be restored to God and His church, then the church leaders will work with those involved to restore them back into fellowship (cf. 2 Cor. 2:5 – 11). Once the restoration efforts are complete, the church will gather to celebrate God's faithful and powerful work of redemption, not just in those removed and restored, but in everyone involved in this journey of faith.[72]

Based on this understanding of God's discipline process through the church, let's look at four implications. First, church discipline is all about *God's ongoing redeeming work* in our ongoing struggle with sin. We can relax knowing that God disciplines every one of His children, without exception, not just when we are outwardly sinning but also when we are inwardly rebelling. We can rest knowing that God is always at work completing the work He has begun in each of us (Phil. 1:6).

Second, God carries out His discipline *through His living Word and people* through the sanctifying work of His ever-present Spirit (Heb. 4:12; 1 Peter 1:2). We can be alert knowing that God carries out His discipline in the quietness of our room as we read and reflect on His Word. We can live humbly and not defensively, knowing that God is actually pursuing and loving us when He uses someone, whether a Christian or non-Christian, to make us aware of the log in our own eye (Matt. 7:3).

Third, God works out His discipline through His people *as they fight the good fight of faith together.* We can be intentional with one another, knowing that God created us to be transformed in community as we encourage and challenge one another to live by faith and not by fear, to live in the Spirit and not in the flesh. We can stir one another up to love and do good works, knowing that life involves a battle with our wicked, unbelieving hearts, where we are prone to isolate ourselves and start believing lies about God and our life with Him and others (Heb. 3:12–14; 10:24–25).

Fourth, God disciplines us *to exalt Christ and protect the purity of His bride.* God loves us enough to discipline us whenever we dishonor our Redeemer by seeking life, hope, and satisfaction apart from Him. We can be overwhelmed by His mercy, knowing He will stop at nothing to ensure that we share in His holiness so that we can enjoy His love and reflect His glory (John 4:14; 1 Cor. 10:31; Heb. 12:7–11). God glorifies Christ and protects His bride when she is compelled by His love to no longer live for herself but to live for Him who died for her and defeated death (2 Cor. 5:14–15).

Take a moment to reflect on this redemptive vision of God's discipline in His church. How does this vision compare with your previous understanding of church discipline? You may begin to see how any other perspective can reduce God's discipline to irrelevant, rigid, or harsh stereotypes that can lead the church to overlook and dismiss church discipline.

Where do you stand regarding church discipline? Perhaps you don't see the need for discipline; we would encourage you to finish reading the rest of the chapter. Maybe you see the need, but you want a list of disciplinable sins so you know whom and when to confront. Unfortunately, the matter is not so simple; such decisions require Spirit-given wisdom and up-close personal involvement with struggling people. Or maybe you are committed to implementing loving discipline and you recognize the complexity of this ministry, but you lack the time, energy, confidence, or wisdom to pursue this path. Regardless of your previous understanding or experience, God is inviting you to prayerfully reflect on how you are carrying out His discipline as His appointed shepherd overseeing His flock.

ANTICIPATING COMMON OBJECTIONS

What are some common objections to church discipline that you or those in your church might raise? And how might we respond to them with humility, respect, wisdom, and pastoral care? Let's consider four. Notice in each case, we seek to affirm the person's concern and then try to lead them toward a more biblical perspective.

"This Is an Unloving Thing to Do."

This is the most common objection, and one that Susan herself voiced: "They talk about being a loving church, but then they go ahead and point out my sin." We must, of course, show love—our Lord's second great commandment requires nothing less. But we must define love as the Lord does and not allow unbiblical notions to cast His redemptive discipline as unloving or to minimize other godly qualities like holiness, obedience, and purity. How do we love members who claim to follow Jesus, yet not only fail to do so but resist every effort by the church to help them?

The Bible shows a direct connection between God's love and God's discipline. Both 1 Corinthians 5 (discipline) and 13 (love) are in the same Pauline letter. The Lord Jesus reminds His church, "Those whom I love I rebuke and discipline. So be earnest, and repent" (Rev. 3:19; cf. Prov. 3:11–12). Proverbs 27:5–6 applies this truth to our relationships, "Better is open rebuke than hidden love. Wounds from a friend can be trusted, but an enemy multiplies kisses." The so-called "love" that ignores or tolerates sin is enemy-like behavior. The parallel truth for parents drives home the same connection, "Whoever spares the rod hates their children, but the one who loves their children is careful to discipline them" (Prov. 13:24). As Dietrich Bonhoeffer put it in his classic book *Life Together*:

> The practice of discipline in the congregation begins in the smallest circles. Where defection from God's Word in doctrine or life imperils the family fellowship and with it the whole congregation, the word of admonition and rebuke must be ventured. Nothing can be more cruel than the tenderness that consigns another to His sin. Nothing can be more compassionate than the severe rebuke that calls a brother back from the path of sin. It is a ministry of mercy, an ultimate offer of genuine fellowship.[73]

Church discipline is an act of loving rescue — mercy — for those heading toward death.[74]

"This Is None of Our Business. We Should Not Interfere with Someone's Private Life."

Several members in Mike and Susan's small group have expressed this very sentiment to their leaders, Tom and Beth. While church discipline is not a ministry to be done by busybodies (Prov. 26:17; 1 Thess. 4:11; 2 Thess. 3:11), caring for each other's spiritual health *is* a major part of the church's business of loving one another (Heb. 3:12–13; 10:24–25; Gal. 6:1–2; James 5:19–20).

This is especially true given the nature of the church as God's family. In fact, virtually all key church discipline passages explicitly refer to the church as "brothers and sisters" (emphasis added below). In some cases, Scripture uses family language to describe the persons needing pursuit:

- Matthew 18:15: "If your *brother or sister* sins, go and point out their fault."
- Luke 17:3: "If your *brother or sister* sins against you, rebuke them."
- 1 Corinthians 5:11: "But now I am writing to you that you must not associate with anyone who claims to be a *brother or sister* but is sexually immoral or greedy." (Cf. 1 Cor. 6:4–6 where Paul protests against Christian *brothers* suing each other.)

In other cases, the family language addresses those who must do the pursuing of each other:

- Romans 16:17: "I urge you, *brothers and sisters*, to watch out for those who cause divisions.... Keep away from them."
- Galatians 6:1: "*Brothers and sisters*, if someone is caught in a sin, you who live by the Spirit should restore that person gently."
- 1 Thessalonians 5:14: "And we urge you, *brothers and sisters*, warn those who are idle."
- 2 Thessalonians 3:6, 15: "In the name of the Lord Jesus Christ, we command you, *brothers and sisters*, to keep away from every believer [lit. *brother or sister*] who is idle.... Yet do not regard them as an enemy, but warn them as you would a fellow believer [lit. *brother or sister*]."
- Hebrews 3:12–13: "See to it, *brothers and sisters*, that none of you has a sinful, unbelieving heart.... But encourage one another daily."
- James 5:19: "My *brothers and sisters*, if one of you should wander from the truth and someone should bring that person back."

In both cases, the identity of both the pursuer and the pursued as brothers and sisters seems prominent.

"The Bible Says, 'Judge Not ...'"

After a confidential members' meeting in which the elders asked the members to lovingly pursue and pray for their sister Susan, several members approached the lead pastor with this concern: "Pastor, the Bible tells us to judge not." Of course, Jesus tells us explicitly in Matthew 7:1–2 that we should not judge. There is an ungodly form of judging that Jesus and His apostles oppose. Church members who have witnessed ungodly forms of "discipline" in previous churches are particularly sensitive to these matters. Yet just a few verses later, in Matthew 7:5, Jesus calls us to discern specks in the other person's eye and make judgments about others (Matt. 7:6, 15–20). Jesus tells His hearers in John 7:24, "Stop judging by mere appearances, but instead judge correctly." Paul commands believers to judge one another in 1 Corinthians 5:1–5, 9–13: "Are you not to judge those inside [the church]?" (1 Cor. 5:12). What Jesus and His apostles forbid is not judging per se, but proud, hypocritical, harmful judging. Righteous judgment proceeds from humility, self-examination, and love for those who need intervention.

"We Are Risking Lawsuits If We Discipline People."

Unfortunately, in our litigious American culture, any seemingly adversarial action can occasion a lawsuit. In the case of Susan, one of the deacons—who is also an attorney—expressed His concern that "we not expose our church to legal risk if Susan hires a lawyer."

At least three perspectives, however, outweigh this fear. First, by proceeding carefully in our discipline ministry with love and wisdom, we greatly reduce the risk. Prudent measures include clear Bible teaching, pre-membership training, membership covenants with signed commitments agreeing to mutual responsibilities of leaders and members, informed consent agreements in counseling, conciliation clauses in church bylaws, employment agreements that require mediation or arbitration instead of litigation, etc.

Second, in some cases not taking disciplinary steps could invite a lawsuit or criminal investigation. If a church knowingly overlooks some offenses and the person continues to sin in those ways, or leaves your church, goes to another church, and continues those practices there, then your church could be liable. Examples could include a member who defrauds other members or a member who commits illegalities, including inappropriate behavior toward minors.

Third, and most important, followers of Christ must trust and obey God, whatever situational risks we might face. We must fear God alone, not people or lawsuits. As Jesus, the Head of the church, has said, "Do not be afraid of those who kill the body but cannot kill the soul. Rather, be afraid of the One who can destroy both soul and body in hell" (Matt. 10:28). Our lives and our churches are in His hands. This was the faith challenge for the deacon in Susan's case. Given the due diligence the church was taking in dealing with her, he was able to commit the situation to God and move forward in full support of the church leaders' pursuit of Susan.

LEADING YOUR CHURCH TO PURSUE PEOPLE LIKE MIKE AND SUSAN

If you are a pastor or church leader, you likely have or will have believers like Mike and Susan in your church. Let's assume that you want to be a faithful shepherd and you are convinced that the above direction is what a Christ-led church must take. You have studied the Scripture along with other helpful resources, and you are prepared to answer the most common objections. What do you do now? Three overall directions seem wise.

Shepherd Those Who Stray and Those Who Suffer from Their Straying

God has called you to shepherd your church members (Acts 20:28; 1 Peter 5:1–4; Heb. 13:17; Ezek. 34:1–6), including people like Mike and Susan. Jesus reminds us in Matthew 18:12–14 that a true shepherd willingly leaves his ninety-nine sheep to search for the one that has wandered off.

Yet pursuing wandering sheep is more than a duty; it is a marvelous opportunity. Our Lord Jesus has authorized and privileged you as one of His appointed pastors to intervene meaningfully in their lives — to bring hope and help to this dear brother and sister. Few occasions bring more joy to the authors of this chapter than being God's redemptive instruments in the lives of those we pastor. Moreover, you have an opportunity to equip and encourage the church body — small group leaders and members — to minister well to Susan and to Mike as you together pursue unity and maturity (Eph. 4:12–16).

Cultivate a Church Culture Most Likely to Implement Effective Church Discipline

Along with shepherding Mike and Susan, there are big-picture themes that wise pastors should cultivate within their church through their various ministries. What marks a church that successfully practices church discipline?

First, a wise pastor will stress a "one-another" body life mindset and a "church as family" mindset, so that members understand that they are called, gifted, and empowered by Christ to minister to each other (Rom. 12; 1 Cor. 12; 1 Peter 4:7 – 11) and to care for each other as brothers and sisters (Mark 3:31 – 35; 10:29 – 31). The more your members own this identity and live out this agenda, the more they will see the need for redemptive discipline when family members stray and the more willing and able they will be to pursue them.

In Susan's case, as Tom and Beth's small group increasingly grasped these realities, their concern for Susan increased. When she vacillated between her husband and the other man, her small group members and pastors pursued her, calling her to repent, promising God's forgiveness to those who do so, and offering to help her break the sinful relationship and reconcile with her husband. Given her divisiveness within the group and her critical comments about the church, the leaders disallowed her participation in her small group's social activities. After several months, the Lord broke down her resistance, using the missing fellowship of her church body. "The persistent love of the church drew me back," Susan said. "I could not continue to remain distant not only from Jesus but also from my Christian brothers and sisters."

Second, since the need for redemptive discipline often arises from relational conflict, a wise pastor will train members in biblical peacemaking.[75] Jesus applauds those who pursue relational peace: "Blessed are the peacemakers, for they will be called children of God" (Matt. 5:9). Paul calls believers to work hard at this: "If it is possible, as far as it depends on you, live at peace with everyone" (Rom. 12:18; also 14:19; Eph. 4:3). When members learn to humbly confess their sins, patiently overlook minor offenses, and caringly confront more serious sins, they are less likely to need discipline and better poised to help provide it.

Third, a wise pastor will cultivate growing measures of gospel humility and gospel hope. Gospel humility means that I am no better than the one needing restoration, and we both know it. In our Lord's parable in Luke 18:9 – 14, the Pharisee brags about his righteousness: "God, I thank you that I am not like other people — robbers, evildoers, adulterers" (18:11). But Jesus instead justifies and exalts the one who humbles himself and cries out, "God, have mercy on me, a sinner" (Luke 18:13). In other words, the only thing worse than *being* a robber, evildoer, or adulterer is *being proud* that you are not one. Those ministering to Susan needed to understand that the only thing worse than Susan's unfaithfulness is being proud that they have not been unfaithful (or thinking that they are above or beyond that possibility).

Gospel hope means no one is beyond God's restorative reach. God can transform even the most hardened heart. To conclude otherwise is unbelief. Mike's notions that Susan will never change and Susan's notions that Mike would never forgive her make them both prophets of doom, excluding God's power to intervene and rescue His people. There is always a way back for those willing to "return to the LORD" (Joel 2:12 – 13). Tom and Beth also needed this gospel hope. On more than one occasion, they were tempted to give up on this difficult couple. But their pastor's ability to bring fresh gospel infusions enabled these leaders and their group to persevere in loving this couple.

Lead Your Church to Implement a Full-Orbed Ministry of Church Discipline

Having been convinced of what God prescribes in His Word for your church, as a pastor you must develop a strategy to lead your fellow leaders and then the congregation to implement this new direction. This involves deciding if this is a direction to take *now*. Many young pastors emerge from seminary bent on immediately making their church more biblical, but the congregation is unprepared for those changes. It might take a few years of faithful pastoral care, expositional Bible teaching, and building trust before a new pastor can safely make major changes.

You will then need to teach the Scriptures to your church leaders, share your vision, discuss their questions and objections, pray together, and secure their commitment. In most cases, bylaw changes will be needed. Space prohibits us from detailing a plan, and each situation brings a host of variables. But it is vital that your fellow church leaders share your vision. It is unwise to address the congregation without unity as a leadership team.

The final stage in developing and implementing a full-orbed ministry of church discipline is teaching and leading the congregation. It will be incumbent on you and your fellow leaders to listen carefully, patiently, empathetically, and non-defensively to their concerns and fears. Realize that every objection represents a specific interest that needs some consideration—however imbalanced, irrational, or fear-based that interest might be. Ask the Lord to fill you with the fruit of His Spirit—"love, joy, peace, forbearance, kindness, goodness, faithfulness, gentleness and self-control" (Gal. 5:22–23) will go a long way in these discussions.

In each of these implementation stages, you should seek counsel from wiser, more experienced pastoral mentors inside and outside of your church.

SOME CONCLUDING THOUGHTS

It is impossible in a brief chapter to cover every aspect of church discipline in sufficient depth. Instead, we focused on the foundational and ongoing aspects of God's discipline in and through the church as we carry out God's mission as a community of faith—brothers and sisters in Christ. Unfortunately, due to the deceitful and destructive nature of sin, there are times when God's people will refuse to listen and submit to His way of living. In such situations, God's discipline can expand—involving more and more people to include church leaders — and escalate — involving pastoral warnings, telling the church, removal from membership, and (hopefully) restoration after repentance. Regardless of where any situation lies on the spectrum of God's discipline through the church, the gospel should always guide us and redemption should always be our goal.

Given the counseling intent of this book, let's address one final question: What is the relationship between biblical counseling and church discipline? Hopefully, after reflecting on the issue of church discipline, you can see that biblical counseling isn't limited to formal meetings with Mike and Susan. Instead, God's redeeming work of biblical counseling appears in every redemptive conversation where the men and women involved encourage one another to look toward Jesus Christ for true life and hope in the midst of a desperate situation. Christ-centered counseling occurs as Mike pleads with Susan to turn from a life of lust and lies to Perfect Love, as Tom and Beth minister to one another amid their struggles with self-righteousness and anger toward Susan and their fears and inadequacies in comforting Mike, and as you patiently shepherd the small group members who express confusion and doubt about church discipline.

The lines blur as you sit back and consider the relationship between biblical counseling and church discipline. Both reflect the ministry of God's Word in the struggles of life where Christ is the focus, the Spirit accomplishes redemptive work in everyone involved, and God the Father is glorified as His people participate with Him in building up His church in love and advancing His kingdom in the world. The Lord designed both to be done in community, not isolated from the church family or separate from the church leadership.

The same dynamic occurs as we consider each ministry of the church. If we focus on biblical counseling, church discipline, discipleship, missions, etc., as distinct entities within the life of the church, we wrongly reduce gospel ministry to compartmentalized functions requiring different skill sets and priorities. And we can overlook and even dismiss God-given redemptive opportunities to shepherd God's people and reach those in the world. Instead, we encourage you to adopt God's vision of a church filled with various members ministering the gospel to various people in various settings with various methods, all united by and flowing from His Spirit and Word. In this way, Mike, Susan, Tom, Beth, and the entire body of Christ will more fully experience the love of God and the beautiful life found in Jesus Christ.

CHAPTER 10

BIBLICAL COUNSELING, THE CHURCH, AND CONFLICT RESOLUTION

JUDY DABLER

John stared at the phone in silence for several minutes. He was still in shock. He knew that his peaceful summer writing sabbatical had come to a sudden end. His closest friend, Bob, the founding pastor of the church where they served together, had just called to inform him that he had left his wife. "I wanted you to hear it from me, John. We tried. We tried to not let what was happening between us take over. I am in love with Janine and we need to be together. I am sorry to do this to you. I know that this is going to be a major shakeup at the church."

To make the bad news even worse, Bob had left his wife for Janine, the women's ministry director for their thriving church of 3,000 members. John thought about his own wife and how this news would impact her. Their wives had been best friends since college. John felt numb as he tried to think. *What do I do now?*

We are surrounded by conflict. It's all around us. International

All Scripture quotations in this chapter are from The Holy Bible, *New International Version*®, NIV® Copyright © 1973, 1978, 1984, 2011 by Biblica, Inc.® Used by permission. All rights reserved worldwide.

conflicts, ethnic cleansings, tribal disputes, marital and family break-down, and neighborhood and work-related complaints—they are all commonplace. And the Christian church and family are not immune to this "conflict" epidemic (consider Paul and Barnabas in Acts 15:36–41 and the Corinthians in 1 Cor. 1:10–17 as two of many biblical examples of conflict among believers). While conflict is almost always painful, conflict in a church context can be emotionally, relationally, and spiritually devastating. Conflict that is accompanied by crisis, trauma, and grief can, for many people, be the most painful reality they will ever experience.

BIBLICAL COUNSELING WITH PEOPLE IN CONFLICT

Conflict is challenging because we experience hurt, betrayal, and deep disappointment when our expectations are not met by trusted loved ones. Unfortunately, many counseling textbooks (Christian or other-wise) often omit interpersonal conflict as a major area of study, and a review of the subject index shows a gap between the words "confiden-tiality" and "confrontation." For whatever reason, conflict models are infrequently taught in graduate level or seminary counseling programs.

Yet the Bible has much to say about this subject and the root causes of conflict, as well as the remedies for it. James 4:1 asks a key question: "What causes fights and quarrels among you?" Answering his question with another question, James provides a compelling diagnosis: "Don't they come from your desires that battle within you?" (James 4:1). Bat-tling idolatrous desires are always at the root of interpersonal conflict (James 4:2–3). Repentance, confession, and forgiveness, the key ingredi-ents of reconciliation, are the remedies for "putting to death" these pow-erful desires that destroy relationships (Col. 3:12–13; Eph. 4:31–32).

Reconciliation, however, is not always sufficient to restore broken trust, respect, and intimacy in damaged relationships. A *restoration process* may also be needed to specifically target rebuilding these three essential attributes. Restoration efforts are markedly different than the typical conflict resolution process. Biblical counseling excels at helping people restore broken relationships, but biblical counseling that effectively addresses conflict with a reconciliation model prior to attempting restoration is far more effective at helping struggling people develop God-honoring and fulfilling relationships.

Conflict counseling should be designed to help struggling individuals identify the desires that battle within and to evaluate the often unknown assumptions beneath those desires. The apostle Paul highlights the importance of taking responsibility for one's own beliefs by refusing to be taken "captive through hollow and deceptive philosophy" (Col. 2:8). Instead, we must take "captive every thought to make it obedient to Christ" (2 Cor. 10:5). Biblical counselors help conflicted people apply a robustly biblical perspective to the beliefs, attitudes, and thoughts of their hearts, all toward the goal of loving God and others more deeply (Matt. 22:35 – 40). Guiding people toward repentance and confession of these battling desires is the goal of biblical conflict counseling.

But what should biblical counselors do when conflict transcends their counselee's immediate relationships, when it is so widespread that it cannot be addressed in the counselor's office? Biblical counseling that focuses on conflict resolution must consider not only the individual's internal world (James 4:1 – 4), but how conflict, crisis, trauma, and grief dynamics are simultaneously lived out in relationships and in communities. Relationships, and communities of many relationships, must become one of the primary focuses in conflict counseling, in addition to addressing the individual. Biblical truths must be comprehensively and intensively applied to individuals, but also to communities as large as John's 3,000-member church. The Biblical Counseling Coalition's Confessional Statement acknowledges this spectrum, from the individual's heart issues to our social relationships with others:

> We recognize the complexity of the connection between people and their social environment. Thus we seek to remain sensitive to the impact of suffering and of the great variety of significant social-cultural factors (1 Peter 3:8 – 22). In our desire to help people comprehensively, we seek to apply God's Word to people's lives amid both positive and negative social experiences.

> We encourage people to seek appropriate practical aid when their problems have a component that involves education, work life, finances, legal matters, criminality (either as a victim or a perpetrator), and other social matters.[76]

Considering the story beginning this chapter, we will soon discover that Pastor John, the most experienced associate pastor at the church and the senior pastor's closest friend, will become the focal point of the crisis about to hit. If managed poorly, this crisis has the potential to lead to conflict that will decimate the church. Managed well, this crisis will drain the energy of even the most skilled team of peacemakers. By looking at conflict from a biblical standpoint, we will see how Pastor John can serve God and the church during this difficult time.

Conflict and crisis have a great deal in common, so much so that for many people, interpersonal conflict *is* a crisis. Crises impact people in predictable ways, and the usual outcomes include anxiety, depression, physical maladies, and poor functioning in everyday circumstances. In a crisis, loss is often inevitable, and the experience of grieving the loss compounds the pain and suffering. The aftermath of a crisis leaves a high price tag. It leads to spiritual depression, emotional pain, relational brokenness, physical suffering, irreversible losses, and a lengthy period of recovery on every level (Ps. 88).

Bernard Mayer, author of *The Dynamics of Conflict*, has written extensively about the many complex realities that impact interpersonal conflict.[77] While not writing from a biblical perspective, Mayer's research findings from chapter 1 of *The Dynamics of Conflict* help us to understand why conflict counseling can be so challenging. Mayer's research points out that different people will experience the exact same conflict in very different ways. Some people experience relational conflict primarily at a cognitive level, while others engage the conflict emotionally. Still others will employ behaviors intended to produce certain outcomes. Conflict resolution efforts can be complicated when an individual's style of dealing with conflict becomes the focus rather than addressing the original conflict. This problem is seen, for example, when an injured individual demands that those who hurt them must see the conflict and respond to it in the same way they do.

The challenges in conflict counseling are increased further when we understand that there are several factors that impact how conflict plays out in our personal relationships. Mayer's research indicates that people's communication styles, the intensity of how they experience and express emotions, their deeply held core values, the social structures in which the conflict is occurring, and the historical contexts in which the conflict originated will all affect the counseling process. And, as we see in James 1 and 4, at the root of conflict exists a heart divided by mixed motives and self-focused demands.

The biblical counselor who navigates the complex waters of conflict must simultaneously recognize these swirling dynamics at play in each person's heart and in each relationship, as well as the matrix of relationships in the larger community. The task can seem daunting. But don't grow discouraged. A well thought out and structured conflict resolution process can go a long way in addressing the challenges of conflict (consider Jethro's advice to Moses in Exodus 18 about structuring a more effective and helpful way of dealing with conflict).

WHAT IS CHRISTIAN CONCILIATION?

When a serious conflict hits a church, like the story we will follow in this chapter, everyone is impacted. Those who are in the best position to lead through the conflict are often deeply impacted by shock, hurt, and anger—even more than those they are trying to serve. So where can church leaders facing conflict and crisis turn for help? Sadly, despite how common conflict is in the church, it's not easy to find highly skilled responders who can be quickly mobilized to meet the immediate need. In the early moments of a conflict crisis, decisions are made that will directly affect how many subsequent conflicts will occur and how serious they will be. Thankfully, there are a growing number of believers who are equipped to effectively respond to conflict in a crisis context. Many of these individuals go by the term "Christian conciliator."

Christian conciliation, as it exists today, means several different things. Originally Christian conciliation was designed to serve as an alternative dispute resolution process for Christian lawyers who were discouraged with litigation's adversarial approach and desired to honor biblical teaching about resolving conflict. Current Christian conciliation efforts span a large spectrum of different activities designed to promote biblical peacemaking, prevent conflict, and equip others to assist people experiencing personal conflict. The diagram below illustrates that current Christian conciliation efforts exist where the gospel intersects with four distinct fields—biblical counseling, alternative dispute resolution, consulting, and education.

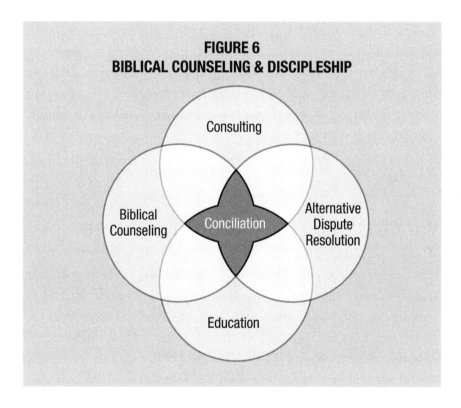

FIGURE 6
BIBLICAL COUNSELING & DISCIPLESHIP

Consulting

Biblical
Counseling

Conciliation

Alternative
Dispute
Resolution

Education

Christian conciliation that overlaps with the world of alternative dispute resolution looks very similar to two or more parties seeking mediation to resolve a dispute, but where there is a commitment to do so in accord with biblical principles. Mutually agreeable solutions to substantive or material issues can be recorded in a legally enforce-able contract while the resolution of personal or relational sin issues (through repentance, confession, and forgiveness) are generally recorded in an informal summary. Conciliation efforts that intersect with biblical counseling look very much like one-on-one hourly coaching sessions in which people in conflict are helped to see their unique contribution to the issues, learn to practice confession, and prepare to seek and offer forgiveness. Conciliation consulting can assist churches and organizations in evaluating corporate policies and documents to set in place structures to prevent or address conflict. Education-based conciliation efforts produce written materials, educational events, and training programs to teach people how to resolve their own personal conflict or learn to assist others who are experiencing conflict.

Today's Christian conciliation movement began with several Christian attorneys in the late 1970s, members of the Christian Legal Society, who had been studying 1 Corinthians 6. In 1980, the first organization was born as Christian attorneys sought to respond to the problem of believers suing other believers. By 1982, several other conciliation services had been formed, and a man named Ken Sande began to play a growing role in furthering the emerging Christian conciliation movement. In 1991, Sande published *The Peacemaker*, his cornerstone text on biblical conflict resolution. After providing leadership for several of the early conciliation organizations, Sande founded his own ministry, Peacemaker Ministries, in 1996. Since then, the Christian conciliation movement has shifted focus toward equipping the local church to deal with conflict in God-honoring ways by changing church culture and training conciliators to assist with conflict resolution.

Using a basic six-step conflict resolution model taught by Peacemaker Ministries, Christian conciliators and peacemaking organizations have developed many different approaches to dealing with conflict in marriages, families, churches, and organizations. Christian conciliation efforts must hold that the gospel of Jesus Christ is central to the message of peacemaking. The local church has the responsibility and authority to help its members deal with conflict in a biblically faithful manner, and biblical counseling is seen as a necessary part of helping confront conflicted parties address the sinful desires that are contributing to the conflict. In addition, God's Word is the authoritative and sufficient source of truth that guides believers in addressing conflict in a God-honoring manner.[78]

David Powlison explains that a comprehensive biblical counseling model has four main components—a conceptual framework that defines the primary issues, a methodology that includes skills and techniques for dealing with the primary issues, a delivery system for providing services to those in need, and an apologetic that critiques other counseling systems while defending its own model.[79] Unfortunately, Christian conciliation is behind the curve when it comes to theologians, theoreticians, and practitioners dialoguing deeply about the concepts related to conflict and doctrine, and how to winsomely and effectively apply the gospel to traumatized, shocked, grieving, and conflicted people.

Delivery systems range from single individuals providing conciliation services as an adjunct to their legal or counseling practices, to teams of individuals serving as members of church-based peacemaking teams, to fee-for-service professional conciliation organizations. Practice methodologies range widely from no-cost hourly meetings resembling traditional counseling to intervention models that span several weeks and cost tens of thousands of dollars. Yet virtually no reliable research exists to evaluate the efficacy of conciliation programs, processes, or services. Biblical scholarship with an eye toward effective reconciliation practice is sorely lacking.

Yet this area promises to be one of the most effective evangelistic and discipleship opportunities available to the church in our postmodern, church-hostile climate. Today, we need people to do for the emerging field of Christian conciliation what Jay Adams did for the biblical counseling movement in the 1970s. We need leaders who will spur debate and discussion, leading to a process of discovery.

As we return to John and his church, we see that having a plan, a process, and people to guide the process helps to navigate the difficult terrain of conflict and crisis, which can make all the difference.

The Need for a Process

After receiving the phone call from Bob, John knew that he had to call the elders together for an emergency meeting. At this point, John felt a need to keep the conflict under tight wraps, though he could not articulate the reasons why. John was aware that he was still navigating his own emotional pain. He began to call each elder to ask them to be at the church in two hours, but no one answered their phone. John left message after message. John also thought about sending an email, but he didn't have access to the emails of the two newest elders installed the previous weekend.

At a loss, John called the church secretary. When he heard Sally's friendly voice, he began to weep as he asked for the email addresses. Sally was instantly alarmed and demanded to know what was wrong. John weakly explained that he could not yet say, but he asked Sally to be prepared for a difficult time ahead. Unfortunately, John forgot to ask Sally to keep his call confidential.

After talking with Pastor John, Sally hung up the phone and immediately went looking for other staff members. Within the hour, the children's pastor, the youth pastor, the director of men's ministries, the choir director, and several administrative staff were aware that something serious had happened. Speculation swirled and various theories were presented. Calls home alerted spouses to a "situation" at the church. When Pastor John entered the building to prepare himself for the elders' meeting, he was intercepted by several concerned staff. Sobbing, John told the staff to be prepared to attend a meeting after the elders' meeting. Stunned and confused, the staff members immediately noticed that Pastor Bob was not mentioned, nor was he present. Tension ran high as Sally began to call all the ministry leaders to attend an emergency meeting later that evening.

When John awoke the next day, he lay in bed remembering the events from the day before. The elders' responses had been surprising. Several elders had raged, demanding that Pastor Bob be fired immediately without severance for his sinful actions. Some elders had quietly wept, suggesting that care teams be established to care for Bob and his wife, and for Janine and her husband. One of the new elders had simply gotten up and left the meeting. The response from the staff had been dramatically different. Most had sat in shocked silence, saying nothing. One assistant pastor kept repeating over and over, "What do you want us to do?" John's wife, Kelly, had sprung into action. She immediately called Bob's wife, Melanie. John had not even thought to reach out to Melanie. At ten o'clock, after hours of painful meetings, John and Kelly sat with Melanie, weeping and praying together. It was 2:00 a.m. before John had finally fallen into bed.

Now, as the phone rang, John saw the time on his alarm clock: 7:00 a.m. Terry Olson, one of the adult Sunday school teachers, was shouting on the phone, "Is it true?" Before John had hung up with Terry, three others had called and left voice messages.

John had not yet gotten out of bed, and already the crisis was out of control.

THEOLOGICAL CONSIDERATIONS

Reconciliation is a key theme at the heart of the message of Christianity (Rom. 5:1–11). Sinful and fallen human beings, in conflict with God, find redemption by being reconciled with God through the saving work of Jesus Christ on the cross (Col. 1:19–22). As followers of Christ, believers are to share the "message of reconciliation" as "Christ's ambassadors" (2 Cor. 5:19–20).

While all believers are called to be "Christ's ambassadors," pastors have a special role because of their unique position of leadership in the church. They formally preach the message of the gospel and guide others in faithful Christian living, including reconciling and restoring relationships in the face of conflict. Duncan Forrester claims that "the way conflicts are handled and resolved should always be of the greatest importance for Christians because it relates to the central stress in the gospel on reconciliation, and may have long-term implications for good or ill."[80] Marsha Lichtenstein makes the claim that "reconciliation is the heart of a spiritually based conflict resolution process."[81] Reconciliation is a product of love and forgiveness, with forgiveness being "a force that heals and builds."[82] Love and forgiveness are made possible when the transformative process of repentance causes the conflicting parties to see how they have contributed to the dispute, and godly sorrow is accompanied by the desire to change with movement toward reconciliation (2 Cor. 7:8 – 13).

In his book *Exclusion and Embrace*, Miroslav Volf states that while reconciliation is possible, it requires that the injured party, out of love, release their demand for justice and for the perpetrator to choose to love the one they have injured — a process made possible only when both the injured party and the perpetrator repent of their sin and forgive.[83] In other words, parties in conflict must learn to embrace each other with love, mercy, and forgiveness.

Roman *Concilium*

C. K. Robertson, in his analysis of 1 Corinthians 6:1 – 11, describes a first-century conflict-resolution process that would have been known to the apostle Paul's readers — the Roman *concilium*. The *concilium* was "an intentional gathering of the adult members of a household network for the purpose of addressing problematic issues and allowing warring siblings to attain compromise and conciliation."[84] In this biblical text, Robertson shows that the apostle Paul chides the Corinthian believers for failing to be as concerned about or as effective as the pagan Romans when it came to dealing with conflict. The Corinthians had not only failed to resolve conflict appropriately, resulting in lawsuits among Christian brothers and sisters, but they also had been defeated by their lack of faith. They had failed to learn the deeper meaning of the gospel message.

Robertson points out that this kind of relational breakdown involves moving relationally from fellowship to enmity. In other words, disagreement alone does not break the bond of relationship. A shift away from valuing familial bonds toward seeking agreement alone will destroy the relational foundation that leads to communion and community in the church. In fact, conflict abounds when parties conclude that previously reached "agreements" have been compromised or violated. According to Robertson, the goal is not simple agreement; rather, the apostle Paul would have Christians honor their family bond as brothers and sisters when resolving conflict, even as the Romans did by using their family *concilium*.[85] In a win/lose battle between Christians, everyone loses. Practical conflict resolution and reconciliation processes must always emphasize the importance of relationships to prevent the adversarial posture that so often results in a win/lose mentality.

A Deteriorating Situation

Several weeks later, John was still struggling through the crisis. Bob would no longer answer his phone calls, but he had agreed to meet with representatives of the elder board. John had just learned that Bob would be bringing his lawyer along to the meeting. Bob's wife, Melanie, was in counseling with a local biblical counselor, and the bills were rapidly mounting. Because of the crisis Melanie and the children were facing, the counseling costs had already totaled $2,400—and there was no end in sight. The elders had quickly arrived at a severance package, conditioned on Bob at least attempting reconciliation with his wife, and many on staff were offended that the dollar amount of the package was more than they made in an entire year.

Two weeks before, when the church family had been notified about Bob's removal as pastor and Janine's removal as the women's ministry director, no one had noticed that Janine's teenage son and daughter were present in the sanctuary until it was too late. Later that day, Janine's husband, son, and daughter had posted a blog about how insensitive John and the elders had been in dragging their mother's name through the mud. They wrote that no one had even cared enough to call to see how anyone in their family was doing. The comments to the blog were filled with outrage toward the church leadership. John had been sickened to realize that he had not even thought about organizing pastoral care for Janine's family, and guilt over his failure consumed him as other blogs added to the flood of condemnation for him and the entire elder board. In the nearly three weeks since the crisis began, John had been working around 100 hours a week. Exhausted, hurt, angry, confused, and discouraged, John wanted to quit. Yet John knew that the elders and the staff were also struggling.

John stared at the name and number written on a slip of paper the church's lawyer had given him. The lawyer recommended bringing in a Christian conciliator to help with the growing mountain of conflicts. But how could anyone help them get through this mess? Still, he called the number. What could they lose?

The conciliation team arrived on Thursday, five days after Pastor John's phone call. The case manager, Jason, was accompanied by three other conciliators, Barbara, Nelson, and Mary. As a first step in the conciliation process, a meeting with the full elder board was scheduled for Thursday evening and a meeting for the church staff was scheduled for Friday morning. The conciliators listened to stories of deep pain and sadly observed how one event had set in motion a series of escalating conflicts and disunity in the church and community.

On Friday afternoon, Jason and Barbara met with Melanie and her children, while Nelson and Mary met with Janine's husband and children. Friday evening's meeting addressed all lay leaders in the church, including small group leaders, adult and youth educators, and Bible study coordinators. Again, the conciliators heard story after story as each participant shared how individuals in the church had formed factions regarding how Bob and Janine should be disciplined and their families cared for. Everyone was encouraged to attend the Saturday morning seminar to educate the church family about how to resolve conflict biblically and to sign up for an individual coaching session to learn how to deal with their own specific conflicts. On Saturday afternoon, Jason and Barbara met with Bob to discuss what a reconciliation process with his wife might look like. Mary compiled the first draft of the conciliation report, outlining a plan on how to address the most visible and damaging conflicts in the church. Nelson prepared to preach the next day's sermon about reconciliation. On Sunday afternoon, a second seminar was provided for anyone who had been unable to attend the Saturday morning event. The team spent all of Monday, Tuesday, and Wednesday meeting with groups and individuals to identify specific mediation needs and to teach principles of biblical peacemaking. The conciliators concluded their first site visit with an elders' meeting Wednesday evening to make their recommendations for a concrete plan to bring healing, reconciliation, and restoration to the church family.

The presence of the conciliation team had already seemed to bring stability into the situation as hurting people were able to share their stories and learn how to apply biblical principles related to repentance, confession, forgiveness, and reconciliation in the myriad of conflicts arising from Bob and Janine's now public affair. On Jason's recommendation, Pastor John finally managed to get two days off to rest and was beginning to recover from the intense emotional, physical, and spiritual drain that happens with frontline crisis and conflict responders. Jason and his team had identified a number of spiritually mature individuals in the church who had the capacity to be trained to help address the escalating conflicts that were damaging relationships in the church.

BIBLICAL COUNSELING AND CHRISTIAN CONCILIATION

Biblical counseling is the life blood of Christian conciliation. The principles and practices developed over the past four decades are essential in guiding hurting and conflicted parties into seeing their own sinful contributions to disputes. The excellent biblical scholarship pertaining to heart idols is particularly helpful as conciliators learn to bring biblical truth to bear in a necessary aspect of conciliation work—examining the heart in a way that leads toward repentance, confession, and forgiveness (Pss. 32 and 51). Biblical forgiveness, a key component of reconciliation work, has seen several helpful resources become available in the last decade. The skills that make biblical counselors effective in their role are the same skills needed by Christian conciliators.

Many of the structures that support biblical counseling efforts (e.g., hourly sessions offered once or twice a week at the counselor's office) will need to be augmented when conflict grips entire families, ministry teams, and churches. While drawing heavily from concepts found in biblical counseling, the addition of alternative dispute resolution processes, consulting theory, and educational philosophy help Christian conciliators design and implement creative and effective strategies for dealing with conflict regardless of whether or not the conflict is "simple" or systemic and widespread.

Many conciliators have adopted a team approach, frequently with both genders represented. Because conflict requires many hours to understand perspectives; identify heart issues; educate people about biblical peacemaking principles; carefully guide parties toward repentance, confession, and forgiveness; and assist the parties in resolving substantive issues through just and wise negotiations, biblical counselors benefit from having skilled and experienced Christian conciliators on their team. They are available to respond to and assist with the sheer time commitment required to comprehensively and intensively address conflict and crisis.

Effective Christian conciliators must have a strong grasp of God's timeless truths and know how to apply them toward reconciliation and relational restoration efforts. Gifted conciliators greatly assist conflicted individuals, organizations, and churches by providing education and training that facilitates true heart change. Biblical counsel is provided on a large scale through education and training as people discover what they should and should not do in the face of conflict, while also experiencing a "renewal of the mind" that permanently shapes beliefs and attitudes contributing to conflict as believers grow in Christ's likeness (Eph. 4:22–24). Christian conciliators who provide consulting draw on biblical truth and their own experience as they help develop custom-tailored processes designed to help prevent future conflict.

Walking It Through

Two months after the disclosure and after many hours of conflict coaching with a conciliator, Bob had come to better understand his heart issues that had contributed to his decision to commit adultery. Bob had also chosen to end his affair with Janine and work toward healing his marriage. Bob and Melanie were planning to attend a weeklong intensive marital reconciliation and restoration process recommended by Jason. While Melanie was anxious, she was hopeful that Bob's repentance was genuine and believed they would be able to work through the relational damage brought about by Bob's affair.

Janine had not yet returned home to her family and was living with a cousin nearby. Neither Janine nor her husband would commit to receiving the counseling assistance offered by the church. Janine's husband had been heard to say that he was planning to sue Pastor Bob for sexual misconduct and would include the church as a named party.

Jason, Nelson, and Mary were on-site to facilitate a reconciliation process between Bob, Pastor John, and the elders, with four lay biblical counselors from the church attending as observers for the purpose of learning more about a conflict resolution process that would help them assist with the mountain of unresolved conflicts that had erupted within the church over the past eight weeks. Friday and Saturday had been set aside for this important first step in bringing peace to a broken church. Bob had listened to the elders' stories of how his sin had impacted them, tearfully confessed his sin, and asked for the opportunity to make a confession to the entire church the following day. Bob, with Jason's help, prepared a written statement for the elders' review. Nelson would again preach on Sunday to help prepare the congregation to hear and respond to Bob's confession. The rest of the conciliation team would provide educational classes for the youth and adults during the Sunday school hour.

Eighteen months after Bob's disclosure of his relationship with Janine, the church is again experiencing energy as gospel-centered ministry is engaged on many levels. Bob and Melanie have reconciled and are continuing to work on rebuilding trust, respect, and intimacy in their marriage. Bob is working at an insurance agency owned by a church member and has had his first conversation with denominational officials about developing a restoration process to evaluate him for possible reinstatement to ministry at some point in years to come. Janine and her husband divorced, and Janine moved from the area and took with her two of her four children. The older two children want nothing to do with their mother. Janine's husband and his older children no longer attend church, but it has been eight months since a negative blog entry has been posted. They have requested the elders and staff of the church to no longer contact them. The elders pray for the family at every elders' meeting.

Pastor John has organized a peacemaking team at the church, and responding to conflict biblically has become a central theme for the entire church body. Each staff member has signed a Covenant of Peace that describes their commitment to handle conflict biblically with one another. All church members have been asked to sign a similar covenant to commit to a biblical conflict resolution process in their own families, marriages, and ministry teams. Three conflicted couples have come forward in the past five months to seek help from the peacemaking team, and the peacemaking team is providing educational classes to the small group leaders and Sunday school teachers. Gossip is addressed when it is encountered, and ministries are working together more collaboratively. The lay biblical counseling team works closely with the peacemaking team as they strive to refer to one another those situations best suited to each ministry.

What Is on the Horizon for Christian Conciliation?

Christian conciliation is about to undergo intense activity as practitioners serve in more and more venues. Marriages, families, churches, and organizations are experiencing the power of the gospel being applied to their conflicts. Through Christian conciliation, believers and unbelievers alike are experiencing the message of God's love for them during some of the most painful experiences of their lives. Counseling conferences, seminary curriculums, secular mediators, and gospel-centered ministries are increasingly concerned about bringing biblical principles of peacemaking into their contexts. Biblical counseling has taken note of Christian conciliation and is beginning a thoughtful dialogue about the principles and practices of conflict resolution. Writings about Christian conciliation are under way, designed to help couples, groups, churches, and organizations navigate complex and painful conflict.[86]

Several organizations with trained conciliators can be found by searching on the Internet for "Christian conciliation." Many will travel to the location of the conflict, and phone coaching is frequently offered. Churches all around the country and around the world have trained conciliators providing volunteer or paid services within their contexts.

A Final Thought

The names and details of the story illustrated in this chapter are a composite of many of the cases in which I have personally served as a conciliator for the past sixteen years. Sadly, this story has been and continues to be played out in our churches. Yet, while these conflicts can be devastating, I have been amazed and humbled to see the gospel magnified as church leaders and members grasp a vision for peacemaking and cling to the overwhelming hope of glorifying God in all they do. Over and over again, I have personally witnessed the stunning beauty of reconciliation when hurting couples, families, churches, and organizations face conflict and relational brokenness out of love for God.

PART 4

EQUIPPING BIBLICAL COUNSELORS

CHAPTER 11

EQUIPPING BIBLICAL COUNSELORS FOR YOUR CHURCH

RON ALLCHIN AND TIM ALLCHIN

O ur family went on a mission trip to the Amazon jungle of Peru in the summer of 1987. Tim was a fifth grader. I (Ron) noticed a tall building still under construction—a vast unfinished steel structure resting on a finished first floor. The local missionary hosting us explained that the building had been started with great promise, but construction had stalled because the building was sinking. In fact, when the second floor was completed, the building sank farther, burying the first floor. The flawed foundation simply could not support the weight of the structure. The building was an eyesore, embarrassing the community, forever sinking!

We believe there is an important lesson here for churches wanting to build a biblical counseling ministry. Launching a biblical counseling ministry *without laying the proper foundation* can undermine any discipleship you hope to accomplish. This chapter details how to equip your church to build a ministry that will continue to multiply into the future. We want to help you customize your ministry for your context as we share several best practices we have developed for implementing a biblical counseling vision. Altogether, we believe there are four sequential steps you will need to follow if you hope to develop a culture and structure of effective biblical counseling in your church: *envisioning*, *enlisting*, *equipping*, and *empowering*.[87]

ENVISIONING: STARTING WITH THE RIGHT PHILOSOPHY

Scripture requires and models effective discipleship through the ministry of the Word. Each church must evaluate how counseling fits into their overall strategy of making disciples. Many churches have a great pulpit ministry, but falter in discipleship because congregants lack encouragement or support to follow through in faithful obedience to the Word. Other churches compromise the authority of the Word by assuming that there is little relevant guidance to be found in the Word to address the challenges of life. However, effective ministry of the Word must go beyond the pulpit, permeating every aspect of daily life for every member.

Acts 20 highlights several characteristics that are important in the formation of an effective vision of discipleship through the ministry of the Word. Paul's relationship to the Ephesians serves as a model of effective ministry that includes both public proclamation of the Word and personal guidance. There are four convictions that should guide the vision of a biblical counseling paradigm within every local church.

Conviction #1: Holistic Discipleship

Your church's vision for biblical counseling should be rooted in a larger conviction that discipleship must be holistic. Biblical counseling's goal is to help people mature and become more like Christ (Col. 1:28–29). These disciples will passionately live out the Great Commission by proclaiming the gospel with boldness and helping new believers to work out their salvation, growing and maturing through obedience and fellowship with the Lord. In Acts 20, Paul's ministry was marked by making disciples through a gospel witness and by teaching them to obey, living out the "whole counsel of God."

Rather than proof-texting, Paul sought to holistically address the thoughts and beliefs, the behaviors, and the emotions of disciples. Publicly and privately, he presented everything "profitable" to help them grow in their knowledge of the Lord and in practical obedience to Scripture. Biblical counseling tears down the wall between "religious problems" and "everyday problems," pointing to Christ as the answer for life's deepest struggles. The *key question* a church must answer regarding this conviction: "Are you committed to provide holistic care and discipleship for your flock?"

Conviction #2: Protective Restoration

A vision for biblical counseling must also take seriously Jesus' teaching about the priority to seek the lost and straying sheep. In Acts 20, Paul modeled Jesus' heart for the lost, lonely, and hurting in how he conducted himself in Ephesus. He reminded the leaders that wolves would come and attack the flock to destroy their faith from both inside and outside the church. Some were wounded and some strayed. Paul challenged his leaders to have an intentional discipleship vision, including prevention, protection, and restoration. The *key question* a church must answer regarding this conviction: "When someone in your local church strays or falls, who is sent to find that person, and what is the process for restoration?"

Conviction #3: Spiritual Leadership

Biblical counseling is one of the most effective means to develop spiritual leadership within the local church. As unproductive members are restored back to spiritual fruitfulness, they have potential to become effective leaders to help others through what they have experienced. Often the most effective counselors are those who have started as counselees!

The spiritual health of leaders in ministry cannot be underestimated because Acts 20 demonstrates that leaders will reproduce their character. In Acts 20:28, leaders are told to pay careful attention to both themselves and the flock while caring for the church. In 20:29–30, we see that even leaders can be led astray and pervert the ministry with which they have been entrusted. Biblical counseling helps leaders by creating a culture of mutual accountability where they learn to sharpen one another through God's truth.

As Paul was leaving the church at Ephesus after three years of ministry together, the leaders demonstrated that they had gained the same heart they had seen and experienced in Paul. Paul had a heart of integrity, compassion, and conviction that marked them deeply. If the highest levels of leadership are not personally invested in making disciples, a biblical counseling ministry will struggle to gain traction. Paul first taught the elders who would have to lead this culture of change. The *key question* a church must answer regarding this conviction: "How is the leadership personally serving as an example of effective one-another ministry, and what will their personal character reproduce in their flock?"

Conviction #4: Missional Compassion

Finally, we believe that biblical counseling should be missional, seeking to reach the community with a much-needed hope. Those who embrace biblical counseling should have a heart to enter into the lives of others in need and to meet that need with the power of Christ. In Acts 20:21, Paul testified to both Jew and Greek of true repentance toward God and faith in our Lord Jesus Christ. His audience was outside of the church and in the surrounding communities. In post-Christian cultures, effective biblical counseling can bridge the gospel into the lives of those who are broken and hurting in the surrounding community.[88]

Missional compassion authenticates the ministry of the Word and helps as God's truth goes deeper into the lives of those reached. Compassionate leaders will have a more receptive audience as they teach the Word. Paul's ministry was characterized by his emotional investment in the spiritual lives of those he served, giving sacrificially and leading selflessly. Rather than seeking to enrich himself by his ministry, he was known for the sacrifices he made to love those under his care. A church where biblical counseling is embraced will become a church that reaches out to the surrounding community. The *key question* a church must answer regarding this conviction: "Does our community see our church as a place where hope and help can be found?"

As you begin the envisioning process, remember that these convictions are about more than starting a biblical counseling ministry. They should fit into the overarching holistic ministry philosophy that guides all of the ministries of the church. Instead of tying particular theological convictions to individual ministries, anchor these convictions to the mission of the church and integrate them into every activity and ministry.

For example, churches that seek to accomplish biblical counseling with only paid staff or elders will always fall short in their ability to shepherd the flock and meet the needs of their people. Equipping leaders at every level to take some responsibility for shepherding is crucial to changing the culture of a church toward embracing biblical counseling. Ministry leaders and small group leaders who embrace these convictions will exponentially increase discipleship ministry in the church. While each person operates from their own unique spiritual gifts, every person is called to participate in "one-anothering" in some way. The late Dr. Bill Goode used to say, "A church should not *have* a counseling ministry, but it should *be* a counseling ministry." This requires both leaders and members to grow in their ability to minister the Word to one another.

It is also important that the vision creates unity. Simply starting a mentoring or counseling ministry that embraces these values will not change the culture of the church if leadership is not personally invested in change. There must be theological unity rooted in a common understanding of the gospel and an understanding of the sanctification process. While some downplay the importance of theology in counseling, unity regarding the sufficiency of Christ and practicality of Scripture is essential if biblical counseling is to take root from the top level of leadership down through the entire membership.

There must also be unity in practice. In Romans 15:14, the church was full of goodness, filled with all knowledge, and able to instruct one another. Every member of the body was expected to embrace some responsibility to care for and instruct one another. Leaders were tasked with equipping the church body for effective ministry.

A culture of biblical counseling will be stunted if church leaders develop convictions regarding the necessity of one-another ministry but fail to equip or allow others in the body to embrace responsibility toward one another. Likewise, if only some members get excited about biblical counseling but church leadership is not on board with the training and direction, disunity and discouragement result. For lack of vision and leadership, the church will return to the status quo.

ENLISTING: CHOOSING THE RIGHT PEOPLE

While all members of the church play some role in one-another ministry, churches need to identify and equip counselors whose primary ministry is focused on restoring brothers from sin (Gal. 6:1–5) and bringing comfort to those who are suffering (2 Cor. 1:3–7). For situations dealing with intense sin or suffering, a response of equal intensity is often needed to help the struggler make progress and grow in faith. The church should equip those whose gifts and passions align well with a ministry of "intense, personalized discipleship." What kind of people will you enlist and equip as a team whose primary ministry is biblical counseling?

Determine the Right Point Leader

In some churches, the pastor is expected to provide the energy, direction, and oversight for every ministry. However, a biblical counseling model that is primarily led by the senior pastor will almost always flounder. The time demands and the weight of walking with those who struggle will bury a pastor who tries to counsel more than a few people at a time. While larger churches may be able to afford a devoted staff person to develop the counseling ministry, most churches will need to find the right point leader to champion, resource, and support those who are learning to counsel. This should be a person who has evidenced a heart for shepherding, has demonstrated wisdom, and has discernment and love for the flock.

The point leader is naturally drawn to hurting people and has already evidenced the ability to reach hurting people within the church and community. This person walks into a room, spots those who are struggling, and is compelled to first listen and understand, and then to do whatever possible to help or to enlist others to help.

Giving compassionate care is already the point leader's heart desire, but the next step is multiplication by equipping others in the body to have this same heart. The point leader understands the benefits of taking others alongside into counseling situations. This is best accomplished through team counseling where a potential leader is invited by a seasoned leader to first observe and in time participate in the counseling process.

Proper administration comes from one who not only has a lot of energy but also has the organizational ability to structure and manage a formal ministry to its greatest effectiveness. Training schedules, forms, policies, and oversight all take forethought and planning. Good administration requires teamwork, but the point leader must lead!

Determine the Right Personnel

Your ability to care for your people requires you to enlist quality shepherds to get started. In Ezekiel 34, God indicts the leaders for failure to care for the sheep, with tragic results for His people. Counseling is not primarily a transfer of information, but a transfer of character. Character is caught, not taught. It is so important that true followers of Christ disciple those who are less mature, teaching them the Word and modeling obedience to it.

Colossians 3:12–17 gives us the DNA of effective counselors. As you select your team, you will want to look for people who have embraced these five principles that produce effective one-another ministry.

- *They See People as a Priority (Col. 3:12– 14):* Paul reminds us that those who come to Christ should reflect a new way of life. When someone is in Christ, they manifest a new love, forgiveness, and patience for those around them. They build others up and are eager to forgive and reconcile. Effective biblical counselors have learned to manage their own relationships effectively and know the importance of healthy relationships in the body.

- *They Experience Peace with God through the Gospel (Col. 3:15):* Counselors cannot pass on hope if they do not live within the reality of hope themselves. Lasting hope comes through the gospel of peace, and biblical counselors regard this truth with utmost importance. All who desire to counsel may not have embraced the gospel, since some are drawn to counseling that embraces other philosophies contradicting Scripture. The gospel is the treasure that changes lives, and it needs to be proclaimed and cherished through the lifestyle of effective biblical counselors.

- *They Have a Passion for the Word (Col. 3:16):* Notice two important aspects about God's Word in the phrase "Let the Word of Christ dwell in you richly." First, effective counselors remember that the Word of Christ is the wonderful story of redemption through faith in Christ. It is not a moralizing gospel, but rather points always to Christ and His Word. Then, how does the Word dwell in us richly? Rich flavors have a potency that permeates. God's powerful Word acts the same in those who allow it to be their nourishment and mirror. Those who have been trained to counsel effectively savor the rich Word of God and have placed their hope in the Savior it reveals and the wisdom it exemplifies. This passion is then passed on to others.

- *They Demonstrate a Practical Wisdom (Col. 3:16):* Biblical counseling could be aptly defined by the phrase "teaching and admonishing one another in all wisdom." Effective counselors wisely teach about the practical way life works, aiming to relate biblically to God and others. They warn about pitfalls using the vast wisdom in God's Word. They demonstrate relational skills and life experiences that minister God's Word effectively, continuing to grow themselves as they guide others in growth.

- *They Live Out a Passionate Praise for God (Col. 3:16b–17):* Effective counselors have a new song in their heart that reflects excitement and joy found in the gospel. The good news is still alive and burning brightly in them. They naturally point others to Christ as the answer because they wholeheartedly believe and live out that reality. The best counselors are often first a counselee who was restored from sin or suffering. They now minister with authentic gratitude toward God and those who helped, having great confidence in the power of God to change lives because they experienced this transformation personally.

As you equip your team, you are looking for people who have the right mix of gifts to effectively motivate and care for others. Churches that allow anyone with interest to counsel may find unequipped helpers quickly giving biblical counseling a bad reputation. Those needing help may be pushed deeper into hiding and farther away from the church through unbiblical or insensitive counsel. Here are some potential counselors with character qualities you'll want to avoid:

- *They Lack a Balance of Grace and Truth:* Those who value truth over grace often become legalistic and cold to the failures and pain others feel. Truth raises the standard and expects rapid compliance. Rather than pointing people to God's power to change, they often point to legalistic truths that bring about behavioral change, but not heart change. God's grace motivates us to live for God's glory through the principles of His Word and gracious character.
- *They Have More Zeal than Knowledge:* They quickly give generic, simplistic answers that are "one size fits all," based on their own experiences. Those whose lives were impacted by certain programs (recovery groups or marriage retreats), certain medical discoveries (medicines or supplements), or by certain books

(devotionals or popular preachers) can often be strong advocates for such. They often have a genuine love for people and a sincere desire to help even though they may lack the knowledge of truth that sets people free and brings lasting change. While they motivate and encourage people in positive ways, their counsel falls short of the sanctification process.

- *They Manipulate and Control Others:* Counselors who expect others to be obedient to what they say rather than what God says violate personal boundaries. The control may be driven by the counselor's pride or, at times, a counselee may prefer the perceived safety of being controlled. However, neither reflects a healthy discipleship relationship where God is the central focus and the Word is the authority. Manipulation leads to a shame or fear-based relationship with the counselor and even with God. Pleasing the counselor dwarfs the biblical goal of maturity and sensitivity to God's leading through His Spirit and the Word.

- *They Are People Pleasers:* Some counselors may tell counselees what they perceive they want to hear. Rather than possibly offending a counselee, their own fear keeps them from being a bold voice for truth as God calls them to be. They share their own experiences without realizing their great responsibility to speak God's Word.

- *They Are People Who Rely Mainly on Common Sense:* Often they live a moral life that adheres to biblical standards, but without the depth to understand how God's wisdom gives deeper and more satisfying answers than their own wisdom and common sense. This approach can subtly imply that God and His Word are not necessary for a transformed life, just common sense. This sounds more like an advice column or pop psychology whose ideas ring true, but whose motivation for change is self-centered. Rather than bringing a counselee to repentance, they tweak behaviors to obtain temporal change. They fail to understand the motivation for lasting change found in God's sufficient Word.

EQUIPPING: BUILDING THROUGH THE RIGHT PRINCIPLES

Once you have selected leaders who will embrace a biblical strategy of care and counseling, you need to think through the long-range goals and steps it will take to develop a robust and effective culture of biblical counseling. Effective biblical counselors address the real issues in unhealthy spiritual lives so those people can first become fruitful disciples and then disciple-makers to help others.

Don't overestimate the changes you can accomplish in year one, or you may become discouraged and give up. And don't underestimate God's ability to grow the ministry by year five through the exponential compounding of disciples. Those first few counselees may serve as the catalyst for pointing others toward Christ. Be realistic. It takes time for a tree to grow and increase fruitful yield. Creating three key opportunities for your people to grow as biblical counselors is critical if your church wants to develop a culture of effective one-anothering.

Equip Counselors through Formal Training

Nothing is more frustrating than being asked to do a job for which you feel unprepared. Formal training will help your people connect the dots between pulpit preaching, practical theology, and common-to-man struggles. Participants should initially learn to link counseling, discipleship, and shepherding and then to develop a process of how to work with those who hurt. Many organizations, such as ABC (Association of Biblical Counselors), ACBC (Association of Certified Biblical Counselors), CCEF (Christian Counseling and Educational Foundation), Faith Church, IABC (International Association of Biblical Counselors), IBCD (Institute for Biblical Counseling & Discipleship), and BCC (Biblical Counseling Center) have provided training seminars to churches for many years.[89] You can also find organizations through the Biblical Counseling Coalition website[90] and through certifying organizations such as ACBC.

Equip through Life-on-Life Relationships

Bob Kellemen, in *Equipping Counselors for Your Church*, gives four "C" words from Romans 15:14 to develop leaders for effective local church ministry.[91] (See table 2.)

TABLE 2
THE FOUR DIMENSIONS OF COMPREHENSIVE
BIBLICAL COUNSELING EQUIPPING

Christlike Character:	"Full of Goodness"	Heart/Being
Biblical Content:	"Complete in Knowledge"	Head/Knowing
Relational Competence:	"Competent to Instruct"	Hands/Doing
Christian Community:	"Brothers/One Another"	Home/Loving

- *Character:* Leaders don't reproduce what they say; they reproduce who they are! Character matters when it comes to life-on-life discipleship; lack of character can destroy the ministry you are building. Those equipping the counselors cannot allow the needs of hurting people to preempt helping your counselors grow in their own character. First we must apply the principles from the Word to our own life if we expect to transfer them to others as disciples.

- *Content:* Even experienced counselors face new situations and complex struggles that are really just new twists on old problems. People walk into churches with increasingly complex problems and even greater confusion about the solutions. Biblical counseling offers foundational, yet profound, answers. Biblical counselors who can sort through the complexity by listening well to the counselee's story will be able to bridge God's answers into a confused life. If we believe that God's Word has never failed to give us profitable answers for all people and problems, we have confidence when we approach Scripture to find answers. Our main task is to creatively apply these answers in wisdom to hurting and struggling people.

- *Competence:* The first time you gave a speech in front of a crowd, you were likely nervous and lacked confidence. However, if you persisted, it became far more comfortable and natural. As you sit in the counseling chair and know you are responsible to guide the conversation forward, remember, God is there with you. This is both a source of comfort and pressure as you desire to speak His truth faithfully. Effective counselors make time to grow in their ability through reading, consultation, conferences, and practice. Gracious yet honest feedback about how to improve is indispensable to competence.

- *Community:* We become effective biblical counselors by receiving and providing counseling in community. Bob Kellemen suggests two important challenges for growth.[92] Every counselor needs others to challenge and to comfort them as they grow in their faith. Also, effective leaders must take God's call to hospitality seriously and invite others into their homes and lives, often discipling them intensely for a time.[93]

Equip Counselors through Effective Mentoring

Often the best way to develop biblical counselors is to show them what actually happens in the counseling process. When people get a taste of the powerful and practical principles at work, they will often have a passion for more, though it is crucial that propriety and confidentiality be stressed. However, the best means of equipping counselors is not only classroom training but also actual observation and involvement. Below are some models to increase involvement of church leaders in the counseling process, helping some take a first step.

- *Counseling Office:* Often a church's counseling office or conference table effectively allows observers to watch an experienced counselor, enabling them to grow in their own ability to counsel. Initially trainees just watch silently, but over time become more involved in the process. Experienced leaders mentor by inviting others to join them in sessions.

- *Living Room:* Particularly in marriage counseling, inviting a married couple to minister to another couple creates momentum and support for a struggling marriage. Often the informal setting of a home encourages a couple to open up and share.

- *Homework Helper:* Counselees are required to find a wise friend who will assist them in completing assignments given by the counselor. The helper serves for accountability and encouragement, but will also learn from this process how to help others going through a similar struggle. "Without counsel plans fail, but with many advisers they succeed" (Prov. 15:22 ESV).

- *Life Experience Advocate:* Who can better help someone going through cancer than a person who saw God as faithful through the same difficulty (2 Cor. 1:3–7)? Those with addictions, marriage struggles, or other difficulties are encouraged and given hope when they learn from those who have already experienced great victory (1 Cor. 10:13).

- *Small Group Involvement:* When counseling those who have little encouragement in their life, introduce them to a support group from church to help them mature and change. An appropriate group increases their resources and provides encouragement for change. Small groups that avoid ministry to the hurting miss God's heart for discipleship as well as great opportunities to grow past their own comfort zone.

- *Visitation:* Pastors and leaders who demonstrate the importance of one-another ministry should include the younger generations in their visitation work. Whether in hospitals or homes, visitation often leads to open doors for counseling.

EMPOWERING: ENSURING QUALITY THROUGH THE RIGHT PRACTICES

To empower your leaders, guide them toward "best practices" that lead to success. Depending on how formal the counseling ministry is, some issues are more crucial than others. However, as your outreach into the community grows, best practices give your ministry credibility and ensure fidelity to your calling and goals.[94]

- *Who is your target?* Will your counsel be restricted to members and regular attenders of your church, or will it be open to anyone from the community who desires help? Starting first with just those in your church and moving later to others from your community normally allows the best chance for growing success.

- *What is your liability?* Will a counseling ministry expose your church to undue risk? Churches need to be careful to define the roles of their counselors as volunteers, and not as professional counselors.[95] It must be clear that this is a church ministry. You would be wise to consult with your insurance carrier and a local lawyer to ensure legal safety. You will also want to have a clear policy on mandated reporting and a procedure to ensure that such reporting takes place in a timely manner.

- *What is your process for dealing with those seeking help?* How do you determine who handles which types of cases? Will you counsel with those who are taking psychotropic drugs or who are currently under a domestic violence restraining order? What about sexual abuse victims or offenders?

- *What ethical considerations will guide you?* How do you ensure a spiritually healthy environment? What types of precautions will you take to ensure sexual propriety between counselors and counselees? How will you counsel children and youth? Who must be present during counseling in the church building or in homes? What safeguards and reporting mechanisms will you put in place to ensure that your ministry follows a biblical standard of personal ethics?

- *How will your ministry grow?* Be careful not to overpromote the counseling as you get started. Do your job well and let the reputation grow through word-of-mouth referrals.

- *What do you need to do about your facilities?* What does your facility communicate about your desire to care well? Do your facilities mimic the medical model, or do they create a conversational and safe environment? Are there windows in the doors to safeguard the counselors against false accusations? Is there a policy on where it is appropriate to meet?

- *Have you developed the forms you will need?* How do you collect and safeguard information? People are coming to you with burdens on their heart, and counselors often write down sensitive information. Where is that information kept and who can access it?

- *Will you charge fees? If so, how much?* Some church-based counseling centers have as their fee to "Come faithfully and do your homework." Other churches ask for a donation to cover costs of administration. A happy medium would be to charge a "cancellation deposit" forfeited if they do not come or a small fee that pays for ongoing resources and training of the leadership team.

- *Do you have a policy about confidentiality?* Do you have a clear statement of limited confidentiality? This must clearly define limits for confidentiality and make the counselee aware of situations where it must be ethically broken. The best practice is to have them sign a form to keep on file. It must be clear that you will report cases of child sexual abuse or criminal activity and take actions if you believe the counselee is a threat to harm themselves or others. A Matthew 18 restoration/confrontation of sin issues should be mentioned.

Leader Gatherings and Ongoing Training

Think about how you will encourage counselors to collaborate and exchange ideas about the best ways to care for people. Counselors who do not regularly meet with others for support may feel the heavy pressure of counselee burdens. Each ministry must find its own balance, but it's important to not let the needs of the sheep outweigh the need for ongoing support for the shepherds.

In addition, there should be required training for individuals who participate as leaders in a counseling ministry. There is also the need for ongoing equipping and training for lay counselors. Family situations, unimaginable to many thirty years ago, are widely accepted and embraced in modern cultures. Ongoing training helps your leaders think through current trends and popular opinions to address these with timeless truth.

Reclaiming the responsibility to counsel within the local church is a significant undertaking. However, many organizations have successfully navigated this transition and can help you along the way. You wisely build on their effective foundations.

Partnerships can help you move forward without strategic missteps. Reliable training, resources, and consultation from ministries who have trained others to counsel their people well are worth the investment. Ministries like ABC, ACBC, BCC, CCEF, IABC, IBCD, and other training organizations can help your counselors with proven and consistent resources.

For churches that are smaller, a community-based counseling model allows you to reach more people. Perhaps one church has leaders excelling in financial counseling, and another church has many who have restored marriages. Does every church in a small community need a ministry for the grieving, or can churches work together to support those who grieve loved ones? Working together can help smaller ministries disciple more effectively, and the cooperative spirit impacts the community.

Building a biblical counseling ministry is a marathon, not a sprint. Use Sunday services to continually promote the ministry. By celebrating certain milestones, you keep your congregation aware and give your counselors the support they need to succeed. Designate certain days to encourage your counselors and to move your counseling ministry forward with energy.

INTRODUCTION SUNDAY

Knowing when to introduce your intention to increase the biblical counseling for your flock is crucial to effectively implementing a care strategy. Because biblical counseling may be a new idea to many in your congregation, you need to make sure key leadership is on board before you announce plans to the congregation. For instance, we have worked with churches where staff was divided over counseling issues, and launching a biblical counseling strategy caused division and conflict. It would have been wiser to work through this as a staff and leadership team before it was introduced. Your goal is to then make a clear, positive presentation about how biblical counseling can impact your church for good.

GRADUATION SUNDAY

Before you launch the new biblical counseling ministry, it would be good to honor your trained counselors and to recognize their achievements through the preparation process. Not only does this tell the counselors they are valuable, but it also signals to your congregation that the church is committed to providing a top-quality counseling ministry.

LEADERSHIP-GATHERING SUNDAY

From time to time, you should gather for the purpose of continuing to resource, encourage, and equip those doing the counseling. Having some of your leaders share success stories about God at work can help encourage those who are working on particularly slow or difficult cases.

PRAYER FOR THE HURTING ON SUNDAY

Would visitors gather the impression from your services that your church is full of only positive people who had a great week? Where do the suffering and hurting fit into the preaching calendar and worship service? Create a culture where it is safe to come forward with your struggles and to grieve losses. Take the time to pray for the hurting — it will signal to all that you really do want to help.

PRAYER TEAM EVERY SUNDAY

One of the best places to begin counseling is to challenge your leadership team to pray with people during weekend services. If the hurting come and go without anyone noticing, it reinforces that the church and their problems are unrelated. Look for opportunities to introduce the hurting to someone who can pray with them now, meet with them later, or connect them into meaningful community.

CONCLUSION: VISUALIZE AND IMPLEMENT THIS PROCESS TO PERPETUATE DISCIPLESHIP

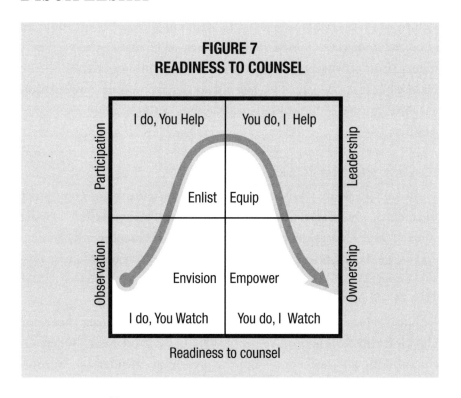

FIGURE 7
READINESS TO COUNSEL

This figure[96] helps to visualize the process we have been talking about that is needed to develop a strong biblical counseling ministry. It will take time and energy to develop, but the effort produces exponentially increased ministry opportunities. A strong foundation begins by envisioning and demonstrating long-term discipleship principles, and then enlisting, equipping, and empowering quality leaders who in turn continue to reproduce others by repeating the cycle of observation, participation, leadership development, and ministry ownership, to again reproduce the cycle. Perpetual discipleship—Matthew 28:20 and 2 Timothy 2:2 fulfilled!

Now is the time for churches to reclaim this responsibility to counsel! As our culture twists deeper and deeper into sinful patterns, effective biblical counseling brings the hope of the gospel and the joy of an obedient life to the struggler. A thriving counseling ministry flows from taking the time to lay a proper foundation through intentional preparation and then continuing to nurture all those involved through perpetual discipleship.

CHAPTER 12

LAUNCHING AND LEADING A BIBLICAL COUNSELING MINISTRY IN A "LARGER CHURCH"

GREG COOK AND JACK DELK

Those in "larger" churches often talk about growing larger and smaller at the same time. They want to grow larger because they take seriously the multiplication mandate of Matthew 28:19–20 and want to reach a lost and dying world with the message of hope in Christ. At the same time, they want to grow "smaller" by cultivating biblical community. The church understands that regardless of the size of our congregation, God calls us to a life of one-another ministry, and biblical community is possible only when we truly know each other and spend time together. This chapter addresses the challenges of developing biblical community through a biblical counseling ministry in a larger church.

What do we mean by a "large" church? At least by one definition, this would refer to any church that has more than three hundred people in attendance.[97] Churches of this size face a unique challenge in launching a biblical counseling ministry because the number of people in leadership and in the congregation can make it difficult to garner widespread support. With many seminaries adopting an integrative approach to counseling rather than a biblical counseling approach, there is a good chance that a larger church will have multiple perspectives on the leadership staff. This can make it difficult to get the entire leadership staff on board with a biblical counseling approach.[98]

Fortunately, having a unanimous commitment by the leadership of the church is not a prerequisite to incorporating and introducing biblical counseling to a larger church. In fact, it may be one of the reasons God has raised you, the one reading this, to your position. You can serve as an advocate, educating and demonstrating in practical ways that the Word of God applies to everyday life and the problems that life in a fallen world brings. In this setting, you have an opportunity to be used by God to increase your church's impact for the kingdom of God. You can do so by bringing the very personal, focused, intense, one-on-one discipleship ministry of the Word — biblical counseling — into a context in which it does not already exist. That was the case for both of us in our church context. Though the leadership of our church did not share our commitment to biblical counseling, we felt convicted to reintroduce this forgotten and overlooked paradigm to our church and the surrounding community.

Disciple-making, pastoral care, and the cultivation of deep one-another relationships are ongoing challenges for large churches. Though there is often a large staff, too often the ratio of staff to congregant is actually smaller, on average, than the average church. Thankfully, many efforts have been made to counteract the lack of community in large churches. The rise of small group ministry has mirrored the rise of mega-churches, beginning in the 1980s and continuing to the present day. Some churches first embraced small groups as a means of attaching new people to the church, while others did it as a means of obeying the biblical command that we love and serve one another. In some cases, this has worked, but in others it may have further exacerbated the sense that a large church is impersonal.

To further complicate attempts to develop community in a large church, many people who attend a larger church come *because* it is large and affords them a degree of anonymity. We must acknowledge that we live in a relentlessly individualistic culture. People like to remain hidden and unknown, even when they come to church.

Soul care and biblical counseling can help by countering our tendency to hide and escape. Large churches need to intentionally offer a safe environment for change where one-to-one relationships can develop. For this reason, we believe that every large church needs to align their small group ministry with their pastoral care and biblical counseling ministries (if they exist).

Yet while there are challenges for larger churches, there are also opportunities. Larger churches simply have more resources. Resource advantages can include a larger budget, larger facilities, more support staff, and a larger congregation from which to find gifted and talented laity to work in and invest in the biblical counseling ministry.

With a church staff of two or three people, the division of labor is often loosely defined. As the size of the staff increases, the division of labor is more defined and specialization occurs. In launching a biblical counseling ministry, this specialization can be a boon and a bane. Positively, leaders tend to become "experts" in their particular area of ministry because they are able to focus much more narrowly on that area. This is equally true in the area of biblical counseling. Negatively, leaders can become so focused on their particular tree that they forget that they are part of a forest. Again, this is true of any ministry area, including biblical counseling. Ministry leaders in a large church have the opportunity to think deeply and carefully and creatively about their particular area of ministry, but the minute they forget that they are just a part of something much bigger, something that God is doing, they have lost their advantage.

Know the History

Regardless of the size of the church, all churches have a history — a story that reminds them where they come from and who they are. It is important to learn this story and to discover where, if at all, biblical counseling philosophies and activities have already been a part of the ministry. You should identify if there has been opposition to a biblical counseling approach in the past and why.

In my own church, I (Greg) began by interviewing the founding elders of the church, and I soon discovered that even though they did not use the label, a significant amount of biblical counseling was already taking place among the staff and elders. There was biblical truth being spoken into people's lives, and there was a great appreciation for loving well, knowing well, and speaking well. I learned that one of the founding pastors was also a bi-professional counselor in the local community. I also found out that some of the connotations with biblical counseling were negative. The first full-time pastor of the church recalled a scathing address by Jay Adams he had heard while in seminary, and it left a bad impression on him.

Know that there will likely be a few contradictions in your own church's history. Some may love biblical counseling, others will not. Still others will not really understand it until you explain it. Addressing misunderstandings about biblical counseling through listening and prayerful consideration gives you an opportunity to address false stereotypes.

LAUNCHING A BIBLICAL COUNSELING MINISTRY IN THE LARGER CHURCH

When you are launching a biblical counseling ministry in a large church, you will want support from the church board as well as the staff. In my church, I needed both, though the elders' support was absolutely essential. When I first proposed the ministry, there was hesitation for two reasons: necessity and liability. This is why it is important to have a well-thought-out proposal. This should include scriptural rationales, mission statements, and ministry objectives. To help you in putting together a biblical counseling ministry mission statement, we recommend an extremely helpful book by Bob Kellemen — *Equipping Counselors for Your Church.*[99]

The second challenge is often the question of liability. A large church usually has extensive resources, and it is wise and appropriate for the leadership board to steward those resources well. If liability concerns are not thoroughly addressed, you should not be surprised if the leadership turns down your proposal. To address liability concerns, we took a careful look at the building and the rooms we were proposing to use for counseling. We also provided written policies, procedures, and release forms for the leadership to review. Another issue that can affect liability is whether or not you charge for the counseling. There are typically greater liability concerns when the counseling ministry is fee-based. In our church, we chose to have cameras placed in every counseling location to record both audio and video. Our counselors counsel only in designated offices that offer plenty of visibility — including windows in the doors.

Apply Change Management Principles

In a larger church, you may also need to consider several change management principles as you transition from launch to leadership. First, remember that humility wins more battles than pride. If you are unable to listen to the concerns of those who resist change, you probably should not be considering a role in biblical counseling (or ministry for that matter). Get leadership buy-in, but don't wait until *everyone* agrees. For some churches, the elder board (or whatever the leadership board calls itself) will be the most important approval body. This is especially true in a large church.

When appealing to the elders to approve the start of a biblical counseling process, it is important that you clarify what is intended for the ministry. Some church counseling ministries form a separate 501c3 nonprofit to protect the larger church from liabilities. This is less needed if the predominant staffing is from nonpaid, non-professionally licensed, non-fee-based ministries. As we mentioned earlier, your liability greatly increases when professional, fee-for-service ministries are offered. An advantage for large churches is that they can afford to dedicate staff and space for a biblical counseling ministry without having to charge a fee.

Bear in mind that the launch process may take several years. This was true for me (Greg) in starting the soul care ministry at my church as well as for Jack in starting a biblical counseling ministry at his church. Don't assume that hesitation or concerns from a key decision maker is a final roadblock. At my church (Jack), I built support and consensus from the bottom up. I recognized that the attention of our church leadership was focused on managing growth (at the time we were in the middle of launching a multicampus vision). I also realized that most of the church leaders did not understand what biblical counseling was or what distinguished it from Christian integrative counseling. Therefore, I started inviting key lay leaders to attend various conferences and training events in biblical counseling.

Over a five-year period, I developed a strong nucleus of respected lay leaders who were as committed to biblical counseling as I was. We proposed to our elders that we start a counseling center with volunteers on one of our campuses without cost to the church or to counselees. The fruit of that ministry initiative produced a groundswell of support from the bottom up, a groundswell that led to biblical counseling becoming a priority in the church. Three years after the start of that counseling center, our staffing structure includes biblical counseling as a stated ministry of the church that will be staffed on every campus. Launching a biblical counseling ministry in a large church can take time, so be patient.

Multisites for Biblical Counseling

In many larger churches today, the growing trend is toward multiple locations or campuses. "One church, many locations." As distasteful as the analogy may sound, creating a multisite is similar to franchising a fast-food restaurant. What are the basic menu items that you carry over from church to church? Typically these include preaching, small groups, children's ministry, and a certain worship structure and style. But biblical counseling can bring some much-needed unity to ministries of care in multisite churches. Ed Stetzer offers a problematic warning to which biblical counseling is the solution:

> Despite a church's best intentions at new sites, sometimes certain pastoral duties get lost: scriptural assignments such as praying over the sick (James 5:14); watching over those placed in your care (1 Peter 5:1); discipline (1 Cor. 5); and breaking bread with the beloved (Acts 2:42). I know that those duties are supposed to be the job of the campus pastor, but we also know it sometimes does not happen. The focus is easily placed on the event more than the community. And sometimes that results in people coming for the show without connecting to the community.[100]

We believe that Stetzer's warning is well founded, which is why those involved in multisite ministries must advocate for a biblical counseling presence and training for multisites. We should not assume that the campus pastor will be able to address the biblical counseling needs of his flock any better than the teaching pastor of a large venue can address the biblical counseling needs of his flock.

There are many avenues for doing biblical counseling in a multisite, but one of the most obvious is the small group process. Casting a vision for caring for people biblically in the small group process is vital (see chapters 5–8 for examples of how this can be done). The biblical counseling advocate should cast this vision and then offer training to ensure that there are multiple points of contact for biblical counseling—especially where there are no separate building structures that house the biblical counseling ministries. Having the space for a counseling center is possible in many large churches, but it is important to make a distinction between the church and the buildings that contain the church. Avoid associating the work of biblical counseling too closely with certain buildings or ministries. Make sure your people keep a broad understanding that biblical counseling is speaking God's truth with care and compassion to God's people.

How Do You Cast Vision?

Counseling in most biblical counseling circles is synonymous with disciple-making. Most large churches have some type of disciple-making process in place, so they want to know: how will this be different? Let the leadership know that the counselee and the counselor are objects of active discipleship efforts—biblical counseling is intensive, focused, one-on-one discipleship. The counselee is being invited into an active, Christ-centered walk with the living God. The counselor is being invited into a disciple-making personal growth project of giving their life away to those in need of direction and hope. Disciple-making is ongoing and finished only when our sanctification is complete (in heaven).

Since a church-wide vision is usually what is needed, most church management experts and how-to conferences for church leaders have a common emphasis: without the support of the senior pastor, do not try to implement change. It's easy to understand why. The senior pastor is a very influential person in the church, no matter the size of the congregation. What that support looks like in a large church may be very different from the support in a smaller church. In a larger church there are likely many strong, thriving ministries, and it is impractical or impossible for the senior leader to personally be the champion of each. It is important to have the support of the senior/lead pastor, but that support does not need to be demonstrated by being a megaphone for the ministry (although a shout-out certainly helps now and then).

The Launch and Development Process

Church size has everything to do with scale—the larger the church, the more resources available. However, it is also true that the larger the church, the greater the demand on those resources. In a larger church, it is possible for a biblical counseling ministry to have dedicated pastoral staff leadership, something that may not be possible in a smaller church. Yet the demands for counseling in a larger church will be more than that staff person can handle personally, so we recruit and train additional counselors. Once trained, these counselors need supervision and shepherding and care. It doesn't take long before that function becomes more than one person can handle, so different levels of counselors are developed.

At Bethlehem Baptist Church, I (Jack) have lay counselors who assist me in the supervision and training of counselors. Large churches increase the size of the recruiting pool and increase the likelihood that you can find one or several trained biblical counselors with high skill levels. I have several lay counselors who have years of biblical counseling training or advanced degrees in biblical counseling. I thank God daily for the blessing of these trained, dedicated, and eager volunteers who assist me in supervision and training.

Yet even with the blessing of these dedicated volunteers, the launch of the counseling ministry needed to happen slowly so more counselors and leaders could be trained and developed. Large churches are blessed by large volunteer pools, but they also have more people who are looking for solutions to life's problems. If we had started off with a big formal announcement and advertised our services, we would have been overwhelmed. Rather, we started without a lot of fanfare and grew primarily through word of mouth. We will start our fourth year this fall with more than twenty trained lay counselors and a vision to add another dozen counselors in the next year. And this fall, a lay counseling ministry will begin on another one of our campuses.

LEADING A BIBLICAL COUNSELING MINISTRY IN THE LARGER CHURCH

When it comes to leading a biblical counseling ministry in a larger church, there are three primary issues you need to address:

- Equipping Counselors by Giving Away Ministry
- The Need for Training and Retraining
- The Need for Careful Screening

Giving Away Ministry

It is very tempting to be the person who helps everyone. But if you are spending all your time holding the "fire hose" and responding to the urgent demands of ministry, you will never be able to build and develop other leaders. And as a ministry develops, it can be very difficult for a leader to let go and hand off ministry to those who are new or less trained. Consider, however, the example our Savior gave to us when He sent the disciples into the neighboring villages and towns to prepare for His arrival (Mark 6:7–13; Luke 10:1–12; Matt. 10). Jesus sent them out with very little formal training to do the work that He had been doing. It was work that He could have done far better than they could (Mark 9:18; Luke 9:40; Matt. 17:16). Jesus sends us out so that we will send others out. Ministry and disciple-making go together.[101]

The Need for Training

Over the years as leaders, it has been our goal to do less direct counseling. We must be oriented toward giving the ministry away and letting others develop their skills. To do this, we need to be developing people to give it away to. In a large church, the counseling pastor's major role must be the training, developing, and shepherding of counselors.

This process of training and developing lay counselors is crucial and never ending. We suggest offering some formal initial training, which, depending on the equipping schedule and sequence, can take between nine and twelve months to complete. Prospective biblical lay counselors should be expected to read several books in preparation for classroom discussions and interactions. This training can occur in formal classroom settings as well as by observing actual counseling sessions. Cameras in our offices (Greg) help us capture all the counseling sessions so that we can learn and observe.

Another method of training through observation is to have a trainee sit in with a trained counselor and observe the counseling process from the first session through the last. Once a potential counselor has done this, we (Jack) switch roles for the next counselee. The trainee takes the counselor's role and the trained counselor observes and offers feedback and critique after each session. Again, this training and observation process doesn't really end. Counselors should be committed to being lifelong learners. As soon as a biblical counselor begins to feel overly competent, they have forgotten that it is the Wonderful Counselor who does the work. We need to remember that we are just a means toward His end.

Careful Screening

A biblical counseling ministry is not a "y'all come" ministry. There should be a careful selection and screening process for bringing in potential new counselors. Remember that the leaders of the church bear responsibility for the care of the flock, and they need to be confident that good, godly ministry is taking place in the counseling room. Beware of gossips, busybodies, and voyeurs. A lay-led counseling ministry tends to attract people with mixed motives and agendas as well as wolves in sheep's clothing (1 Tim. 5:3–5; 2 Thess. 3:11).

While an overemphasis on confidentiality can sometimes undermine community, we must always be careful in handling the things people share with us. Too much confidentiality may help a person justify a lifestyle of hiding (i.e., If I tell you, I don't have to tell others). But we are also admonished to care for and protect the flock. A good biblical counselor must be biblically and theologically grounded. After all, biblical counseling is all about seeing life as God sees it and responding to life in ways that glorify Him. Look for spiritually maturing people to staff your counseling ministry. Just as we can grow and develop counseling skills, we can grow and develop our knowledge and understanding of God and His Word.

Embedding into the DNA

I (Jack) remember my parents' first microwave (and dishwasher, but I further age myself). It was a mystery surrounded by fears of irradiation on the one hand or bold claims that this one appliance could eventually replace all other heating appliances in the standard household kitchen.

Neither claim ultimately proved to live up to the fear (or hype), though it is certainly true that what started as a mysterious luxury for a few has become a standard fixture in the kitchens of America. It's difficult to imagine a kitchen without a microwave (or a dorm or motel room, for that matter), but when they were first introduced, there was a confusion of hype and skepticism. Many thought of them as an unnecessary nuisance.

By crude analogy, our hope is that biblical counseling will eventually become a "standard appliance" in the makeup of every church. For this to happen, we need to move beyond vision and mission and embed biblical counseling into the very DNA of the congregation. This begins by linking the vision of the counseling ministry to the vision and mission of the church. If your biblical counseling ministry does not fit with the vision and mission of your church, it will not survive. It is that simple. Everything that a large church does must be vision and mission driven. You can link biblical counseling to a church-wide mission statement like, "We are committed to helping you become a fully developing follower of Christ, or what the New Testament calls 'a disciple' based on Colossians 1:28" (Greg), or, "We exist to spread a passion for the supremacy of God in all things for the joy of all peoples through Jesus Christ" (Jack).

In addition to the mission statement, the DNA of your church includes the traits and qualities that characterize your church. Working a vision for a biblical counseling ministry into the DNA of your church changes everything; it becomes part of the identity of the church and the people who are the church. Linking your biblical counseling ministry to the vision and mission of the church can be accomplished with a well-crafted document, but making your biblical counseling ministry part of the DNA of the church takes time, energy, and intentionality.

We want to conclude by emphasizing the need for intentionality. You must have a plan and a strategy if you want to make biblical counseling part of your church's DNA. At Christ Chapel (Greg) this strategy began at the top (elders and pastors) and moved down to the people and ministries of the church. At Bethlehem (Jack), it started from the ground up; that is, we started with a core of like-minded laity who already had made biblical counseling part of their DNA and were dedicated to seeing the church transformed by biblical counseling. That core group began to target key lay ministry leaders and select pastors and elders to spread their vision by inviting them to conferences, bringing in speakers with a biblical counseling background, and beginning a biblical counseling ministry that produced fruit. That fruit in turn invited greater inclusion, recognition, and blessing from the top leadership.

Whatever strategy you use to implement a biblical counseling ministry in your church, expect it to take time. Turning a large church is like turning an ocean liner; it takes time and it takes space. But when biblical counseling is part of the DNA of your church, people will begin to see that our biggest problem is inside of us, not outside of us. They will look to and embrace the Redeemer who is mighty to help and save. The church will recognize that we don't need to look outside of the church to find help; God's Word equips us to help one another. People begin to see that it is okay to not be okay; they become more transparent. We are all in process and have not arrived; none of us are perfect, but we are being perfected. Martin Luther said it well:

> This life therefore is not righteousness, but growth in righteousness, not health, but healing, not being but becoming, not rest but exercise. We are not yet what we shall be, but we are growing toward it, the process is not yet finished, but it is going on, this is not the end, but it is the road. All does not yet gleam in glory, but all is being purified.[102]

Regardless of the size of your church, we are all being conformed into the image of Christ. Our roads may not all look the same, our experiences may not mirror one another's, but the process includes growth, healing, and exercise and is not finished until we see the Savior face-to-face. "Beloved, we are God's children now, and what we will be has not yet appeared; but we know that when he appears we shall be like him, because we shall see him as he is. And everyone who thus hopes in him purifies himself as he is pure" (1 John 3:2–3 ESV).

CHAPTER 13

LAUNCHING A COUNSELING CENTER IN A "MIDSIZE CHURCH": BIBLICAL COUNSELING FOR THE CHURCH *AND* COMMUNITY

JIM NEWHEISER AND ROD MAYS

A biblical counseling ministry has the potential to strengthen the midsize church from within while also giving the church an opportunity to make an impact on the broader community. We define a midsize church as a congregation that has fewer than five hundred but more than one hundred people attending on a Sunday morning. In addition to a full-time preaching pastor, there will typically be one or more pastors or staff who have multiple responsibilities (i.e., counseling, youth, worship/music, outreach, etc.) because the church cannot afford to hire a staff pastor for each separate function.

GETTING STARTED

Before anything else is done, it is essential that the preaching pastor be committed to the sufficiency of God's infallible Word, that the responsibility of the pastors/elders to shepherd the flock of God is clear (1 Peter 5:1–4), and the call is for all members to be one-another ministers (Rom. 15:14). The preaching should set an example to the congregation of how the Scriptures can be applied to all of life. The church should have a culture of seeking biblical answers to life's practical problems.

It is also important that the preaching pastor is engaged in caring for individual members of the flock. Counseling will keep the pastor connected to the real-world problems people face, which will make the preaching better. This public exposition of Scripture will continue to equip the pastor to more effectively use God's Word in counseling.

In a midsize church with a membership that can run as high as five hundred people, a single pastor does not have the time or the ability to do all of the shepherding/counseling. Just as Moses was overwhelmed by the responsibility of judging all the people of Israel (Ex. 18:13–16), the preaching pastor can quickly become exhausted with the responsibilities of study, administration, and counseling. And just as Jethro counseled Moses to appoint others to apply God's Word to the people's problems, pastors must be encouraged to equip others to care for and disciple church members. The lead pastor should be excited about a biblical counseling ministry in the church because it will take some of the burden so he can be devoted to his calling to the ministry of the Word and prayer without wearing himself out or neglecting his family.

Some preaching pastors have been well trained in counseling and are equipped to train and disciple their fellow leaders in soul care. Others graduate from seminary well prepared to publicly proclaim God's Word, but not as well equipped to counsel. They would benefit from joining fellow leaders in receiving basic counseling training. Often the other staff pastor or a lay leader may take the lead in promoting biblical counseling in the local church. That person can begin by getting trained as a biblical counselor to be equipped to guide other key leaders (elders, deacons, home group leaders, women's ministry leaders) as they are trained. The entire church will benefit by having many members equipped to build one another up through the Word (Eph. 4:15–16).

Thankfully, there are many excellent training options available, including conferences, DVD sets, and online training. While all who attend such training will find benefit (often first in their own lives and then in helping others), we believe that pursuing some kind of certification or credit is beneficial. Just as one tends to learn more in school when taking a course for credit (instead of attending as an auditor), the process of certification gives students the opportunity to receive correction or clarification where needed and to demonstrate that they have learned the material. Certification also provides a standard by which a church or a counseling center can have confidence that the counselors have a solid grasp of biblical counseling theory and methodology. For many years ACBC[103] (formerly NANC, National Association of Nouthetic Counselors) certification, which includes instruction, reading, observation, and counseling under the supervision of a mentor, has offered a high standard for biblical counselors. Ideally, at least one staff pastor and a few of the other key leaders will become certified through ACBC. For those who are not yet ready for the rigors of ACBC certification, IBCD[104] offers three certificates in care and discipleship which are more attainable for lay leaders and can be steps leading to ACBC certification.

CARING FOR THE CONGREGATION

The first call of the leaders of any church is to shepherd the flock entrusted to their care. The elders/pastors, along with other equipped leaders, may form a counseling team to fulfill this responsibility. People who need spiritual help typically go to the most visible pastor. While that pastor, like Moses in Exodus 18, may get involved in some of the toughest cases, the other gifted counselors can share this load.

When someone in need contacts the preaching pastor or the church office for help, there needs to be a point person who can distribute the cases according to the abilities and availability of the counseling team. Some couples may be designated to help with premarital counseling and marriage conflicts. Mature godly women (Titus 2:3–4) can be prepared to meet with women struggling with fear, anxiety, child-training issues, loneliness, etc. Godly men can meet alone with a brother who is losing the battle with lust or anger. In order to help the members of the congregation to accept someone other than the preaching pastor as their counselor, the pastor might participate in the first session, with the trained counselor taking the lead. It also is wise to keep the congregation informed about the counseling ministry and to make it clear how members can seek help and the kind of help they can expect. A goal would be for your church to have a reputation for being a place where the Word is faithfully proclaimed publicly and where people can get solid biblical soul care privately (Acts 20:20).

EXPANDING THE VISION TO CARE FOR THOSE OUTSIDE YOUR CHURCH

Just as every Christian has a special gift to use to serve the Lord and His people, different local churches have different strengths that can have an impact on the broader church and even on the community/world. Some churches may excel in outreach to different segments of the community. Others serve as launching pads for missionaries and church planters. Some churches excel in offering biblical counsel and care. Your counseling ministry may really start to grow when church members refer their friends and family to the care team. Then those who have been helped tell others. And they tell others. When God is using a ministry to care for needy souls, the word gets out and people come.

There are many benefits to opening up your counseling ministry to those outside your church. In addition to being a blessing to sister churches, a counseling ministry is often used by God to evangelize the lost[105] and to guide unchurched believers to commit to a local church. We have had the joy of seeing many unbelievers who came for free biblical counseling, then came to a saving faith in Jesus Christ.

Issues to Be Addressed When You Counsel Those Outside Your Local Church

The expansion of the counseling ministry of a midsize church needs to be done carefully and deliberately, lest the resources of the church be overwhelmed (Prov. 21:5; Luke 14:28–30). You want to be a local church that has a counseling center, not a counseling center that has a church. Several important questions need to be answered.

DO YOU HAVE SUFFICIENT COUNSELING RESOURCES TO EXPAND BEYOND YOUR LOCAL CHURCH?

Do you have enough counselors? Make a list of those who are equipped and willing to offer counsel and the number of hours each is available. Is there enough supply to meet demand beyond that of the local church? Be careful not to burn out your counselors. Understand that some counselors have the capacity to handle several cases in a week while others can deal with only one or two cases. Counseling is emotionally, spiritually, and physically draining.

Where and when will the counseling take place? Does your church facility have appropriate offices and waiting spaces for the counseling ministry? During what hours do you plan to make counseling available? Many churches offer counseling to outsiders one afternoon and evening a week. It is good to limit the times that such counseling is available so that staff members and counselors can devote the rest of the week to caring for the local body.

Who will manage the counselors' schedules, confirm appointments, and greet counselees? The maintenance of counseling schedules is like running a doctor's office. It will take more time and effort than you may expect, and it needs to be done well. You don't want counselors sitting around because the counselees don't show. Nor do you want available counseling hours to go to waste while needy people are on a waiting list. This may be added to the responsibilities of the church secretary/administrator, but it is possible that you will have to hire someone part-time to keep up with this important aspect of your ministry.

HOW WILL YOU DEAL WITH FINANCES?

Will you charge for your counseling? If so, how much? Or will you post a suggested donation for those who receive counseling? Because counseling is a church-based ministry of the Word, we have chosen not to charge, but to accept donations. Because counselors, staff, and observers often make great sacrifices to make themselves available for our counselees, we do charge a no-show fee.

How will you deal with insurance and possible legal issues? Welcoming troubled outsiders into your counseling center increases the possibility of conflict.[106] Will your present insurance cover your counseling ministry in case of a lawsuit, or do you need to add a rider to your policy? How can you reduce your exposure to liability? We have our counselees sign a statement that clearly states that we are not offering state-licensed therapy, but pastoral counsel from Scripture. We try to avoid even the outward appearance of being professional psychologists or therapists. We also make it clear that we cannot promise absolute confidentiality in cases in which we are required by Scripture (i.e., church discipline) or law (i.e., the abuse of a minor) to involve others. The counselee also commits to biblical conciliation/peacemaking in case of any dispute. You also will need to establish a policy as to how you will deal with maintaining counseling notes and records and how you would respond if these are subpoenaed or if a counselor is called to testify in court.

Will you pay your counselors or will you expect them to work on a volunteer basis? Most midsize churches can't afford to pay full-time counselors, which means we rely on pastors and staff members who counsel in addition to their other responsibilities and on trained volunteers. As resources have allowed, we have paid a nominal fee per case to our counselors, but when finances have been tight, we have been greatly blessed by men and women who have been willing and able to serve without pay.

Consider the financial impact on the host church. The counseling center, like all other ministries, will consume both financial and people resources. Parameters need to be established and agreed upon by key leadership. The counseling center needs to live within its budget. Staff members need to fulfill their responsibilities to their local church.

WHO WILL RECEIVE PRIORITY IN YOUR COUNSELING MINISTRY?

Our policy is to offer counsel to church members as quickly as possible. We often, however, have a waiting list for people from the community. We sometimes give priority to certain emergency situations and when a leader from the counselee's local church is willing to participate in the counseling.[107] We also give priority to church leaders and missionaries who urgently need counsel because many others may be affected by their restoration or disqualification.

WHO IS QUALIFIED TO COUNSEL FOR YOUR COUNSELING CENTER?

While there are many excellent counselors who have no formal certification, we have found that ACBC certification is a good and reasonable standard for those who will counsel outsiders through our counseling ministry. You also will need to decide whether you will allow counselors from other churches to work in your center. We welcome ACBC-certified counselors who are members in good standing of supportive sister churches in our area to counsel with us. We also make sure that their leaders approve of their counseling for us. We would not use a counselor who is not a member in good standing of a biblical local church.

HOW CAN YOU GET THE CHURCH TO SUPPORT THE MINISTRY OF COUNSELING OUTSIDERS?

Help the congregation to get behind this ministry with prayer and support as an important way the church is reaching outside its walls to bless the community and reach out to the lost. While this can be done through various announcements and other forms of communication, the public enthusiastic support of the preaching pastor is vital. Tell the congregation what God is doing through this ministry. It is exciting that a midsize church can have a great impact for the kingdom of God.

Counseling Those Outside Your Local Church

Many counselees come to us because they are not being shepherded elsewhere. Often this is a crucial aspect of their problem. If they are not yet committed to a local church, we show them from Scripture (Heb. 13:17) why church membership is vital and then make their pursuit of commitment to a biblical local church a condition of receiving ongoing counsel. If they are not sure where they should go, we will suggest a few excellent churches near where they live.

Counselees may come to you from churches you believe to be weak. It is our policy to try to work in harmony with all churches that affirm the gospel of salvation by God's grace alone, through faith alone in Christ, and the authority of Scripture.[108] We assume the best of all churches that profess to believe and proclaim the truth (1 Cor. 13:7). We don't want leaders of evangelical churches in our area to see us as a threat to steal their sheep. Rather, we want them to view us as a resource to help them to shepherd their sheep. We do not make attendance at *our* church a condition of receiving counsel. We also believe that it is important that our counselees' church leaders know that they are meeting with us and that we want to cooperate with them. When a church isn't following through with its duties (i.e., discipline, benevolence, discipleship), we offer to help their leaders work through the process biblically. We have had some leaders who had never dealt with certain situations express gratitude to us for our help. When a counselee has a problem with his/her local church, we seek to mediate so that these issues can be worked out. Sometimes counselees conclude on their own that their church falls significantly short of biblical standards. Rather than telling them to come to our church, we give them a booklet[109] that sets forth biblical criteria for choosing a church (and when to leave a church) and make a few suggestions based on what we know about churches in their local area.

There are some disadvantages to consider when helping those who are not members of your local church through counseling, at least when you compare this ministry with the counsel of church members. Within the church, you already know a lot of background about most of your counselees, while in a center you are usually meeting a person for the first time. Counseling in a center typically lasts for a few months, and then the counselee must go back to their own church for ongoing care.[110] That slot is then taken by someone on the waiting list. The local church, on the other hand, is designed by God as a place of ongoing care. Counseling in a center typically operates on a rigid hour-by-hour time schedule and in an office, while the time and venue of counseling people in the local church has more flexibility. A counselor can offer advice from God's Word, but doesn't have formal authority over counselees. The pastor/elder from the counselee's church has watch over that person's soul (Heb. 13:17) and the authority to initiate church discipline when needed.

One problem we face is that some leaders of other churches don't counsel (shepherd) their own people, but instead send them to us to get free counseling. Sometimes this is because the leader is focused on other things and doesn't want to become involved in counseling, claiming to be too busy. Other leaders don't feel equipped to deal with tough counseling cases and feel safer referring them to "experts."[111] To avoid misuse, we offer priority to counselees who come with a leader from their church (not necessarily the preaching pastor) who will participate and, hopefully, be equipped to counsel others after observing our counseling. Sometimes we make participation of a church leader a condition for ongoing counseling, or we will contact a church leader to gently exhort him to fulfill his calling to shepherd Christ's sheep (Acts 20:28) and to encourage him to consider pursuing training in biblical counseling for himself and his other church leaders.

EXPANDING THE VISION TO EQUIPPING OTHER CHURCHES

There are many reasons why you should consider taking this next step from counseling outsiders to equipping leaders from other churches. There is a great need for local churches to be strengthened in their counseling/ care and discipleship ministries. Many church leaders feel unequipped. Others are overwhelmed and need trained people to help them in their setting. Some even outsource their counseling to unbiblical secular counselors. The best place for sheep to receive care is from their own shepherds on an ongoing basis, rather than at a counseling center on a temporary basis.

Furthermore, we quickly realized that we cannot meet all of the need/ demand for biblical counseling in our region. No matter how many hours we would make available, they would be filled. It's really just the old "teach a man to fish" principle. The focus of our counseling center is to equip people to counsel the Word in their own local churches. We count it a privilege to bless other evangelical churches in our region with this ministry. And a primary purpose of our counseling is now to equip trainees from other churches through participation in live observation of counseling sessions. The ideal observers are leaders in training from the counselee's local church so that those being trained can carry on care and discipleship after the temporary counseling relationship with us is over. We also are happy for our more experienced counselors to be a resource to equip church leaders as they deal with more challenging cases.

We have been thrilled to see other churches catch the vision for biblical counseling. First they begin by sending people to us for counsel. Then they begin sending people for training. Several church leaders get through the basic levels of Care and Discipleship certification while a few will even attain ACBC certification. One of our greatest joys has been to help churches establish other counseling centers.

Issues to Be Addressed When You Open a Training Center

The first stage in launching a training center is to develop a philosophy of counseling that is clear, easily communicated, and easily understood.

Once you have done this (see later in the chapter), you will need to assess whether you have the resources to be a training center. Do you have gifted and qualified people who have time available to teach the counseling courses? Is there a need in your area? Probably the answer is yes (especially if people from other churches are flocking to your center for counsel). On the other hand, there may be another local church in your area that is already doing an excellent job training people in biblical counseling with whom you can partner. Or there may be other like-minded churches with which you can pool resources to establish a new ministry.

Then you will need to determine which curriculum you will use. It is probably easiest to start by using a curriculum developed by others, rather than developing your own from the beginning.[112] This could involve showing DVDs and having an experienced counselor lead a discussion and answer questions after each training session. Or the experienced counselor might be able to teach from someone else's syllabus. Over time those who teach for your training center may personalize the curriculum, which would ultimately lead to the creation of your own training course. Your training center also might choose to affiliate with ACBC, which certifies training centers into their network.

A fourth issue to ponder relates to how you will handle logistics. When will you meet for counseling and training? Many midsize churches/counseling centers have found it best to offer counseling and training one night a week. We (Jim) meet on Monday night. Most of our cases have live observers who then meet with the counselors to discuss the cases (while making every effort to protect the privacy of the counselees). You will also want to think about the resources you will make available for counselees and trainees. When homework is assigned in counseling, it is convenient to have the needed materials available in the counseling office. You can develop a collection of books, booklets, CDs, and DVDs available for purchase.

A fifth issue relates to how you will handle finances. You may choose to charge for training. Large training events can also provide financial resources which help to fund the counseling ministry during the rest of the year. As your counseling ministry expands, it may not be possible for your midsize church to bear the financial burden alone. Because your ministry is blessing people beyond your church, it is appropriate to receive financial help from churches and individuals who have benefited and who believe in the mission of biblical counseling.

Finally, you will want to consider how your counseling center will be organized. Some choose to make their counseling center a separate ministry with its own 501c3 status. Most centers that use this model have a staff director who runs the center on a day-to-day basis and a board of directors with representatives from various churches in the community that has final say in the operation of the center. Other churches choose to keep their counseling center as a ministry of their local church. While the leadership of the local church has ultimate oversight and authority, you can have an advisory board consisting of leaders from various like-minded churches in your area that works with the staff to provide vision and direction for your counseling ministry.

Expanding the Vision to Reach Out to Other Churches

You may find yourself quite busy simply counseling and training those who come to you by word of mouth and referral. Yet as a midsize church and counseling center, there will still be many churches in your region that are unaware of your ministry and may even be unaware of the basic principles of the sufficiency of Scripture and the power of the gospel to change lives through biblical counseling. You want to reach and bless these brothers and sisters also.

One way the vision for biblical counseling can be spread is by having leaders of your counseling center meet with leaders of area churches to explain your ministry and to answer any questions they may have. Some pastors may be concerned that you might try to persuade those who come to your center for counsel or training to join your church. You want to assure them that your desire is that counselees go back to their home churches where they will be cared for and thrive, and that the purpose of your training ministry is to equip people to counsel in their own churches so that counselees will no longer need to come to a center like yours.

Some church leaders have a negative view of biblical counseling because they have been misinformed. Meeting with such a pastor gives you the opportunity to address such concerns. For example, we make it clear that biblical counseling is not merely bashing people with the biblical imperatives, but explain how the gospel of grace is central in our counseling. We also do not deny the existence of brain diseases, nor do we say that it is always wrong to take psychotropic medication. We give examples of how God has used the ministry of biblical counseling to transform lives of individuals and the entire culture of many local churches.

Well-publicized training events are another great way to introduce people to biblical counseling and to get more churches and leaders on the path to being equipped to become more engaged in soul care. In addition to our ongoing weekly counseling and training, we hold two major annual events. In the spring we have an all-day seminar on a topic of interest (e.g., marriage, child training, finances, sex, knowing God's will, etc.). During the summer we have a major conference (Thursday night through Saturday noon) with well-known speakers/ authors speaking on subjects of wide interest around a theme in our general sessions while also offering several breakout options for issues that might be of concern to a smaller group (e.g., helping counselees who have been sexually abused). In the week leading up to the conference, we offer our complete care and discipleship training (for certification) as an intensive course (all day Monday–Thursday) in two tracks. Another approach used by some counseling centers is to offer training over a few weekends[113] (Friday night and all day Saturday).

While a well-known speaker may attract a larger crowd, the attendance at biblical counseling training events typically grows over the years as people are equipped and then bring others in future years. Some churches will send (and pay for) groups of key leaders to attend these training events.

DEVELOPING A PHILOSOPHY OF COUNSELING MINISTRY

Though we are covering this last, it is typically one of the first things you will want to develop when you are launching or starting a new biblical counseling ministry: develop your philosophy of counseling ministry. The term "philosophy of ministry" refers to a unique set of presuppositions, principles, and goals that flow from the study of Scripture applied to the ministry of pastoral care and counseling. A philosophy of counseling ministry is an aid in evaluating the practice of biblical counseling. It is also an aid in assessing the actual process and methodology applied to counseling, establishing the purpose for counseling, and determining what practices and purposes might need to change in order to see Scripture become an effective force in people's lives.

In his article "The Sufficiency of Scripture to Diagnose and Cure Souls," David Powlison states, "To recover the centrality of Scripture for the cure of souls demands two things: *conviction* backed up with *content*."[114] Our conviction or belief about Scripture must contain an understanding of the processes of justification and sanctification in the believer's life. True change by the Holy Spirit, through the Scripture, can occur only in the lives of those who have been justified by faith alone, in Christ alone. It is true that there are techniques, coping mechanisms, and training in better decision-making practices which may bring some relief and help to those who are not followers of Jesus, but real change in a person's perspective and worldview is possible only by a work of God in the heart.

A philosophy of ministry protects us from our own personalities in this practice. Some counselors/pastors may be able to function on their own talents and abilities as articulate, persuasive speakers. Because a ministry tends to take on the personality of the one doing ministry, a solid dependence on the work of the Holy Spirit will be a guard in the heart of the counselor. A well-defined philosophy of ministry will also protect the counselors from speaking primarily from their own experiences. This is important in the forming of a counselor's worldview.

Our frailty as human beings with our fallen tendencies to frustration and exhaustion may cause us to believe our philosophy of ministry is a "system" which is not working well for us when we have a bad day or we see counselees making poor decisions and defeating themselves over and over. A biblical philosophy of ministry will protect the pastor or counselor from being tempted to try a different methodology or counseling philosophy which may seem to change behavior and thinking patterns, but avoids the issue of the heart.

We should not think that the effectiveness of our counseling or the accomplishment of what we believe God's goals for the counselee to be is directly dependent on our gifts, skill, or wisdom. God uses all of us in our weakness to accomplish His goals (2 Cor. 12:9). We faithfully, prayerfully, and obediently act with dependence on the Holy Spirit, pointing people to God's Word. As counselors recognize their own sinful natures and weaknesses, they find it is easier to meet others who have been "caught in any transgression" (Gal. 6:1 ESV) or who may be confused and overwhelmed by circumstances. The words of Galatians 6 go on to warn those "who are spiritual" to watch themselves, so they will not be tempted in the same way as the one who has been caught in sin (Gal. 6:1–3).

It is imperative that the counselor understand the counselee through the grid of scriptural truth, rather than forcing the client through a standardized "assembly line" approach of programs and/or models. Our methods, strategy, and materials must be tailored to individual needs and the personality and abilities of the counselor/pastor. Careful examination of the Scriptures yields no formulaic approach to Christian faith and practice. There is no one-size-fits-all strategy for ministry. Rather, the whole of Scripture must be seen as one sweeping story of redemption and reconciliation, ending in the hope of restoration at the end of the age. The pattern of Creation, Fall, Redemption, and Future Glory (Restoration) is seen as the pattern for every human life as well as the pattern for God's universal work.

Individual ministry of the Word is completely dependent upon the context of the relationship between two people, whether pastor/counselor and church member/counselee or two friends, family members, or coworkers. The depth of the relationship and the level of suffering will dictate the style of communication (face-to-face, email, telephone, over meals, coffee, casually, or at a set appointment), methods (conversation and listening, Bible study, praying together), and strategy (accountability, frequency, shared experiences). No two counseling relationships or personal ministry opportunities will ever look exactly alike.

A set philosophy of ministry, which allows for a fixed theology and a flexible methodology, will aid the pastor/counselor in deciding what the next move should be in a ministry relationship. The truths about who God is, as seen in the outline of Creation, Fall, Redemption, and Future Glory/Restoration, will never change. These are biblically based foundational events that shape the theological basis for all counseling. What we believe about God as the Creator and Sustainer of the universe, His holiness, and the justice and love which motivated and continues to motivate His redemption of all things will inform how we help other men and women to view God and themselves. This framework and the truths of justification and sanctification which are inherent to it form the building blocks of the worldview the counselor/pastor/friend will speak to as he or she patiently listens, understands, and encourages the one who is struggling to find a sure place to rest and begin to think clearly about the real beliefs found in the heart.

Paul Tripp provides one additional example of a biblical/practical philosophy of ministry. In his book *Instruments in the Redeemer's Hands*, Tripp writes about the four elements of personal ministry. He outlines them as *love* (building relationships in order to care for others), *know* (discovering the heart of the other person by asking good questions that help the counselee think through the issues of his or her own heart), *speak* (applying the gospel worldview to a counselee's situation, presenting truth in order to see real change), and *do* (walking with and encouraging the counselee to think correctly, to handle emotions well and to become accountable for behavior).[115]

A clear and concise practice of pastoral care and counseling in the church exists to teach saints an understanding of the Scriptures, the ministry of the Spirit, and the principles of sanctification so that they may grow in grace and develop healthy relationships in the community of God, the church of Jesus Christ. The purpose of biblical counseling is to help believers develop a biblical worldview that allows the gospel of grace and the wisdom of Scripture to speak into every area and every circumstance of life, including emotional responses.

A philosophy of ministry will not only establish guardrails for our own church's ministry but also for those who want to learn from us. A midsize church of up to five hundred members will obviously attract outsiders who are interested in counseling. Will our philosophy of ministry attract them (because this is what they are looking for) or will it divert them (because this is not what they are looking for)? We will train our own people in this philosophy as well as those from other churches who agree in principle but need further instruction.

CONCLUSION

While not every midsize church will become a training center for other churches in its region, every local church needs leaders who are equipped to minister God's Word to those who face various spiritual problems. It was never God's design for all of the soul care for Christ's sheep to be accomplished by one leader. All mature Christians should be able to help one another with the basic struggles of the Christian life (Rom. 15:14). Churches also need several who are equipped to deal with the harder cases.

We live in a great day. Wonderful resources are available by which those whom God has called can receive excellent training. Once local churches start down this path of biblical faithfulness in caring for one another, they may be amazed at all God does through them.

CHAPTER 14

LAUNCHING A COUNSELING MINISTRY IN A "SMALLER CHURCH"

RANDY PATTEN

We've looked at several different ways to launch a biblical counseling ministry in a large church (over five hundred weekly attendees) and how to launch a biblical counseling center in a midsize church (between one hundred and five hundred attendees). But what about smaller churches and church plants? Do they have the resources to facilitate a biblical counseling ministry? Certainly! A biblical counseling ministry can and should flourish in a smaller church and/or church plant. It will require the lead pastor to understand, embrace, and actively participate in face-to-face ministry of the Word. These actions will lead to a gratifying pastoral ministry marked by effective disciple-making, restored relationships, humble servants, and gratefulness for God's love and wisdom revealed in the Scriptures.

LIVING EXAMPLES

Kevin Carson, a church planter in Ozark, Missouri, planted a church about a dozen years ago with a core of twelve people, including two who had been trained in biblical counseling. Today, almost everyone in the congregation of two hundred has had some instruction in biblical problem solving. This has been taught through sermons, small group fellowship, by receiving counseling, or by participating in one of the formal training sessions the church offers. The congregation is marked by love, unity, and an "others" mindset.

Pastor Carson has said, "No part of our ministry is exempt from the influence of biblical counseling." The church, Sonrise Baptist Church, offers biblical counseling not only to its members but also makes it available to the community. And Sonrise has now become a certified biblical counseling training center with the Association of Certified Biblical Counselors (ACBC) to make equipping in biblical counseling readily available to area church leaders. Sonrise is having a disproportionate impact for the cause of Christ compared to its size, largely due to its biblical counseling emphasis and skills.

Another example of a church planted with a biblical counseling focus is Grace Fellowship Church. Brad Bigney came to Florence, Kentucky, in 1996 to pastor a new church plant with eighty people who were part of the nucleus of the plant. Biblical counseling was a prominent part of his philosophy of ministry from the beginning, having seen the benefits in his own life and marriage. That emphasis, coupled with vibrant public worship services, clear and practical exposition of the Word, and teamed with an effective small group ministry, contributed to the congregation's significant growth. Since the initial plant of eighty people, the church has grown to over 1,800 who now call Grace Fellowship their church home. Their counseling ministry frequently has a substantial waiting list of people from the community seeking help. To help meet that need, the church has also become a certified training center with the Association of Certified Biblical Counselors (ACBC). In the greater Cincinnati, Ohio/Northern Kentucky area, Grace Fellowship has earned a reputation as the place to go if you need help with personal or family problems. Grace has become what I call a "Bishop Church," that is, one that other church leaders look to for direction and help. The emphasis on biblical counseling principles and procedures has contributed to this happening.

Both of these examples are stories of church plants that have since grown and expanded to develop larger biblical counseling ministries. But what does it take to start out and launch a counseling ministry if you are a leader in a smaller church or a church plant?

I was twenty-five years old and in my final year of seminary studies when I was called to be the pastor of a congregation with seventeen members and an average attendance of thirty-eight on Sunday mornings. What once had been a thriving church had been decimated by problems that had not been handled biblically, resulting in two splits. A significant number of people left after each one. Those who remained desperately wanted their beloved church to survive, but they were on the edge of hopelessness.

Hurting congregations, like hurting individuals, start looking for someone to help them. A wise, seasoned pastor with vision for what might happen encouraged the small congregation to call me as their pastor. He even raised money to help pay my salary for the first year!

Though my congregation was small, it took less than two years for me to realize that my counseling skills desperately needed improvement. I enrolled in a training program a couple of hours away that met every Monday for eleven weeks. The assigned reading, case studies, and morning lectures were very helpful, but what changed my life and ministry were the afternoons and evenings.

It was during those time periods that I sat at the end of the table and watched one of our three trainers take the Sword of the Spirit out of the sheath and use it to help a hurting person sitting across from him. My heart yearned to handle the Word with such confidence, skill, and compassion!

I drove home late each Monday evening eager to use what I had learned. God gave me plenty of opportunities to practice and develop my counseling skills. I learned that hurting people know hurting people, and when you help someone to get real answers and direction, they tell their friends.

Before long I had a full counseling schedule, and our congregation was growing as a direct result of my counseling ministry. Other leaders followed in my footsteps and, over time, by God's grace, our church became a counseling ministry.

So what were the lessons I learned along the way? If I were talking to a young church planter or the pastor of a small church of less than one hundred people, what would I say to them about launching and leading a biblical counseling ministry?

If your church is theologically sound, it is likely that your congregation is already receiving biblical counseling in a general discipleship format. Typically, this comes in the form of sermons, Sunday school classes, weekly Bible studies, and small group meetings. There is one message for all who are present regardless of individuals' circumstances; that is what makes it general discipleship.

Preaching and teaching the Bible are important because it teaches the listeners how to think and act Christianly. That is why pastors are commanded to "Teach and preach these principles" (1 Tim. 6:2 NASB). The public declaration of God's truth is certainly giving advice/instruction/warning/counsel, but it has to be recognized as general, not applied specifically to one's circumstances. Biblical counseling is intensive discipleship, not general discipleship.

Church leaders also need to acknowledge that members of their congregation are both counselors and counselees. That is, they are regularly giving and receiving counsel/advice on personal issues. Much of that informal counseling takes place before and after services or while serving together in a ministry. But just because this takes place on church property and with church members does not mean it is biblical. A lot of bad counsel has been given in the church parking lot! Begin by acknowledging that counseling takes place on your church property, but it is not always organized, scheduled, or evaluated.

Four passages of Scripture provide motivation for a smaller church to begin a biblical counseling ministry. First, Matthew 28:18–20 states, "Go therefore and make disciples of all the nations, baptizing them in the name of the Father and the Son and the Holy Spirit, *teaching them to observe all that I commanded you*" (NASB, emphasis added). "Teaching to observe" means instructing individuals to apply biblical principles and precepts to their own circumstances. Biblical counseling is one very effective way of accomplishing this.

Second, Ephesians 4:11–12 records, "And he gave the apostles, the prophets, the evangelists, the shepherds and teachers, *to equip the saints for the work of ministry,* for building up the body of Christ" (ESV, emphasis added). A biblical shepherd must equip his sheep to handle anger, fear, worry, temptation, discouragement, rejection, success, failure, guilt, bitterness, communication struggles, and self-discipline, to name a few. A shepherd must be equipped for the ministry of being a godly husband, wife, child, parent, employee, employer, and friend. These are all frequent topics of study and application in biblical counseling.

Second Timothy 2:2 (ESV) instructs pastors, "And what you have heard from me in the presence of many witnesses entrust to faithful men who will be able to teach others also." A biblical pastor will view himself as a helpful coach, not as the star performer. He will seek to multiply his efforts through those he has trained and positioned for fruitful ministry. A team approach to biblical counseling is a very effective way to do this and will be discussed later in this chapter.

Finally, Colossians 1:28–29 (ESV) provides a particularly motivational text in my own life and ministry. "Him we proclaim, warning everyone and teaching everyone with all wisdom, that we may present everyone mature in Christ. For this I toil, struggling with all his energy that he powerfully works within me."

The doctrine of progressive sanctification teaches that all believers need to be growing and changing to be more and more like the Lord Jesus Christ in our thoughts, motives, and actions. That is what it means to mature in Christ. Biblical counseling sets the stage to speak truth into people's lives when they are about to take a step either toward or away from spiritual progress. Sometimes face-to-face ministry of the Word demands that we warn; sometimes we teach; sometimes we encourage; sometimes we comfort. Regardless, it is always with the goal of helping that person to become more like Christ.

That said, the pastor must be the one to take the lead in a smaller church. In most cases he will be the best-trained theologian in the congregation and will have the greatest versatility in his schedule, since counseling will be viewed as pastoral work. But he must make it clear that he is biblically mandated to train and equip his congregation for this ministry as well. One of the most effective ways of doing this is to provide opportunities for members to observe you ministering privately to hurting people, using the Bible. Team counseling has multiple benefits, and the training aspect is prominent.

In a small church, it will be difficult for a pastor to train someone beyond his own level of skill. In addition to growing in his own proficiency, a wise pastor should consider the following options.

Attend Biblical Counseling Training Conferences
There are more training opportunities and formats available today than ever before. Start by visiting the website for the Association of Certified Biblical Counselors (ACBC). When you do, note the multiple Counseling and Discipleship Training Conferences they conduct around the nation (*http://www.biblicalcounseling.com/training/*) as well as the annual conference. ACBC also certifies biblical counseling training centers. At this writing there are more than sixty across the United States. Other organizations also provide helpful training. The best location to learn about these would be the Biblical Counseling Coalition's (BCC) website: *http://biblicalcounselingcoalition.org/.*

But don't attend a biblical counseling conference by yourself. Many pastors have found it wise to take key members of the church with them as part of their equipping strategy. It will also help them catch a vision for how God might use a counseling ministry at your church home.

Read Selectively and Regularly
Not every book that purports to be about biblical counseling is theologically accurate. Some books that are theologically accurate are more

helpful than others. Where to begin? Start with the books recommended by ACBC (*http://www.biblicalcounseling.com/certification/reading-and-observation-logs*). Also visit the book review section of the BCC website (*http://biblicalcounselingcoalition.org/books/*) for very helpful recommendations. The blogs on both of these sites can also be insightful on a wide variety of topics frequently encountered by biblical counselors.

Ten pages per day on average is the regular reading I recommend. I know from personal experience how demanding the life of a solo pastor can be. With all the reading typically done in sermon preparation, it can be difficult to make time to read in an area where you know you need to grow. There are some days when you cannot read anything to develop your skills, but there are other days when you could read twenty to fifty pages.

If you average reading ten pages per day, you can typically finish at least one book a month. A very effective way to be growing in understanding of biblical counseling is to always be reading something about it, even if it is only ten pages per day.

Observe Someone More Skilled Than You Are

I was blessed in my initial training in biblical counseling to observe three men who knew much more about how to minister to hurting people using the Scriptures than I did. I believed the Bible had answers and I wanted to help people—that is why I pursued vocational Christian ministry. Watching those three men conduct more than twenty counseling sessions over a period of three months lit a fire in me to learn how to minister to people with confidence, skill, and compassion the way they did.

Ideally, try to watch in person as someone conducts a counseling session. That allows the opportunity for discussion about strategy and questions about procedures. Even though I have a few thousand hours of counseling experience, I still find it enjoyable and informative to observe someone else leading a counseling session. I urge you to find someone a little further down the counseling skill path than you who will allow you to sit in as an assistant. If an in-person session is not an option, you can watch counseling observation DVDs from Faith Biblical Counseling Ministries (*http://www.faithlafayette.org/counseling*) and the Institute in Biblical Counseling and Discipleship (*http://www. IBCD.org/*). These are profitable for both individual growth and for training others in counseling methodology.

Pursue Certification as a Biblical Counselor

The Association of Certified Biblical Counselors (formerly called NANC, National Association of Nouthetic Counselors) has a thorough and time-proven strategy to help individuals develop biblical counseling skills. There are three phases in the certification process: learning, exams and application, and supervision. You can learn more about each of these at the ACBC website.

Hundreds of pastors and other Christian leaders have entered the ACBC certification process and testify to its benefits. My own counseling skills skyrocketed as a result of working through the various steps. The requirements are rigorous but doable. It is both humbling and encouraging to now have people who observe me counseling tell me that they want to learn to do what they watched me do, just like I did many years ago with the three men who trained me.

Pastor, isn't that what you want your people to say to you? Then it is reasonable to make it a priority to have your knowledge and skills examined by an organization such as ACBC for the purpose of being the best equipper you can be.

ANTICIPATE SMALL CHURCH SPECIFIC ISSUES

The leader of a small church who is starting a counseling ministry will face three challenges that are significantly exacerbated by church size. They are the matters of priority, place, and policies.

A church planter or pastor of a church with under 100 in attendance is typically a solo pastor. He lives a life of strongly competing priorities and frequently feels overwhelmed. His personal expectations coupled with those others have of him are daunting. He has to preach, teach, marry, bury, and meet with every committee, plan worship services, and visit newcomers, established members, and the hospitalized. When someone has misplaced their key, he is the first person they call to unlock the building. He is seeking to build relationships in the community and evangelize the lost. Finances are both a church and a personal burden. In addition, he knows God expects him to study, pray, and meditate. Oh, and be a model husband and father.

Under such circumstances, some men have said, "I'll start counseling others when I can get my own life shaped up." I suggest you reject that thinking. Instead, recognize that God chooses to use people in need of change and growth to help other people who need to change and grow so that He gets the glory. Just as proclaiming the Word publicly is a conviction, so it must be a conviction-driven priority that you will minister the Word privately to hurting individuals.

Having an acceptable place to counsel is frequently another specific issue unique to the small church or church planter. If the church is using the local movie theater, lodge hall, school building, or Seventh-Day Adventist church building for Sunday services, those spaces are typically not desirable or available for counseling during the week. Counseling in one's home, especially if there are younger children, can also be problematic. One solution is for the pastor/church planter to become comfortable counseling in an informal setting. Kevin Carson, the church planter referred to earlier, jokes that he has done more counseling at Panera on a napkin than he has done in a church office. Effective biblical counseling can take place at a restaurant, coffee shop, on a park bench, or in the cafeteria during lunch break at work, but it will require the church leader to be flexible and adjust procedures appropriately.

Another way to address the place problem is to identify and make arrangements to use a desirable space on a regular basis. This may be a meeting room at the local library or nearby motel or rooms at a business owned by someone sympathetic to your cause. A nearby church may also make space available or may already have space.

Particularly tough for leaders of small churches are policies about certain frequently encountered issues, such as counselees attending your church services and men not counseling women alone. Many biblical counselors, including me, think it is wise to require counselees to attend at least one public service per week at the church that is providing the biblical counseling free of charge. Hopefully a pastor of a small church or church plant can honestly say that what happens in the public services will complement and enhance what is discussed in the private sessions. The policy is wise and works well until a local supporting church requests that you counsel some of their people but makes it clear that you are not to expect them to attend your services. My experience is that people expect smaller churches and younger pastors to be more willing to adjust their policies to meet the desires of supporters, friends, or other pastors than they would be of a larger church with a veteran pastor. Wisdom will be needed in determining when to be flexible and when to hold to an announced policy.

There are multiple well-known reasons why it is not wise for a man to counsel a woman alone. Adhering to this policy becomes a specific challenge to the small church pastor or church planter because he is often the only employee. Frequently he is alone in the building or in his home office. This will demand that he schedule counseling at a time and place where he knows he can have someone else nearby. I know of small church pastors who counsel before, during, or after evening services, youth group meetings, and worship team rehearsals, just because they know people will be in the building. Another pastor identified a couple of retired individuals who would come to the building when asked and sit outside the office area during his counseling sessions. Sometimes, though, a woman will call with an urgent matter and ask to see you quickly. The frustration of trying to find someone to join you can become a powerful incentive to get some of your godly women trained as biblical counselors so that such calls can be referred to them.

DETERMINE YOUR SCHEDULE

There are many benefits to setting aside specific times and days for counseling. First, counseling calls for a different mindset than sermon preparation, making phone calls, responding to emails, or event planning. Once you are in the counseling "groove," it is best to remain there rather than bouncing back and forth between disparate activities. Also, having one day of the week when you provide counseling allows you to recruit trainees to come and observe as your assistant. They can plan their schedule to be present with you each week. Yet another advantage to selecting set days and times is that it makes it easy for you or whoever answers the church phone to respond to queries about the availability of counseling. "Yes, our church loves our community, and we provide free counseling, by appointment, every Tuesday afternoon and evening ..."

Designating a day and certain hours when you provide counseling, especially to those in the community, will provide some boundaries for you so that counseling does not take over your schedule. Personally, I suggest considering either Monday or Tuesday afternoon and evening. Many churches, even smaller ones, have some kind of programming on Wednesday evenings that makes it difficult to meet that night. And if you are like most families, things seem to get busier at home as the weekend approaches, so Thursdays seldom are ideal. Fridays and the weekends typically do not work well, so that leaves you with Monday or Tuesday. Again, don't just consider your own schedule in choosing; think about the availability of other people to serve as assistants/trainees.

For me, a typical counseling day will be scheduled with sessions beginning at noon, 1:30, 3:00, 5:00, 6:30, and 8:00 p.m. Our staff eats dinner from 4:30–5:00, and each session is planned to last approximately an hour or a bit longer. This will give you time to interact with your trainees after the counselee leaves, visit the restroom, get a snack, etc., and then start the next session on time.

You should also make sure that the rooms you use for counseling are attractive and functional. To be attractive for counseling, the room needs to be free of unnecessary distractions. It may need to be cleaned up and spruced up. A functional room for counseling is one that is private with adequate soundproofing so that conversations are not easily overheard. It should have comfortable chairs, a desk or table to sit at, and a whiteboard and markers.

ESTABLISH GUIDELINES AND PROCEDURES

Certain philosophical guidelines should be established to assist you in making decisions about how your counseling ministry will operate. These are wisdom issues, so what one small church may decide is wise to do may be different from what another church decides. Whatever you decide, the important thing is that you establish a policy. If you do not, every counselor will feel free to do what is right in their own eyes.

Here are the nine guidelines we have for our ministry:

1. Counseling will be done in teams of two or three.
2. All counselors must be biblical counselors, not integrationists.
3. All lead and associate counselors are expected to pursue ACBC certification.
4. All lead or associate counselors must be church members.
5. We do not charge for counseling, but counselees are expected to pay for materials used to assist them.
6. Appointments are scheduled after counselees return the Personal Data Inventory and Basic Information sheets.
7. Counselees are expected to attend at least one scheduled service or small group meeting per week at our church while they are receiving counseling.
8. On our counseling day, if there is an open hour or a counselee no-show, the time will be spent in some form of staff development (e.g., reading, completing ACBC exams, discussion of case studies, watching instructional DVDs, etc.).
9. Child care will be provided at church expense for counselors' children.

Most counseling ministries have some means of learning about the people seeking counseling and their concerns prior to the first session. These frequently include but are not limited to a Personal Data Inventory and a Basic Information sheet. I would also recommend having a medical release form, an agreement to receive biblical counseling form, carbonless duplicate paper for homework assignments, and a case report form. You should be exposed to these when you take a basic course in biblical counseling.

Even if you are starting out as a team of one, you should anticipate eventually recruiting others to your counseling team. There is great wisdom in choosing titles that reflect where an individual is in development as a biblical counselor. Below are three suggested titles and some criteria for each designation:

1. *Lead Counselor:* Someone who is ACBC certified or has completed a basic course, completed the ACBC reading requirements, and completed one of the exams. This individual leads counseling sessions and has an associate or assistant counselor observing sessions.

2. *Associate Counselor:* Someone who has completed a basic course in biblical counseling and has read at least one basic biblical counseling textbook, has demonstrated faithfulness and fruitfulness in other ministry settings, and is working on the ACBC theology and counseling exams. This individual participates in the sessions under the guidance of a Lead Counselor and may also be assigned cases as part of development. The goal is for an Associate Counselor to one day become a Lead Counselor.

3. *Assistant Counselor:* Someone considered spiritually mature enough to have been put in a teaching position, has demonstrated faithfulness and fruitfulness in other ministry settings, and has read at least one basic biblical counseling textbook. This individual is evaluating whether to pursue further training with the goal of someday becoming a Lead Counselor.

SECURE FUNDING AND PURCHASE RESOURCES

Once you have your philosophy and procedures in place, you will need to secure funding for the launch of your counseling ministry. This money will be used to purchase resources for counselees that will be frequently recommended by counselors. As funds allow, you might be able to develop a resource library for counselors, provide meals and refreshments for staff on the weekly counseling day, fund staff training and development, cover costs for ACBC application and supervision fees, and pay child care providers.

What churches value they fund, and the counseling ministry merits being a line item on the budget. It should be seen as a key part of both the church's evangelistic and discipleship efforts. Though it does not require a lot of money to get started, it will require some funds, just like every other ministry in the church.

While you are securing money and resources, make sure you do not neglect prayer. One person described biblical counseling as hand-to-hand spiritual combat. The enemy of our soul will not be pleased with our efforts to make disciples of Jesus Christ. In 2 Corinthians 10:3–4, Paul says, "For though we walk in the flesh, we are not waging war according to the flesh. For the weapons of our warfare are not of the flesh but have divine power to destroy strongholds."

Recruit a prayer team that will make it a priority on the counseling day to intercede on behalf of the counseling ministry administrator, scheduling secretary, counselors, and the counselees. Periodically during worship services it is wise to encourage the whole congregation to pray for this important ministry of the church.

FINALLY, SET YOUR LAUNCH DATE AND START!

Ask the congregation to spread the word about the availability of free faith-based biblical counseling. None of us live where there is an absence of broken relationships, life-dominating sins, suffering, and emptiness. We are surrounded by hurting people. Many of them would welcome the opportunity to talk to someone who would genuinely care and seek to help them find answers for their difficulties.

These are great days for loving our communities by organizing and formalizing your church's counseling ministry. The size of the church does not matter to people who are hurting and looking for answers. Launch your counseling ministry and immediately begin seeking to improve it as weaknesses become apparent. God uses imperfect people to minister His Word to hurting people so that He gets the glory.

Pastor, the congregation you serve can have an effective counseling ministry even if your church is small. It will need to start with you, but it should not end with you. As I said before, it will require you to understand, embrace, and actively participate in face-to-face ministry of the Word. These actions will lead to a gratifying pastoral ministry marked by effective disciple-making, restored relationships, humble servants, and gratefulness for God's love and wisdom revealed in the Scriptures.

And after a few years, you probably will find people in leadership at your church counseling others, people you first met as counselees. That is disciple-making come full circle, and it is possible through a ministry of biblical counseling in your church.

CHAPTER 15

Launching and Leading a Biblical Counseling Ministry in a Multicultural Church

Nicolas Ellen and Charles Ware

In 2004 I (Charles) was an attendee of the Lausanne global Forum on World Evangelization. After a long flight and a 2 a.m. check-in at the hotel in Pattaya, Thailand, I woke up the next day, tired but ready. My emotional excitement somehow overcame my physical exhaustion as I joined with several thousand leaders from around the world. The number of attendees from the United States had been intentionally limited so that the discussion on *world* evangelization would not be dominated by Western leaders.

The attendees at the conference were divided into *issue groups*. My group was assigned the issue of "Reconciliation as the Mission of God: Faithful Christian Witness in a World of Destructive Conflicts and Divisions." The forty-eight believers within our group represented a variety of cultures, some known historically for being hostile to each

255

other. The group included an Israeli and a Palestinian, a Hutu and a Tutsi, blacks and whites from the United States. The bold question we were going to discuss was this: "Is the gospel powerful enough to both penetrate and unite different cultures for the glory of God and advancement of His kingdom through a unified church?"

It was enlightening and challenging as we shared stories and searched the Scriptures together. I recall one participant from a country deeply divided by cultural and tribal wars saying, "The 'gospel of the West' is too weak to help us!" The conclusion of the group was that the gospel of grace is sufficient to evangelize and unite cultures, in Christ, for the glory of God and the advancement of His kingdom through a unified church.

MORE THAN MY IMAGINATION

I often dream of the church on earth reflecting the reality of Revelation 5:9. This passage paints us a mosaic of redeemed believers from every tribe, language, people, and nation singing with unified hearts, "Worthy is the Lamb!" This future vision leads me to believe that relationships between believers of differing cultures who are united in Christ offer us a foretaste of heaven on earth. A multicultural church with a mosaic of different cultures is a beautiful sight to behold. It is refreshing to see God's redeemed worshiping together in one service bound together by grace. But does a corporate gathering of people of diverse cultures necessarily indicate the unity of their minds and hearts in Christ?

Any pastor who has been around for a while will tell you that the unity you see in the congregation during worship can often be an illusion. People in the pew have not always been equipped to apply what they hear from the pulpit to *real life*, and this can be especially true in a multicultural congregation that has learned to "get along" in public—while remaining divided within their hearts.

We need to encourage mature and honest conversations about race and culture in the church. But how can we do this? How do we engage one another across cultural lines to discuss things that often offend, embarrass, marginalize, confuse, and hurt us? The potential for dissension increases when we bring up past problems in the church, historical divisions that are not easily solved and have deeply wounded people. Sadly, many of us suffer in silence simply because there is no place for us to talk openly and honestly.

In *Aliens in the Promise Land: Why Minority Leadership Is Overlooked in White Christian Churches and Institutions*, editor Anthony B. Bradley shares several powerful stories of believers who feel lonely and marginalized within the family of God where they serve. Each of these stories captures the person's dream of a better tomorrow. And we must not lose sight of the truth that God's grace offers us a better tomorrow, far better than our hopeless imagination! This is where a biblical counseling ministry can help. Biblical counseling can facilitate conversations by creating an environment where gracious interactions can occur. This can lead to the development of deep unity and loving relationships. God's grace creates a family where we have a sense of security and belonging, even with those who are culturally different.

Count the Cost?

Before you consider launching a biblical counseling ministry in a multicultural church, you must count the cost. Effective biblical counseling will bring to light dark, sinful attitudes that believers may have masked for years. When you begin digging into cultural issues, unresolved pain, deep distrust, insecurity, jealousy, and pride may be exposed and can lead to greater tensions and possibly dissensions within the body. You may wonder, Can the gospel really bring healing to these deep, historic divisions?

The answer is "yes!" We wholeheartedly believe that the gospel of grace can produce trusting, loving relationships among believers from different cultures. These relationships are a reflection of the wisdom of God, visible through the church (Eph. 3:9 – 11). But it takes the entire body, working together, to make it happen. We believe that *every* saint has a responsibility in this regard. Christian pastors and teachers must explain the Scriptures' affirmation of unity in Christ. Christian families must train their children to love and respect all people. Christian businesses must financially support efforts toward biblical unity. Christian organizations and businesses must work hard to weed out prejudice in principle and in practice. Individuals and organizations must work at creating cross-cultural relationships and mutually beneficial partnerships. A biblical counseling ministry within a multicultural church is uniquely positioned, in dependence upon the Spirit of God, to enlighten and transform God's people through the Word of God into the likeness of the Son of God.

There are five areas you need to address before launching a biblical counseling ministry in a multicultural church: integrity, education, compassion, modeling, and a final assessment from the Lord. The church leadership must personally clarify each of these areas in writing, and the church needs to work to establish a church culture that reflects each of these. We'll begin with the first: integrity.

INTEGRITY

Why do you want to launch a biblical counseling ministry? Why do you want to do it in a multicultural church? Your motivation will directly affect your policies, practices, procedures, and, most of all, your perseverance. Personal integrity is a matter of the heart. It requires a commitment to search for biblical wisdom, a willingness to submit to biblical wisdom, and the intentional influence of others to live out a life that reflects biblical wisdom.

Integrity of Purpose: Why Do I Desire This Relationship?

The first motive for doing this should be the Great Commandment, love for God and our neighbor (Matt. 22:37 – 40; 1 Cor. 12:31 – 13:3).

We should desire to create a biblical culture of grace within the church (Titus 2:11 – 14) because such an environment provides understanding of fallen humanity and highlights the power of the cross and the Scriptures in developing relationships that exhibit the redemptive grace of God.

Biblical counseling is grounded in good theology. Paul lays a strong biblical foundation for the multicultural nature of the New Testament church in Ephesians 2 – 3. Next, he prays for personal, experiential enablement for the believers to perceive the incredible love of Christ (Eph. 3:14 – 21). In chapter 4, Paul calls the Ephesians to apply the doctrine of unity by "walking worthy of their calling" as a multicultural community. This is more than five simple steps they need to apply that day. Paul goes right to the heart of the matter — a change from the inside out. Walking worthy of one's calling *in unity* means living a life of lowliness, gentleness, with longsuffering, bearing with one another in love, and striving — exerting real effort to maintain the unity created by the cross (Eph. 4:1 – 3).

We must have integrity in our purpose, not manipulating people or creating a false sense of unity based on other things. The truth is that heart change is hard work. If we set up expectations of microwave results or promote unity through relationships built on misunderstandings and hurts, we lack integrity. Real love and constant work are the ingredients for maintaining the peace created by God, especially in a multicultural community.

Integrity of Commitment: Doing the Right Thing among One Another

Integrity also manifests itself as a commitment to do what is right. People will have strong, diverse views on everything from the right Bible versions, to marriage and divorce, interracial marriage, education, justice, racism, war, politics, and immigration. You will encounter differing theological positions and even different philosophies of counseling. Close relationships will invite serious questions, including questions about the past. Some will wonder how Christian leaders with good doctrine could support slavery and segregation and resist civil rights. How could American Christians support a war against England to assure religious freedom while at the same time denying African-Americans similar freedoms? How could we proclaim from our pulpits love for all while denying some people groups the opportunity to attend our schools, sit at our tables, or be members in our churches?

We must be willing to acknowledge that many of our past evangelical leaders sincerely believed their positions were biblical — even positions that some of us would argue today were biblically wrong. Some of these positions were rooted more in the culture than the Scriptures, and the church was silent and, in some cases, an active participant in the mistreatment of individuals, destroying families in the name of God.

There will also be questions for today. Some will wonder, Is the evangelical position against homosexuality and same-sex marriage just an outdated culturally discriminatory view like racial discrimination in the 1960s? What should Christians believe about the immigration debate? Biblical counselors may answer these questions differently. But we must be able to have the conversations. We must learn to cultivate an environment where we can address these questions within our ministries.[116]

The Integrity of Commitment to Both an Inclusive and Exclusive Message

As we seek to navigate through our culture today, one dominated by secular tolerance, we must imitate the courage and commitment of past leaders by remaining faithful to scriptural absolutes. There is no room for compromise on the truth. We must also be diligent in examining our beliefs, personally and institutionally, to root out cultural biases that unnecessarily divide us.

Some of the institutions we lead today were originally founded by segregationists, and though our doctrinal positions may have changed, the institution may have a residue of segregation. Where we eat, vacation, live, and work may have elements that are subconsciously carried over from the past. Cultural tensions continue to exist in part because we have grown up ignorant of one another.

A multicultural church must proclaim from the pulpit and live out in practice biblical inclusion *and* exclusion. Biblical counseling is rooted in an exclusive gospel where salvation is through Christ alone, and our moral values are defined by the Bible rather than the culture. But how should the church deal with the need for biblical diversity without drifting into the moral abyss of secular tolerance? God's people must engage in relationships of integrity and provide proper biblical education that enables them to see the wisdom of God in creating a multicultural church (Eph. 3:1 – 13). We need churches that deal with real-life cultural issues from many different viewpoints—all with the Bible as the ultimate authority—where we test all things through the lens of Scripture.

PROPER EDUCATION: A BIBLICAL VIEW OF HEALING CULTURAL DIVISIONS WITHIN THE CHURCH

Proclaiming from the pulpit and practicing in the pew biblical inclusion and exclusion will require educating the congregation. Some people will have formed their views on diversity and multiculturalism from secular and cultural educators who may see believers as ignorant, racists, bigots, or as chauvinistic, homophobic people blinded by unreasoned faith. We will need to remind people that the Scriptures are where we turn for wisdom in addressing these issues. We should humbly admit that past interpretations may have been in error or have led to a mistaken application and overall misdirection for the church. Emphasize the need to properly interpret texts and apply them with wisdom. Model what it looks like to wrestle with the Scriptures and show people how to apply them to life.

There is a danger within a multicultural church to make simplistic statements in the name of unity: "Love unites, doctrine divides. We

EQUIPPING BIBLICAL COUNSELORS

are only dogmatic about the gospel, everything else is acceptable." But these statements usually aren't helpful, and they lack biblical support. We cannot define love without doctrine. And while we believe the gospel is essential, we need the truth of the entire Bible, not just portions. God's people, especially in a multicultural church, should be biblically educated on the core, doctrinal absolutes. These are the beliefs that form the foundation on which the church stands. But people will also need to understand how to address personal freedom, and where it is allowable and appropriate to disagree. We need to learn how to find unity that allows for disagreement and brings glory to God. Can we have conversations about difficult issues with a commitment to finding scriptural answers that bring unity, rather than allowing our disagreements to fragment our relationships? Again, these conversations may be extremely difficult, if not humanly impossible. Having unity on what we believe in the Bible can lead to compassion for one another as we continue on the journey together.

COMPASSION: I REFUSE TO WALK AWAY FROM YOU!

True compassion leads us to reach out to, rather than walk away from, one another. It is easier to walk away from a troubled relationship than it is to walk through the storm together. Yet deep and trusting relationships are often birthed in the womb of adversity. Prepare yourself for trials. Leaders who lead with compassion are often misunderstood and alienated—sometimes by the very groups they are seeking to unite. You may be called derogatory names or falsely accused of impure motives. Your loyalty to one group will be questioned. Doors of opportunity may close to you.

Sometimes, the road is lonely when you are living between groups. One believer said in despair, "I am too white for blacks and too black for whites." Another believer said, "When I reached out to help, I was called a racist. How should I respond?" These are the unspoken stories

262

in the multicultural church. Are you listening to them? Biblical compassion exhibits a willingness to listen to the life stories of our fellow believers. There is a genuine desire to know the circumstances that God has used to shape each of us into the people we are today. And leaders can encourage these conversations by asking, "Where were you born?" "What were your parents like?" We can ask people to share stories about their childhood home, their friends, and the community they were raised in. We can ask about their salvation experience, their cultural experiences, and the food and music they like. An anonymous church survey might help leaders discern whether members feel offended, marginalized, insecure, or lonely within the church. In the church service or in small groups, there may be creative ways to provide opportunities for people to get to know one another. Members of different ethnic and/or cultural backgrounds may share before the congregation personal experiences and prejudices that God's grace and people are helping them to overcome. These times should be mixed, with both positive and negative experiences, representative of a variety of ethnicities and cultural groups. Sometimes you may want to gather two groups together with a good leader to honestly discuss their experiences within the church. These meetings need to be within the context of a larger plan so you know what to do with the information that surfaces. When legitimate concerns are brought to light and nothing is done about them, members may walk away and rebel or retreat in silence.

JESUS' MARKETING PLAN: MODELING THE MESSAGE AMONG ONE ANOTHER

Jesus provides some helpful marketing and branding advice for His church when He says, "By this all men will know that you are my disciples, if you have love for one another" (John 13:35 RSV). We believe that a multicultural church can shine a bright light onto Christ's message as it models the people of God caring for one another across multiple cultural divides.

And what might a watching world see? Picture biblical counseling within a multicultural church where people of different backgrounds are working together to create an environment of grace. A place where relationships demonstrate all six of the critical elements of a grace-oriented community. What are those elements?

First, biblical repentance—having the humility to acknowledge and release our personally held cultural views that contradict Scripture. We must reject views that offend or exclude others unnecessarily (Acts 10:25–28; James 2:1–9). Second, transparency—the willingness to share both the negatives and positives of our personal stories to develop healthy relationships across cultural divides. Third, authenticity—communication without hypocrisy across cultural divides that seeks the welfare of the entire body (Eph. 4:15–16). Fourth, trust—placing one's confidence in God first and then in our fellow believers, and allowing for vulnerability and risk in sharing our lives with one another. Fifth, unity with diversity—preferring others before ourselves for Christ's sake and for unity within the body (Phil. 2:2–9). And sixth, commitment—intentionally persevering until relationships reflect the love of Christ. We want to demonstrate a love that sacrificially perseveres even when it receives nothing in return (John 3:16; Rom. 5:8). When these six elements are in place, we are ready to showcase gracious relationships through biblical counseling ministry within a multicultural church. But this raises a final question: How will we know when we've arrived?

FINAL ASSESSMENT REPORT

Leaders have been entrusted with two priceless "gifts"—the Word of God and the people of God. One day we will receive a report card from the Judge of all the earth. We will be graded on our faithfulness to the proclamation of the Word (2 Tim. 4:1–5) and the quality of the lives we built (1 Cor. 3:9–17). This work requires great skill when you are serving in a multicultural church.

The good news is that the multicultural church is God's idea, so we know that His grace is sufficient for the challenges we face. The launching of a biblical ministry within a multicultural church creates a wonderful environment in which to manifest the wisdom of God so that all can see the "mystery hidden in past ages." This mystery, Paul tells us, is the oneness of believers in Christ manifested through our relationships in the church.

When I (Nicolas) went to seminary, I discovered that even though I was surrounded by brothers in Christ of different cultures and ethnicities, I was still somehow different because of my culture and color. Interactions with my colleagues led me to believe that my culture was "liberal" and out of sync with God and His will, and their culture was "conservative" and in sync with God and His will. In the courses I took, we discussed various political or socioeconomic issues, and it was clear to me that if I did not follow the views of the status quo, the majority culture (not necessarily the Bible), I would need to check my theology for errors or question the validity of my Christianity. In conversations, helping people with physical and economic problems was labeled "the social gospel," which clearly was at odds with evangelical Christianity.

I remember going to my dorm with a sense that I was somehow different than my fellow students. There were many interactions I had with other students where the "one-anothers" of Scripture were especially hard to apply because of these misunderstandings—even though we were still all "brothers in Christ." Because I am African-American, some would try to connect with me by talking about "rap music" or "black people in sports." Some tried to connect by talking about how much they loved "fried chicken"! I saw a genuine desire to connect, but a lack of understanding of how to do so in a loving, thoughtful way. This led me to reflect on how we can be one in Christ, yet quite different in how we apply God's Word in our own particular life and cultural context. We need to keep this reality in mind as we seek to develop one-another environments in the context of a multicultural ministry. We cannot privilege one cultural perspective over another.

We must learn to value the different insights that diverse people bring to the discussion.

DEVELOPING A ONE-ANOTHER MINISTRY INTO THE VISION OF A MULTICULTURAL CHURCH

A God-honoring church should preach, promote, and provide a context for understanding and living out the "one-another Scriptures." These are Scriptures that emphasize loving one another, being kind to one another, and giving preference to one another. As we learn to live out the one-anothers of Scripture, we are better equipped to do effective evangelism and discipleship. This can take place in the larger context of a biblical counseling ministry. In what follows, I'd like to suggest some strategies to consider if you are in a multicultural church setting.

Develop a Biblical Understanding of Ethnicity

First, you will want to carefully develop a biblical understanding of ethnicity. The biblical narrative indicates that we all are descendants of the first Adam, yet there exists a wide variety of cultures and people groups that make up the single Adamic (human) race. We cannot ignore the values, tastes, and experiences of these various groups if we wish to have an effective one-anothering ministry in a multicultural church. So we should begin with a biblical understanding of race and ethnicity. Look at what the Old Testament teaches. Consider how ethnic issues and concerns are discussed in the New Testament. Evaluate the implications this might have for today, in your local church context, and get specific. Try to understand the origin and history of the people groups in your community. Highlight the creativity and the diversity God has embedded into His creation.

Acknowledge that Racism Exists in Your Community

As you develop a biblical and contextual understanding of race and ethnicity, you will need to acknowledge that racism is alive and well in your community. Racism is the result of human sin, and you will want to study the impact of racism on the people groups in your community. Evaluate how the sin of racism has progressed and spread. Learn about the impact racism has had in your community and consider hosting a time of discussion where you connect present-day relational challenges with the sin of racism. Ask people in your church how racism has impacted their life on a personal level and family level. Ask how racism has impacted their communities.

Learn to be biblical without being blind to reality. Don't minimize what people share with you, even if it is different from your own experience. Seek to promote Jesus Christ and His agenda *within* their cultural existence. Promote the powerful message of Jesus Christ while considering the context and condition of the people to whom the message is being articulated. You want to communicate without compromising the message or expressing condescension to that particular culture.

This takes practice and will likely result in many mistakes. It is a learning process. We must grow in self-awareness and learn to consider our own personal opinions, political views, media biases, and personal experiences so that we can bring them under the scrutiny of the Word of God. In addition, we should study the Scriptures to see how Jesus and His disciples engaged non-Jewish people groups to promote God's agenda without being condescending to the people they were seeking to reach.

The goal in all of this is to promote unity, but never at the expense of diversity. Ethnicity is not a barrier to inclusion among God's people. And individuals of any people group who put their trust in the person and work of Jesus Christ to save them from sin are sealed by God with the Holy Spirit and are now part of the body of Jesus Christ. We are one in Christ—yet still diverse in our cultures. And where our cultural practices do not compromise or contradict the biblical standards, there must be respect. We should not seek to "correct" practices simply because they differ from our own. Again, we should be biblical without being blind to race.

Prepare for Misunderstanding

Even with good intentions, misunderstandings will occur. Words and their meanings are misunderstood and misinterpreted. Body language is taken the wrong way. And when misunderstandings happen, we should address the offense immediately and bridge the gap of misunderstanding accordingly. Seek forgiveness for the offense and explain your intentions. Learn how to say something in a way that isn't culturally offensive, using appropriate words to articulate your message. Learn what certain gestures mean and the appropriate gestures to use. Don't run from these misunderstandings—embrace them and learn from them!

In addition, look for people who fit the biblical criteria for leadership who also have an understanding of the unique challenges of ministry in a multicultural environment. Having like-minded leadership made up of differing ethnicities brings glory to God and gives the world a wonderful picture of the God who unites us. Multiethnic leadership also says to the body that you are serious about this. Make sure that these leadership roles are real, with legitimate power and authority to make decisions and to lead, not just quotas to fill.

IN SUMMARY

We can tie everything together in this chapter by using the acronym CONNECT.

C: Consider the people you are counseling before the counseling session.

Ask questions of the people group you are seeking to counsel that will allow you to learn about the norms, the struggles, the honors, the accomplishments, or even what they would consider embarrassments. Identify the key social issues and movements that have had the greatest and the worst impact on the people group you are seeking to counsel. Explore the norms of their family structure and various other structures unique to that particular people group. Connect your information to the person(s) you are seeking to counsel from that people group.

O: Omit stereotypes knowing they can only create discord within the counseling session.

Don't take what you have learned from television or personal bias as a means to connect with the people group you are seeking to counsel. Instead, ask questions from a position of humility. Do not make assumptions and reveal pride and ignorance. For instance, don't assume that because someone is African-American, that person likes rap music, grew up in the projects, or is on welfare. This could bring unnecessary offense. Taking time to ask questions and do research on the culture will help you to counsel from a position of facts instead of presumptions.

N: Notice the central themes that need to be addressed and seek to deal with them according to Scripture.

Learn to identify the common biblical themes of sin. Look for pride, idols, lust, worry, fear, etc. Evaluate how those common themes manifest themselves within the cultural context of the people group you are seeking to counsel. Take the information and analyze it within the context of systematic and biblical theology in order to draw some conclusions on some strategic ways you can counsel that people group accordingly.

N: Notice the central themes that need to be addressed and seek to deal with them within the context of the cultural experience.

As you learn the central sin issues and the biblical solutions that address the situation, show your counselee how to apply the truth within the context of their cultural experience. For instance, think through ways a young African-American male might learn to submit to his nonbiological father (the man married to the boy's mother) and to the boy's biological father, who seeks to plant seeds of division in the mind of his young son. Think through the implications without compromising the truth.

E: Eliminate any parenting mentalities and partner with your counselee and serve accordingly.

Too often I have seen counselors connect with a people group different from their own in a condescending manner. The counselor treated the people group differently from their own people group, as if they were children in need of a parent. You must be careful not to assume that you are smarter than the people group you are seeking to counsel. You must be careful not to think you have all the answers to their problems, thereby assuming all they need to do is just shut up and listen to you as a child should listen to a parent. They just might surprise you with what they know. When seeking to counsel people from a group that is different from your own, seek to be a partner with them, not a parent to them. Seek to identify what they know about various issues of life and learn how you can serve them accordingly.

C: Confront all sin with compassion and care.

We have a saying in my church, "We don't condone sin or condemn sin, but we do confront sin with compassion and care." Sin is sin no matter what people group you are addressing. As a counselor your goal is to love people by speaking the truth in love, support people in their sufferings, and confront sin to lead individuals in the process of putting off sin, renewing the mind, and putting on righteousness. You must not be careless or condescending. You must be compassionate and caring. You cannot overlook sin out fear of being misunderstood or rejected. You must deal with it accordingly to the glory of God and the good of the individual, no matter their ethnicity.

T: Treat the counselee the way you would want to be treated.

As you are working through various issues with others, think about the way you would want to be treated and treat the person that way. Don't let ethnicity drive you in your counseling. Let love drive you. Be considerate of one's ethnicity, but don't be consumed with their ethnicity when counseling. Let the basic insights of the nature of man, sin, salvation, sanctification, and love dictate your direction with the counselee. You would not want anyone to patronize you, so don't patronize others in counseling. You would not want anyone to be inconsiderate or condescending to you, so do not do that to others in counseling. Just as you want to be loved, understood, and respected, seek to love, understand, and respect others.

We close by urging you to think less about "race" relations and more about "grace" relations. Learn to take into account differences of culture, context, and condition and to value the contributions of other ethnic groups and cultures. But do this in a way that does not minimize or maximize their unique cultural existence. Instead, seek to promote Jesus Christ and His agenda *within* their culture. Grace relations are not blind to diversity, nor does a focus on unity in Christ mean that we should ignore our real and valuable cultural differences. When we are gracious in our relationships with those of different cultures, it promotes a powerful message to the world—that the love we share in Christ values our uniqueness while bringing us together to glorify God.

CHAPTER 16

LAUNCHING AND LEADING A BIBLICAL COUNSELING MINISTRY FOR THE CHURCHES OF THE NATIONS

WAYNE VANDERWIER

For over a decade, a single question captured my heart: "Who is helping pastors to counsel?"

You see, I was a pastor. And even though counseling training had somehow been skipped in my seminary education, once I had begun pastoral ministry, God gave me a crash course in learning how to skillfully use the Scriptures to restore broken believers to the love and grace of God. Over the past decade, I had completed the process of certification with the National Association of Nouthetic Counselors (now the Association of Certified Biblical Counselors — ACBC).

I was also a teacher. God had opened doors of opportunity for me to teach biblical counseling at several Bible institutes and colleges in America. And through this teaching experience, I saw firsthand the profound impact that learning to practically apply God's Word was making in the lives of my students and in their ministries.

I should add that I was also what you would call a "missionary." During my early years of pastoral service, I was honored to travel to several nations to teach introductory college-level courses on biblical counseling.

So you can understand why I was haunted by the question, Who is helping the *pastors to counsel*, specifically pastors in other parts of the *world*, pastors who don't have ready access to training resources or seminaries? I was very aware of the blessings that those of us who live and serve Christ in America have had. Even today, the church in America continues to develop rich soul care resources like this book you are reading. Students both here and abroad are excited to learn as much as they can about biblical counseling and the personal ministry of the Word. But there remains a gap between the abundance of resources in the West and what is available to pastors elsewhere. The gap is one of training. Who is training the *pastors* in *other* parts of the world, places with little or no formal theological education, pastors with no practical theology training? Who is training them to compassionately and competently minister God's eternal truth to hurting hearts and point them back to the gracious, open arms of their loving Lord, Jesus Christ?

That simple question nagged me for over a decade. And no matter what I did, I couldn't shake it off. Eventually, after studying the Scriptures and through some God-ordained circumstances in our lives, my wife and I determined that we would be the answer to our question. We began a ministry called Overseas Instruction in Counseling (OIC) out of a desire to glorify God through the spiritual strengthening of believers and churches in the nations. Our mission statement was—and still is—*Training Biblical Counseling Trainers Around the World.*

In this chapter I want to raise this concern, help you to understand what is at stake, and give you a suggestion of how we can address it by making our own cross-cultural counseling more effective.

WHAT ARE YOU TRYING TO DO?

If God is calling you to minister through biblical counseling to people of another culture, your first task will be to determine your goal. This simple idea was impressed on us very early in the development of our ministry. We were asked to go to Russia in partnership with another US-based missions agency to conduct a series of biblical counseling training seminars. It seemed like a wonderful opportunity. But we wondered, what was the end goal? Why, ultimately, were we doing it? What did we hope to accomplish?

Not sure of the answers to these questions, I asked the director of the agency these questions, and he began wondering the same things. We thought to ourselves: Isn't it okay to just go there to train? But that didn't seem like a sufficient objective. We knew that Russian pastors might not be interested in or able to pursue a credential from an American-based organization, so directing them toward ACBC (or any other similar organization's) certification was not an option. But that line of thinking sparked a bigger goal in our minds. What if we could eventually train enough pastors in enough locations in Russia who would eventually ignite a new movement of biblical counseling. Perhaps this movement of like-minded Russian pastors would eventually be able to start their own credentialed ministry. These questions gave birth to a strategic objective: We would train pastors as a way of *assisting in the initial creation and/or continuing development of national biblical counseling training and certifying organizations.* Our goal was not just to train pastors — it was to start a national movement.

Seven Phases of Understanding

Out of this initial experience I have developed a process for thinking about the goals and purposes of biblical counseling training. The grid below (figure 8) tells my own story, and I've found that it is similar to many others from leaders in the biblical counseling movement:

The fact that you are reading this chapter means you're probably already through the early phases of this development. Perhaps your focus is now on those last two or three items on the list. What do each of these points mean, and how are they different?

Let me start by making a simple observation. *Talking about* biblical counseling (i.e., conducting a seminar or conference) is not the same

FIGURE 8
SEVEN PHASES IN OUR COUNSELING UNDERSTANDING

1. **You Discover Your Need for** ... (Biblical Counseling Training) ... Training in Biblical Sufficiency-Based Redemptive Discipleship
2. **You Learn about** ... (Biblical Counseling) ... Truly and Purely Biblical Soul Care
3. **You Train to** ... (Counsel Biblically) ... Do the Biblically Based and Personalized Ministry of Soul Restoration
4. **You Do** ... (Biblical Counseling), meaning you ... Engage in the Ministry of Using the Scriptures to Graciously Restore Broken Believers to a Vital Relationship with Jesus Christ
5. **You Talk about** ... (Biblical Counseling) ... the Impact of Practical Theology That Is Personally Applied
6. **You Train Other Believers** ... (Biblical Counselors) ... to Use the Bible to Help Their Fellow Believers with the Challenges of Life
7. **You Train Christian Leaders** ... (Biblical Counseling Trainers) ... to Train Other Christians

thing as *training* biblical counselors. And *training* biblical counselors is not the same thing as *training* biblical counseling *trainers*. There will be some places where all you can do, at least initially, is *talk about* the concept of using the Bible to address the challenges of life. That's a good place to start. And when you do that well, over time, God may eventually use those discussions to provide future opportunities for you to *train* or even to *train trainers*.

As you identify and clarify the goal of your international biblical counseling ministry, you may want to think through questions like these:

- What are the short- and long-term objectives of your biblical counseling–related ministry in other nations?
- How will you discover the expectations of those you serve? (Do they think your training will lead them to a career as a counselor?)

- How will you—or your national partner—promote this training? What will be communicated about the end result of your work?

Once your objective is clearly in mind—and in print—you must begin the process of thinking biblically about answering God's call to cross-cultural ministry. To help you in doing this, I recommend studying the stories of those who engaged in some form of cross-cultural ministry in the Scriptures. A comprehensive listing is impossible to provide here, but some obvious examples include:

- Abram traveled to an unknown foreign land.
- Joseph went from pit-dweller to prisoner to prince in a culture that was radically different from his own.
- Moses moved millions of God's people from a known and settled place to an unknown and scary place.
- Joshua later marched those millions into foreign territory to confront people who were peculiar to them in frightening ways.
- Daniel and his colleagues experienced cross-cultural education—and testing.
- Zerubbabel and others, a few generations later, returned "home" to a place significantly changed by the occupation of several generations of "others."
- The apostle Paul traveled his world to share the gospel, plant churches, and strengthen the believers.
- And Jesus, the ultimate cross-cultural missionary, left the glories of heaven to live among broken, wicked people.

In addition to biblical examples, you may want to read several missionary biographies or study the history of cross-cultural ministry and the rise of the modern missionary movement.

So What's a "Culture"?

If you've decided that God is calling you to invest your life in ministry to another culture, you will want to think more intentionally about the concept of "culture." Despite years of research and study, there is not yet a broadly agreed upon definition for the concept of "culture." We know that a person's *worldview* drives their *beliefs* and that their beliefs determine their *values*. Culture includes all of these elements, but it is a broad concept.

At a practical, experiential level, you will notice that the people you live among may look and sound different than you. They will probably do some things differently than you. They will eat—and offer to you—foods that you've not seen or tried before. But these obvious differences only begin to describe the complexity of what culture involves. The real challenge for the cross-cultural servant is to attempt to understand the ways people in this new place think, make choices, and interact with others.

Let me give you an example. Our ministry in the Philippines is done primarily in English. Because we conduct most of the ministry in English, it leads some Americans to believe that because the nationals listen to us and speak to us in our own language, they understand what we are saying. But the social, educational, and cultural grid through which they hear us makes it very unlikely that they understand what we are saying *in the same way* we understand it. Why?

First, while English may be the language of education and commerce in the Philippines, it's probably the second or third language for most Filipinos. Second, Filipino culture is collectivist (*Tayo* or *Barkada*), not individualistic. So when we say something in English with our American cultural assumptions, it gets filtered through the collectivist lens of their own culture. Third, Filipinos are event-oriented, not time-oriented. We can use the same words, but the meanings we attach to those words will vary based on our cultural understanding of time. Fourth, interpersonal relationships in the Philippines are dictated by a desire to yield to the will of the leader or majority (*Pakikisama*) and perhaps by a lifelong debt of gratitude toward a benefactor (*Utang na Loob*). Again, this sense of gratitude or the impulse to yield to leaders will influence the way we interact, the answers people share, and their experience in counseling. Fifth, in Filipino culture, the role of restoring or preserving interpersonal relationships is the work of a "go-between" (*Tagapamagitan*), a mediator. So this cultural expectation affects how they interpret the biblical counseling experience. These five illustrations are just a small sample of the larger cultural differences Americans have with this one people group.

Consider how many of these cultural distinctives might affect the way we give instruction in our personal ministry of the Word. If personal, private confrontation of sin (Matt. 18:15; Gal. 6:1) is one aspect of biblical counseling,[117] you need to be aware that you are teaching something that is directly at odds with the culture. That's not to say you should avoid confronting. It just means that you need to do it with cultural sensitivity. You cannot assume that what works in an American cultural context will work in exactly the same way in a Filipino context.

Understanding culture is even further complicated by the fact that cultural boundaries do not follow national boundaries. One of the courses in our graduate-degree curriculum is titled "cross-cultural counseling." When I shared the title of the class with a room of students during a class we were teaching in Egypt, one of our students objected. "Why do we need this? We're all Egyptians!" Thinking quickly, I asked him a question in response: "Yes," I admitted. "You are all Egyptians. But is there any difference between living in Cairo and living in Upper Egypt?" Immediately, everyone understood why they needed this class. Cairo and Upper Egypt are completely different worlds, yet they exist within the same nation. Even in a room filled with Egyptians who will be counseling other Egyptians, there is a recognized need for cross-cultural counseling skills. Case closed.

And if Upper Egypt and Lower Egypt are two different worlds, the same is true in other places as well, sometimes just a few miles away from each other. I was raised in a farming community in West Michigan, and I attended an all-white high school. Farming drove the local economy, and people in my town were religious and moral, if not always born-again evangelicals. Gerald Ford, a conservative Republican, was my congressman.

In 1981, I was called to pastor a church in Northwest Indiana in an urban, multicultural, multilinguistic area. Steel mills and unions were the basis of the local economy. Crime and political corruption were pandemic. Adam Benjamin, a liberal Democrat, was my congressman.

I had moved only slightly more than 100 miles from my hometown, but these were huge changes. I experienced a great deal of culture shock. To give you another example from our ministry in Russia, we've learned that there is no such thing as "Russian" culture. Our friends in Siberia remind us: "There are two Russias—Moscow, and everything else." The same is true in the Middle East. There is no such thing as a single "Arab culture." Lebanon and Jordan, although neighboring nations, are very different places. There is no such thing as a single "Australian culture." Life in Sydney and life in the Outback could not be more different. What's the point to all of this? It's a reminder that you cannot transfer your assumptions from one culture to another. To minister effectively you'll need to take what the Bible teaches, learn the particular nuances of the culture you are ministering to, and then interpret the Scriptures by applying them to life *in that cultural context*. There are typically three steps in this process: learn, fail, and grow.

First, you need to become aware of your own ethnocentricity, the belief that your ways of doing things are "right." For example, should Christians give to God? Yes. But what is the "right" way to collect the monetary gifts of God's people when the assembly of believers is meeting? A processional to the front? A cloth bag on the end of a stick? An offering plate? A box in the back of the room? Giving is biblical, but the method of collecting the giving is cultural. How do you learn? Reading about the experiences of others can help. I've listed some helpful books in the bibliography to get you started.

Let me also encourage you to begin the cultural learning process by doing cross-cultural ministry right where you live. Communities of people from other cultures are probably living near you and you may not even know it. Build relationships, make friends, and earn the right to be heard among "strangers."

That said, it is inevitable that you will fail. You will eventually do something that is culturally inappropriate or even potentially embarrassing. Don't worry! God will use these experiences to check your humility and humor. Failure is an essential part of the learning process. And know that as you fail and learn, you will grow. All of this is similar to the process of progressive sanctification. It's lifelong. Veteran missionaries will tell you that as helpful as it is to learn a new language, it's just a small part of the never-ending process of learning and adapting to a new culture.

WHO CAN HELP US — OVER THERE?

Let's assume that you know what you want to accomplish — you have some specific goals in mind. Let's also assume that you've started the process of learning something about the culture in the place you'd like to serve. The next step is to find and develop a national ministry partner.

Creating Ministry Partnerships

Generally speaking, American Christians tend to be quite generous and they love to support missions-related projects. But if all of the sacrifice and effort put into a ministry project is borne by one party, that's not a *partnership*. A partnership is two-way. It is a relationship between equals, each bringing their unique skills and gifts to the relationship. American churches typically assume that if they can do something, they should do it. But the question is not *can* we do it? The question is: *should* we? The issues at stake relate to two concepts — ownership and sustainability.

In our ministry, we believe that foreign nationals who request the assistance of our ministry should share in the responsibility of bringing that skill (biblical sufficiency–based counseling training) to their setting. Our OIC Partner Agreement sheet specifies what we do and what the nationals are expected to do. It is intended to be a real partnership between two equals.

WHAT WE DO

So what do we do, as a ministry? We provide teachers and teaching. Specifically, our "Associate Teachers" are responsible to provide for their transportation to the ministry location. This typically involves support discovery (fund-raising), a process that allows the instructor to include their church, their family, and their ministry colleagues in the time-and-effort investment they are making. This also generates needed prayer support from those who have financially invested in the work. In addition, we provide the general curriculum plan and sequential modular materials, i.e., what will be taught.

WHAT THEY DO

What do we ask our national partners to do? We ask our partners to provide:

- An appropriate facility, including necessary technology.
- Promotional materials that include registration instructions.
- Ground transportation (from and to the airport) for our team (usually 4–6 persons).
- Lodging and meals for our team during the period of our ministry.
- Translation (if necessary) of the printed materials. (This would include both student notes and presentations.)
- Interpretation (if necessary) of the lectures and other conversations.

This is just an example. It may not work in every situation, and the way you share the responsibilities does not have to follow our template. But the point we are making is the same: we *strongly* encourage you to involve your national partner in the work.

This means that you may need to decline invitations for ministry if the inviting group will not help to carry the load. We've experienced this problem as well. Years ago I met with a ministry leader from another nation and shared with him the responsibilities detailed above. We agreed on a ministry date a year from that time. Just two months prior to the start date of the program and, with promotional materials already disseminated, the national leader called me with a different plan. He asked if OIC would be responsible for the transportation and room-and-board of the national pastors who would be attending and if a gift book could be provided for each of them. We declined and ended up canceling the program. Why? I explained that even if we had the funding to do these things, we wouldn't. We are committed to the belief that our national partner and the attending pastors all need to have "skin in the game."

WHAT YOU SHOULD CONSIDER FOR THIS ROLE

As you consider potential partners, you should begin with doctrinal agreement. In America, most churches and ministries with a biblical counseling ministry are typically conservative evangelicals. Though the leaders of US-based biblical counseling organizations represent a wide variety of denominations, they typically coalesce around statements of faith that are very specific on some issues and very general on others. You will need to decide the degree to which disparity on theological issues is acceptable. Will the potential partner need to agree with you on eternal security? What about limited atonement? Can they have a different eschatological view than you hold? Some foreign churches may have female pastors. Will you train them?

If your goal is to do more than just *talk about* biblical counseling in one setting, you'll want to select a ministry partner who is respected and influential. Because the objective of OIC is to help establish and strengthen national biblical counseling ministries, I use this analogy: "We want to hitch our horse to the wagon that's able to carry the most weight."

God has been kind to give our ministry a variety of partner ministries. We have worked with missionary agencies, local churches, a government-approved denomination, an underground school, a biblical counseling organization (started by one of our students!), a fellowship of churches, and various Bible institutes and theological (graduate) schools. So which kind of ministry is best for partnership? Truthfully, each one is best—in their own cultural context. In fact, if we were to limit ourselves to just one "type" of partner ministry, it would severely hinder our work around the world!

So how do you find qualified ministry partners? To get started, there are two simple steps you can take. First, pray. Do you lack wisdom on this issue? Me too! But our brother James told us what to do (*ask God* ...), how God would respond (*it will be given, generously* ...), and the encouragement to do it (*there will be no reproach for asking!*) (see James 1:5). Then, after you've prayed, plan a visit. Before you commit to and schedule ministry in another culture, take (what we call) a "survey trip." This will allow you to experience the local culture, observe the potential partners in their ministry environment, and interview a variety of potential partners in various locations. These conversations will give you an opportunity to share your vision and the goals you have established, review the curriculum plan and the focus of each module, determine how often and at what intervals you will return to serve in this nation, and detail the partnership responsibilities.

Maintaining Ministry Partnerships

As is true with all relationships, ministry partnerships require continued communication and understanding. Our core values statement focuses on several of the priorities and qualities that we want to define in our relationships with our partners:

- Biblical Priorities in Our Relationships
  - Humility (Prov. 22:4; James 4:10)
  - Love (John 13:34–35; Rom. 12:10)
  - Orderliness (1 Cor. 14:40; 12:18)
- Excellence in Our Work
  - Diligence (Eccl. 9:10a; Prov. 12:24)
  - Dependability (Prov. 28:20; Matt. 25:21)
  - Enthusiasm (Rom. 12:9–11; Gal. 4:18)

- Mutual Blessing through Our Partnerships
  - Unity (Eph. 4:4–6; 1 Cor. 1:13)
  - Generosity (2 Cor. 8:9; 9:7)
  - Dependability (1 Cor. 4:2; Prov. 25:13)

In addition to these qualities, what can you do, practically, to manage and strengthen your relationship with your international partner? Let me share one example with you. In 2009, OIC, in partnership with the National Theological College and Graduate School, began a master of biblical counseling (MBC) degree program in Egypt. At the time, Hosni Mubarak was president. Two years later, the Arab Spring of 2011 led to the election of Mohamed Morsi. His tenure as president was tumultuous and short-lived. More recently, in the spring of 2014, General el-Sisi became the new president. By the time our first MBC cohort graduated in the fall of 2014, our students had endured two revolutions, the collapse of Egypt's once-thriving tourism industry, an economy on the verge of ruin, and the permanent emigration of millions of their countrymen.

These seismic cultural shifts, created by political and economic upheavals, were changes we could not ignore. We wanted to serve our students well through this period of uncertainty, so we needed to listen, to be flexible, and to respond to changes in the culture and the world around us.

PROVIDE BETWEEN-MODULE INSTRUCTION AND ENCOURAGEMENT

Another way to maintain healthy relationships with a partner is to provide instruction and encouragement between the times of ministry. This is something we stumbled on after a request from one of our groups in Siberia. Following our Module 2 program, they asked if we would return a few days early, prior to the next module, which was scheduled six months later. Why? They wanted a day or two of practical training. We did this, and we discovered that this time was tremendously valuable for them — and for us!

Because our ministry is structured as a curriculum-driven, multi-modular training program, we require "Projects for Growth" between the modules. Completion of these projects qualifies the participant to continue in the program. But after several years we discovered that our Module 1, Biblical Counseling: What Is It? (Defining a Biblical Sufficiency – Based Model of Personal Ministry), is so enthusiastically received that there are people who want to attend the second module when we return. Our answer is yes, if…

- The national partner takes the responsibility for teaching Module 1. (We're *training trainers*, right? We provide all the handouts and presentations through the partner ministry.)
- They do the Projects for Growth (to become "Module 2 qualified").
- They commit to finish the program.

In one of our locations in the Philippines, Baguio City, the partner pastor, Robbie Casas, facilitated and hosted a "Module 1 Makeup Session" meeting using the video recordings of our teaching. As a result of this diligent "between-modules" work on the part of our excellent ministry partner, our Module 1 attendance increased by twenty-two additional people in Module 2!

STAY CONNECTED THROUGH SOCIAL MEDIA AND OTHER AVAILABLE TECHNOLOGIES

While social media and other technologies can be used for nefarious purposes, they can also be pressed into the service of our King. Our graduate students in Ukraine have created a closed Facebook group to stay in touch with us and with each other. Our modular program partners in the Philippines have created and posted video clips of our training on YouTube as promotion for future events. Our work "down under" through Biblical Soul Care Australia has developed a newsletter and website for its expanding physical and electronic mailing lists. Applications like Voxer, Skype, Twitter, and GoToMeeting are just some of today's invaluable tools for communication with ministry partners between on-location training sessions.

HOW DO WE DO THIS?

Your goal is set; your commitment to cross-cultural ministry is resolute; your selected national partner is joyfully anticipating your scheduled ministry. Now you have to decide: what will you teach?

THE GOLDILOCKS SYNDROME

In the well-known children's fairy tale, Goldilocks faced some extremes — porridge that was too hot and too cold, chairs that were too big and too small, and beds that were too hard and too soft. We've seen training programs that suffer the same kinds of problems with extremes — too many sessions and too few, too academic in tone and too informal in presentation, too much between-session work and none at all. The one thing all these programs have in common is a high rate of attrition. One such program reported a dropout rate of 70 percent!

But Goldilocks always found something that was "just right." And we need to find that balance in the structure of our training programs too. Still, balance in the way we *plan* our training doesn't require compromise in the way we *do* our training. The philosophical idea popularized by Aristotle that the moral thing to do is the "mean" thing to do — neither excessive nor deficient — militates against striving for excellence. Your program should be *excessive* in the thoroughness of its preparation, the clarity of its communication, and the passion of its presentation.

Rather than imposing an Americanized "one-size-fits-all" training program onto our national partners, we need to be willing to customize our training to the unique needs of the receiving culture. This creates a lot more work but yields a much better result. As our first master of biblical counseling degree cohort in Egypt was nearing completion of the course, one of our students, a well-known and highly respected medical doctor, Yasser Farah, asked if we would partner with the biblical counseling organization he had started, New Renovare Ministries, to conduct modular training there. But in asking this, he was also asking something else—that we change our modular curriculum plan to accommodate the culture. How would we do this?

Yasser argued that even though OIC isn't a theological education ministry, our Module 1 should begin with two sessions on the Bible: the inspiration of Scripture and the inerrancy of Scripture. Why? Because the concept of verbal inspiration (and the concept of inerrancy that flows from that) is not something widely taught in Egypt. In addition, an allegorical hermeneutic has typically been taught in Egypt ever since it was developed and codified in Alexandria in the second century. Yasser reasoned that if our students didn't first get the Bible right, they wouldn't get biblical counseling right. And he was correct.

PERSONNEL AND MATERIALS

Our practice, and our strong recommendation, is that biblical counseling training be done through teams of teachers. Recruiting and preparing at least one other person for each session avoids the "cultic" feel that can creep into a program developed or taught by just one person. We prefer and encourage our OIC Associate Teachers to bring their spouse on their international ministry trip. In addition, we frequently ask those considering future ministry with OIC to take "observation trips" to personally experience biblical counseling training in a cross-cultural environment.

What materials do we bring and provide? Student handouts should be in the hands of the national partner early enough for them to translate, copy, collate, and bind the sets. (Suggestion: let the partner tell you how early is early enough.) In preparing the notes, remember:

- Most of the world uses a different paper size than the USA.
- Use a standard font and size of type. Avoid "fancy" styles.
- Documents transferred electronically often become corrupted because of the various versions of the application on which they were created.

- The notes should be in "evacuated outline" format, not manuscript.
- Avoid fill-in-the-blanks. The translator can't guess the "fill" and the syntax of the other language is probably different.
- Outlines should not be alliterated. The words you want do not all begin with the same letter in the other language.
- Avoid idiomatic expressions and figures of speech.

If you're sending visual presentations (Microsoft's PowerPoint or Apple's Keynote) for translation, remember...

- The national language should precede and be larger than the English.
- The work of translation may ruin the spacing and design you built into the slides.
- Your students will use your presentations as an English lesson!

If possible, try to point your students to biblical counseling–related resources in their own language. While there is no coordinated database of biblical counseling–related books available in various languages, OIC is working to provide information to those seeking help in this area. In languages without resources, OIC is spearheading efforts to remedy this problem. For example, through the sacrifice of hundreds of donor families and supporting churches, OIC was able to have 21 books and 35 topic-specific booklets translated into Arabic between 2010 and 2014. This investment leaves practical help in the hands of our Christian Arab brothers and sisters not only in the nations in which we work (Egypt, Lebanon, and Jordan) but also for the rest of the nations in that region as well.

CAN THIS REALLY BE DONE?

Hopefully, by this point you are excited about the possibility of launching and leading a biblical counseling training program in a cross-cultural environment. Understandably, you might be a bit nervous about taking this huge step of faith. Let me assure you: we were too! When God led us to begin OIC in 2006, we wondered...

- Will anybody even ask us to come?
- Will the Christians in America support this kind of church strengthening—not church planting—missionary work?
- Will the Christians in other nations understand and appreciate the necessity and value of this kind of soul care training?

God said, "Yes!" to all these questions. We have seen Him do what we never could have imagined.

CHAPTER 17

ETHICAL AND LEGAL ISSUES IN BIBLICAL COUNSELING IN THE CHURCH: CARING LIKE CHRIST

BOB KELLEMEN

Physicians swear an oath to "do no harm." Soul physicians commit to Christ and the body of Christ to "care like Christ." When we care like Christ, we commit to more than avoiding harm; we engage in doing much good. I find it helpful and instructive to read counseling ethical codes. I know I'm likely in the minority on this. In the vast majority of these, they choose to highlight all of the boundaries that *must not* be crossed and everything a counselor must *not* do. The emphasis is typically on the negative vices to avoid, and they fail to mention what a counselor should positively pursue. And while it is wise, good, and necessary to outline what *not* to do (and I have included examples in this chapter), we cannot stop there.

Jesus, in instructing us in how to care for His sheep, told us what *not* to do as well. But He did not stop there. After stating the negative, He would add the word "instead ..." In teaching His disciples about humble service, Jesus illustrated what they should avoid—arrogant, dictatorial leadership—but then He went on to teach them the positive virtue to pursue instead—servant leadership:

> You know that the rulers of the Gentiles lord it over them, and their high officials exercise authority over them (negative vice to avoid). *Not so with you. Instead,* whoever wants to become great among you must be your servant, and whoever wants to be first must be your slave—just as the Son of Man did not come to be served, but to serve, and to give his life as a ransom for many (positive virtue to pursue).
>
> Matthew 20:25–28, parentheses and emphasis added

Jesus would often follow this pattern: *Don't do this, but instead be this.*

Perhaps learning from his teacher and Lord, Peter also follows this pattern in his letters. While equipping his fellow elders, Peter exhorts them not to lord it over those entrusted to them, *but instead* to be examples to the flock. He urges them not to be greedy for money, *but instead* to be eager to serve. He encourages his fellow shepherds not to serve out of compulsion, *but instead* to be humbly willing to serve as God calls them to do (1 Peter 5:1–5). As Christ emphasized His own servanthood as *the* model to follow, so also Peter points to Christ as the ultimate example of the servant leader—be shepherds who serve those under your care by following after the model of the Great Servant Shepherd.

Peter's teaching mirrors the Old Testament focus on God's shepherds caring for God's sheep. In Ezekiel 34, the Sovereign Lord says, "Woe to the shepherds of Israel who only take care of themselves! Should not shepherds take care of the flock?" (Ezek. 34:2). And the rest of this passage then provides us with a litany of *instead* instructions. What ought shepherds and church-wide counseling/shepherding ministries offer to God's flock? Instead of harshly and brutally ruling over them (Ezek. 34:4), we should care for the sheep like the Great Shepherd did by strengthening the weak, healing the sick, binding up the injured, bringing back the strays, searching for the lost, looking after the flock, tending them in good pasture, and by shepherding the flock with justice (Ezek. 34:4–16).

The Bible is careful to tell us what not to do. But we dare not stop with "doing no harm." Biblical ethics and Christlike loving care require a heart-motivated commitment to doing great good as well.

CARE CAREFULLY BY CARING LIKE CHRIST

In my consulting, I have found that it is easy for churches to fall into one of two extremes regarding the ethical and legal issues surrounding biblical counseling. On one extreme we see churches that retreat in paranoia because they fear lawsuits. Ethical and legal concerns are the unspoken elephants in the room, and fears motivate church leaders to squelch emerging biblical counseling ministries. At the other extreme, you will find churches that ignore ethical and legal issues. In so doing, they place at risk their church, their counseling ministry, and, most importantly, the people to whom they minister.

Rather than fearing legal and ethical concerns or ignoring them, we should seek to understand and embrace them as shadows of the higher ethical values we find in God's law. *We obey the law of God and the law of the land in the fear of God and not the fear of man.* As shepherding biblical counselors, God calls us to be ethical, not as a legalistic obligation, but as a part of our ever deepening relationship with God in Christ. Thus, biblical counseling standards seek to help us to apply the message of Christ's gospel of grace to our counseling ministry. "Whatever happens, conduct yourselves in a manner worthy of the gospel of Christ" (Phil. 1:27).

The Law of Love

It is no accident that Paul links the law of the land and the law of love in Romans 13. Paul teaches us to submit ourselves to God-established authorities, to the law of the land (Rom. 13:1–7). Then, in the very next breath, Paul writes about the law of God—the law of love. "Let no debt remain outstanding, except the continuing debt to love one another, for he who loves his fellowman has fulfilled the law" (Rom. 13:8). Paul explains that "whatever other commandment[s] there may be, are summed up in this one rule: 'Love your neighbor as yourself.' Love does no harm to its neighbor. Therefore love is the fulfillment of the law" (Rom. 13:9b–10).

Paul is simply building upon Christ's ministry. Jesus reserves His most scathing judgment for ministers who abuse their power by abusing those to whom they minister. His list of woes to unethical, unloving shepherds in Matthew 23:1–39 should cure every ministry leader of a lax attitude toward ministry relational standards. Jesus warns of certain and severe judgment for anyone who mistreats the little child (Matt. 18:1–9) or fails to minister to the lost sheep (Matt. 18:10–14). Jesus and Paul contrast the hireling and the true shepherd, the savage wolves and the good shepherds, the true apostle and the false apostle (John 10:1–21; Acts 20:13–38; 2 Cor. 10:1–12:21). Paul and Peter, in outlining the requirements of God's shepherds, highlight godly character and ethical conduct (1 Tim. 3:1–16; 1 Peter 5:1–5).

These specific law-of-love requirements flow from the most foundational requirement of God. "And what does the LORD require of you? To act justly and to love mercy and to walk humbly with your God" (Mic. 6:8). Even more importantly, all ethical ministry behavior flows ultimately from the very character of God. "But just as he who called you is holy, so be holy in all you do; for it is written: 'Be holy, because I am holy'" (1 Peter 1:15–16). This God-like holiness has specific life, ministry, and relationship application. In the same text, Peter writes, "Now that you have purified yourselves by obeying the truth so that you have sincere love for your brothers, love one another deeply, from the heart" (1 Peter 1:22).

Why do I begin here? Because it is important for church leaders and biblical counselors to understand that practicing ethical and legal wisdom in ministry is nothing less than being Christlike. It is assuring that every possible safeguard is in place so that the hurting people we minister to are not harmed, *but instead* helped, served, and cared for carefully. It is making sure that our biblical counseling ministry fulfills God's law of love. When we do that, while fulfilling the law of the land may still be necessary, it will likely be undemanding in comparison.

As you read this chapter, my hope is that you will learn that while we must take the law of the land seriously, we must take even more seriously God's law of love that demands that we not only do no harm, but that we care like Christ. God's law of love holds us to a higher standard of counseling ethics than any law of the land ever could—caring like Christ. The ultimate goal of following ethical (the law of love) and legal (the law of the land) standards is not simply protecting the church from lawsuits, but ensuring that our ministries and ministers remain above reproach, and, much more importantly, protecting the sheep from harm by caring like the Great Shepherd.

With these goals in mind, we'll explore the following three overarching aspects of caring carefully:

- The Qualification of the Caregiver: Be Comprehensively Equipped to Care like Christ
- The Scope of Care: Communicate Honestly and Accurately about Your Ministry
- The Quality of Care: Building Safeguards into Your Ministry

I should also add, as we get started, that I am not a legal expert. Don't take this chapter as equivalent to legal counsel for your church or ministry. I provide this chapter simply as a synopsis of best practices. I encourage you, if you are reading this, to take responsibility to talk with a qualified and informed lawyer and to remain current on this, as legal interpretations change over time. I also encourage churches to contract with an attorney who is an expert on the pertinent laws in their state, as laws vary from state to state. At minimum, churches should maintain and provide malpractice and liability insurance that covers the church, its pastors, trustees, and elected leaders, and those trained in the biblical counseling ministry. I encourage churches to follow both the law of the land and the even higher law of love. The nature of your training ministry (informal one-another ministry or more formal biblical counseling) will play a significant role in how you may need to address these issues.[118] With these considerations in mind, let's begin with the qualifications of the caregiver.

THE QUALIFICATION OF THE CAREGIVER

When I state that there are qualifications for giving care, some might wonder, "Doesn't the Bible say that every member is a minister? Aren't we all counselors, called to engage in one-another ministry?" These are fair questions. When the Bible talks about every member ministering by speaking the truth in love, it does so in the context of pastors and teachers preparing and equipping God's people for works of service (Eph. 4:11 – 16). It is understood that those who lack spiritual maturity and fail to demonstrate Christlikeness are not prepared to speak the truth in love (Eph. 4:13). Those who are infants in biblical knowledge and who are tossed back and forth by every wind of doctrine are not prepared to speak the truth in love (Eph. 4:14).

When Paul talks about brothers and sisters being competent to counsel, he does so in the context of maturing believers who are full of goodness and complete in knowledge (Rom. 15:14). The one-another ministry that Paul calls the believers to in Romans 15 – 16 presupposes that these brothers and sisters are growing in the grace and knowledge of the Lord Jesus Christ — qualifications for caregiving.

Like Ephesians 4 and Romans 15, Galatians 6 is a third "non-professional" setting. Paul writes, "Brothers, if someone is caught in a sin, *you who are spiritual* should restore him gently. But *watch yourself*, or you also may be tempted" (Gal. 6:1, emphasis added). Paul makes it clear that brotherly restoration requires the growing spiritual maturity that comes from consistent self-counsel.

So whether we are sitting down at a Starbucks and offering informal one-another care or sitting across from a counselee and sharing formal biblical counsel — all Christian caregiving requires qualification.[119] The question is, "What résumé qualifications demonstrate our eligibility to be caregivers who care like Christ?" Fortunately, in Romans 15:14, the apostle Paul has already completed the biblical counselor's résumé. "I myself am convinced, my brothers, that you yourselves are full of goodness, complete in knowledge and competent to instruct one another." In this verse, the surrounding context, and other biblical passages we discover the four résumé qualifications of a qualified biblical counselor (see table 3).

For the biblical counselor, Christlike character (application of gospel wisdom to our lives), biblical content (rich knowledge of God's Word), counseling relational competence (sharing Scripture and soul with others), and Christian community (embedded in a 24/7 relationship with Christ and the body of Christ) all unite to qualify us to minister to one another.

TABLE 3
THE FOUR DIMENSIONS OF COMPREHENSIVE
BIBLICAL COUNSELING QUALIFICATION

Christlike *Character:*	"Full of Goodness"	Heart/Being
Biblical *Content*/Conviction:	"Complete in Knowledge"	Head/Knowing
Counseling *Competence:*	"Competent to Instruct"	Hands/Doing
Christian *Community:*	"Brothers/One Another"	Home/Loving[120]

Character in Biblical Counseling: Christlike Character—A Call to Integrity

Competent biblical counselors have résumés with "full of goodness" as their first qualification. "Goodness" is the same word Paul uses in Galatians 5:22–23 as one of the nine aspects of the fruit of the Spirit. When I first read Romans 15:14, I wondered why Paul would pick the fruit of goodness. Why not love, joy, peace, or any other fruit of the Spirit?

So I explored goodness. The Old Testament highlights the basic confession that God *is* good because His love endures forever (1 Chron. 16:34). It also emphasizes that our good God *does* good (Ex. 18:9). That is, He displays His goodness in active social relationships. Further, I noted Christ's statement that only God is good (Matt. 19:17). Then I noticed the linkage of goodness and godliness with god-likeness—with *Christlikeness* (Matt. 5:43–48; Eph. 2:10; Col. 1:10). In each of these passages, goodness displays itself in active, grace-oriented relationships, as when our good Father causes His sun to shine on and His rain to fall on the righteous and the unrighteous.

William Hendriksen, in his commentary on Galatians, explains that goodness is a virtue that reveals itself in social relationships; in our various contacts and connections with others.[121] Theologian and linguist Walter Gundmann demonstrates that biblical goodness always displays itself in relational contexts through undeserved kindness.[122] Thus, in Romans 15:14, Paul is talking about *Christlike character* that relates with grace. The powerful biblical counselor reflects the ultimate Biblical Counselor — Jesus. We are qualified counselors to the degree that we reflect the loving character of Christ. Paul is teaching us that the competent biblical counselor is the person who relates well, who connects deeply, who is compassionate, and who has the ability to develop intimate grace relationships.

We often talk about Christlikeness in ways that are vague and general. But the Bible makes it more practical and realistic. Christlikeness is our inner life increasingly reflecting the inner life of Christ. In my book *Gospel-Centered Counseling*, I developed a biblical portrait of our inner life as relational, rational, volitional, and emotional.[123] Based on that biblical understanding, I identified four marks of Christlike character that every biblical counselor must cultivate.

FIGURE 9
FOUR MARKS OF CHRISTLIKE CHARACTER THAT EVERY BIBLICAL COUNSELOR MUST CULTIVATE

1. **Relating like Christ:** Loving God and Others Passionately
2. **Thinking like Christ:** Renewing My Mind to View Life from God's Eternal Perspective
3. **Choosing like Christ:** Dying to Self and Living Sacrificially for Others
4. **Feeling like Christ:** Facing Life Honestly and Managing My Moods Biblically

Christ's caregiving law of love is a call to integrity—maturing Christlike character. If we are going to care carefully by caring like Christ, then we need to cultivate the character of Christ.

Conviction in Biblical Counseling: Biblical Content— A Call to Wisdom

Paul lists "complete in knowledge" as the second qualification on the biblical counselor's résumé. "Complete" does not suggest that we become walking biblical encyclopedias with absolute knowledge of all theological truth. Instead, by "complete" Paul means that we become so filled with God's Word that it claims our entire being and stamps our whole life, conduct, attitude, and relationships. We are captured by God's truth.

Paul could have chosen any of several words that highlight content or factual knowledge alone. Instead he chooses a word for knowledge that highlights the combination of information and transformation. Paul's word focuses on insight and wisdom—the wisdom to relate truth to life. Competent biblical counselors understand how to apply God's Word first to their own life. They also have the insight to see how God's Word relates to their friend's life. Additionally, they have the biblical vision to see how God is relating to their friend. They have discernment to see life from God's perspective.

Ethical training in biblical counseling should seek to equip biblical counselors with the wisdom to relate biblical truth to people's daily lives and relationships—changing lives with Christ's changeless truth. In *Gospel-Centered Counseling*, I outlined and developed eight ultimate life questions that every biblical counselor must address.

While others may craft a different outline of required biblical content/conviction, it is clear that Christ's caregiving law of love is a call to wisdom—biblical truth applied to life with grace. If we are going to care carefully by caring like Christ, then we need to develop the mind of Christ.

FIGURE 10
EIGHT ULTIMATE LIFE QUESTIONS THAT EVERY BIBLICAL COUNSELOR MUST ADDRESS

- The Word: "Where do we find wisdom for life in a broken world?"
- The Trinity/Community: "What comes into our mind when we think about God?"
- Creation: "Whose are we?"
- Fall: "What's the root source of our problem?
- Redemption: "How does Christ bring us peace with God?" "How does Christ change people?"
- Church: "Where can we find a place to belong and become?"
- Consummation: "How does our future destiny with Christ make a difference in our lives today as saints who struggle against suffering and sin?"
- Sanctification: "Why are we here?" "How do we become like Jesus?"

Competence in Biblical Counseling: Counseling Competence—A Call to Excellence

Paul says that the typical Christians in Rome with character and conviction are qualified or "competent to instruct." The word "competent" means to have the power to accomplish a mission, the power necessary to fulfill God's call to minister to one another. "Competent" also means to have the ability, capability, resources, and strength to function and relate well. Paul is confident that believers can be relationally competent in Christ.

Powerfully competent to do what? Powerful to "instruct" (*nouthetein*). Jay Adams, Founder of the National Association of Nouthetic Counselors (NANC) (now the Association of Certified Biblical Counselors), describes nouthetic counseling as confronting for change out of concern.[124] "Instruct" contains this nuance, especially when the proposed change emphasizes inner heart change leading to relational change. In fact, the foundational meaning of *noutheteo* comes from the root *noeo*, meaning to direct one's mind, to perceive, and from *nous*—the mind, heart, seat of spiritual, rational, and moral insight and action. The mind is the place of practical reason leading to moral action. The stress is not merely on the intellect but also on the will and disposition. *Noutheteo* means to impart understanding, to set right, to lay on the heart. Nouthetic impartation of truth can take on many forms, such as encouraging, urging, spurring on, teaching, reminding, admonishing, reconciling, guiding, and advising.

Paul never intended Romans 15:14 to be the final or only word on the nature of biblical counseling. Nor did he use *noutheteo* as the only or even the primary concept to describe the personal ministry of the Word. For instance, in 1 Thessalonians 5:14, Paul uses five distinct words for biblical counseling. "And we urge (*parakaleo*) you, brothers, warn (*noutheteo*) those who are idle, encourage (*paramutheomai*) the timid, help (*antechomai*) the weak, be patient with (*makrothumeo*) everyone" (parentheses added).

Among the many New Testament words for spiritual care, *parakaleo* predominates. Whereas *noutheteo* occurs eleven times in the New Testament, *parakaleo* (comfort, encourage, console) appears 109 times. In 2 Corinthians 1:3–11, Paul informs us that we are competent to comfort (*parakaleo*) one another. Those who have humbly received God's comfort, God equips to offer comfort to others.

The word *parakaleo* emphasizes personal presence (one called alongside to help) and suffering with another person. It seeks to turn desolation into consolation through hope in God. The duty of comfort in Old and New Testament thinking fell not on professional helpers, but on close relatives, neighbors, friends, and colleagues. Comforters come alongside to help struggling, suffering people through personal presence coupled with scriptural insight.

When Christ ascended, He sent the Holy Spirit to be our *Parakletos*—our Comforter and Advocate called alongside to encourage and help in times of suffering, trouble, grief, injustice, and hardship. The Spirit performs His ministry by being in us and by revealing truth to us (John 14:16–17).

The Spirit's name is "Encourager" and "Advocate," and His strategy is to speak the truth in love about our justification and acceptance in Christ.

Our end goal is to become competent to care like Christ—the Wonderful Counselor. In another of my books, *Gospel Conversations*, I outline *parakaletic* biblical counseling as counseling focused on sustaining and healing people facing suffering and moving toward sanctification. And I outline *nouthetic* biblical counseling as reconciling and guiding people battling sin and moving toward sanctification. Each area of counseling has counseling competencies associated with it.

FIGURE 11
FOUR CORE RELATIONAL COMPETENCIES THAT EVERY BIBLICAL COUNSELOR MUST DEVELOP

- Sustaining Competencies for *Parakaletic* Biblical Counseling
- Healing Competencies for *Parakaletic* Biblical Counseling
- Reconciling Competencies for *Nouthetic* Biblical Counseling
- Guiding Competencies for *Nouthetic* Biblical Counseling

While you will craft a different outline of required biblical counseling competencies, it is clear that Christ's caregiving law of love is a call to excellence—the competence to care like Christ to help people to become like Christ as they face suffering and sin. If we are going to care carefully by caring like Christ, then we need to mature in our ability to shepherd others like Christ.

CHRISTIAN COMMUNITY: CONNECTING IN JESUS—A CALL TO COMMUNITY

Every word Paul has written about competent biblical counselors he has penned in the plural—"brothers," "one another," "you yourselves." Qualified biblical counselors live and grow together in community as they commune with Christ and connect with the body of Christ.

Paul sandwiches his words in Romans 15:14 around a one-another community context. In Romans 12:3 – 8, he writes of each member belonging to all the others and of using gifts in the context of the body of Christ. In Romans 12:9 – 21, the context reflects one-anothering. Be devoted to one another in love. Honor one another. Share with one another. Practice hospitality with one another. Rejoice with one another. Weep with one another. Live in harmony with one another.

In Romans 13, the context is loving one another: "Whatever other commandment there may be, are summed up in this one rule: 'Love your neighbor as yourself.' Love does no harm to its neighbor. Therefore love is the fulfillment of the law" (13:9 – 10). Paul continues his one-anothering theme in Romans 14:1 – 15:13. Don't judge one another; instead mutually edify each other. Bear with one another. Please one another. Build up one another. Be united with one another. Encourage one another. Accept one another. Worship with one another.

In Romans 16, Paul writes about meeting together with one another in house churches where believers connect intimately. Connecting in community is the context, before and after Romans 15:14. Effective training in biblical counseling is learned in community. Put another way, growth in character, content, and competence occurs in the context of community. We become effective biblical counselors by giving and receiving biblical counseling in community.

According to Paul, transformed lives occur as we connect together in the body of Christ (Rom. 12:3 – 16:27) *and* as we connect with Christ (Rom. 12:1 – 2). Conformity to Christ is the result of communion with Christ (2 Cor. 3:16 – 18; 4:16 – 18). Effective biblical counselors add another important qualification to their résumé: connection in community.

FIGURE 12
TWO KINDS OF CHRISTIAN COMMUNITY THAT EVERY BIBLICAL COUNSELOR MUST PARTICIPATE IN

- Communion with Christ: Our Vertical Relationship
- Communion with the Body of Christ: Our Horizontal Relationship

THE SCOPE OF CARE: COMMUNICATING HONESTLY AND ACCURATELY ABOUT YOUR MINISTRY

An important law-of-the-land and law-of-love issue that biblical counseling ministries must address is informed consent. Technically, informed consent means that the caregiver has a duty to disclose fairly the scope and nature of the care provided and alternative modes of care so that the person seeking care can make an informed voluntary decision. Adequacy of disclosure is judged by what a reasonable person would want to know to make that informed decision.[125]

Practically speaking, this means that in our biblical counseling ministries, we need to communicate honestly and accurately who we are, what we are offering, and what we are *not* offering. We never hold out ourselves to be more than we are trained and qualified to be. In *Equipping Counselors for Your Church*, you will find sample informed consent forms. One form states, in part:

> I have been informed that the spiritual care I will be receiving from _____ (Name of Biblical Counselor) at _____ (Name of Church), is Christian and biblical in nature. I have also been informed that _____ (Name of Biblical Counselor) is an encourager and discipler trained at _____ (Name of Church) as a biblical counselor and spiritual friend in the church's Biblical Counseling Ministry. Under supervision from one of the biblical counseling trainers, _____ (Name of Biblical Counselor) offers to provide biblical encouragement and discipleship on personal and relational matters from a spiritual perspective guided by biblical principles. He/she is *not* trained, authorized, or licensed to provide professional counseling, psychological treatment, or psychological diagnosis. I understand that if I request professional counseling, then I will be provided with a resource list. I give my consent to _____ (Name of Biblical Counselor)

to discuss any and all of the information that I talk about in our meetings with his/her supervisor(s) in the Biblical Counseling Ministry.[126]

Clearly Communicate Who You Are

Consent forms should carefully label the type of care being offered. In the sample above, *biblical counselor* is the primary label chosen and defined. It is supported by other terms, such as *spiritual friend, encourager, discipler, soul care,* and *spiritual direction.* Second, the sample uses terms like *ministry* and *church* to highlight the non-licensed, spiritual nature of the help offered.

Practitioners in best practice churches often debate whether or not to use, in any form, with any modifiers, the term "counseling" or "counselor." Some people choose to avoid terms such as "lay counselor" or "biblical counselor" because of the possibility of someone mistaking this non-professional, non-licensed counseling for professional licensed counseling. Instead, they choose other legitimate words and descriptions used in the Bible and/or in church history—words with less potential for causing confusion in the mind of the person seeking care. Others strongly desire to claim/reclaim the mantle and label of "biblical counselor," seeing it as a legitimate scriptural description that the church should not allow the world to usurp. They then carefully explain what they mean and do not mean by their terms.

Whatever term you use, never label your biblical counselors as something they are not trained to do. Regardless of which term you choose, the vital issue is how you describe and define your terms.

Clearly Communicate What You Offer and What You Do Not Offer

A central aspect of defining your label involves stating what goals you aim to address and what goals you do *not* aim to address. What is the scope and nature of the care you are offering? Your *consent form* should outline specifically what you mean by *biblical counseling.* It should clearly distinguish between what is offered and what is not offered, what the biblical counselor/spiritual friend is and is *not* qualified to do. From the example above:

> The biblical counselor offers to provide biblical encouragement and disciple-ship on personal and relational matters from a spiritual perspective guided by biblical principles. He/she is *not* trained, authorized, or licensed to provide professional counseling, psychological treatment, or psychological diagnosis.

Quality of Care: Building Safeguards into Your Ministry

We can compare scope of care and quality of care in a nontechnical, nonlegal sense:

- Scope of Care: Claim to Do Only What You Are Trained to Do
- Quality of Care: Do with Integrity and Propriety What You Claim to Do

In terms of legal theory, quality of care relates to negligence and/or malpractice. George Ohlschlager sees overlap in negligence and mal-practice; even the definitions he provides are similar. Malpractice is an act or omission by a professional practitioner in the treatment of a patient or client that is inconsistent with the reasonable care or skill usually demonstrated by ordinary, prudent practitioners of the same profession, similarly situated.[127] Negligence can be defined as an act or omission to act which was unreasonable in light of an established duty of care, which was breached, resulting in harm of another.[128] There are four elements of a negligence suit:

- *Duty of Care:* The caregiver's responsibility to ensure the safety and welfare of the person receiving care.
- *Breach of Duty:* The caregiver either does something he/she should not do (for example, sexual involvement with a counselee) or does not do something he/she should have done (for example, failure to refer when necessary or failure to inform a third party in danger of harm from the counselee).
- *Injury:* Harm done to a person's physical or mental well-being,

reputation, pride, rights and privileges (lawsuits in this area may include issues related to church discipline and public disclosure of information).

- *Proximate Cause:* The counselor's breach of duty of care was the proximate (or direct) cause of the injury.[129]

While these matters can seem technical and even intimidating, they involve practical and necessary safeguards. Seven pertinent issues summarize the quality-of-care matters that every biblical counseling ministry should address: propriety, humility, referral, confidentiality, church discipline, documentation, and supervision.

Propriety in Biblical Counseling Ministry

We have all heard the horror stories of sexual involvement between a counselor and a counselee. Obviously, the motivation for safeguarding this area must be much greater than simply avoiding a lawsuit. Propriety should be motivated by our desire to honor God and to minister in healthy, helpful ways to hurting, vulnerable people. Safeguards include the following:

- Perform Background Checks on All Biblical Counselors: This is increasingly a common, necessary, and expected practice in all church ministries.
- Do Not Allow Counseling Sessions Off Premises
- Require All Counseling Sessions to Meet in a Building When Others Are Nearby
- Require That Counseling Sessions Meet in Rooms That Have Doors with Windows: While this can be problematic in some buildings, it is worth the cost.
- Discourage Mixed Gender Sessions without a Third Person Present: Have a trainee or staff member present.[130]

These safeguards protect everyone. Of course, we want to protect the hurting person in need of trustworthy care. We also want to protect the caregiver. All it takes is one false accusation or one moment of succumbing to temptation to destroy a person's reputation, family, and ministry.

Humility in Biblical Counseling

God's Word commands us not to think more highly of ourselves than we ought, but rather to think of ourselves with sober judgment according to our gifting and training (Rom. 12:3; 15:14). We all have limits and limitations. Thus, we should never allow any of our biblical counselors (or ourselves) to counsel beyond their competence, ability, or training. A detailed intake policy and procedure (see *Equipping Counselors for Your Church*) provides a safeguard so that the person needing care is assigned to a person qualified to care for that individual with that specific issue.

We should never give cross-disciplinary advice — advice related to any profession for which we are not trained, such as law, medicine, and psychiatry. Regarding medications or physical issues, defer and refer to qualified medical personnel. It is a wise best practice to maintain a consulting relationship with trusted medical professionals. Those who lead the biblical counseling ministry need to have access to other pastors, counselors, and educators with whom they can confer and consult.

Seeking certification from national biblical counseling ministries for yourself, your other biblical counselors, and/or for your biblical counseling ministry can be another sign of humility. It communicates that you are part of a group larger than yourself. It typically provides opportunities for outside continuing education, and it often offers collegial relationships and supervisory connections.

Referral and Biblical Counseling Ministry

Referral is one specific way that we demonstrate humility in biblical counseling. No one is equipped to minister to everyone. No training program has the time to equip trainees for every possible issue. Your informed consent form should list the areas where your ministry will focus. Counseling issues outside those areas should be referred to others with pertinent expertise. It is imperative that your ministry identifies professional resources to refer people to when issues arise beyond the competency of your team.

Related to referral are the issues of wrongful termination, abandonment, and follow-up care. The duty of care operates continually until the counseling relationship is validly terminated. If the counselee desires continued counseling, but the counselor believes that ongoing counseling would no longer be effective, then the counselor is responsible to recommend an appropriate referral.

Ideally, the decision to end counseling should be made mutually. If the decision is made because the initial issues that brought the person to counseling have been satisfactorily addressed, then the final counseling session should address a summary of the initial goals, a summary of the growth resulting from the meetings, insight concerning any unresolved areas, suggestions for further growth (including appropriate follow-up care), and the reasons for concluding counseling. Counselees should know that if an issue returns or new issues develop, they are invited to contact your offices again. Often it is helpful to schedule another appointment three months (or a mutually determined time) later for a "check-in/check-up."

Confidentiality in Biblical Counseling Ministry

Like each of the quality-of-care issues, confidentiality has legal meanings as well as biblical/ethical implications. In the legal realm, most states do not recognize a confidentiality privilege for lay biblical counselors who are not pastors. Privileged communication is codified in the law and means that a minister acting in his professional capacity as a spiritual adviser cannot be forced to reveal the content of confidential communications to any outside party, including a court of law. Confidentiality, on the other hand, is an ethical decision not to reveal what is learned in the context of a professional relationship, and it does not have legal protection.[131]

Our focus is on the ethical and relational nature of confidentiality in biblical counseling and on a counselee's expectation of confidential communication. Each biblical counseling ministry must develop clear organizational policies. These policies need to be in writing, explained to the counselee at the start of counseling, and signed. Here is one sample statement:

> Confidentiality is an important aspect of the biblical counseling relationship, and we will carefully guard the information you entrust to us. All communications between you and our Biblical Counseling offices will be held in strict confidence, unless you (or a parent in the case of a minor) give authorization to release this information. The exceptions to this would be: (1) if a person expresses intent to harm himself/herself or someone else; (2) if there is evidence or reasonable suspicion of abuse against a minor child, elder person, or dependent adult; (3) if a subpoena or other court order is received directing the disclosure of information; (4) if/when our biblical counselors consult with their supervisor; or (5) if a person persistently refuses to renounce a particular sin (habitual unrepentant rebellion against the Word of God) and it becomes necessary to seek the assistance of others in the church to encourage repentance, restoration, and reconciliation (Matthew 18:15–20 and our Church Discipline Policy). Please be assured that our counselors strongly prefer not to disclose personal information to others, and they will make every effort to help you find ways to resolve a problem as privately as possible.

Some people assume that discussing and signing a policy like this would have a chilling effect on a person's willingness to share personal information. However, every legitimate counseling organization and ministry will have such a statement, so counselees will not find this out of the ordinary. By discussing this openly at the outset, you put counselees at ease.

Church Discipline and Biblical Counseling Ministry

As noted in the confidentiality statement, church discipline is one of the exceptions to confidentiality. The potential legal ramifications include invasion of privacy, defamation of character, publication of private facts, and infliction of emotional distress.[132] Biblically, God's Word contains guidelines designed to restore errant believers by bringing them to repentance and reconciliation with Christ and the body of Christ (within or outside the context of a formal biblical counseling ministry).

Within the context of biblical counseling, counselees frequently bring to counseling their struggles to overcome besetting sins. Struggling against sin is not a cause for increased levels of church discipline intervention. However, persistent refusal to renounce a particular sin (habitual unrepentant rebellion against the Word of God) can lead to the initiation of a church restoration/discipline process.

Churches should create a written Church Discipline Policy (see *Equipping Counselors for Your Church*). It should be discussed with and signed by every new member, and it should be read at least once a year at an official church meeting. The policy should clearly spell out the biblical principles and practices, the spiritual motivations and goals, and the step-by-step process to which every member agrees to adhere.

To date, case law seems to support a church's right to discipline members who have agreed to such discipline as part of the membership process. However, when members under discipline remove themselves from membership, at least some case law suggests that this withdraws the person's consent to participate in a spiritual relationship. Therefore, disciplinary actions no longer have First Amendment protection.[133] Some would suggest that you discipline only members.[134] Others would suggest that the church discipline policy explain that resignation from membership after the initiation of church discipline does not void the church's responsibility to carry on the church discipline process.[135]

If a counselee evidences continued unrepentant rebellion, it is essential that the church restoration/discipline policy be followed carefully. Each step of the process should be documented. If the process continues to the step of public discipline, the discipline announcement should be discreetly shared at a members-only meeting.

Documentation and Biblical Counseling

Documentation serves both to organize the ministry and to assist in caring carefully. If scope-of-care or quality-of-care issues arise, it will be extremely helpful if you have carefully documented the *training* that those in your biblical counseling ministry receive. Maintain a basic outline of your training structure, have available copies of your training materials, and keep copies of your completed evaluations of trainees.

Counselors should also document each counseling relationship with basic case notes. Case notes should include the name of the person seen, the date, the session number, a review of the previous session, goals for the current session, an in-session summary, a listing of post-session homework, and the next meeting date and time. On the back of this form, include a treatment plan that matches your training model. In this way, all record-keeping stays consistent with the training received. In case notes, do not use psychological labels and diagnostic categories. The use of such labels could be perceived as movement away from spiritual care to psychological and even licensed counseling.

Keep these records on site in a secure location—they should never leave the building. There is no clear, uniform standard for how long to keep such records. Best practice ministries tend to keep them for three years, after which they are destroyed.

CONCLUSION: CARE CAREFULLY, CARE LIKE CHRIST

Though it should go without saying, I'll conclude by adding that all lay biblical counselors should be supervised by qualified individuals. As part of supervision, the supervisor should discuss all counseling evaluation forms completed during the final session, and these evaluations should be maintained. You should also document and keep records of all continuing education.

I realize that many of us would rather not think about these legal and ethical issues. However, we must deal with the law of the land to which God commands us to submit and with the law of love that God commands us to obey. God calls us to be prudent in regard to our responsibilities to abide by and respect the law. And He calls us to be loving and above reproach as we minister to His people. By carefully thinking through the legal and ethical issues related to biblical counseling, you honor God and care for the people who come to you, seeking help in their time of need.

PART 5

BIBLICAL COUNSELING AND OUTREACH

CHAPTER 18

BIBLICAL COUNSELING AND EVANGELISM

KEVIN CARSON AND RANDY PATTEN

Evangelizing lost people in a counseling session has been compared to fishing in a barrel. That is, many of the obstacles have been removed and the opportunities for success are great. What are the obstacles to evangelism? They often include things like a lack of relationship, an appropriate opportunity, and sufficient time for follow-up discussion. In biblical counseling each of these hindrances is overcome, and there are often opportunities to present the claims of Jesus Christ in a meaningful way. By God's grace, when we are faithful in sowing the seed of the gospel and watering it, there is life-transforming repentance and conversion.

That is what happened to Johnny and Diane. They married shortly after Johnny graduated from college with a degree in engineering and soon moved to the city where I (Randy) was serving as pastor. There were many stressors in their lives, some predictable, but a few that were unique to them. They had the typical challenges of being in a new city: finding your way around in unfamiliar territory, loneliness due to living far away from all family and friends, long and stressful hours at a new job, and long and boring hours at home alone while your husband is at work. But what made their circumstances particularly challenging were their ethnic differences. You see, Johnny came from an Asian heritage, while Diane was born and raised in the Deep South of the United States. Their cultural differences presented some unique challenges, including questions about the spiritual side of life. Johnny was fairly indifferent to spiritual matters, while Diane longed for the warmth and friendliness of the church she had attended as a child.

As they struggled through this, they felt led to seek God's blessing on their life. But how? And where? They chose to go to a church close to their apartment complex. Fortunately, it was our church! They liked it and began attending services regularly. I visited them in their home soon after the initial visit, and we began building a relationship. I encouraged them to take advantage of our biblical counseling ministry.

I wish all of my stories ended the way this one does. During our fourth counseling session, Johnny called out to God to forgive his sins and save him. Over time, he grew in his new relationship with Christ and eventually became one of the leaders in the church.

There is nothing better than a front-row seat as God changes lives. When I (Kevin) first started counseling, I was told that you cannot counsel an unbeliever. But over the years I have found that this is not true. I have discovered, in fact, that the process of counseling unbelievers is no different from counseling believers. The *process* is the same: you enter into conversational ministry with an individual who needs the truth of God's Word, the power of the Spirit, the grace of Jesus Christ, and the patience of a biblical counselor engaged in the process with them. To be clear, long-term, God-honoring change is impossible without a relationship with Christ. However, with an unbeliever, you can patiently help them as they maneuver through life's pressures while pointing them toward the life-giving, life-sustaining, life-changing grace of Jesus Christ (2 Peter 1:2–4). In this chapter, we want to highlight the priority for evangelism in counseling, the challenges of evangelism in counseling, the practice of evangelism in counseling, and, finally, end with several cautions when practicing evangelism in counseling.

THE PRIORITY OF EVANGELISM IN COUNSELING

Biblical counselors are men and women who have personally experienced the powerful, life-changing effect of the gospel. And they know that counselees need that gospel to radically change them as well—either the gospel of salvation or the gospel of sanctification. So sharing the gospel of Jesus Christ is of first priority in biblical counseling.

Necessary for Heart Change

Evangelism is necessary for true and lasting heart change. When Jesus explained to the disciples what defiles a person, he said, "But what comes out of the mouth proceeds from the heart, and this defiles a person. For out of the heart come evil thoughts, murder, adultery, sexual immorality, theft, false witness, slander. These are what defile a person. But to eat with unwashed hands does not defile anyone" (Matt. 15:18–20 ESV). Here Jesus teaches the necessity of dealing with the heart if we want to see real change. What the mouth says or what the hands do is indicative of what is taking place at the heart level. Jesus made a similar point using fruit trees. Is it possible to get good fruit from a bad tree or bad fruit from a good tree? No. Jesus continued, "The good person out of the good treasure of his heart produces good, and the evil person out of his evil treasure produces evil, for out of the abundance of the heart his mouth speaks" (Luke 6:45 ESV).

And the apostle Paul concurred. No one who is unregenerate can please God, nor does he or she have the ability or desire to do so (Rom. 8:7–8, 14). Without the Spirit of God, the unsaved are incapable of understanding, applying, or living consistent with the gospel (1 Cor. 2:11), as they are dead in trespasses and sins (Eph. 2:1–3), facing an eternity without Christ because of their unbelief (John 3:18, 36). Therefore, biblical counseling must aim for true transformation through heart change—and that begins with the gospel of Jesus Christ for salvation. No one can experience any meaningful or fundamental change outside of the life-transforming power of Christ in salvation. Salvation goes to the root of the problem — the heart.

Anything less than the gospel of salvation is akin to placing a Band-Aid over a deep wound requiring surgery. The work of a counselor is to explain the universal call of salvation, that is, repentance for sin and belief in Jesus Christ, to the unsaved counselee in recognition that only the gospel can bring true life change. As Thomas Sigley aptly stated it, "Therefore, when we counsel an unbeliever, we must work evangelistically. Our techniques must show people the relationship between their nature and their behavior, the link between sin and its consequences, the relevance of God's grace to our real need. Only then will the unbeliever profit from our counseling efforts."[136]

A Central Part of the Discipleship Process

Jesus concluded His earthly ministry to His disciples by reminding them of their personal responsibility to continue making disciples of the world (Matt. 28:18–20). Jesus gave the command to make disciples of all nations, transitioning the mission from a centripetal to a centrifugal strategy where disciples are to take the gospel out — to the world. Jesus also provided the strategy to fulfill this mission: going, baptizing, and teaching.[137] The command to make disciples is comprehensive, including both salvation and sanctification components. The discipleship process includes nothing less than teaching the disciple to observe all things Jesus commanded.

How, then, are disciples created? The process begins with what we call evangelism: taking the gospel message and going. This can be applied to the counseling process more specifically, since your goal in counseling is to help this counselee learn, love, and live Jesus. As Paul aptly stated it, "How then will they call on him in whom they have not believed? And how are they to believe in him of whom they have never heard? And how are they to hear without someone preaching?" (Rom. 10:14 ESV). Evangelism always begins the discipleship process and should be a high priority in counseling.

Essential to Who You Are: An Ambassador

As Christ's disciples, Paul names us as ambassadors of Christ (2 Cor. 5:18 – 21). Here he is emphasizing two important points. First, that God reconciled us to Himself through Christ, and second, the responsibility we have as ambassadors for the ministry and message of reconciliation. Reconciliation here refers to the relational change between God and man, from enemies to friends, because of Christ's work on the cross where Christ became sin for us so that God, in turn, can treat us like Jesus. The relationship between God and the believer is transformed through the death of Jesus, who sacrificially bore the wrath of God. Then, after we have been reconciled to God through Christ, although we are undeserving and weak, God entrusts believers in Christ with this special ministry of the word of reconciliation.

As entrusted ones, those who have been reconciled with God, we are called ambassadors of Christ. God makes His appeal of reconciliation through the very people who needed reconciliation. God is calling your counselee to a relationship with Him through you as His ambassador, as imperfect and weak as you may be. As the voice of God, you present the hope of the gospel — righteousness in Christ. Therefore, we must first know and understand who we are in Christ. Since we speak on behalf of God, we adopt God's agenda, His message, and His passion toward the counselee's need. God is making His appeal through us, and we implore the counselee, on behalf of Christ, to be reconciled to God.

Consistent with the Life of a Christ-Follower

Counseling often happens during times of suffering. And at times, as we all know, a believer suffers in spite of doing good. Peter challenges his readers to respond to unjust affliction, ill treatment, and persecution with a good conscience and Christ-honoring conduct. He encourages them not to be afraid while still honoring Christ in their hearts. He instructs them: "But in your hearts honor Christ the Lord as holy, always being prepared to make a defense to anyone who asks you for a reason for the hope that is in you; yet do it with gentleness and respect"

(1 Peter 3:15 ESV). In other words, Peter expects the believer to respond to persecution in a Christlike manner so that an unbeliever will want to know *how* that type of response is possible. The response of a believer in the midst of suffering shows their hope in Christ that motivates their Christ-honoring response. And as they describe the incredible implications of the gospel and living for eternity rather than for this moment, Peter challenges them to do all of this in humility and with respect.

If believers are to respond to unjust affliction with a readiness to explain how Christ changes their life, shouldn't we, who counsel others, be ready to do the same? As believers live and counsel, it should be natural for them to respond to all of life by sharing the hope of the gospel. Evangelism is more than a technique or a program; it is an essential by-product of living consistent with the gospel as a Christ-follower.

This is one reason why every biblical counselor should prioritize evangelism in the counseling process. Yes, evangelism is one of the goals of counseling since it is necessary for heart change and is a key part of the discipleship process. But evangelism also is essential to our ministry as an ambassador, and it is consistent with the lifestyle of a committed Christ-follower. As the counselor considers the personal life change he has experienced through the gospel, he should passionately and purposefully share the gospel with the counselee.

THE CHALLENGES OF EVANGELISM IN COUNSELING

Knowing that there is a priority for evangelism in counseling is just the beginning. Many counselors would agree with this in principle, but in the give-and-take of a typical counseling session, there are often challenges that hinder the reception of the gospel or, for the counselor, hinder the presentation of the gospel message.

Pluralistic Society

Counselees never come to counseling in a vacuum. They live in a world filled with messages that are contrary to the gospel. Paul described believers at Ephesus, prior to their salvation, as those who "once walked, following the course of this world, following the prince of the power of the air" (Eph. 2:2 ESV). The world system is filled with disorienting voices, similar to the sound in a gym prior to a large event — noise everywhere, but nothing distinct can be heard. Truth claims compete against each other; many have declared all truth claims relative, and it is left to each individual to choose what is best for his or her own life.

This counselee often comes to counseling without any commitment to a particular system of beliefs. In fact, the counselee's commitment may be to the lack of any authoritative system of truth. This is a challenge! So how should a counselor respond? As one committed to the truth (Rom. 10:17), you should patiently, gently, honestly, and lovingly answer the counselee's question while continually pointing back to the truths of the Scripture. We may not be able to address every question or solve every problem brought to us, but as counselors we trust the gracious work of the Spirit in the life of the counselee. We believe that God is working through the proclamation of the gospel in the process of counseling, and that His truth is the antidote to unbiblical thinking.

Affluent Society

Another potential hindrance to the reception of the gospel is the affluent nature of the American society. In contrast to most of world history, the typical American counselee enjoys a life of relative ease and prosperity. Yet throughout the Bible we see God using circumstances of poverty and persecution to help individuals develop greater sensitivity to God and His ways. Solomon writes, "It is better to go to the house of mourning than to go to the house of feasting, for this is the end of all mankind, and the living will lay it to heart.... The heart of the wise is in the house of mourning, but the heart of fools is in the house of mirth" (Eccl. 7:2, 4 ESV). Solomon is suggesting that the sadness of the funeral home is good because it makes one think through the biggest issues in life. In a similar manner, James reminds his readers that their extreme poverty and pressure-filled circumstances are used by God to help them think through life's problems in relationship to God (James 1).

A good counselor will be aware of this and will recognize that the pressures of life provide a window of opportunity to help challenge these hindrances. These pressures can take many different forms. You may have a middle-aged man who learns he has stage 4 liver cancer, or a young mom whose husband walked out on her, or the parents of a teenage boy who got arrested for drug possession. When your counselee is faced with these kinds of trials or heartaches, the counselor encourages them in words similar to the psalmist: "Teach us to number our days that we may get a heart of wisdom" (Ps. 90:12 ESV). Wise biblical counsel, spoken in love, can open a door in the heart to present the gospel to an unbelieving counselee.

Moral Lifestyle

Many times counselees come to counseling because of a troubling issue, yet on the whole they feel that they are living a relatively good or moral life. Counselees may rehearse to you their kindness to others, their reliability in business, their loyalty to friends, or try to show that they have integrity of character. And it might be true, that according to worldly standards they are living a morally acceptable lifestyle. Of course, this fosters self-righteousness, and, similar to the Pharisees, the counselees fail to see their need for salvation in Jesus Christ because of their own spiritual blindness. This blindness is nurtured through their own positive lifestyle choices. Again, as a counselor, you need to lovingly confront this self-righteousness and help counselees to recognize their need for the gospel of Jesus Christ.

Professing Christian

Sometimes one of the biggest challenges in this regard is the counselee who has been raised in the church and is already a professing Christian. You may come to recognize that the person seeking counseling is an unsaved person. It's important to understand that many counselees will come to you with a great deal of Bible knowledge, sometimes even an academic degree. They have heard the stories, learned Grandma's rendition of the Proverbs, and have received an inaccurate sense of security through religious rituals. They have a functional theology of living, based on their church of origin. As you talk with the person, you may begin to question if they are truly regenerate.

There are at least two passages to keep in mind as you engage this person. As you minister to this individual, you can present a warning motivated by love and share what Jesus taught on this:

> "Not everyone who says to me, 'Lord, Lord,' will enter the kingdom of heaven, but the one who does the will of my Father who is in heaven. On that day many will say to me, 'Lord, Lord, did we not prophesy in your name, and cast out demons in your name, and do many mighty works in your name?' And then will I declare to them, 'I never knew you; depart from me, you workers of lawlessness.'"
>
> Matthew 7:21–23 ESV

You can point out that Jesus challenged the idea that any kind of righteous work would make one eligible to enter into heaven.

In addition, after multiple sessions where the counselee fails to make any meaningful change, the counselor can gently challenge, "Given your response to the Scriptures over the past few weeks, please take some time and convince me you are a Christian." A good follow-up assignment would be to pick key passages in 1 John to have the counselee read and consider.

Personal Fear

To this point, we have looked at obstacles that exist in the life of the person being counseled. But there are also obstacles that the counselor may need to deal with as well. One of the most common hindrances to sharing the gospel is personal fear. There are many reasons for this fear, including rejection, failure, loss of relationship, and concern over saying the wrong thing. Yet fear is also an opportunity, providing us an occasion to depend on God in our weakness (2 Cor. 12:9). This gospel-sharing opportunity is not something that takes God by surprise; instead,

God desires to use you to do His work as an ambassador of Jesus Christ (2 Cor. 5:18–20; Eph. 2:10). God uses all kinds of people (and sometimes angels and animals) to share the message of redemption. Your skill is not the most important issue at hand; the most important issue is allowing the Spirit to use the message of the gospel in the heart of this counselee.

When you are faced with the opportunity to share Christ with a counselee, recall the words Paul spoke to Timothy: "For God gave us a spirit not of fear but of power and love and self-control. Therefore do not be ashamed of the testimony about our Lord" (2 Tim. 1:7–8 ESV). Recognize that God grants you the power and courage to share the truth, to share the most important message—the message of reconciliation.

Lack of Know-How

Another hindrance to making a clear and effective gospel presentation in counseling is the simple lack of know-how. As we have supervised counselors over the years, many have admitted that they simply do not know how to present the gospel in a counseling situation. The following section is provided to help you better present the gospel in counseling.

THE PRACTICE OF EVANGELISM IN COUNSELING

Begin with the issue or concern that has brought the counselee to see you. Whether informal or formal counseling, God has provided an occasion to create this conversational ministry opportunity, so that is where you should start. I (Randy) get as much data as I can in the first session so that I begin to understand the person's story and possible spiritual condition. Before they leave, I assign them homework. The written homework assignment becomes the agenda for the next week. We may rearrange the order in which we talk about it (rather than top to bottom), but will work through the homework as the primary structure for week two. I have found it very fruitful to assign homework that speaks to the presenting issue as well as the gospel. It's a starting point for the evangelism process.

Sowing the Gospel and Watering the Gospel

Using 1 Corinthians 3:5–6 as my guide, I think about evangelism in two parts. First is the concept of sowing a seed. "What then is Apollos? What is Paul? Servants through whom you *believed*, as the Lord assigned to each. I *planted*, Apollos *watered*, but *God gave the growth*" (ESV, emphasis added). Here is the idea of planting (or sowing) and watering. To sow or plant the seed means that you present the gospel. You give some kind of witness to Christ, but it does not have to be a full-blown gospel presentation. To sow the seed means that we do something to cause people to think positively about the claims of Jesus Christ and we share the basic tenets of the gospel.

If sowing the seed is presenting the basic tenets of Christ, then watering the seed is encouraging people to seriously consider the claims of Christ. Christians can water the gospel through kindness to people, acts of love, and the way we speak or act that causes people to think highly about Jesus.

During counseling, the homework you assign between sessions can be part of the sowing and watering process. As we go over homework during the session, I ask: "What did you learn?" "What are your thoughts?" "What are your concerns?" "What questions do you have?" Use multiple questions as you go through the material to uncover further opportunities for follow-up discussion.

Homework That Helps in the Gospel Presentation

As I mentioned earlier, beginning in week one, I assign homework assignments that facilitate this process of sowing and watering the gospel. My goal is that by week three's session, I can make a full gospel presentation. Over the years, I have found that people will continue to think about the things we discuss, and most of those who get saved in counseling have gotten saved somewhere between weeks four and six. Here is a brief summary of some of the homework I assign.

READING THE GOSPEL OF JOHN

One of the simplest ways to get started is to have the counselee read three chapters, three times a week from the gospel of John. Typically, I have them read John because we know that John's gospel was written specifically to bring people to faith in the Lord Jesus Christ: "Now Jesus did many other signs in the presence of the disciples, which are not written in this book; but these are written so that you may believe that Jesus is the Christ, the Son of God, and that by believing you may have life in his name" (John 20:30 – 31 ESV).

I ask them to pay particular attention to who Jesus Christ said He is, why He came to earth, and what others said about Him. I discuss how in our post-Christian culture most people know very little about the Bible or about Christ in particular. I've found that if I try to present the gospel right away, it is like a stranger talking to a stranger about a stranger. Instead, I have found it valuable to do some things that build and establish our relationship first, then get them reading in the Scriptures so they learn something about Christ. Finally, I talk with them about what the word *believe* means. Usually by the third session, I give a full presentation of the gospel—a three-point outline that explains the meaning of the word *believe*.

I start by sharing that a key word in the gospel of John is the word *believe*. It is used 98 times in 21 chapters. To believe in Jesus involves three key concepts. The first is to know *Facts*. You cannot believe in Christ without knowing some things about Him. That is why it is important to read the gospel of John because it starts when Christ comes to earth and ends when He goes back to heaven, so it is an overview of the life and ministry of Christ.

The second concept related to believing involves *Commitment*. People who read the gospel of John and learn about Christ are forced to come to one of three conclusions:

1. You determine that Jesus was a liar. He was not the Son of God, He knew He was not, and He purposefully deceived people. If that is what you conclude, no one will expect you to become a follower of Christ.

2. You determine that Jesus was a lunatic. That is, He was not the Son of God, but He thought He was and got a following. If you think He was a lunatic, you are certainly not going to follow Him.

3. The only other option is that Jesus is exactly who He said He is. He is the Son of God and is the way, the truth, and the life and nobody can come to the Father but through Him (John 14:7). If you believe that, if that is what you conclude, it should prompt a commitment to Him.[138]

This leads to the third concept related to believing, and it involves a *Change in Life*. Believing in Christ is not just adding some religious thoughts to your current lifestyle. Believing in Christ changes everything, because it means that you rely on Him totally as your Savior and He becomes the Lord of your life. His love for us is what motivates us in life as we are committed to Him.

I often use the human illustration of meeting my future wife, Cindy, at Cedarville College when I was still single. After dating several girls, my attention focused on one gal. As I got to know her and understand who she is, her passions, her background, her goals for life, and her character, the facts about her drove me to make a commitment. And I determined, of all the women I knew in the world, she was the one I wanted to spend the rest of my life with. I convinced her to marry me. That commitment changed my life. This is similar to what it means to believe in Jesus.

After I have written these three points on the board (Facts, Commitment, Change), I tell the counselee that many people who say they are a Christian have believed in Christ only in numbers one (Facts) and two (Commitment). But that is not what it means to believe biblically.

Just knowing facts or making a commitment will make you a religious person or it may mean that you've had a religious experience, but it does not mean that your life has changed—that you have been born again as a follower of Jesus. "If any man be in Christ, he is a new creature: old things are passed away; behold, all thing are become new" (2 Cor. 5:17 KJV). I also make it clear that getting baptized or going to membership classes or reading books about Christ is not enough.

Sometimes I will ask counselees to memorize John 3:16–18 (usually just one verse per week). If I'm counseling a couple, I ask them to quote the verses to each other and check each other. My goal is that they can quote John 3:16–18 word-perfect. This is the key passage I use to discuss with them the word *believe*. I have also used various versions of gospel tracts over the years to have them read the first week. I assign them to read it and be ready to discuss it. Depending on their understanding, I probably would reassign it on week two.

THE CAUTIONS OF EVANGELISM IN COUNSELING

In the process of counseling, a counselor must always juggle various priorities and emphases. And as we have supervised many aspiring biblical counselors over the years, we have recognized several areas of concern related to evangelism and biblical counseling. There are concerns related to the importance of truth in general and to the counseling practice specifically.

Remain Ethically Consistent

Sometimes, a new biblical counselor will wonder if they should present the gospel if someone comes to them for counseling but does not ask any questions about Jesus or the Bible. Is it appropriate to bring this up if the person has not? First, it should be said that this is not a new question. Many years ago, Gary Collins admonished Christian counselors who in their counseling practice never mentioned Jesus, challenging them not to separate their professed theology and professional practice.[139] On the other hand, I (Kevin) recall a national biblical counseling training conference where I heard a presenter say that we should not mention the Bible unless the counselee brings it up. A military chaplain I know also advocated this view, arguing that we should show sensitivity and not try to impose our standards and values upon another. He suggested that it was wise to never mention God to a soldier unless the soldier asks about God first. So which view is correct? Should we bring Jesus into the conversation or wait until the person asks?

My own view is pretty clear on this. While I would admit that in the ebb-and-flow of counseling there may be an instance where a counselor would choose to not share much Scripture, to be ethically consistent with our theological beliefs we *must* share the gospel with counselees. As ambassadors of Christ we have the responsibility of communicating the message of reconciliation, and we must share truth that provides the only hope of real life change. If we know a message that can ultimately provide real and lasting change, yet choose not to share it, we have not fulfilled our calling as an ambassador. We are inconsistent with our moral obligation to share the gospel, and this is a colossal mistake. Paul was clear, "How then will they call on him in whom they have not believed? And how are they to believe in him of whom they have never heard?" (Rom. 10:14 ESV). We *must* tell them of Jesus.

Rehabilitating or Exchanging Lusts, Lies, or Idols

Another concern to keep in mind is the ease of rehabilitating or exchanging lusts, lies, or idols if one fails to point the counselee to ultimate truth. Salvation is necessary for any true or lasting heart change. The counselor who decides to focus on other secondary or tertiary issues becomes an accomplice in aiding the counselee to manipulate his idolatry so that life outside of Christ is easier.

Choosing not to share Christ—not to evangelize a counselee—will lead to two things. First, it introduces confusion and ultimately fails to provide the necessary ingredient for life change—Jesus Christ Himself.

To imply that life can be better without Christ robs the heart out of the incarnation of Christ. Jesus came because people do need radical change that only He can provide, and yet we are somehow implying that life change is possible *outside* of Christ.

Second, when we choose not to share the gospel, we leave the impression with counselees that life is feasible with their existing lusts, lies, and idols. We give them a false assurance that life is fine as long as it is practically workable and pleasant to the feelings. But this leads to even greater problems in the future. If life remains doable, then we are simply making people comfortable on the road to hell. And when life gets hard again, as it inevitably will, the counselee will inaccurately assume that biblical counseling just didn't work, or worse, that God's solutions are not adequate to deal with real problems. Both of these conclusions are avoidable if the counselor begins with the gospel of salvation in Jesus Christ.

Neglecting Valuable Data Gathering

As the counseling process begins, there is a temptation to neglect good data gathering once a counselor knows the counselee needs regeneration. The counseling session may begin like any other, confirming the details on the initial intake form and beginning to ask questions related to the presenting problem. Then, at some point, upon learning that the counselee is not saved, the counselor is tempted to shift methods and jump into a gospel presentation. The focus of the session shifts abruptly to evangelism. All other counseling concerns are minimized while the counselor seeks to share the good news of a relationship with Christ.

If you haven't realized it by now, this is not what we are suggesting. As we have strongly encouraged, the counselor must be motivated biblically and have a passion for evangelism, but if the session transitions from its initial focus to a purely evangelistic focus, the counselor runs the risk of losing future opportunities to present the gospel further. The counselee may get confused by the shift in flow of the session and fail to understand what is happening. Furthermore, the counselor's change in focus means he will miss other important details he would have uncovered through good data gathering. At the end of the counseling session, the counselor may actually know less than he needs. It's likely that the counselee will feel confused or manipulated by the change, sensing that the counselor has another agenda and did not focus on counselee's personal concerns.

By the counselor simply asking questions and continuing to gather data, the counselee would have a greater sense of hope that the long-term goals were being addressed. And the information gained is far from useless. This new information can form the basis for conversations and the homework for the next week. It provides further opportunities to better unpack the gospel and pray for regeneration. And the counselee still has hope that the presenting problem is being addressed.

Misrepresenting the Gospel

The final concern relates to the gospel presentation itself. At times, armed with a passion to see someone become regenerated, the counselor misrepresents the gospel. Instead of calling for the counselee to acknowledge sin, admit a need for a Savior, repent of sins, and follow Christ, the counselor presents a false gospel in one way or another. Possibly the counselor invites the counselee into a new relationship with Christ and emphasizes the fact that Jesus can become a friend, can help one feel better, can provide for needs, among other true observations about Jesus.

The functional result: a counselee desires a relationship with Christ out of self-interest—not from an awareness of sin and desire for forgiveness. The counselee believes everything is better, yet has not been regenerated. The counselee loves the promise of friendship, but does not acknowledge sin as the barrier to a true relationship with Christ.

SHARE THE GOSPEL

Our hope and prayer for you, the reader, is that God might grant you the opportunity to share the gospel. That's our passion as biblical counselors. That's our passion as followers of Christ. That's our passion as recipients of grace. Share the gospel of salvation and sanctification. Share the hope that is found only in Christ. Share the power of Christ that saves. Trust God to use His Word for its intended purpose. By God's grace, you can also celebrate with the Johnnys of your world that God graciously entrusts to you in the sowing and watering process.

CHAPTER 19

BIBLICAL COUNSELING, THE CHURCH, AND COMMUNITY OUTREACH

ROB GREEN AND STEVE VIARS

The Lord has created a resurgence in more thoughtful and careful approaches to soul care in local churches. Just as diet, exercise, regular medical care, and proper sleep are important for the well-being of the physical body, conversations focused on Christ, addressing life issues, and learning how to live worthy of our calling are important for the well-being of our souls. While soul care occurs at many levels and in many places, biblical counseling is emerging as one of the more important ways to equip believers for the ministry of soul care. Conferences are well attended, books are being published, counseling ministries in churches are being established, and growing numbers of people are getting involved.

For all of this we shout, "Praise the Lord!" We could not be more excited about the Lord's work in these areas. In this chapter we want to push our thinking, as a larger movement of biblical counselors, to the next logical step. We want to encourage readers to consider several additional ways that biblical counseling can be used to serve and reach the community for Christ. Let's begin by going back to the basic mission of the church.

FAITH CHURCH'S MISSION AND CORE VALUES

One of the best ways to share these ideas is by telling you the story of our church, Faith Church in Lafayette, Indiana. At Faith Church, we have personally seen how biblical counseling is effective in providing soul care within our church body as well as providing a resource to the surrounding community. Much of this chapter will be testimonial in nature, describing what we are doing and the thinking behind our efforts. We will be the first to admit that we still have much to learn about caring for people and how to best serve the community. We do not believe that we have arrived. We are fully aware that sinful pride can easily blind us to areas of struggle that may seem so obvious to others. We struggle with making the right decisions and ensuring that our efforts always remain focused on the message and glory of Jesus Christ. At the same time, we are hopeful that our story will encourage you as you see the Lord's mighty hand at work. We trust that you will praise Him as well and then ask the Spirit to direct you in your response.

Our primary desire is to live for the glory of God and to be consistent with the theological truths that we hold dear. The mission statement of our church is based on our understanding of Matthew 28:19–20 and Ephesians 4:11–16, both scriptural texts that explain the mission of *the church*—the body of Christ. Faith Church's mission states:

> The mission of Faith Church is to glorify God by winning people to Jesus Christ and equipping them to be more faithful disciples.

Our church mission statement may be similar to your own. The words can change, but as a mission it emphasizes the purpose of glorifying God and the activities we will engage in, winning people to Jesus and equipping them. We believe that biblical counseling fits hand in glove with both the purpose and the activities of this mission. But we still need to flesh this out in the context of our ministry, so we have created a diagram of concentric circles to show how we believe biblical counseling functions in the daily life of the church (see figure 13).

CIRCLE ONE: THE FOUNDATION — THE GOSPEL OF JESUS CHRIST

The message of the death, burial, and resurrection of Jesus Christ is central to everything we do in biblical counseling. Without Christ at the center, there is no counseling ministry. This, of course, applies to every ministry of the church as well. The story line of Scripture finds a crescendo at the cross of Christ. For it is at the cross that God's plans come together. The Old Testament looked forward to a coming Messiah who would suffer for His people, yet Jesus made it clear that He had to leave, to ascend to the Father, in order for the Spirit's work to

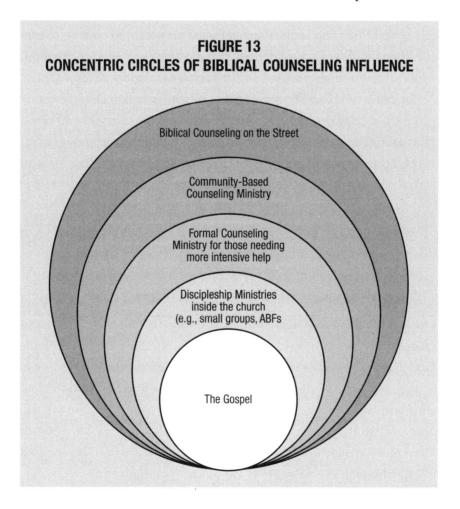

FIGURE 13
CONCENTRIC CIRCLES OF BIBLICAL COUNSELING INFLUENCE

Biblical Counseling on the Street

Community-Based Counseling Ministry

Formal Counseling Ministry for those needing more intensive help

Discipleship Ministries inside the church (e.g., small groups, ABFs

The Gospel

expand from its Old Testament boundaries. The church, which forever eliminates the Jew and Gentile division and racism, was established, and there is now one body and one spiritual house. The gospel communicates the truth about Jesus—His life, death, resurrection, and ascension—and the good news of the gift of the Holy Spirit. Without the gospel, there is nothing of value remaining. This is why, for our biblical counseling ministry to properly care for souls, the gospel message must be front and center.

CIRCLES TWO AND THREE: DISCIPLESHIP AND CHRIST-CENTERED COUNSELING TO OUR LOCAL CHURCH

The next two circles represent the most obvious and natural connections between the church and biblical counseling. If we are going to equip believers to be more faithful disciples, then we must provide teaching and training about life. The church family needs soul care in the context of community (Heb. 10:23–25). Obviously, one aspect of soul care is a biblical counseling ministry. We all wish that our worship services, our small groups, our service opportunities, and our discipleship structures would automatically produce faithful disciples of Christ. But the reality is that we face personal struggles in our daily lives. Our answer to these struggles has been to provide the personal ministry of the Word—biblical counseling. We use biblical counseling to help our church family deal with the pressures and challenges of life, regardless of whether the source of those difficulties is from the outside (suffering), or from their own heart (sin), or both. In addition, we provide ongoing training within our church family so that some of these challenges are handled as members live in community with one another. Ongoing training and equipping serve to accomplish the mission, allow for difficulties to be handled early in the process, and eliminate the need for additional staff.

Through the years, we have seen the Lord work mightily as more and more churches have answered the call to shepherd their own flock. Churches and leaders are learning that sickness and cancer are more than physical issues requiring a physician; they are soul issues in need of the ongoing grace of Christ and the comfort, encouragement, and even correction of the church community. In addition, we've seen the emergence of the Biblical Counseling Coalition and the growing numbers of certified training centers through the Association of Certified Biblical Counselors. But biblical counseling does not stop there. This is just the first step in the mission of the church, as we win people to Christ and train them to be faithful disciples.

CIRCLE FOUR: OFFERING COUNSELING SERVICES TO OUR COMMUNITY

Most people know that biblical counseling is a necessary ministry within a healthy church body. Yet there came a time at Faith Church when we realized that biblical counseling could be one of the ways that our church showed its love for the community. We figured that if we could minister to people inside the church who were struggling, why not seek to help folks outside the church as well? Circle four represents this shift, an opportunity to let one's light shine before people (Matt. 5:16). Biblical counseling for the community represents an opportunity to win others to Christ (1 Cor. 9:19–23), and it can impact your community-based ministries in at least two ways.

Providing Christ-Centered Biblical Counseling to People in Our Community

In the 1970s, Pastor Bill Goode, Dr. Bob Smith, and several others in our church decided to offer their services to the community, providing free Christ-centered biblical counseling. The operation was rather small in those early days, and to keep the organizational challenges to a minimum, they decided that Monday afternoon and evening would be the most appropriate time to serve the larger community. Since there was still a church family to shepherd, they determined that all counseling to those outside of the church would be limited to those Monday hours. Pastor Goode explained that many pastors took Monday as a day off, but that his "day off" would be used to serve a greater purpose. The church saw his desire to serve and supported it. After all, church members would still be counseled on the other days and times in order to ensure that the pastors were properly caring for those inside the church family.

Since those early days, the ministry has expanded from four counselors to twenty-five, including eight who serve at a location near Purdue University. Most of the twenty-five who serve weekly are laypersons who counsel because they care about their friends and neighbors in the community. The participation of laypeople is an indication that the church body has seen the value of the Monday counseling ministry. And as the number of counselors has expanded, so has the number of hours of counseling offered per year. At the most recent count, the ministry is offering almost 3,000 hours of free counseling each year to those in our community.

We understand that some churches have decided not to engage in a biblical counseling ministry to the community because they fear a lawsuit or some in church leadership are concerned that too much time might be devoted to people who are not members of the church. But arguments like these are often expressions of fear rather than expressions of mission. Our mission is to glorify God, and we do this by winning people to Christ and equipping them as disciples.

In addition to aligning with our mission, there have been several by-products of the ministry to our community. The three most exciting have been an increased passion for evangelism, the clear connection people see between counseling and the local church, and the opportunity to serve other local churches. Our advertising, our consent forms, and our opening interactions with potential counselees explain that we are a biblical counseling center operated by a church. There is no pretending, no surprises. In addition, we make it clear that our counseling is not something separate, an entity functioning on its own. We are a church providing Bible-centered resources for anyone who would like help.

Hundreds of individuals have been won to Christ, and their first contact with Faith came through the door of the biblical counseling center. Unlike some evangelistic outreaches, these evangelistic opportunities occur because someone came to the ministry and wanted to talk with us about what God is doing in their life. What an opportunity! Here are people coming to our church and inviting their counselor to speak directly from Scripture about their struggles. Sometimes the only "hook" to biblical counseling is a neighbor or a coworker who explained how they were helped through the church's counseling ministry. It simply does not get much better than that. Oftentimes these individuals have had little to no spiritual influence. Many of them do not have a conversion testimony or even have knowledge of the Bible. These dear folks have to be taught that the Bible is made of sixty-six books, each book with chapters (those are the big numbers), and verses (those are the little numbers). They have to be taught the gospel message. They have to be shown what a meaningful relationship with Christ would mean right now and in the future.

I recall one young man who came—rather, was made to come—to our counseling ministry because his father committed suicide. His mother was deeply concerned how the death of his father might impact her son. This young man had no clue how God might want to work in his life. During his first week, he explained that he did not want to be there and he had zero interest in counseling. His counselor did not try to convince him to stay, but said that if he would return, then he, as his counselor, would serve him in two particular ways. First, he would help the young man to put his father's death in the larger context of what the Lord might want to do in his life, and second, he would explain how the truth found in the Bible would help him and his mom get along much better. The young man decided to return. Three months later, he had made a profession of faith, and he and his mom were working together instead of against each other. They were attending church and could celebrate the fact that this young man had memorized the names of the books in the New Testament.

A second story is so amazing, it is something only God could have orchestrated. Years ago, a couple were separated and on the verge of a divorce. The wife chose to come to biblical counseling, and she was saved. The Lord did such an amazing work in her life that her husband decided to come to learn for himself what had changed her. He was saved. Ten years later, she contracted cancer and died. At the funeral, several friends of this couple heard their full story for the first time and repented as well. We should never forget that the Lord is capable of taking our biggest messes and making them beautiful. We rejoice to have a front-row seat to the Lord's work!

In addition to evangelism, biblical counseling to the community has been an open door to develop a larger connection to the local church body. Our church membership classes regularly include those who initially came to Faith Church through the door of the counseling ministry. The counseling ministry has become one of the most effective outreach tools for our church. As hurting people receive help developing a relationship with Christ, they inevitably want more than the counseling session. Some of our most passionate servants are individuals who were former counselees in the Monday program. These people are not transferring in from other churches; they are often weak Christians who are not connected and feeling very alone. We have the joy of meeting these folks where they are and connecting them to a loving church family who will "one-another" them as Christ commands.

The counseling ministry has also been a means of blessing for other churches. One of the core values that our church adopted was "strengthening others." We learned that some of our Monday counselees were faithfully attending other evangelical churches, and in some cases the leadership teams at these churches had asked if we would counsel certain individuals through our ministry. In these cases, our counseling staff has the privilege and opportunity to work with other church leaders to

339

restore a member of another church to full function in their body. We often invite the pastors of these churches to the counseling so they can be better equipped to shepherd their own people. In other words, we give our time to serve a sister church by counseling a member until they are ready again to serve, give, lead, and contribute to the body. Sometimes this also results in the further equipping of a fellow shepherd.

Over the years, we have counseled many pastors from our larger community as well. These men, and sometimes their families, are often weighed down by the pressures of ministry and the pressures of their own sin. It is a great joy to see a person on his way out of the ministry restored to strength. Sometimes, that Monday night session is a time for them to decompress and reflect on all that the Lord has done in their life and ministry.

Our community counseling outreach also includes a ministry we call Vision of Hope (VOH). VOH is a residential program for young women primarily between the ages of fourteen and twenty-eight who struggle with habits of self-harm, eating disorders, drug or alcohol addictions, or unplanned pregnancies. While this program has nominal fees, it is incredibly cost effective when compared with other residential programs throughout the country. Every month there are young women from all over the country (and a few internationals) who move into a beautiful home to begin biblical counseling. As a girl reaches certain milestones that are tailored to her unique situation, she progresses through three phases until graduation. All three benefits (evangelism, church connection, and blessing other churches) have occurred through the six years of VOH's operation.

One story from our VOH ministry is particularly memorable. A young girl came to us dealing with abuse. Her life was in shambles. She felt doomed to a subsistence existence moving from one abusive relationship to another. Many times, she had been told that she would never amount to anything. But Jesus intervened. Shortly after moving into the home, she began having questions. She wanted to know *why* the people cared about her and loved her. And the answer was simple

... because Jesus does! This girl, a bruised reed and smoldering wick if there ever was one, was lifted out of her pit by the Lord and given a new life. Her conversion was obvious. For the next year she learned just how much Jesus loved her and cared for her, and learned all about her new identity. She learned that a meaningful relationship with Jesus would impact everything about her. She was transformed from a bruised reed to a trophy of God's grace. After graduation from VOH, she decided to stay at Faith Church, as she now had friends who loved her and cared for her ... rather than abusing her. She also attracted the attention of a single guy in our church. By the time this work is published, she will be a married woman, active in the ministries at Faith, and living a new life. In her case, we had the privilege of using biblical counseling to evangelize and to connect a person to the community at Faith Church. Stories like this are why we are passionate to emphasize the connection between biblical counseling and community outreach. We believe this is simply the Great Commission in action.

Providing Excellent Resources to Enrich the Lives of Those in Our Parish

The driving motive for our community outreach is to win people to Christ. I (Steve) remind our leadership team on a regular basis that "we want Lafayette to be a place where it is really hard to get to hell from." I say this as a reminder that we want to share Christ with every last person in our community. Many church leaders with a passion for evangelism will share that sentiment, but *how* one goes about doing outreach is the real challenge. In our community there is a desire to see the church reclaim its place in the life of our community. In the past, the church was the place where people gathered, where people held important meetings. It was the center of community life. But over the years, the center of community life has gone other places, and it is a challenge to reclaim that space. We believe that this begins by communicating to the community that the church cares, that we love them and have something to offer them. Jesus spoke about this in His Sermon on the Mount:

> You are the salt of the earth, but if salt has lost its taste, how shall its salti-
> ness be restored? It is no longer good for anything except to be thrown out
> and trampled under people's feet. You are the light of the world. A city set
> on a hill cannot be hidden. Nor do people light a lamp and put it under a
> basket, but on a stand, and it gives light to all in the house. In the same way,
> let your light shine before others, so that they may see your good works and
> give glory to your Father who is in heaven.   Matthew 5:13–16 ESV

Jesus is simply reiterating what the Lord had expected from the nation
of Israel. The nation of Israel was placed by God at the crossroads of
the world in order to be a testimony to the Lord to all the nations of the
earth. And the Lord continues that goal with His church. God's people
exist to proclaim the greatness of Jesus Christ (1 Peter 2:4–10), but the
means by which that happens is not just a declaration from the mouth,
but also, as Matthew 5:16 states, by works of service.

Our church has always been engaged in works of service in our
community, but a major shift happened in 2000. The local chapter
of the Red Cross had a Christmas program for needy children in our
community, but some of their donations were behind schedule. Faith
Church launched an immediate push to fill the need. One week later,
the need was met. After that, the Red Cross came to see Faith Church
as a helpful partner in accomplishing its mission. The next year, the
Red Cross was facing administrative challenges and was considering
canceling the entire donation program. Faith led the charge to admin-
ister the program and involve other churches. We gave the credit to
the Red Cross. This not only strengthened the church's relationship
to the Red Cross; it was a statement to our local community leaders.
They began to see our church as a partner that loves the community
and is ready to serve the community, rather than a church that threw
rocks. Shortly thereafter, Faith decided that instead of building a new
auditorium for our worship gatherings once a week, we would invest in
a community center that would serve as salt and light to those in our
community. Best of all, it would be used seven days a week.

Not that any of this came easily. There were challenges, and one
of the first challenges was determining exactly what services the

community would value. Rather than try to guess, we created community surveys and tried to listen and learn from those who lived around us. We began referring to the people who lived within a two-mile radius of the church as "our parish." Our parish represented the people the Lord had sovereignly put near us, and our parish began talking to us. They let us know that they wanted a place for community meetings, low-cost day care, gymnasiums and fields for various sports leagues, and they even wanted a skate park because there were no ramps in our area. We added a fitness area and a zero-depth pool and the design of the new community center was completed. Today there are nearly 3,000 members who use the community center, and roughly 80 percent of them are *not* from Faith Church. On any given day the facility is used by our police department, by an outside group hosting a conference, by a group of Mothers of Preschool Children (MOPS), or even to host a six-year-old girl's birthday party.

What does this have to do with biblical counseling, you might ask? The principles that govern our interactions with others are taught in our biblical counseling classes, and they impact the way we do each ministry. The pool is used by a group that serves children in our community who have special needs. The gyms have hosted basketball and volleyball leagues where hundreds of people from the community participate. The fields outside have been the site of over 1,000 people gathering to watch five-year-olds play soccer. The preschool serves nearly 100 families, many of whom are not connected to a church. The community center and our associated community ministries have been a bridge to our community. Through the center, we introduce our community to people who care, and, more importantly, to a God who cares.

In 2013, a second community center was added on the campus of Purdue University. This community center hosts worship services on Sundays, biblical counseling to the community on Mondays, and a Purdue college ministry on Friday nights. It hosts numerous community events as well. Hundreds of women from India who were studying at Purdue used the facility for a cultural night to give them a "taste of home." We've hosted events and picnics that have drawn many of the neighbors from the surrounding area. There is a community park on the property specifically designed for our church to engage in conversation and relationship with those in the community. And once again, the neighbors helped set the agenda. We asked our neighbors what they wanted and how they could be served. Now, when they come to utilize the services they asked for, these personal interactions provide opportunities for us to provide them with biblical counsel. We know that sometimes the services simply make Lafayette a nice place to live and the church property a nice place to visit. But our experience is that these interactions have often led folks to seek biblical counseling help as well.

Doing good works in the community glorifies God. It points the community toward the Lord and gives opportunities for conversations about the death, burial, and resurrection of Jesus. Sometimes those who see the ministry from the soccer field are interested in a much more personal interaction through the doors of the counseling center. There is a synergy that exists between all the ministries that reaches people and glorifies God.

CIRCLE FIVE: TAKING BIBLICAL COUNSELING TO THE STREETS

To this point our discussion has centered on how biblical counseling impacts local church soul care and community outreach where the community *comes* to the church. Can there be more? What would it look like if we took biblical counseling to the community? Over the last two years we have seen some development on this front, in two ways in particular.

Christ-Centered Biblical Counseling and the Community Development Corporation

Our federal government allocates funds to local governments for the purpose of community revitalization. One of the ways this is done is by restoring homes that are in such poor condition that the real estate brokers and flippers will not pursue them due to the high risk of financial loss. Picture the very worst homes in your community. The government wants those homes restored because they view restored homes as an investment in America that ultimately increases the tax base and helps citizens become productive in their community. However, these funds cannot be spent directly by local governments; they must have a nonprofit partner. In 2013, the city of Lafayette approached Faith Church and asked the church to be its nonprofit partner. Without the city's request, this avenue of work would not have been open to us.

Here is how the program works. Government funds are used to help restore a blighted home in a community to livable standards, and then a low-to-moderate income family is found that can move into the home. What does this have to do with biblical counseling? Keep in mind that the city did not ask Faith Church to do this because we have a unique ability to restore homes. Several other organizations could accomplish that work. The city asked us because they wanted the holistic, wraparound services Faith provides, and this includes our counseling services. They wanted the entire package to be available to a potential buyer so that the buyer would be a productive and helpful member of the community. The partnership indicates that the city sees value in what we do; the city was willing to find a faith-based community partner to do good works together. In this case, both the city and the church are able to take steps toward accomplishing their respective missions.

This initiative has also encouraged our church to consider additional ways that God-honoring ministry could occur. Our church has launched a "city missionary" initiative out of this. Home buyers must meet eligibility requirements, and they are awarded homes through a board selection process approved by the city, but it is possible that some of those buyers might be people in our church who see downtown neighborhoods as potential mission fields. While all prospective buyers will receive training in the normal issues, like finances, caring for properties, and job security, in some cases a home buyer from our church will be trained in leading small groups, problem solving, hosting neighborhood parties, biblical counseling, and organizing Bible studies. Not every home we rehabilitate will be sold to a "city missionary." Still, we hope to have many "city missionaries" scattered over these downtown areas so that we can reach people in these neighborhoods with the gospel.

A revitalized piece of property is just one step in the process. The more important piece is seeking to evangelize the city—one house, one city missionary at a time. Lord willing, ten years from now, there will be Bible studies and small groups happening all over the downtown neighborhoods, groups started by our city missionaries who have been trained to take biblical counseling directly to the neighborhood. We continue to be amazed that the Lord would allow these amazing developments where our concern for good works is embraced by the larger community.

It may be that your ministry context may not allow you to be involved in this kind of project. However, that does not mean that you should not think and pray about taking biblical counseling to the streets of your community. Is it possible that the Lord might be calling you to take your counseling ministry outside the walls of your building? By God's grace, if you open yourself up to this possibility, we believe you will discover the opportunities He has for you.

Christ-Centered Biblical Counseling Meeting Community Needs

In addition to the home rehabilitation program and the city missionaries we are developing and training, we offer two courses of training at several downtown locations. While Faith Church operates two community centers, there are additional community centers which have served as the loci of social services for many years in the downtown area. While we offer training at our community centers, this aspect of the ministry involves going to the social service "meccas" for community outreach.

For years our church has had a clothing closet and food pantry to serve those who are needy, but now we are partnering with an organization called Jobs for Life and offering training to interested individuals in their neighborhoods. The premise of Jobs for Life is that poverty is not broken by a food pantry or by another handout. Poverty is overcome when individuals find work that pays the bills associated with a normal household. Thus, our church members serve as coaches helping individuals write résumés, learn basic job skills, learn how to work in order to keep a job, and, most importantly, our members serve as friends so that spiritual conversations occur. The Jobs for Life program, in our eyes, is about more than dealing with generational poverty (which would be valuable since we believe that all human beings are God's image bearers) ... it is dealing with our spiritual poverty.

In addition to Jobs for Life, we are also offering financial counseling in these downtown locations. While many people in our community do not live paycheck to paycheck, many who live in the poorer downtown neighborhoods certainly do. They are susceptible to questionable, if not downright sinful, loan practices. They are susceptible to generational poverty where the cycle is not easily broken. They are susceptible to the sinful attitudes that often accompany those who are in financial trouble. Thus, financial classes are one of our opportunities to take biblical counseling to the city. These folks will not travel to our suburban locations, at least initially, but they might walk to the place where they have received hundreds of social services in the past. That opportunity allows us to talk not only about their financial bankruptcy but also everyone's spiritual bankruptcy.

Biblical counseling has an important relationship to the local church and to community outreach. It can influence the ministries to the community from within the boundaries of the church property, but the Lord may open additional ways in which He wants His glory shown by taking biblical counseling to the streets of your community.

IN SUMMARY

We hope that you can join us in praising the Lord for all that He is doing in His church to care for souls. We join with others in praising the Lord that more and more churches are learning how to counsel their own members. And we join together in thanks for the continued interest in biblical counseling training and development that makes these ministries stronger and more effective. Yet biblical counseling as a discipleship tool inside the church is only one part of the equation.

It may be that the Lord wants you to expand your counseling ministry to those in your community for purposes of evangelism, outreach, and serving and strengthening other churches. Maybe it is time to train your leadership that offering biblical counseling to your community is part of the broader mission of the church. Maybe it is time to organize a team for community-based outreach through biblical counseling. Maybe it is time to encourage your church family to tell their family, friends, coworkers, and neighbors that biblical counseling is available to whoever wants it.

It may be that you are using biblical counseling in your church for soul care and in your community for outreach, church growth, and blessing other churches. Maybe now is the time to take the next step in community outreach. Listen. Learn from your parish. Implement the ideas they give you. The Lord calls us to proclaim His greatness, to tell of His wonderful actions, and to call people to repentance of sin and faith in Christ for His honor and glory. May we be found a faithful steward busy in the Master's work.

CHAPTER 20

BIBLICAL COUNSELING, THE CHURCH, AND THE PARA-CHURCH

HEATH LAMBERT AND DAVID POWLISON

In a book on counseling in the church, it is natural to ask about the relationship between para-church counseling ministries and local church ministries. This chapter will consider that question. We are both deeply committed to and active in our local churches as well as in various para-church contexts. Our passion for understanding the relationship between church and para-church can be expressed in two narratives. The first story is personal, the second historical.

TWO MODERN STORIES

On a cold afternoon just before Christmas, the two of us sat together by a warm fire in Pennsylvania. I (Heath) was nearing the end of my doctoral work under David's supervision and had just been offered a faculty position in biblical counseling at Southern Seminary. I had been happily serving for the last several years as a local church pastor, and I wanted to continue this important and fruitful work. I shared this with David, informing him that because of my commitment to the local church, I was going to decline the invitation to serve as a professor.

Hearing this, David pushed back. He suggested that my strong commitment to the local church could actually lead to my accepting the position at Southern. It was a question of personal calling, and there was not an "automatic" answer that was true for every person. He pointed out that remaining in my current position would allow me to impact *that* congregation. Serving as a professor, he argued, could impact *hundreds*—potentially *thousands*—of congregations.

His point was well taken. A decision to accept a ministry position in a para-church institution, such as a theological seminary, was not at odds with my commitment to the local church. In fact, I came to be persuaded that, for me, this would actually be the strongest demonstration of my commitment to the local church.

That's the personal narrative. Now, the historical one.

Nearly a half century ago, the vision for reestablishing wise, biblical counseling in local churches arose within a para-church context, significantly influenced by a perception of the needs of local church ministry. Jay Adams, an experienced local church pastor, was serving as a professor of practical theology at Westminster Seminary. Like most new intellectual and practical proposals, the idea of biblical counseling began with difficult questions and problems: "How can I help struggling people? What should I teach pastors-to-be about their responsibility for hands-on pastoral care? Should the church's practice be subordinate to secular models of understanding people and of trying to help them with their problems? Does the Bible say anything specific about people's deepest personal and interpersonal problems?" Adams concluded that our faith does speak to these questions—and that a faith that can't speak to counseling needs becomes essentially irrelevant.

It is not surprising that the next steps of growth also arose in para-church settings. Churches that lack a vision for counseling ministry need to hear it and learn it from someone. So the first initiatives in model-building, in training and education, in offering counseling services, and in developing published resources also originated in para-church ministries.[140] But, from the start, the goal was to serve local churches, to help God's people grow in grace and wisdom, to help the church's ministries become more faithful, probing, and effective.

Today an alphabet soup of para-church ministries continues this work of casting vision, developing the counseling model, training men and women to counsel, offering counseling to people not being served by a local church, and producing literature and other resources. To this day, each of these para-church ministries operates out of a conviction that a biblical model of counseling ministry will find its most fruitful expression as one of the core ministries of local churches. Thousands of churches have caught that vision and taken steps to implement their vision practically.

And it is a two-way street. The need arises in the practical problems of churches and individual Christians. Para-church helps to meet the need, in significant part by helping churches to better meet the need. And churches exert a significant check on the tendency of para-church institutions to take on a life of their own that would separate them from the life of the church and would substitute for the church.

These two narratives illustrate something of why our commitment to rich and deep counseling in the context of the local church also leads us to a commitment to para-church ministry. And these stories demonstrate the potential for church and para-church to live in a dynamic, constructive relationship. A mutually reinforcing dynamic can take place between the working of churches (where all Christians gather in community) and the work of para-churches (organized for a specialized mission, either reaching back to strengthen the community or reaching to outsider populations that the community isn't reaching).

THE OLD, OLD STORY

This story is as old as Scripture. And it has appeared repeatedly throughout church history.

Here is the deep structure biblically. Local churches are an extension of the creational principle of the *family*. This is where the work of God began, where redemption also began, and where all God's purposes in Christ will culminate. A marriage feast and a family reunion are coming. But along the way, a second institutional dynamic also participates in the journey toward that destination. Para-church activities are an extension of the redemptive principle of the *called individual*, who reinvigorates the family and who goes out to invite strangers in.

In the Old Testament, the extended family of Israel gathered to worship and learn both as family units and in the temple under the leadership of priests. In homes and on a hill the assembly happened, the *ekklesia* of God. But, simultaneously, prophets and wisdom-writers served in para-church roles, outside that organizational structure, yet serving its welfare and growth. They spoke and wrote to inform, reform, and disciple the community, and to proclaim the Lord's name, promises, and will to the nations.

At the time of the incarnation of the Messiah, the community was still gathering in the temple and at home. In God's providence, synagogues had also arisen as a further development of the familial principle, gathering locally for Sabbath worship and teaching. But, simultaneously, Jesus, His disciples, and other followers formed a para-church movement of reform, intensive discipleship, and outreach. The Christian movement began as a para-church movement to revitalize and expand the family of God.

After Christ's resurrection, the para-church missionary band of apostles went out to gather Christian believers into new synagogues — pointedly establishing local churches. They went out to call all peoples to come into the family of God. They intensively discipled these new churches through their teaching and writing. Para-church served local church; it was never an end in itself.

Throughout both Old Testament and New, we repeatedly see a close relationship between the open-to-all congregational pattern of the church family and the selective, disciplined pattern of para-church calling, serving a specialized mission. Neither is a guarantee of goodness and truth. Both can stray and do harm. Either can become a source of renewal for the other and for the body of Christ as a whole.

Two thousand years of church history repeatedly shows that the Spirit continues to use variations on the same two kinds of organizational structure in order to build and nurture the people of God. Familial congregations welcome all, and all participate. The more selective and specialized para-church focuses in on a particular mission. Over the centuries, a host of monastic, evangelistic, discipling, educational, medical, mercy, justice, and missionary organizations have mobilized dedicated Christians called to serve particular purposes that went beyond what a local church could do. When they have served well, they specifically serve the greater cause of the church.[141]

We will develop the remainder of this chapter along two tracks. First, we will discuss the philosophy of how para-church and local church counseling ministries interrelate. Second, we will sketch the topography of para-church ministry roles for men and women committed and trained to counsel biblically.

BIBLICAL COUNSELING, LOCAL CHURCH, AND PARA-CHURCH

Let's start with two crucial principles for understanding the relationship between church and para-church when it comes to biblical counseling. After that, we will consider three ways that this relationship can best be lived out. In this, we hope to lay a foundation for establishing wise, careful, and rich connections between local churches and para-church ministries.

Two Crucial Principles

The first crucial principle defines God's overarching goal. Christ has chosen to gather His people into countless congregations—which, in the end, will gather as one great assembly before the face of God.

Effective para-church ministry must be grounded in this reality and must faithfully serve this familial principle. God has chosen to establish the church community as the institution by which He best expresses His mission in the world. He is gathering His children to make disciples of them—i.e., to raise children who will live as dependent children are meant to live, to raise children who will become wise adults acting in the image of Christ.

The Father is patiently teaching His children to do the things churches are meant to do well—and to do these things together, because they are inherently relational. Worship Him. Listen to Him. Seek Him. Be washed in the fresh water of grace. Be nourished in the bread and wine of Christ's love. Bear each other's burdens. Forbear and forgive the failings of others. Forbear and give thanks for the innumerable differences between people. Serve the common good. Invite outsiders in to drink the Water of Life. Protect the purity of both message and people. Learn to love God and others.

Jesus Christ is continually working to build this church—His church (Matt. 16:18). Christians are members of the church, the very household of God (Eph. 2:19). If we actually love our Father, we will love our siblings (1 John 5:1–2). This living church—literally, a new people-group united to Christ and each other, even now gathering, congregating, assembling in Christ's name—is the pillar and buttress of the truth (2 Tim. 3:15). When Christ returns in glory and power, He comes to redeem His bride—the church, each and all of us (Rev. 19:6–10)!

The church is central.

The centrality of the church does not mean that there is no room for the multitude of activities that we refer to today as para-church work. Instead, it legitimates a rich proliferation of ministries to address the many problems that need addressing. Historically, Christians have understood a distinction between particular local churches and the various other levels in which the universal church operates. The Bible talks about the church in a layered way. Sometimes church means a local congregation of believers—Aquila and Priscilla (Prisca), together with the church in their house, send hearty greetings (Rom. 16:3–16). The Bible also talks about the church as a citywide entity—Paul, Silvanus, and Timothy, to the church of the Thessalonians (1 Thess. 1:1). The church can be referred to as a regional reality—the church throughout all Judea and Galilee and Samaria had peace and was being built up (Acts 9:31). Finally, Scripture understands the church as a universal body—Christ loved the church and gave Himself up for her (Eph. 5:25). That all-encompassing body of Christ is built up into maturity by the innumerable ways that each part does its part (Eph. 4:11–16).

This diverse use of the term "church" in the Bible provides a strong biblical justification within which Christians may organize themselves to serve in activities that we call para-church: e.g., schools, relief agencies, publishing, college ministries, chaplaincies, and so forth. It is no surprise that individuals who form organizations for such purposes do faithful work for the sake of Christ. They are doing their part as part of the universal church. Those individuals and organizations are drawn from and are dependent upon many local congregations.

This is the pattern that para-church biblical counseling ministries seek to fulfill. The important work that para-church does in and for the church does not make it a substitute for the congregation. Para-church ministry can often be helpful, even necessary, for a season. But when all is said and done, it is dispensable. At the end of history, the gathered familial church will remain. All para-church auxiliary ministries will have finished their temporary purposes. These dispensable, "seasonal" ministries must be aimed at strengthening and supporting what God has chosen to be indispensable, namely His church.

So the centrality of the local church congregation is actually an argument for principled para-church ministry—so long as such ministries direct their energies toward the church's thriving. That is so for seminaries, prison ministries, counseling ministries, and international mission societies ... and every other form of para-church organization. The mission of local churches endures throughout history. The mission of a para-church is seasonal, according to a specific need, and that mission must result in the welfare of local churches.

The second crucial principle defines one specific "seasonal" need in our time. Biblical counseling is an essential part of what every church should be doing. Candid, constructive, prayerful, fruitful conversations are a characteristic of a church whose people are alive to God and each other. But, on the whole, we haven't been doing it, or haven't been doing it well. So a need exists. A wide gap exists between what our biblical DNA calls for and what our lives together manifest. In hundreds of different ways, the Bible urges Christians to do the work that we moderns call "counseling." We should be having significant conversations with each other, talking through things that matter in ways that are helpful. We are to help each other grow wise and loving, in the midst of the ways each one of us struggles every day with our sins and sufferings.

Scripture doesn't use the word "counseling" for the things we use that word to describe, but the reality is present everywhere. Listen to familiar passages (slightly paraphrased).

- Take the judgmental log out of your own eye — then you will see clearly to gently take the blinding speck out of your brother's eye (Matt. 7:5).
- Speak into each other's lives in ways that are true, relevant, and helpful (Rom. 15:14).
- Find God's comfort in your own troubles — then you will be able to comfort any person facing any trouble (2 Cor. 1:4).
- Think hard about how you can stir each other up to love and good works (Heb. 10:24).
- Encourage one another every single day so that none of you are hardened by sin's deceitfulness (Heb. 3:13).
- Admonish the unruly. Encourage the fainthearted. Hold on to the weak. Be patient with them all (1 Thess. 5:14).
- Learn how to sustain with a word anyone who is weary (Isa. 50:4).
- Pray specifically for your brothers and sisters, that their love will abound more and more in knowledge and discernment (Phil. 1:9).

- Let every word you ever say be nourishing, constructive, timely, giving grace to anyone who is listening to what you say (Eph. 4:29).

Sit with those passages. Realize what they are actually saying. Every one of us needs help, and needs to learn to give help—and honest conversations are intrinsic to what counts as help.

Don't let our culture's office-bound, fee-for-service, professional depiction of "counseling" control how you think about counseling. And don't let the fact that churches often do everything except have honest, constructive conversations control how you think about counseling. Regardless of what we call it, God wants His people to be having personal, prayerful, change-oriented conversations with one another. God wants that because He is an intrinsic part of the conversation. Sitting under good preaching and developing a good devotional life don't eliminate the need for counseling—instead, they should create a community of wise counselors and awaken your awareness of your own need for the input and prayers of others. That's the message of those Scriptures mentioned above. If it's not happening, then some disconnect is occurring in the preaching, devotional life, worship, programs, and fellowship.

When the church loses sight of this crucial work—as happened throughout most of the nineteenth and twentieth centuries in the American church—it is incumbent on believers to restore the church to faithfulness. To become faithful is to become wise. And wisdom is a verbal virtue, able to comfort the disturbed and disturb the comfortable. This restoration to faithfulness has been and continues to be the work of para-church ministries involved in biblical counseling.

These two realities—the centrality of the local church and the crucial nature of biblical counseling—form the principled argument for the existence of para-church ministries dedicated to biblical counseling. Such organizations exist to restore wise, faithful, loving, excellent biblical counseling in local churches. With this understanding, how can the relationship between para-church and local church best be lived out? We will discuss three relational realities by which para-church can serve churches.

THREE RELATIONAL REALITIES

The first relational reality is *training*. Para-church biblical counseling ministry can serve the church by training people in local churches to do counseling well.

All ministry requires skill. Of course, the Holy Spirit is the person who imparts giftedness (1 Cor. 12:11). This conviction, however, does not make it unnecessary to hone giftedness through careful training. The Spirit uses people. People organize their work together into institutions that put a variety of gifts to work.

Preaching provides a clear historical example. For centuries local churches have relied on para-church institutions such as theological seminaries to train the ministers who will be called to preach to the flock. Most of us with rock-solid convictions about the significance of preaching in the local church learned many of our convictions, insights, and skills during our theological education in a para-church seminary. We read books produced by para-church publishers. We gathered with like-minded believers in para-church conferences to find fellowship, further teaching, and role models of how to do preaching well.

Training in counseling is as crucial as training in preaching. Counseling training may be even more essential. A pastor-to-be who desires to learn how to preach has no shortage of opportunities to do so. He gets exposed to the ministry of preaching from his local church pastor every week. He can hear preaching at any number of conferences. He can hear the Word preached on countless websites and podcasts. Most books about "ministry of the Word" and about the application of Scripture to life are books about preaching. Pastors are taught how to speak a prepared, scripted message that moves from the biblical text out into general life experience.

But usually only one or two people preach in a church on a regular basis. And everyone, including preachers, will do counseling—either well or poorly, either intentionally or unwittingly, always informally and perhaps formally on occasion. But no abundance of resources is available for counseling ministry. Seminaries were slow to even teach counseling. They have been even slower to consciously build their teaching from Scripture, rather than relying on secular models. Few books on "ministry of the Word" and application direct their attention to the dynamics of interpersonal conversations. Pastors and laypersons are not taught how ministry of the Word and prayer unfold within an unscripted, improvisational conversation that moves from particular life experiences into biblical truth.

This is an odd imbalance and omission, when you think about it. In the Gospels we listen in on how Jesus conducts significant, personalized conversations far more often than we listen in on his preaching. And the expression of love, the problem-solving, the perspective giving, the prayers, the candid self-disclosure, the direct personal exhortation, and the vigorous sense of relationships expressed in many New Testament epistles is much more like the immediacy of counseling than like expository preaching. We should be able to both preach and counsel.

Because counseling ministry happens in a private conversation, not out in public, there are no counseling podcasts or opportunities to listen in. Even when men and women in a local church are doing dozens of hours of faithful biblical counseling every week, that work remains invisible to most people in the congregation. So if the church of Jesus Christ is going to grow in our ability to counsel wisely, we need experts in biblical counseling to train us in this work.

This is precisely the need that para-church biblical counseling ministries seek to meet. A hallmark of the para-church aspect of the biblical counseling movement is the training offered through instruction in seminaries, colleges, and other teaching ministries. Teaching also happens through published resources (books, articles, blog posts). A number of biblical counseling ministries have developed distance education courses through the Internet. There are a variety of regional and national training conferences both here and in various countries around the world. These efforts have brought training to tens of thousands of men and women, training otherwise unavailable in their local churches. It could become available in churches. And it will become increasingly available there, as this season of para-church ministry succeeds in fulfilling its mission. The para-church and the local church honor each other and advance the cause of Christ when the para-church offers training in biblical counseling that gets spliced into the operative DNA of local churches.

The second relational reality is *collaboration*. Collaboration is a powerful force in ministry. For example, one of the most positive arguments for the existence of denominations is that our churches — and the Christians in them — can accomplish more for the kingdom together than we can apart.

One historical example of collaboration is the cooperative program of the Southern Baptist Convention. Local churches collaborate to work in a para-church way and fund para-church ministries. Started in 1925, the cooperative program receives financial gifts from millions of Southern Baptists and thousands of churches to fund gospel ministry all over the world. No one person or church could ever raise the billions of dollars used to fund six seminaries, publishing ministries, and a wide range of missionary and evangelistic projects nationally and internationally. But when that work is supported by 16 million people and more than 40,000 churches, it creates a powerful impact.

Collaboration works.

This kind of collaboration is what biblical counseling para-church ministries have accomplished in partnership with local churches, becoming a biblical counseling *movement*. Every church, whether large or small, can implement biblical counseling ministry in some fashion. But it takes the collaboration of many churches and many para-church organizations to create a movement.

Christians all over the world have discovered biblical counseling. They have grown and are growing in their ability to counsel wisely, because a movement has arisen. Countless numbers of Christians have attended training events, earned a degree, gained experience, received certification, read books, been supervised and mentored, been able to observe counseling, or have themselves received counseling through para-church efforts in biblical counseling. We have much more work to do, of course. But what has already been accomplished would have been impossible for one local church to do. The collaborative effect of para-church biblical counseling ministries, working with and through thousands of local churches, has made what has been accomplished a reality.

The church's ability to offer wise counsel will be strengthened as Christians participate—individually and as churches—in para-church efforts to help congregations collaborate and advance the cause of the personal ministry of the Word.

A final relational reality is that of *accountability*. Accountability is an essential part of faithfulness in Christian ministry. Christianity is a religion of truth, faith, and love. Truth has standards. There are true and false ways to explain the human heart, or to weigh the significance of suffering and personal history, or to describe the goals of human flourishing. Faith takes both wise and foolish forms, either trusting rightly or misplacing and distorting trust. Attempts to love and help another person are sometimes loving and helpful, but sometimes unloving and unhelpful. "Counseling" can fall anywhere across the spectrum. Accountability helps us to clarify our convictions and our counsel, to deepen our faith, and to make our love more true.

For example, in 1646, 121 clergymen gathered in Westminster Abbey to draft guiding documents for the reformation of the Church of England. The document they produced came to be called "The Westminster Confession of Faith." This document has been used ever since as one measure of confessional accountability in multiple denominations for countless pastors, elders, and laypersons in thousands of congregations. Other churches, ministries, and denominations use other confessional statements directed toward the same end of establishing accountability.

The practice of using para-church standards of accountability has enjoyed broad acceptance with Christians through the centuries. Biblical counseling para-church ministry can also serve local churches by providing the accountability that is so necessary to the practice of personal ministry of the Word.

For example, one complicating factor facing the biblical counseling movement, and the churches offering it, is the current popularity of the very term "biblical counseling." All kinds of counselors today are quick to say that they engage in biblical counseling. Organizations that once openly advertised that they "integrated Christianity and psychology" now say that they are offering "biblical counseling" — though what they actually do and say has hardly changed. The term "biblical counseling" was often derided from the 1970s and through the 1990s — but now it has become a popular term. So counselors who have never received any instruction in biblical counseling, and who do not really believe that God intends Scripture to play a central role in counseling, may use the term. This poses a problem. When a term comes to mean anything, it becomes useless. We need accountability with regard to the definition, ideas, and practices that make counseling worthy of the adjective "biblical."

This task of creating standards of accountability is something that para-church biblical counseling ministries have sought to do from the beginning. Leaders have written books proposing to define the content and methodology of biblical counseling.[142] Organizations have sought to recognize and certify faithfulness and skill in biblical counseling practice.[143] There have been efforts to create standards for the belief and conduct of biblical counselors.[144] Of course, none of these efforts or secondary standards are final and infallible. But they are a work in progress toward a good end — that we as Christ's people will be increasingly able to articulate and practice what it means to counsel in fidelity to the mind and heart of our Savior Jesus Christ.

As para-church leaders create a faithful context for accountability in the practice of biblical counseling, local churches will benefit, able to grow in their conscious faithfulness to this important task.

Biblical counselors should be the first to understand that training, collaboration, and accountability are a two-way street. Of course this is so—many of the leaders and participants in para-church ministries have been or are pastors of local churches, and all, whether or not they are pastors, are active in local churches. The differences between local church and para-church are not absolute—because the persons involved live easily and fruitfully in both institutional worlds.

WHAT DO "COUNSELING MINISTRIES" LOOK LIKE IN A PARA-CHURCH SETTING?

It is helpful to remember that wise counseling should be one component in *every* aspect of local church ministry. Think about that. To help another person calls for skills in understanding how Scripture maps onto life experience relevantly and in detail. It calls for skills in understanding the varied needs, struggles, and troubles of various kinds of people. It calls for skills in understanding how God works change in people—and how He works in the midst of what doesn't change. It calls for skills in conversation.

- How is it that kindness, pastoral intention, and genuine inquiry draw out otherwise unspeakable things, the fine china of a person's heart?
- When do you speak up, and when do you listen hard and quietly mull over what you are coming to know?
- When do you ask questions—and what questions do you ask?
- When do you press in with a thoughtful response?
- When and how do you encourage?
- When and how do you confront?
- When do you draw out what a person already knows, and when do you teach what they don't yet know?
- When and how do you pray personally and relevantly for someone?
- When and how do you help a person get practical?

The many wisdoms that go into good counseling are basic aspects of distinctively Christian wisdom.

This means that every role within the church is strengthened to the degree that counseling wisdoms are present: pastors, elders, youth workers, secretaries, janitors, worship leaders, deacons and deaconesses going about mercy ministry, evangelists, small group leaders ... and anyone who is simply a friend, a family member, a brother or sister in Christ—as well as those who might be designated and more specifically tasked with hands-on pastoral care. The rest of this book is about these things.

The same skillful wisdom applies to para-church ministry. What counseling roles thrive in para-church settings? Here is a sampler.

Chaplaincies are a long-established para-church role that calls for candidly Christian counseling. Historically, chaplains have served in hospitals, the military, nursing homes, and schools, with occasional opportunities in business and industry.

Missionaries doing evangelism and church-planting: Counseling operates within world missions in two obvious ways. First, missionaries themselves need care, counsel, and prayer. Counseling wisdom is one obvious key to caring well for missionaries—and mission agencies increasingly recognize that need. Second, and even more basic, life-changing conversational wisdom ("counseling") is intrinsic to the entire missionary endeavor. Evangelism, repentance and faith, baptism, and forming churches express the "come through the door" first half of the Great Commission. The making of a disciple begins with new life in union with God and His people—the import of "baptizing into the Name" of the triune God. And counseling savvy makes the evangelistic message cut deeper by making the personal relevance more obvious. The making of a disciple continues on with Christian formation, the "live in the family" second half of the Great Commission. "Teaching them to keep all I have commanded" speaks to our growth in grace, in faith, in love, in obedience, in wisdom. Counseling savvy also makes this formation cut deeper and more personally. Personally relevant conversation encourages the deeper self-knowledge that corresponds to a more grounded knowledge of God. Mission work that does honest conversations well bids to produce deeper and more honest conversions, and then more intentional Christian growth.

Crisis pregnancy workers are presented with huge counseling opportunities. Some practical information and services are needed, of course, but everything else is counseling.

Similarly, *rescue missions* offer many practical services as part of their mercy ministry: health care, detox from addictions, improved diet and hygiene, safety, education, and job training and placement. Everything else — Bible study, mentoring, discipleship, accountability, small groups — is ministry of the Word and prayer with a counseling slant.

Prison ministries: Everything is counseling. The sins, sufferings, troubles, and temptations parade in the open — so admonish the unruly; encourage the fainthearted; hold on to the weak; be patient with them all.

Campus ministries in colleges and high schools: Like youth workers in a local church, para-church campus workers build friendships, lead Bible studies, and organize events. But most of what they do is talk and pray with students about their struggles and troubles. Biblical counseling skill is a must.

School teachers, guidance counselors, and school disciplinarians: There are objective jobs to be done when teaching content, helping plan the next step after graduation, and intervening in problems. But schools deal with people, so counseling skills are always operating just under the surface and, often enough, will have opportunities to come out in the open.

The same is true for *medical doctors and nurses*, and for *lawyers and mediators/conciliators/peacemakers.* A Christian does not reduce personal problems to a body gone awry or reduce relational problems to a legal conflict. Medical people know that there is always a person inside every diagnosis, and that health problems often arise from personal problems and always trigger counseling needs. A Christian wants to heal both body and soul. Similarly, legal people will always deal with the "material issue" in contention, but they are also dealing with persons in broken relationships who may be aggrieved, obsessed, angry, frightened, guilty, vindictive, or confused. A Christian does not reduce the law to achieving victory over an adversary. Biblical counseling skills are most welcome and useful in these neighboring professions.

Social workers, relief missions, and other mercy ministries: Again, whatever the tangible need being addressed, there is always a person in need of pastoral care, in need of Christ, in need of hope, in need of growing in the faith that works out into love.

Publishers: Christian publishers choose works to print according to some philosophy. Some Christian publishers are self-conscious that the entire genres of "counseling" and "self-help" need to be candidly, wisely Christian. Other publishers should join in promoting biblical understanding and help.

Professors in higher education: Christian seminaries, universities, colleges, and Bible colleges. Campus workers and college fellowships aim to serve students as persons and as members of a community—but who nurtures the mind? The *content* of seminary counseling classes and of college courses in psychology and counseling should conform to the wisdom and worldview of Scripture, instead of being secularized. The current state of affairs is spotty at best.

Ministries to the elderly: We mention this one because it is so neglected and so needed. Most churches hire an energetic youth worker to disciple young people. Why is pastoral care for the elderly rarely approached with a discipleship vision to grow the faith and love of those who are living under the encroaching shadow of death, who are living through a cascade of losses, and who are facing their last enemy?

Ministries that provide counseling services: We put this last because it is too often the first and only thing people think of. But it is wisest to envision counseling as one component in every form of para-church ministry, not to begin with the "I am a biblical counselor" role. Get things in biblical perspective, and then consider how direct biblical counseling services might be delivered to otherwise neglected populations and to people who may not be reachable by local congregations.

There is room for a great deal of institutional and organizational creativity in designing appropriate ways to meet particular needs afloat in the community, while pointedly serving the growth of local churches.

That is only a sampler of possibilities. Currently there are relatively few "routinized career tracks" in place, either in churches or in para-church organizations, for a person described as a "biblical counselor." That will change—it is already changing. But thinking creatively about how counseling wisdom enhances *every* church or para-church role is a good place to start. From there, wisely conceived para-church ministries can be built to serve specialized missions, extending the blessings of grace beyond the church, complementing the work of churches, and serving to strengthen the churches of God in every community.

CHAPTER 21

BIBLICAL COUNSELING, THE CHURCH, AND THE ACADEMY

LILLY PARK AND JEREMY PIERRE

Depraved minds want to know. So do virtuous ones.

What do we mean? Simply that regardless of who we are or what we do, we are seeking knowledge. We all want to know. Knowledge is a means of arranging the world to conform to our plans, and people were designed to pursue it. The pursuit of knowledge, and the greater human capability that results from it, is a magnificent aspect of how human beings image their Creator. God fashioned in us inquiring minds as an instrument for worship.

But knowledge for the sake of greater human capability is not *necessarily* a virtuous pursuit. Increased human capability, as history has shown, can be hijacked by any number of atrocious motivations — dominance over other people groups, the self-destructive greed to consume more, the mitigation of consequences from unhealthy and immoral ways of living. Increased human capability is virtuous only when motivated by virtuous purposes.

Virtuous purposes seem quite rare these days in higher education — at least virtuous as God would define it. But if it's any comfort,

Christian thinkers from the beginning have complained about the philosophical concerns or research interests of the academies of their time. All of this may give the impression that higher education as a means of pursuing knowledge is not worth the risk for those who want to be faithful. Why not do all education through the church, where the dangers of intellectualism or philosophical error are lower?

Such reasoning commits two great errors: first, it assumes the danger of false teaching is higher outside the church (an assumption not shared by the apostle Paul). Second, it ignores the rich theological vision of the world displayed in Scripture that all disciplines, occupations, and industries are the jurisdiction of God's glory. Thus, the institutions that prepare people for these pursuits, though not the church, can glorify God.

But educational institutions do not glorify God as they ought to simply in the transference of knowledge, as we've established. The pursuit and transmission of knowledge must be done for virtuous purposes as God defines them, and He defines them according to His own central purpose in redemption: to establish the kingdom of God through the proclamation of the gospel. The church is the only earthly steward of this purpose. Any educational institution that claims to be Christian must see itself as a servant to the church, the only community Christ has pledged His undying loyalty to (Matt. 16:16 – 19).

THE ACADEMY AS SERVANT OF THE CHURCH

The church's privileged role as the center point of redeeming grace is why Christian institutions of learning must be self-conscious servants of the church as the primary means of serving humanity. Christian institutions of higher education are not the church, and thus they do not carry out the mission of the church in her place. Neither do they ignore the role of the church as unimportant to the benefit of humanity. Rather, Christian institutions of higher education pursue and transmit knowledge of the scholarly disciplines for the purpose of enabling people to work for the benefit of the world in Christ-honoring ways.

More specifically, Christian higher education glorifies God and serves His church by engaging in the pursuit of knowledge for its proper application to human conduct, in conscious attendance to the central mission of the church to proclaim a crucified, risen, and reigning Lord. We will unpack this simple thesis with three main assertions, all the while keeping an eye toward the discipline of biblical counseling.

First, the purpose of the church directs the purpose of the academy. Second, the academy allows for the theoretical pursuit of knowledge that is necessary to practical application in ministry. Third, the academy must value practical application as necessary for transference of knowledge and transformation of lives.

The Purpose of the Church Directs the Purpose of the Academy

Stephen Dempster points out that something *inherent* in Christianity necessitates the pursuit of knowledge, but always bound to the specific goal of love—love to God as His image bearers exercising dominion of the world as His agents, and love for neighbor because this God-directed dominion is mutually beneficial to all.[145]

The pursuit of knowledge for the good of humanity is a thoroughly Christian doctrine, rooted deep in the Protestant heritage. One of the precious developments of the Reformation was the doctrine of vocation in which Christians "were to serve God in whatever their occupations, not just in special 'religious' vocations. Hence university learning, even apart from theological preparation, could be a means of glorifying God."[146]

But virtue and love are motivations that no longer come naturally to human beings. Scripture represents people both in glorious terms as divine image bearers and in dubious terms as corrupted sinners. So the very function that makes them like God can be used to make them very much *not* like Him. None of the biblical writers are particularly impressed with the human pursuit of knowledge apart from a covenantal relationship with the self-revealing God. The pursuit of knowledge apart from the revelation of God, and the community to which it is entrusted, always leads to disaster—starting with Adam and Eve's pursuit, running through their son Cain's line, through the Tower of Babel, and continuing on in the efforts of all nations and institutions that ignore the covenant Lord.

So educators, as those concerned with the pursuit and transmission of knowledge, must always ask the question, Learning to what end?[147] The end must be to glorify God. But glorifying God in itself is a broad answer that can be hijacked by any number of ideologies. Is the core of the task to bring glory to God feeding hungry children? Revitalizing cities? Caring for the environment? Purging evil from the culture?

Human beings find out what it means to glorify God by listening to what He says will glorify Him. He communicates this through Scripture. And the community entrusted with Scripture is not the academy, but the church. The question, Learning to what end? can only be answered for the academy by the church. Thus, we make the bold assertion that the church's mission is necessary to give direction to the academy's pursuits. Dempster goes on to point out that not only does Christianity inherently necessitate the pursuit of knowledge, but it does so "bound ... to a specific spiritual goal."[148]

As the community shaped by the Word of God, the church bears the responsibility of being a prophetic witness to a thousand cultures, each with different values and priorities that vie for the right to answer the question, Learning to what end? Is the end of learning to increase the standard of living for the most people in the precarious reality of a world economy? to evolve humanity into a higher existence collectively? to attain human autonomy individually? to decrease human consumption of its surrounding environment? Each culture has multiple ideologies working hard to pursue knowledge for a more powerful voice. And the church alone is the community of God that proclaims His Word, which chastens every culture.[149]

The church as the community of the kingdom of God rebukes aspects of every culture by insisting on the glory of Christ in all pursuits of knowledge.[150] The church keeps the gospel central to the understanding of human flourishing and progress, a gospel that redeems sinners to rule the world on God's behalf in ways that reflect His character and goals. The church alone is the final earthly steward of the confession that Jesus is the Christ, the Son of the living God (Matt. 18:12–20), as well as the word of that Messiah (Eph. 4:11–16).

Two implications of this first point come to mind. First, Christian institutions of higher education will remain loyal to the church's mission only if they have codified confessions that guide them. In other words, academies that wish to preserve the centrality of the gospel must be confessional institutions. They must have clearly defined statements of belief that guide hiring of faculty and the teaching and writing that faculty practice. The historic trend away from confessions by institutions such as Yale, Harvard, and many other Christian-founded universities began as a desire to be "nonsectarian" but ended up being not much more than an awkward blending of Christian and other competing worldviews.[151] Confessions ground institutions more closely to the church's mission by guarding a plainly stated set of common beliefs and guiding principles. This is especially true for institutions that teach biblical counseling, which requires a world-and-life view saturated with a high view of Scripture's authority.

Second, faculty and administrators should be personally involved in serving the church as members of the body necessary to its growth. Ecclesiology is a flatly practical doctrine, requiring the personal allegiance of any who claim Christ (Rom. 12:3–8; 1 Cor. 12:12–31; Eph. 4:11–16; Heb. 10:23–25). If the individuals making the decisions about institutional priorities, research funding, administrative involvement, and faculty promotion are personally disengaged from the church, they are less likely to be motivated by the values of the kingdom. We will say more about the practical aspects of this in our third point below, but for now it is sufficient to say that if biblical counseling is to retain its rich ecclesiology, those who develop it as a discipline must personally be dedicated to the church.

The Academy Allows for the Theoretical Pursuit of Knowledge That Is Necessary to Practical Application in Ministry

Many times, theoretical knowledge and practical ministry are pitted against one another, for reasons that at first seem understandable. We are all sensitive to the stories of Christian college students living like villains, seminary graduates blowing up churches with inept people skills, graduate students once vibrant in their faith growing cold and cynical. No one likes an egghead. But we must be equally on guard against intellectually reckless pastors, undiscerning pragmatists, or sleepy and unthinking congregations. No one should like a numbskull either. The church should tolerate neither intellectualism nor anti-intellectualism.

The reason for this is the nature of theology, and all other disciplines as servants to it. Theology can be considered both science and wisdom, *scientia* and *sapientia*. Both aspects must be carefully considered in every discipline. If we ignore the importance of *scientia*, pursuing theoretical knowledge, we become vulnerable to subtle ideological shifts that have momentous practical consequences. If we ignore *sapientia*, the wisdom of practically applying that knowledge, we become useless in carrying out the call of God to live as His agents in the world.

Our point is that academies labor to increase *scientia* — knowledge of a definite subject matter using a definite method of investigation and verification, coherent regarding its subject matter, and communicable with other subject matters.[152] If we emphasize application too much by only valuing knowledge that has instantly identifiable usefulness, our wisdom will be poorer in the end. One scholar points out the dangers of pursuing knowledge only for its perceived usefulness:

> Utilitarianism is a threat to utility ... a rigid application of the utilitarian criterion could deprive the next generation of the very means it will need for the tasks that it will face, which will not be the tasks that this generation

faces and which therefore cannot be dealt with by those particular instrumentalities that this generation has identified as "useful."[153]

We should maintain valuing knowledge for its own sake, confident that because God creates nothing purposeless, it will be effective for shaping wise ways of living, even when those ways are not immediately apparent. One writer gives an excellent example of this. The eleventh edition of *Encyclopedia Britannica*, published in 1911, devoted nine folio columns to "Delian League" and only two columns to "Uranium," concluding that there was no significant use for the "metallic chemical element."[154] Uranium is now one of the most coveted and talked about objects of study, and no one has a clue what the Delian League was. This is a good reminder that scholars rightly pursue knowledge that is not immediately applicable, and academies give a stage for such study.

Churches can, of course, pursue the science of theology, biblical counseling, and many other subjects apart from the academy. The church shows the ability to pursue knowledge apart from immediate applicability every time a pastor studies the character of God in his private office with no intention of teaching a lesson on it.

But churches are usually unable to employ scholars to specialize in a given field. Specialization is an important part of faithfulness, not just visible progress. Researching and staying abreast in an academic discipline is a vital way for Christians to engage the culture and help its members who live in that culture discern truth from error and live appropriately. Carl Henry pointed out that the secular conceptual schemes floating around in academia often merely "put on parade the spirit of contemporary culture, setting its ruling assumptions in the context of comprehensive theory," rather than question "the controlling ideas of the present period."[155] It is vital for Christian thinkers to be given a platform to know and assess these theories as well as the controlling ideas of a culture.

The academy guards this pursuit by employing scholars and theoreticians who serve to progress the knowledge of their field and to transfer both that knowledge and the tools to acquire that knowledge to students. They are able to see how the knowledge shaped by revealed truth at times resonates and often contradicts the controlling ideas of the age.

The biblical counseling movement has witnessed the importance of engaging *ideas*, not just practice. As a discipline, biblical counseling has to engage *scientia* externally, both the mass of secular psychologies as well as the litany of attempts to integrate those psychologies with Christian doctrine without solid theological method. It also has to engage internally. This means having dedicated scholars to study such things as theological process and application, the person and work of Christ and the knowability of God, human experience as image bearers, models of epistemology, the process of change, hermeneutical method, the function of language, legal and ethical issues, cultural contextualization, and counseling methodology. In other words, those involved in biblical counseling have a significant stake in the direction of Christian education. The academy is an important tool in the development of a biblically faithful model of counseling.

As we have, hopefully, made plain, the church, as the community of the Spirit, is a greater institution than the academy. But the academy can nevertheless serve the church by progressing theoretical knowledge on such topics in conscious service to the church's mission. Still, theoretical knowledge is not an end in itself, as we now would like to demonstrate with our third assertion.

The Academy Must Value Practical Application as Necessary for Transference of Knowledge and Transformation of Lives

Along with theoretical knowledge, the academy must value practical application as another essential component of a holistic approach to learning. A holistic approach to learning engages *whole persons*, mind and body—or, to be more specific, thoughts, emotions, will, actions. Because all of these aspects of human nature are interrelated, learning addresses not only cognitive knowledge but also behavioral movement.

In fact, a team of educators who researched best practices in teaching stress the importance of challenging students at the level of thinking, acting, and feeling for transference of knowledge.[156] As a result, students tend to grasp knowledge more comprehensively and remember it more enduringly when learning with their whole being. For instance, in the context of Christian education, it's one thing to learn about the doctrine of man, but how does it affect our ministry to single parents, widows, and divorced persons? How does progressive sanctification affect our children's ministry? Such questions confront students with the implications of theoretical knowledge and increase their motivation to study diligently.

Educational pedagogies should not overemphasize either extreme. Exclusively lecturing on a topic overemphasizes theoretical knowledge. Exclusively working on projects underemphasizes it. No universal teaching formula exists for every class, but it seems that an optimal one will provide theoretical knowledge as a foundation to the necessary step of modeling and testing application. Well-known Christian educator Howard Hendricks discusses the necessity of maximum involvement for maximum learning.[157] He points out that given the option to learn about the Holy Land from a lecture by an expert authority, seeing a photographic presentation, or actually going there personally, most students will likely choose the last option as the most influential learning experience.[158] Hendricks acknowledges the role of lectures and visual presentations, but his point is that a student who is more involved in learning will be more invested in the learning process. How practical learning is required in each class will look different, but faculty should seek to intentionally incorporate it.

TRANSFERENCE OF KNOWLEDGE

We cannot measure the preparedness of a student for biblical counseling or any other field merely based on academic performance. In a way, it is like sending a medical student who studied only books to perform surgery. Thus, many academic programs require practicum or internship for graduation. It takes time and practice to develop skills;

consequently, practical application should be integrated in courses as early as possible.

But competent skills alone do not indicate that knowledge has been properly transferred, if our goal is to glorify God with our knowledge. In Christian education, wisdom should characterize the transference of knowledge. Wisdom, *sapientia*, is applying knowledge, *scientia*, in a way that glorifies God. Wisdom, then, is the goal in transferring knowledge. Understanding of that knowledge is best displayed in the accurate practice of it. From a counseling perspective, wisdom requires being sensitive to individual needs and situations. Such wisdom allows a person to discern what themes from Scripture are pertinent to the situation and how best to express those in ways that will lead to virtuous outcomes. It is one thing to know what Scripture says about a certain issue and quite another to know how it ought to be conveyed productively in a given situation.

Jay Adams points out the need for both insight and creativity in counseling: "Neither true biblical insight nor creativity may attempt to do the job on its own. Each, in its own way, contributes; the one provides the flexibility that is necessary to adjust to each particular case, while the other produces the framework and the base for what is to be adapted."[159] Adams' observation describes an aspect of wisdom, because insight and creativity are based on the right knowledge being used in the right way, depending on the situation. As students practice counseling at home, work, school, church, and in society at large, they learn numerous ways to apply the same principle in various contexts.

Throughout this process, faculty and church members play influential roles in how well students transfer their knowledge to situations, allowing them to make mistakes in an environment where those mistakes can be pointed out and improved upon. Mistakes made apart from the process of education do not benefit from the same immediate feedback and guidance, thus they can perpetuate. Experienced educators who allow room for feedback on the practice of counseling greatly increase the efficiency of a student's growing experience.

Transformation of Lives

John Frame helpfully points out that theology *necessitates* application. He builds into the very definition of theology its practical results by saying theology is "the application of Scripture, by persons, to every area of life."[160] The necessary purpose for the study of theology warrants this definition: "The theologian states the facts and truths of Scripture for the purpose of *edification*. Those truths are stated not for their own sake, but to build up people in Christian faith."[161] The study of the theoretical aspects of theology is indeed a necessary foundation, but equally necessary is its application to every area of life. Theology transforms the full spectrum of the human experience.

Biblical counseling is a tool of practical theology and shares in this purpose. If biblical counseling is to be taught in the academy, it must share in this purpose, which requires a personal touch not typically characteristic of academic teaching. If biblical counseling is intended to help people transform their understanding of life and conduct within the full spectrum of life as the outflow of a personal relationship with Christ through His Word, then those who teach and those who learn in an academic setting must incarnate this intention. In other words, a person not actively seeking transformation himself is hindered in his application of Scripture to others.

Biblical counselors are chastened by the theology they teach others. As they help others to learn to walk, they have a bit of a limp themselves. In an academic setting, this means that while professors ought to be experts of various aspects of the discipline of biblical counseling, they never arrive at the application of theology to life. Even in the expert culture of a university, the common saying in biblical counseling applies: Good counselors are good counselees. Good counselors compare their lives to biblical teachings and the counsel that they give to others. They are mindful of their own weaknesses and sinful inclinations. In sum, in order to remain effective in the discipline of biblical counseling, instructors must maintain awareness of their own need for the personal grace of the Lord Jesus in applying His Word to their lives.

SOME PRACTICAL GUIDELINES FOR ACADEMIC PROGRAMS IN BIBLICAL COUNSELING

Students will perceive that the academy serves the church but does not replace it when they consistently encounter faculty and administrators who prioritize the church. Faculty members need to be people of the church. Only by being personally invested in church life will lectures and exercises be rich with practical wisdom on how transformation happens in community. If church is tangential to the life of a professor, that implies that one can be successful in this discipline without the church. In his classic book on biblical counseling, Jay Adams writes:

> A teacher teaches theory (perhaps not the theory he consciously wishes to teach) all the time by his practice, and in this he inevitably communicates well. What the teacher does, says, what his (her) attitudes, moods, etc. are, all are a part of teaching *by modeling.* The teacher is the integration of principle and practice.[162]

The reality is that students face temptations to compromise church attendance and fellowship when facing seemingly unending amounts of reading and assignments. Inadvertently, they replace church fellowship with academic association. In the study of practical theology, students need the church as the necessary context for seeing what they are learning come alive. Students who are overcommitted between work, family, and school should consider extending the program of academic study to maintain this vital connection to church life. Students need to see faculty members willing to do the same.

Faculty members ought to model personal concern for students as well. Obviously, faculty members have varying degrees of availability, but they should schedule into their workload informal contexts outside of the classroom to influence students. A few simple ways to create space for this is to post weekly office hours for students, take a group of students to the cafeteria before or after class, or even show hospitality at the instructor's home. Discipleship does occur in the academy as well, but will be consistent only when faculty members intentionally schedule it.

Course objectives should include both theoretical engagement and application for ministry because scientia *and* sapientia *are both necessary to excellence in ministry.* From lectures to labs, academic programs that incorporate these course objectives will educate well-rounded students who think critically and practice wisely. Course objectives are standardized educational requirements and can seem insignificant, but they serve a useful purpose in shaping the outcomes of a course and keeping faculty accountable in addressing theory and practice.

Observation, in both directions, is essential for counselors. Students develop competence and character as they are observed by and observe church leaders and members. Curriculum should include opportunities for constructive feedback on strengths and weaknesses in counseling practice. Nothing develops skill more efficiently. Schools that teach biblical counseling may not be able to arrange counseling practicums in private practice or clinical contexts, but that does not mean that quality skill development is impossible. Two suggestions may be helpful here.

First, on-campus counseling practicums assist in preparing students for off-campus counseling. Instructors could arrange a course in which students counsel each other on real-life problems, preparing counseling sessions and homework.[163] They also benefit by receiving counseling, which reinforces the concept that biblical counselors never stop learning from others and need to continually examine their lives. This allows them to be more cognizant of how a person receiving counseling might feel or think. How practicums are arranged will differ based on class size. In smaller classes, students tend to have more opportunities to counsel each other in class, but students should also counsel each other outside of class time for more accountability and relationship building.

Second, churches can provide opportunities for counseling. Even if a church does not have a counseling ministry or a formal internship program in place, a counseling student can become immersed in ministry, both to serve the church and to increase personal knowledge and experience. If a church does have a counseling ministry, students can simply make use of the existing structures. Regardless, the key to improvement is supervision on the instructor's part. This supervision can occur by means of video or audio recording or by written report.

CLOSING

In 1911, Benjamin Warfield, a well-known theology scholar, warned seminary students that learning theology could lead to a slippery slope of missing theology. If theoretical knowledge or practical application is pursued without adoration for God, then learning becomes the end and not a means to glorify God. Over a century later, his admonition is still applicable for Christians not only in the academy but also in the church:

> Are you, by this constant contact with divine things, growing in holiness, becoming every day more and more men of God? If not, you are hardening!... You will never prosper in your religious life in the Theological Seminary until your work in the Theological Seminary becomes itself to you a religious exercise out of which you draw every day enlargement of heart, elevation of spirit, and adoring delight in your Maker and your Savior.[164]

If the academy is to glorify God, then those directing it must listen carefully to what God says in His Word about what glorifies Him. The steward of God's Word is His redeemed bride, the church, which alone has this privileged role. All pursuits of knowledge find their purpose in knowing and worshiping the One who rules over all knowledge, all people, all disciplines—including biblical counseling.

CHAPTER 22

THE MISSIONAL
VISION OF BIBLICAL
COUNSELING

ED WELCH AND SAM WILLIAMS

Missional work (taking the gospel and biblical counseling to the world) begins with the global and compelling nature of the kingdom of God. Author C. John Miller describes this grand vision well.

> A look at the universe about us reveals that God has a certain style: the massive and the majestic. God's workings in the spiritual realm follow the same pattern. It should not surprise us that the prophet Isaiah would refer to the coming of the Messiah as a "strange deed"—a work so sweeping in magnitude that it would sweep away all evil and lay the foundation for a whole new order.[165]

From there, we work back to the details of what this looks like within the body of Christ. Then we move out, beyond the borders of the church—and aim to speak winsomely about the counsel of Jesus to the world.

The apostle Paul gives a version of this missional mindset and ministry in 2 Corinthians 4:14–5:21. Christ's love, he writes, compels us because He died for all, and now we live for the One who died for us rather than for ourselves. We see those who are in Christ as new creations. Next, Paul moves to complex relational matters, generosity and other details that are local expressions of this global commission. But he doesn't stop there. He reminds us that we are ambassadors for reconciliation to those who do not belong to Christ.

The writer of Hebrews promotes this larger vision by showing that Jesus is worthy of greater honor than Moses. His message is weightier than that of angels. His high priestly work is more effective than the sacrifices made by the line of Aaron. And His covenant is a new and better covenant. As with Paul, these global realities lead to a response in the realm of local details, which reminds us that the kingdom is, in fact, now in us and among us, so it is our job to act accordingly.

Most Christians are aware of this expansive nature of the kingdom of heaven. The issue of this chapter is how biblical counseling is living out God's global mission that reaches to the ends of the earth.[166] We will project a vision for biblical counseling as one part of God's compelling and global mission for this world. To do that, we will start with our perspective of the way this mission plays out in our counseling offices, then we will consider what this might look like in local church communities, and we will expand the focus to the world Jesus calls us to be in, but not of.

A MISSIONAL VISION FOR PERSONAL COUNSELING

Since most biblical counselors are, in fact, counselors, the mission starts in our counseling offices. If the kingdom of heaven has gripped us, it will come out first in the details of personal face-to-face ministry. Those details should sound better than counseling offered outside of the realm of the Spirit that relies on human insight alone. Our vision is for biblical counseling to go deeper, peering into the spiritual center of the human heart. And, our vision is for biblical counseling to go broader, extending meaningful help to all ages, addressing all our human struggles, and in all contexts.

Here are three ways we can focus on growing so that we might enact that vision with individual counselees: we grow in humility, we grow in expressing kindness and mercy, and we grow in knowing others well. Each of the three takes seriously Micah's charge, "He has told you, O man, what is good; And what does the LORD require of you But to do justice, to love kindness, And to walk humbly with your God?" (Mic. 6:8 NASB). Let's look more deeply at each.

We Grow in Humility

Humility is fundamental to our missional vision. A theological textbook began with this preface from its author: "The material in this book has not changed for thirty years." He was trying to defend Scripture's timeless truth. And it *is* timeless truth. But biblical counseling's books and models are not timeless truths. So we must be careful that we are not blinded by our personal and cultural limitations that can hedge us in from a fuller understanding of Scripture and people. Because our insights, theories, and methods are not as true as Scripture, we are always a work in progress. Thus, humility demands that we grow in our knowledge of the Word and its application.

To this end, we merge great confidence in Scripture with a healthy dose of self-doubt about our minds, models, and methods. That doesn't mean inserting a few "Ah, shucks" in our counsel, or "Maybe someone else could be more helpful than I am." We are confident in Christ and that God's Word contains the only grand unifying theory of the cosmos, and that all truth emanates from this living and active Word. Self-doubt and humility simply mean that we believe our application of that biblical truth is not always the best.

Furthermore, the people we counsel are complex in ways that challenge our discernment of counseling priorities and the most suitable Scripture. Discerning God's agenda and making sure we do not sully it with ours can be complicated. It is an honor and a challenge to sort out which of the thousands of truths in Scripture is most appropriate for this person in this particular situation at this particular time in their life and at this stage in their spiritual development.

Missional counseling is a collaborative partnership with the Spirit of God and a person crafted by, and like, and for Him. We bow under the Word of this God and consider with this counselee, "What are the particular words of God to you now, in these present circumstances?" (And, of course, the same question applies to the counselor.) In addition, when it is feasible, we counsel with the help of others. That means that another person might be invited to join the counseling time (e.g., a pastor, spouse, friend). At least we will ask for prayer and wisdom from others who are not physically present.

We Grow in Love That Is Characterized by Kindness and Mercy

Love is integral to God's missional vision (John 3:16). Mercy and kindness should pour out of us in ways that make us stand out among our neighbors in the secular world.

The broader field of counseling has known for decades that helpful care comes from the co-mingling of (1) a system that makes sense of, and to, the person and the particular problem at hand, and (2) a genuine relationship. Secular counseling, however, is often relationally restrained by its interest in professional boundaries and clinical objectivity.

That is not to say that biblical counseling has no boundaries. We are limited in how much we can do and how much time we can give, and we certainly do not want to give the slightest hint of relational impropriety. But we do expect to love those we counsel, we expect that love will grow, and we expect the love to be edged with glory in such a way that it is noticeable and blesses others.

How might that sound in a conversation?

"You have been on my heart this week. Here is how I have been praying for you."
"This is a unique time—to meet together before Christ, needing the Spirit, asking for mercy and grace. What a privilege."

We grieve with those who grieve. We celebrate with those who celebrate. We keep an eye out for the work of the Spirit in this person and savor it, and then we get on board with what He is doing.

385

When people are stuck in sin, our kindness is more than a veneer. We are burdened because someone we love is flirting with death. Our appeals are personal; we are not mere technicians with a biblical script. We express how we have been affected; we may shed tears as we plead for and with those who do not know the goodness of God in Jesus. Our desire is that counselees leave the counseling session sensing that they were loved wisely and well.

We Grow in Our Understanding of People

A missional vision includes love that strives to know people deeply. We will address this characteristic in-depth, because this has been an area where we believe the biblical counseling movement has been historically weak.

In our movement, there has seemed to be a lack of skill in knowing others in a way that they truly felt known. This weakness may come from this line of thinking: If we already know what the Bible has to say about people, then why take time to hear a person's story? Although this is surely an extreme caricature, we believe it is a weakness for some biblical counselors. Sermons can be effective even when the preacher has little personal knowledge of his hearers. But that is rarely true in counseling.

This may be one reason why biblical counseling is not known for its three-dimensional descriptions of people. Our case studies have tended to flatten people into occasions for us to make theological points. In view of 1 Corinthians 13:2 ("If I ... know all mysteries and all knowledge ... but do not have love, I am nothing" [NASB]), this should make us wonder if we are biblical *enough* in our counseling. If this critique is on target, then here is a suggested course correction: a combination of love and biblical insight yields in-depth knowledge of people that is matchless.

Practically, memoirs, testimonies, and careful case studies can help rehabilitate this weakness — and biblical counseling has demonstrated progress by our recent attention to these. Some of the best descriptions of mental disorders come from memoirs. For example, addiction memoirs help us to understand the tragic enslavement of addicts. Our compassion grows as we listen to real stories of real people. Bipolar memoirs help us to understand the euphoric flights that move quickly into painful chaos. Kay Jamison's *An Unquiet Mind: A Memoir of Moods and Madness* has been a perennial favorite among CCEF (Christian Counseling and Educational Foundation) students. She takes us inside a manic mind and describes what has been helpful and what has not.

Biblical counselors have grown in wisdom and understanding through these memoirs. And biblical counselors have written a growing number of book reviews on secular memoirs. In these reviews, we demonstrate how Scripture can always see more than what is overtly obvious. For example, consider the biography *A Beautiful Mind: The Life of Mathematical Genius and Nobel Laureate John Nash* by Sylvia Nasar. This chronicles the descent of John Nash's mind into the emotional detachment of schizophrenia. It illustrates the incessant and bizarre connections made in an unstable mind. Random numbers suddenly hold the key to the universe. A word that appears in two different newspaper articles about murder proves a link between the two perpetrators. These details take us into the inner world of an unusual mind and give us secondhand experience. But schizophrenia was not the entire story. Nash struggled with feeling inferior. To compensate, he aspired for personal glory. Coupled with this arrogance was a need to solve the unsolvable problems. Then there was the guilt for betraying his spouse, fears related to growing old, and struggles with loss. Indeed, Scripture reveals the human heart, and in Nash's heart we find pride, guilt, suffering, fear, and shame—matters to which Scripture speaks directly and that are beyond the scope of medication.

In addition to reading and reviewing memoirs, the biblical counseling movement is also making headway in writing and sharing our own stories. At Southeastern Baptist Theological Seminary, students in the problematic emotions, addiction, and psychopathology classes who have struggled with an issue are asked to give testimonies to help their colleagues understand the experience. The students answer just three questions: What was it like? What didn't help? What really helped? These stories move dry *DSM* (*Diagnostic and Statistical Manual of Mental Disorders*) diagnoses into the neighborhood where people actually live and give students a much better feel for what it is like trying to live with panic attacks, or raise a child with autism, or do battle with alcohol or drugs. Course evaluations at the end of the semester always point to these stories as among the most helpful parts of the class.

Ed took a bold and highly educational step recently when he reflected on a bout of panic attacks on CCEF's blog. I (Sam) told him I learned as much from his testimony about panic as I did in reading his 324-page book *Running Scared*. The book is very good, but it doesn't match his story when it comes to getting into the shoes of a person with panic. Particularly helpful in Ed's story was listening to precisely how Jesus mattered in times of panic, even though He was not a panacea.

Every time we read a memoir or biography or listen to a testimony, it adds to our experience and case wisdom, and with that growth comes humility and carefulness. They teach us that human experience is rarely as simple and straightforward as we imagined. These stories also challenge some of our assumptions about the potential role of psychiatric medication and the types of personal interaction that are genuinely helpful. And they improve the practicality of our theology. Indeed, we have much to learn from real-life stories, whatever package they come in. Yet while we are learning, we are listening with scripturally tuned ears, so we hear more than what a memoir intended. We are challenged to broaden our application of the Bible to experiences we have not yet considered. And we are encouraged as we see that the Spirit and Scripture open our eyes to see more than anyone can see apart from them.

We aim to grow in these three ways because they all help deepen and strengthen relationships, and we represent a very personal and very relational God. He is the God who knows us better than we know ourselves—and joins that knowledge with compassion. Therefore, we represent Him poorly when a counselee feels better known at AA or better understood by a *DSM – 5* description. Our vision is to know our counselees in such a way that they are blessed by being known, they tell others that they have been so known, and they themselves grow in how they know others. This is one way the mission goes and grows.

We want those who receive biblical counsel to become our best apologists. We hope they find in biblical counseling more love, deeper insight, and more extensive transformation than can be found in any secular competitor. The Father sends Jesus, who sends us after He breathes His Spirit into us. Under the inspiration of this Spirit Counselor, we then send our counselees into this world to be wise counselors to family, friends, and coworkers (John 20:21 – 23). That's the mission — an expanding circle of counselors, filled with the Spirit of Christ: wise, kind, and humble. Now let's think about the mission lived out when nonbelievers seek one-on-one help from a biblical counselor.

Counseling People Who Do Not Know Christ

Sometimes people who have not placed their hopes and trust in Jesus come to us. They may come with Christian family members, or are referred by a believing neighbor, or they just want a counselor who shares their conservative values. How do we counsel those who do not share our understanding of the authority of Scripture and the lordship of Jesus Christ? This might be the most frequent question among students of biblical counseling, whether those students are lay, graduate, or undergraduate. When a question like this surfaces, it should open our missionary eyes. To begin to answer the question, the missional vision might be rephrased like this:

> We have been given something very precious, and we want to give it to our family and friends and anybody else who is hurting and without hope.

So what should we do? Biblical counselors should pray for encounters with unbelievers, especially for those whose world with all its strategies and ways of coping no longer works for them. Most of us have known someone who is immune to evangelism and mocks the Christian faith. Then a spouse commits adultery; a child becomes a drug addict; depression renders everything black and meaningless. Suffering tends to make humanity's suppression of the truth much more difficult. People who were atheists yesterday are so encouraged that you are willing to pray for them today.

To this end, we aim to write and counsel in ways that attract and invite, catching people off guard in the best of ways and revealing a relational world where God is different than who they imagined Him to be. We aim to avoid the trite and predictable. We say things we want them to hear, so we take care that our words are not misunderstood. We work to excise in-house jargon that communicates to unbelievers that we prefer to speak our own language rather than learn theirs. A missionary's goal is to render theological terms in the receptor's language, accessible and meaningful while yet faithful to the "better than" words of God.

Up to this point, the focus has been micro—on the one-on-one dimension of biblical counseling. Now let's go macro and broaden the focus. The Great Commission of Christ is big, going everywhere the curse is found.

BIBLICAL COUNSELING'S MISSIONAL VISION FOR THE WORLD

In the Biblical Counseling Coalition's Confessional Statement, we read:

> We believe that Christianity is missionary-minded by its very nature. Biblical counseling should be a powerful evangelistic and apologetic force in our world. We want to bring the good news of Jesus and His Word to the world that only God can redeem. We seek to speak in relevant ways to Christians and non-Christians, to draw them to the Savior and the distinctive wisdom that comes only from His Word (Titus 2:10–15).

As we move outward to the secular world, perhaps our most needful constituency is non-Christians who are active in psychology and psychotherapy. We believe, however, that our direct engagement with this group is negligible and much less than missional. Jesus' version of a mission trip is to go into this world and yet not be of it. We have the second part of this down pat, but we seem to have neglected the first part. Yes, we are not of this world, but we are, or at least should be, in it. Biblical counseling has been weak in interacting with the secular world. This is our vision of what biblical counseling's engagement with the secular world might look like.

Again, the Biblical Counseling Coalition's Confessional Statement addresses this mindset:

> We want to present the claims, mercies, hope, and relevance of Christ in a positive, loving Christlike spirit (1 Peter 3:15). We seek to engage the broad spectrum of counseling models and approaches. We want to affirm what is biblical and wise. Where we believe models and methods fall short of Christ's call, we want to critique clearly and charitably.

We aim for charitable, merciful engagement with this beautiful and broken world, and yet we remain acutely aware of the fundamental incompatibility between Scripture's model of care and this world's. We know that observations and reasoning that do not recognize God and His character in creation are always, sometimes more and sometimes less, blind. Part of being missional means that we are alert to the world's influence and can (God help us) respond with something much better. These influences operate at both the level of worldview and counseling method.

Responding to Worldviews

At the level of worldview, we have two recurring critiques. First is that psychotherapeutic psychology conceives of people as autonomous, self-contained individuals and is utterly blind to how life is always lived vis-à-vis the triune God. G. C. Berkouwer writes, "We may say without fear of contradiction that the most striking thing in the biblical portrayal of man lies in this, that it never asks attention for man in himself, but demands our fullest attention for man in his relation with God."[167] To try to understand the person apart from God is to perpetuate a delusion.

A second and related critique is that secular theories of the person typically zero in on one piece of humanity, but miss the whole.

Whereas they do identify something important about humanity—e.g., the present impact of a painful past, the challenge of untethered emotions and irrational thoughts—they miss other elements that are essential. Secular theories, because they have no access to Scripture's breadth, are always reductive. Our contribution is to establish an alternative that is better because it captures the complexity of humanity in all its pain, its goodness, and its badness.

An illustration of this reductionism is Dialectical Behavior Therapy (DBT), which is a very popular and eclectic brand of psychotherapy, bringing together a diverse blend of Western and Eastern methods. It is entirely pragmatic, open to almost anything that might help. Yet it avoids essentially human questions about meaning and purpose that underlie most human struggles.

Responding to Particular Counseling Methods

At the level of counseling method, secular psychology has recently fallen in love with "evidence-based" secrets deemed essential for helping people. In response, we note that secular psychology has largely forgotten that it begins with assumptions about human nature that are not evidence-based, and that evidence for effectiveness is a very difficult matter to establish in the multifactorial world of human relationships and personal change.

We do not stand alone with this concern, as a rising tide of psychologists voice similar concerns that, to summarize, sound like this: "Your counselees (manifesting only one clearly demarcated symptom or disorder) and counseling (highly structured manual-based techniques that are carried out in lock-step form) are not like the people I see in my clinic, and your counseling seems more suited for a robot than a person."

We have seen how counseling theories and methods come and go, and particular methods have a limited shelf life, which then give way to new theories and methods. Biblical counselors are not alone in observing that modern psychotherapies are more art than science, and that this art, like all others, is draped in culture that does not easily export to other cultures.[168]

Biblical counseling will always expose assumptions and debunk the overstatements of the psychotherapies. However, we place a lower priority on this than we once did. Critiques of chemical imbalance theories, our overmedicated culture, and psychotherapeutic goals have always been mainstream, taken up by others who offer even more precise critiques than we do. Furthermore, biblical counseling's prominent vision has always been to bring the person and work of Jesus to struggling people in a way that is helpful, surprising, and beautiful. Critical analysis of other counseling theories and methods will remain important, though secondary.

Writing and Talking to the Secular World

It has been our observation that not many biblical counselors ever attend—let alone present papers at—secular conferences, and we have very few non-Christian readers of our writings. It is our opinion that biblical counseling is a small outpost that the world never had to forget because it never knew it in the first place. In terms of missional outreach to the secular counseling world, it appears that we have little like Stanton Jones' article in the *American Psychologist*[169] or Paul Vitz's *Psychology as Religion: The Cult of Self-Worship*.[170] As far as we know, there is no biblical counseling version of Alvin Plantinga, who first made his mark in analytic philosophy and whose philosophical defense of theism earned respect in the secular academy. We haven't aimed for publishers that focus on the secular market. We rarely seek out critique of our manuscripts from secular professionals. We can claim a few op-ed pieces and not much more.

Reading and Learning from the Secular World

First, let's take some credit. Most biblical counselors we know read much more secular material than the secularists we know read our material. Most of us are quick to affirm useful observations from non-Christians before we discuss the underlying assumptions and inadequacy of their conclusions—and that is a significant step outward that the biblical counseling movement has taken. However, it would be hard to call that *missional* because we are listening to them. But it does suggest that our dominant stance is not separation and isolation. Rather, our stance is engagement that seeks to understand. And yet, we would like to see another step toward more meaningful dialogue.

One place to find meaningful dialogue partners may be in the fields of medicine and psychiatry. We should look to dialogue with these two fields first because they readily intersect with our perspectives and they make observations that are more easily reframed in biblical categories.

DIALOGUE PARTNERS IN THE SECULAR WORLD: THOSE IN THE FIELD OF MEDICINE AND PSYCHIATRY

Medicine and psychiatry are longstanding neighbors of biblical counseling. Most biblical counselors have adopted human unity-in-duality as a faithful representation of Scripture: we are embodied souls, created of two substances that are mysteriously and wonderfully joined together (though they possess the capacity for separation at death). Whereas Scripture fills out the details of the soul (spirit), Scripture identifies only the essential category of the body and leaves it to other disciplines—like neurology, neuropsychology, and psychiatry—to fill out useful details.

For example, neurological and neuropsychological case studies illustrate that our emotions can be shaped by brain and body dysfunctions. We then take this research data back to Scripture and use it as a catalyst as we deepen our biblical theology of emotions. With the medical data in mind, emotions illustrate the interdependence of spirit and body. Emotions can reveal the affections of the heart or the peculiarities of brain dysfunction—and, most often, both.

This broader view of emotions is relatively unique among psychological theories, which tend to be reductionistic in either the biological or the cognitive direction. Our perspective, therefore, would be worth promoting and could be a good foray into meaningful missional interaction.

As a second example, we can consider how human duality can expand the understanding of despondency or depression. Depression rooted in the heart may have its causes in being sinned against, in guilt or shame, or in an inaccurate knowledge of God. Yet this certainly does not exhaust the causes for despondency and depression. Depression may be caused by bodily weakness. If so, it is not rooted in spiritual matters (though it is always a spiritual challenge). Rather, it is a result of living in a fallen body that groans until the day of final redemption.

Notice the prominent bodily symptoms of depression: insomnia, lack of appetite, lethargy, slowness of movement, and slowness of intellect. These are not in and of themselves moral issues, which could point to spiritual causes. Physically induced depression can *affect* the susceptible heart and move it toward despair, hopelessness, and an unbiblical view of one's self. Nevertheless, the physical features of depression are just that—physical—and they can be treated medically and behaviorally. Even if depression originates in a person's heart, which is not always easy to discern, the accompanying physical features can be treated medically.

This is not to say that spiritual help is irrelevant or even secondary. Although medication and other behavioral or physical treatments may alleviate the feeling of depression in some people, spiritual help for depressed persons is essential. Depressed persons are just like everyone else. They need practical, biblical teaching that will daily call them to faith in Christ (Heb. 3:12–13). But depressed persons need this even more. When depressed, it is easy for unbelief to gain ground and undermine the ability to resist temptation. The human heart is notorious for taking advantage of depression and transforming it into something that is self-consuming and guilt-provoking. Consequently, depressed people might feel despair, hopelessness, and anger. Satan knows that depression can be a test of faith that leads to greater spiritual maturity (James 1:2). Scriptural advice to counselors of depressed persons begins with:

"Encourage the fainthearted" (1 Thess. 5:14 ESV) and then is scattered throughout the canon, with a whole category of psalms (of lament) that are tailor-made for those in the pit of despair.

This is only one application of the embodied soul. Other applications extend to the gamut of *DSM–5* diagnoses. This is one place where the missional nature of biblical counseling is bearing fruit. After years of maturation, CCEF's 2011 conference on psychiatric disorders was attended by an unprecedented number of psychiatrists and mental health professionals as compared with previous conferences. It was followed by well-received psychiatric conferences in India. In addition, recent Internet discussions about psychiatric problems, initiated by Bob Kellemen and Heath Lambert, have generated unparalleled interest from the larger church.

BIBLICAL COUNSELING'S MISSION TO THE CHURCH

The church is at the very center of biblical counseling's missionary vision. This is a distinguishing mark of biblical counseling and perhaps the most important way it can gain traction in our world. Although we counsel individuals, we always have the church in view. This vision is expressed in three primary ways: through the pursuit of unity with other biblical counselors that reflects the unity of Christ's church, through the pursuit of the local church's wisdom for our counseling cases, and through our willingness to listen to the church's critiques of biblical counseling. Let's explore each of these three ways to live out biblical counseling's mission to the church.

Biblical Counselors Interact with One Another in Ways That Reflect That We Are One Body

Some counselees and professional counselors have been so impacted by a particular approach that they become evangelists for it. Or, they have been helped so much by a particular person and his or her method that they want everyone to be helped by that person. This has contributed to disunity in some churches and denominations. We understand that the church universal has always had a tendency to follow a charismatic leader (1 Cor. 1). As such, biblical counseling does best when it avoids allegiance to a particular person or institution and aims for a corporate movement that imitates the body imagery of the church. In short, we do not want to harm one another, and we can best avoid that by remembering that we are one body with many members. When any member of the body is harmed, the whole body is weakened.

With respect to our different perspectives within the biblical counseling world, we want Scripture to guide us in how we dialogue and adjudicate these. We should be good at building bridges with other biblical counselors and with the church. Our goal is not to enhance the reputation and growth of the "biblical counseling" brand, but to contribute to loving and wise interpersonal care that could be referred to as "biblical counseling," but that decidedly avoids proprietary motives. Our desire is for peace and unity within the biblical counseling movement to serve to enhance the peace and unity of the church (Matt. 5:8).

Biblical Counselors Act like Associate Church Staff

Another means for biblical counseling to bless the church is to keep the church and its leaders in mind all along the way when we counsel its members. It is not natural for counselors to keep the larger church in view. Our ministry is to individual people. We hold confidences. The inertia of personal ministry is toward privacy. It is easy for us to act like solo artists, but Scripture redirects us to the resources of the larger body of Christ.

One expression of this vision is the sheer number of biblical counselors who *are* on church staffs and the number of para-church biblical counselors who wish they were. Good biblical counselors who serve churches but are not formally on a church staff should act as though they are, insofar as it is reasonable and biblical. They can work within the theological contours and distinctives of a counselee's church and seek the wisdom of that pastoral staff. For example, a biblical counselor who is not on a church staff was counseling someone who had been caught in sin. The counselor had a concern about the proper scope of the counselee's confession. The counselor had an opinion, but realized that he was venturing into Scripture application more than clear scriptural directives. So he made a call to the person's pastor. The pastor brought it to the elders and made a decision that differed from the counselor's, to which the counselor readily submitted. There is, indeed, wisdom when there is a convergence of counseling with pastoral guidance.

Biblical Counselors Listen to Critiques

One clear evidence of a healthy missional vision is our willingness to self-critique, search out critiques, and listen to critiques from the church and the broader Christian community. If our vision is to be carried out through relationships, then listening to others is essential, as noted in the Biblical Counseling Coalition's Confessional Statement:

> We want to listen well to those who disagree with us, and learn from their critiques. Our mission to spread the truth and fame of Jesus Christ includes a desire that all counselors appreciate and embrace the beauty of a Christ-centered and Word-based approach to people, problems, and solutions.

Scripture and the Spirit give us certainty about Jesus and His mission, and we are not wishy-washy in matters where Scripture is clear, but our fallible and fallen humanity is always before us. We can say a right thing at the wrong time, we can miss themes in Scripture that are most apt for that moment, we can misunderstand what is most important, and the list continues. Our missional vision is not enhanced by triumphal proclamation. It is enhanced through relationships that include the back-and-forth of speaking and listening.

That includes eliciting the concerns of others about our counsel. This is even more important as we move outward to the larger Christian community, since many pastors and Christian counselors already have questions about biblical counseling. To assume a blank slate in our conversation with the church is, at least, naïve. We have been in the neighborhood for a while, and most people have heard about us. It is good to elicit feedback from our brothers and sisters, listen well, understand their concerns, and carefully answer their questions.

AS OUR COUNSELING GOES, SO GOES THE MISSION

A culture-crossing, all-nations vision is essential to biblical counseling, if it takes Christ's Commission seriously. A biblical missional vision clarifies our goals and is possible because Christ promises to go with us always into all places. It is daunting because it assumes a working knowledge of Scripture and people and culture. We will accomplish it to the extent that our mission is God's mission, derived from His Word, inspired by His Spirit, compelled by His Christ.

Bringing it down to ground zero, we could summarize our missional vision and impact this way: As our counseling goes, so goes the mission. If our counseling captures the majesty of the gospel and provides a glimpse into the ever-expanding kingdom of heaven, we will find others naturally and supernaturally compelled to be part of this mission that we call biblical counseling.

PART 6

BIBLICAL COUNSELING IN HISTORICAL PERSPECTIVE

CHAPTER 23

THE LEGACY AND FUTURE OF BIBLICAL COUNSELING IN THE LOCAL CHURCH

HOWARD EYRICH AND JONATHAN HOLMES

In his twentieth-anniversary celebratory article about the Christian Counseling and Educational Foundation (CCEF), John Bettler, the first Executive Director, offered a caution for those writing or reading history. "We remember our past as we are at the moment of remembering.... History easily becomes nostalgia."[171] Dr. Bettler was warning us that we tend to color history. In other words, there is a second dimension to these personal historical accounts that pulsates with life. Objective historians cannot fully summarize the real story: the angst, the emotions, the frustrations, the excitement, the joys, and the wonder that constituted the sinews actually binding the movement together.

These observations provide the backdrop for my (Howard) personal perspective on the history of the modern biblical counseling movement. In the pages that follow, I will share some personal reflections on the beginnings of the movement. Why? Because this history is vital if we are to understand and contextualize the work in this book on biblical counseling and the local church. We cannot forget the past, and some-times, just hearing the stories of what God did years ago can spark fresh understanding and new vision for the future.

THE LEGACY OF BIBLICAL COUNSELING: WHERE HAVE WE COME FROM AND WHY?

I begin with my earliest interest in counseling. It started when I (Howard) was a student at Bob Jones University. During that time, several of my close acquaintances were dismissed from the school. In each case the school took justified action based on a strict interpretation of the rule book. But I found myself wondering and thinking about the reasons why students had broken the rules. In each case I felt that there were underlying causes, causes that were not fully considered, that had led to the student's poor choices. My interest in looking into these motives was pricked.

Several years later, I graduated from Faith Theological Seminary in 1965 with a BD (an MDiv for the younger readers). During those years my wife, Pam, and I served as youth leaders on church staff, where we were confronted with many difficult family issues. These situations raised some of the same questions: What led to these? What were the underlying causes? In 1968, I completed a ThM from Dallas Seminary and took my first full-time church position as Pastor of Christian Education and Youth at Colonial Hills Baptist Church in Atlanta, Georgia.

Settled into my role as a youth pastor, I soon began searching for answers to my nagging questions about motivation. I was looking for practical insights to help those I was mentoring. All of this led me to the next stop in my professional journey as Dean of Men in a Bible college. Still, I didn't find the answers I was looking for. After four years in a Christian university and four years in two fine conservative seminaries, I still felt like I didn't have good answers to my questions.

My search eventually took me into the world of Carl Rogers, Steward Hiltner, and Howard Clinebell.[172] Howard was an early advocate of training in psychotherapy for seminarians and was a prime mover in the establishment of the pastoral counseling movement of which he served as its first president (1964–65). In the summer of 1969, I enrolled in an MA counseling program at Millersville State University. But after nine hours, I abandoned the program. When asked why, I was honest: "I put everything I read and heard into my theological sieve, and it all ran out on the ground." Still searching, my next move was to interview with Clyde Narramore to seek enrollment at the Rosemead Graduate School of Psychology. But after a two-hour interview I told my wife, "Scratch that one. He is a warm Christian man but has a humanistic anthropology."

If you have had the chance to read David Powlison's dissertation, you will realize that I was not alone. In those years there was a growing number of us who were experiencing the same frustrations.[173] One of those men was Jay Adams. God had uniquely gifted, trained, and platformed Jay to lead a new charge in this area. Jay's practical emphasis was more focused on changing behaviors and, as a result, his nuanced exploration of motivation was often missed. Additionally, Jay was embroiled in polemics from the day *Competent to Counsel* hit the streets. Many charged him with being a "Christian behaviorist." The prominence of *confrontation* and the *put off/put on dynamic* in his writings and lectures certainly fueled this charge and unfortunately overshadowed anything he had written that touched on the question of motivation. He even developed some friction with his first trainee, John Bettler, over their differing emphasis on the issue of motivation.

I was privileged to observe Adams engaged in over a hundred hours of counseling, covering a variety of cases, and I participated in weekly roundtable discussions of cases of which Adams was a contributor for almost five years. These roundtables included usually four counselors and ten pastoral trainees. In those early years the counselors included me and men like Dr. Richard Ganz, Dr. John Bettler, and Dr. George Scipioni. We spent many hours discussing the question of motivation, but at that point in the development of biblical counseling, we did not have categories to describe the various motivations. We were still just figuring it out on the go. To give an example of this, I share a story Bettler recounts about how he and Adams would travel to New Jersey to counsel one day each week in the year 1967. On the drive up they would theorize and meditate together on Scripture and its application. Then they would go to work counseling and implementing what they were working out in their thinking. On the way home they would debrief the day's work.[174]

My own experience was similar. Less than ten years later I found myself living in Atlanta, working for CCEF under contract. Twice a week Andrew Boswell, who came as an intern with me and became my first employee, would travel the hour and a half to Macon. On the way to Macon we would discuss case approaches and issues and work on strategies regarding the use of Scripture in counseling. On the way home I would have Andrew review his cases and I would offer supervisory comments. Often we would engage in great doctrinal discussions regarding motivation (how we understand biblical anthropology and progressive sanctification in the counseling context). We were not attempting to replicate what Adams and Bettler had done; we were simply doing what we had to do. At that point, no one was talking about mentorship, but in retrospect, I was mentoring Andrew just as Bettler and Adams had mentored me.

Back in 1970, when I enrolled at CCEF, it was a very small organization, so small that when I came on staff in the summer of 1971, we "expanded" the ministry into the nursery (which became my office). At the end of each day we would put everything (including our phone) in the closet and leave. Several years later, in Atlanta and Macon, we ran things the same way. We didn't have fancy offices, yet people from all walks of life were coming to see us for counseling. We were seeing marriages healed. We were seeing depressed people returning to normal functioning. We were learning how to work with women suffering from PMS and menopause. And we were teaching and mentoring others.

In the late 1970s, Faith Baptist Church of Lafayette, Indiana;

Granada Presbyterian Church in Miami; Kirk of the Hills (PCA) in Saint Louis; Westminster Presbyterian in Fort Myers, Florida; and a scattering of other churches and free-standing organizations arose that followed the model, both in theory and teaching methodology, that Adams had initiated at CCEF. We had no textbook other than *Competent to Counsel*. Some of us had the fun of working with Jay as he was hammering out his second book, *The Christian Counselor's Manual*. Then, in the mid-1970s, came a request from Adams for each of us on the staff at CCEF to write up ten of our cases to help him formulate *The Christian Counselor's Casebook*. In 1975, I edited *What to Do When*, the plenary sessions of the National Association of Nouthetic Counselors, and in 1976, I published *Three to Get Ready*. Soon afterward, in 1979 Wayne Mack published *Homework Manual for Biblical Counselors I*. These early works were the trickle that has now become a torrent of resources.

In those years during the mid-1970s, we had five counselors at CCEF, and perhaps 300 or 400 biblical counselors spread around the country were loosely connected. The National Association of Nouthetic Counselors (NANC) was launched to provide some semblance of consistency of training and thinking by providing certification. Unfortunately, NANC stumbled and almost died. But in 1986 the Lord provided Dr. Bill Goode to be the Executive Director. Bill brought with him the support staff of Faith Baptist Church in Lafayette, Indiana, which breathed new vigor into the organization. Today the organization is thriving, with over 1,000 certified counselors. The model of NANC (now known as the Association of Certified Biblical Counselors) has also birthed several other certifying organizations that are similar in commitment.

Why do I share these reflections? Well, as of this writing, I am celebrating my seventy-fifth birthday. Today, there are not many of us around who were directly associated with Jay Adams or involved in the beginnings of the modern biblical counseling movement. We were developing an approach that was theologically and anthropologically consistent with our commitment to the integrity of Scripture, and Adams became the lightning rod around whom we rallied. This group includes a few men who are still around today, including John Bettler, Earl Cook, George Scipioni, Bob Smith, Wayne Mack, and Richard Ganz.

REFLECTIONS FROM EARL COOK

In recent years, I was able to interview one of these men, Dr. Earl Cook. Earl, like many of us, attended the training program in the early 1970s, before the first curriculum component was added to the twelve-week training program. He continued to engage with CCEF training, eventually joining the staff around 1979 to take up the position of Pastoral Liaison. I asked Earl, who had just celebrated his eighty-sixth birthday, what he would include if he were sharing the story of those early years. His responses all relate to the continued growth and expansion of the biblical counseling movement.

First, Earl talked about the early growth and development of the movement. He said he would travel in a radius of fifty to seventy-five miles of Philadelphia to regularly visit with local pastors. He would ask them if they were familiar with CCEF. Most of the time, the answer was negative. He would then ask if they knew anything about biblical counseling. Again, most did not. Then he would ask if they had heard of Jay Adams. Most of them knew of Adams or had read something he had written. Earl would follow up with some one-on-one instruction, hoping to ignite a hunger to know more about the movement. I believe this early example is something we can learn from, a reminder that personal contact with pastors and leaders is often the best way to promote understanding.

Earl also talked about the structural development of biblical counseling and how it evolved rapidly. He mentioned the development of a formal curriculum and the strategic hiring of faculty like David Powlison, Ed Welch, and Winston Smith at CCEF. Again, this is a good reminder to us today that movements need resources and structure.

And we need good people, leaders who have diverse interests and who will carry the movement forward to the next generation.

The third and final element that Earl noted was the development of CCEF through extension centers and the burgeoning staff positions in local churches—the point that is most relevant to this volume on the local church. In the early years, CCEF began satellite operations in Princeton and Cherry Hill, New Jersey; San Diego, California; and Atlanta and Macon, Georgia. Most of these centers became independent of CCEF in less than a decade. For a movement to grow and develop, it needs to reach into the local church. It cannot be confined to academic institutions, but must be integrated into local churches where ministry and counseling centers are organized.

REFLECTIONS BY RICHARD GANZ

Another of the early pioneers in the biblical counseling movement was Richard Ganz, who eventually settled in Ottawa, Canada. Richard engaged in church planting, establishing a Theological Hall, and lecturing worldwide on the message of biblical counseling, bringing it into unlikely academic settings. In 1993, Ganz published *PsychoBabble*, in which he explained the dichotomy between secular counseling and biblical counseling. He demonstrated the dangers of incorporating secular techniques into a Christian approach.[175] Like Earl Cook, I also had the chance to interview Dr. Ganz via email.

Dr. Ganz began by sharing his thoughts on the key *person* God raised up in those early days: Jay Adams. Ganz wrote:

> For this movement to survive, let alone thrive, Jay Adams was perfect. He didn't care about criticism leveled at him. In fact, criticism just spurred him on to sharpen ever more his biblical methodology.

Clearly, for a movement like this to grow and spread, we need leaders, like Adams, who can deal with criticism and respond appropriately.

Next Ganz emphasized the importance of having a *strategy*.

> God raised up this man who was totally given over to the inspired, infallible, inerrant Word of God. Jay Adams believed in the sufficiency of the

Scriptures for counseling problems. The Bible, Adams held, was sufficient to deal with the full range of sin-related issues and all the other problems of living that had been cast onto the laps of the eagerly waiting secular psychotherapists by the church.

Today as well, we need a clear strategy. We must know what is foundational to our practice and ministry, the nonnegotiables, and align our practice accordingly.

Third, Ganz talked about knowing your *demographic*.

God raised up Jay Adams who was concerned to reach *the church*. Believers were tired of having their faith attacked by the secularist psychotherapists. *Competent to Counsel* came out at exactly the right time (1970) for a Bible-believing community that had been receiving counseling that was dismissive of their faith. Churches around the world became churches committed to biblical counseling.... The Revolution had begun![176]

Our demographic has not changed. Like Adams and others in those early years, biblical counseling is first and foremost a ministry of the church, for the church.

Some Strengths and Weaknesses of the Modern Biblical Counseling Movement

Knowing the past is helpful. It provides a guide to the future, as we look at what God has done. What are some of the strengths of the modern biblical counseling movement? For one, biblical counseling has resisted the pull of becoming a professional discipline with its own esoteric vocabulary. It has not become an academic *cult* that speaks to itself, and it has developed a wide following among the laity of the church. As a movement it has encouraged every Christian to engage in the process while understanding that there are varying levels of giftedness and skill sets among practitioners. As a ministry of the church and for the church, it has encouraged the church to search the Scriptures and to grapple with everything from Tourette's syndrome to bipolar disorder. The momentum has produced an ever-increasing quality of literature that is academically responsible and practically accessible to the laymen who so capably labor in our midst.

As with any movement, there are also potential weaknesses, areas where we need to be cautious. First, we must be careful that we do not erode our foundational commitment to the sufficiency of Scripture and the Christ presented therein. If we lose this rooting, we will find ourselves with the same *wood, hay,* and *stubble* that characterized the pastoral counseling of the Rogers and Hiltner brands.

Second, we must not allow the biblical counseling movement to grow complacent. As we develop an ever-increasing knowledge base, as science develops and our technology changes, we must exercise vigilance. Yes, we must engage science, but we can never allow science to rise to the level of authority over revelation. But we cannot ignore science either. To do so is to compromise the sufficiency of Scripture. There is always a balance. And we must not grow complacent, turning this into a monument to those who established the movement.

THE FUTURE OF BIBLICAL COUNSELING: WHERE ARE WE HEADED?

It is a daunting task to write about the future of biblical counseling. To this point, you've heard some reflections from some of the first members of the movement. As one of the youngest members of the Biblical Counseling Coalition, I (Jonathan) realize the enormous debt I owe to men like Howard Eyrich, Jay Adams, John Bettler, and David Powlison. I've heard a frequent critique of my generation that we often eschew the old and embrace the new (much of which is just the "old" reformatted). There is pride in this, of course, as we search for something new, for constant reinvention and relevance. As we think about the future, this is a pitfall we need to avoid. Any discussion about the future of biblical counseling should rightly acknowledge our indebtedness to the sacrifices of men like my coauthor, Howard, and others.

As a younger member of the movement, let me share a bit of my story, for background. Growing up, there were two things I consistently told people I wanted to be: a teacher and a psychologist. Yes, a psychologist. There was just something intriguing about the idea of talking and helping other people. When it came time to pick a college, my parents were fairly firm in their desire to see me attend a Christian college. My dad was familiar with John MacArthur, and when he discovered a college led by him, that sealed the deal for him. For my part, I wasn't convinced it was where I wanted to go. I remember looking at the majors offered, and psychology was not even listed! There was, however, something called *biblical counseling*. At the time, I had no idea what biblical counseling was, but I listed it as my intended major because it sounded close to psychology.

Well, the rest is history. Those four years at Master's College were transformational, not only for my Christian life but for my growing understanding of biblical counseling. I came to realize and believe that biblical counseling was different than anything I had ever encountered or read about. It was during college that I encountered the writings of Jay Adams and studied under wise and godly professors like John Street and Stuart Scott. During those years I had a front-row seat to see some of the maturing and development of the biblical counseling movement.

As he looked back on the early years of the movement, Jay Adams has said, "Looking back isn't always so pleasant. Often skeletons in the closet won't stay put. Heartaches and problems may characterize the past. Broken friendships and bad relationships may dominate the scene."[177] Yes, looking back can be difficult, but as I, a younger member of the movement, look at the past of biblical counseling, I firmly believe that the prayers, efforts, tears, and sacrifices invested in bringing biblical counseling into the mainstream conversation of evangelicalism are bearing much fruit today in the local church.

As a movement, biblical counseling continues to grow and mature, for which we can all give thanks to God. What originally began as a reaction to the secularization and outsourcing of care has now grown into a recognized and viable discipline of care.[178] At a symposium of biblical counselors, Steve Viars noted the growth of biblical counseling in that the *movement was maturing, more was being written*, and a *greater number of people were involved.*[179] Truly, as Viars commented later, these are exciting days for biblical counseling.

We need to avoid the ever-present danger of navel-gazing. However, with that in mind, I think it is good for us to ponder where biblical counseling is situated in the larger conversation of things happening inside and outside the local church. Looking ahead, there seem to be four promising trends emerging as biblical counseling matures as a movement: a cultural trend, a relational trend, an academic trend, and an ecclesiastic trend. Here are the four, with the trend I see emerging:

- *Cultural:* A deepening awareness of people in search of hope
- *Relational:* A growing sense of unity among biblical counselors
- *Academic:* A developing partnership among Christian colleges and seminaries
- *Ecclesiastic:* A flourishing of church-based care and counsel

Cultural: A Deepening Awareness of People in Search of Hope

It's no secret that rising demand for mental health care is at an all-time high. A recent article noted that more than 60 percent of adults and 70 percent of children with a diagnosable disorder are not receiving any form of mental health care.[180] Of the $2.6 trillion we spend on health care, only a small amount is actually dedicated to counseling and therapy.[181]

Approximately 90 million Americans live in a community where there is one psychiatrist per 30,000 residents.[182] According to the National Institute of Mental Health, one in four Americans suffers from a mental health disorder.[183] Of those, a staggering 60 percent of adults with a diagnosable mental health disorder receive no form of treatment.[184] Robert Whitaker in his book *Anatomy of an Epidemic* writes, "In 2007, we spent $25 billion on anti-depressants and anti-psychotics, and to put that figure in perspective, that was more than the gross domestic product of Cameroon, a nation of 18 million people."[185]

What does this mean for biblical counseling specifically in the local church? It means the local church has an amazing opportunity to offer a stark alternative to what is currently offered. Melinda Beck writes in the *Wall Street Journal* of a Seattle-based psychiatrist who has over 500 patients ... *most of whom she will never meet.*[186] The psychiatrist goes on to say that she oversees ten case managers, each of whom helps her administrate this counseling load. This seems shocking to us, but this detached level of care is necessary because of the number of people searching for therapy.

What these articles and statistics are voicing is the ever-increasing need for help coupled with a diminishing pool of people to offer it. Into this cultural milieu, the local church can step up and offer not only an alternative but an alternative that brings with it the full weight of the Person and work of Jesus Christ.

David Powlison notes, "In the pages of the Bible we have a social model to die for (and the secular world would kill to get even an approximation!): a seamless joining of nurturing and remedial functions, a seamless joining of comfort for those who suffer and transformation for those whose lives are misinformed."[187]

It is within the context of a local church that people in need of care and counsel can receive it within an embedded environment, which provides more than an hour of care every other week. The local church can offer personal change, centered on the Person of Christ through the personal ministry of the Word.

Relational: A Growing Sense of Unity among Biblical Counselors

Another promising trend within the biblical counseling movement is the development of intra-movement relationships. The Biblical Counseling Coalition's Mission Statement expressly includes a desire to foster collaborative relationships.[188] Prior to the founding and formation of the BCC, there was a general sense of agreement that ministry in the biblical counseling movement could be advanced better together, rather than apart, in separate silos of ministry.

Each December since 2011, the Council Board and Board of Directors of the BCC have met together for this express purpose. These men and women represent a growing and diverse movement — professors, pastors, practitioners — all brought together by their common desire to see biblical counseling flourish and thrive.

These relationships, which have formed over the past decade, have fostered and facilitated a much-needed dialogue across the spectrum of biblical counseling. As with any movement, there is a diversity of opinion and belief. Knowing a person's particular position or belief is good and helpful, but knowing the person behind that particular belief is even more helpful. It's biblical relationships in action.

I am confident that the relationships among the BCC Council members have helped us as a movement become less suspicious of one another and more trusting and willing to partner with one another to advance the kingdom.

Academic: A Developing Partnership among Christian Colleges and Seminaries

When the modern biblical counseling movement was launching, there was not nearly the interest or acceptance of biblical counseling that you see today in colleges and seminaries. John Bettler observed, "I remember ... leaving a class (Westminster Theological Seminary) in Apologetics in which Dr. [Cornelius] Van Til railed against the incorporation of unbelieving thought into a consistent Christian world-view and then walking to a class on pastoral care where Rogerian methods were taught and practiced uncritically — and nobody blinked."[189]

Initially the focus of biblical counseling was largely on training and equipping vocational pastors for the work of counseling ministry. David Powlison noted this dynamic as early as 1988 when he wrote on crucial issues facing the movement:

> We have generally spoken to the conservative pastor in the trenches and to the counseling-minded layperson. We have given them tools to counsel more confidently and effectively. Our target audience has been the local church.

Biblical counseling must cultivate other audiences. We need to do so for our own edification as a truly biblical movement. We need to do so in order to edify others with what God has given us. I would like to propose one particular audience into which biblical counseling must be contextualized. We need to speak with Christian academics. We have barely begun to generate meaningful dialogue with the faculty and students in Christian colleges and seminaries.[190]

While there is still much work to be done in this area, today many well-known accredited colleges and seminaries have degree programs or courses offered in biblical counseling. The following list represents a broad sample of various academic institutions:

- Southern Theological Seminary[191]
- Reformed Theological Seminary – Charlotte[192]
- Westminster Theological Seminary[193]
- The Master's College & Seminary[194]
- Southeastern Theological Seminary[195]
- Redeemer Seminary[196]
- Faith Bible Seminary[197]
- Baptist Bible College and Theological Seminary[198]
- Crossroads Bible College[199]
- Birmingham Theological Seminary[200]

This development in biblical counseling is particularly helpful for the local churches in several areas. Many onlookers have observed, rightfully or wrongfully, that biblical counseling was *anti*-science, *anti*-psychology, and *anti*-intellectual, thus leading to a common understanding of biblical counseling as being overly simplistic,[201] more known for what it is against than what it stands for.

Admittedly, there is reason to arrive at this conclusion, but as David Powlison notes, Jay Adams' initial presentation of biblical counseling was to a "pastoral audience." Powlison explains:

Critics have misread simple for simplistic. Biblical counseling is informed by a highly developed theological tradition. Its roots are as intellectual as they are practical.... The counseling world, Christian and non-Christian alike, guards its turf by creating technical vocabularies and professional structures into which would-be counselors must be initiated.... We have opposed their pretension to proprietary rights over knowledge and efficacy in the arena of counseling. We have opposed the professional elitism inherent in secular psychology, an elitism mirrored in most Christian counseling.... We even have thought that academia was not the primary arena in which to discuss counseling. It is a secondary arena with well-institutionalized pretensions to primacy. So we have addressed the church because *biblical* counseling is meant for the daily lives of God's people. The grass roots always will be and always should be the primary constituency for biblical counseling.... We need to reach out to the educational wing of the church of Christ. If we neglect Christian academia, the development and spread of biblical counseling will be seriously hindered.[202]

Over the past decade this relationship between Christian academia and the development of biblical counseling has changed and is being addressed and discussed. As biblical counseling seeks to flourish in the local church, we rightly recognize colleges and seminaries as a place where many are being trained for this work of ministry.

By God's grace, I believe it is evident that a quarter of a century later, significant strides have been made, but the future of biblical counseling, specifically in the local church, will need to cultivate this audience of Christian higher education. One of the ways colleges and seminaries are aiding counseling in the local church is through the writing, publication, and distribution of solid books and resources which many churches need and utilize in their counseling ministries.

An area in need of attention pertains to the academic coursework required for seminary graduates in the area of counseling. In most seminary graduate programs, the number of courses dedicated to counseling is fairly disproportionate to other disciplines. Bob Kellemen, at an Evangelical Theological Society meeting, encouraged the consideration of additional training in counseling in seminary master of divinity programs.[203] As these institutions train men and women for the work of ministry, it is crucial to include practical instruction in the area of biblical counseling.

Ecclesiastic: A Flourishing of Church-Based Care and Counsel

In 2002, David Powlison noted:

> We who call for the centrality of the church in counseling face a dilemma. The very thing we believe in and aspire to lacks many of the necessary components to define, enable, and regulate the hands-on cure of souls.... It is fine to call Christians to practice and seek cure of souls in submission to the doctrine and life of the local church. But the church needs to become a far better place to come into and come under.[204]

By God's grace, I believe we are seeing a promising future for biblical counseling in the local church. Of the sixty-plus BCC Board and Council members, more than half are local church pastors. Our Confessional Statement puts it best, saying, "We believe that the church should be both the center and the sender of Gospel-centered counseling (Rom. 15:14)."

As the evangelical church has a renewed interest in gospel-centered, Christ-centered ministry, the ministry of biblical counseling has grown and thrived. Many have commented about the recent recovery and renewed interest in the doctrines of grace. In this context, biblical counseling offers a real-life test tube where these doctrines come into contact with real people in real life. Biblical counseling in the local church offers a place where espoused theology becomes practical theology. The local church can offer a place where life can be lived out.

Well-known and respected pastors have brought on board counseling pastors who are committed to biblical counseling in the context of the local church.[205] I believe it is a testimony to the nature of biblical counseling, and its interest in *personal change centered on the Person of Christ through the personal ministry of the Word*, that it can cross many denominational barriers.

CONCLUSION

As biblical counselors, it is our desire to see counseling flourish in the context of the local church. We believe the local church offers an alternative and an environment in which true, Christ-centered change can work itself out. There are still several areas where the local church can continue to improve and grow.

As a movement, though, biblical counseling would be keen to heed Augustine's reply to the question on the three distinguishing virtues of Christian faith: humility, humility, and humility. With the rich past we have inherited and the present dynamics which appear favorable to biblical counseling, let us remain humble as we look ahead to the future, remembering:

"Now to him who is able to do far more abundantly than all that we ask or think, according to the power at work within us, to him be glory in the church and in Christ Jesus throughout all generations, forever and ever. Amen" (Eph. 3:20–21 ESV).

LIVING FOR THE CAUSE

ERNIE BAKER

It is late in the afternoon on July 2, 1863, and the 20th Maine Volunteers are about to enter the annals of American military history. They are being led by Colonel Joshua Chamberlain, who is completely dedicated to the cause of preserving the Union during the American Civil War. He left his home, family, and a comfortable teaching position as a college professor to march hundreds of miles south to fight to restore the Union and was about to face the ultimate test of resolve.

As they rushed uphill through the woods at Gettysburg, they were placed on the extreme left of the entire Union Army. His commanding officer told him that he must "hold to the last man." Being the end of the line, he could not retreat. Already the rifle fire from the enemy could be heard growing louder to their right as other units were enveloped in the fighting. As the smoke grew thicker, their opponents could finally be seen approaching through the woods and preparing to charge their line. His Maine men were outnumbered almost two to one, but he had the advantage of the high ground. His men quickly dug in and awaited the crush of the attack. Then, for over two hours they fired volley after volley as they were attacked with desperate charge after desperate charge. At one point the lines of the two foes were totally enveloped with one another as brutal hand-to-hand fighting took place. Men were falling all around him and Colonel Chamberlain was knocked over by a bullet.

As the enemies' lines regrouped for yet another assault, Chamberlain realized his men were almost out of ammunition. It became a stark reality that if they were attacked again, he would have to retreat. Knowing that this was not an option, he did what the desperate moment called for. He ordered a bayonet charge! Rather than waiting, he would take the fight to them, but with mostly empty guns. As they charged down the hill, the Southerners were so startled, they ran. Hundreds were captured. The day was saved by this desperate move, and for his bravery and sacrifice, Colonel Chamberlain received the highest award an American military hero can be given — the Congressional Medal of Honor.

What inspires people to be willing to lay down their lives like this? It is obvious there must be a grand cause to be willing to sacrifice for, to potentially die for. In Chamberlain's own words, "The inspiration of a noble cause involving human interests wide and far, enables men to do things they did not dream themselves capable of before, and which they were not capable of alone. The consciousness of belonging, vitally, to something beyond individuality; of being part of a personality that reaches we know not where, in space and time, greatens the heart to the limits of the soul's ideal."[206]

This conclusion is written with the conviction that the cause that has been unfolded in this book is such a grand cause. In fact, it is the greatest cause in the history of the world. It is a cause worth dying for and therefore worth sacrificially living for. This cause is the making of disciples, and God's chosen vehicle to do it is the church (Matt. 28:18 – 20).

A vision for how to do it has been laid out in this book, and we believe this is not just another theory of church or discipleship ministry. We have endeavored to present thoroughly biblical thinking based on such passages as Ephesians 4:11 – 16. Not only that, but each author is a person dedicated to the church and experienced in serving the local church as it endeavors to fulfill this mission in a biblical way. Or, as we say in the Biblical Counseling Coalition, "Promoting personal change, centered on the Person of Christ, through the personal ministry of the Word." It has been written with the conviction that ministry is about people, not running programs.

We have emphasized that our Lord's main vehicle for accomplishing this mission is through the local church. The church is the most amazing organism on the planet and has amazing potential to impact a lost and desperate world. Unfortunately, many churches are intimidated by the culture, can't see the potential, and do not understand the mission.

In a day when Islam, secularism, and atheism are on the rise, wouldn't it be great if we saw a church that is wide awake and focused to the point of sacrifice? I know you agree. But what's holding us back? What will keep us from fulfilling the mission? I believe the answer is simple — *competing causes*. I only have so much energy, and there are many things competing for time and finances.

COMPETING CAUSES

Let's consider some of the causes that compete with *the* cause. In 1 John 2:15 – 17, the apostle John writes, "Do not *love* the world or the things in the world. If anyone *loves* the world, the *love* of the Father is not in him. For all that is in the world — the *desires* of the flesh and the *desires* of the eyes and pride of life — is not from the Father but is from the world. And the world is passing away along with its *desires*, but whoever does the will of God abides forever" (ESV, emphasis added).

Notice that according to John, the problem is not a list of do's and don'ts. The problem is deeper and internal. It is about loves and lusts, wrong desires and soul-deadening delights. If we are loving or strongly desiring the same things as our culture, then we are on a different mission or our mission will be diluted. It is too easy for other things to become our cause, what we live for, which then consumes our time and resources. Let's briefly explore John's categories.

Desires of the Flesh

Many things could be highlighted under this category, but I would like to address one I see as a plague — living for comfort. Life is about taking it easy. I've known some so focused on taking it easy that it seems like their mentality is, "I don't want to push too hard. I might break myself." That type of mentality doesn't fit the wartime mentality illustrated at the beginning. It is obvious how this thinking distracts from the mission because there is not a willingness to sacrifice.

Desires of the Eyes

There are so many ways we can give in to the desires of the eyes. For example, is our obsession with watching movies and being tuned in to social media keeping us from fulfilling the mission? The "I need to relax" mentality sure can fill up time that could be used discipling and fulfilling our mission "to equip the saints" (Eph. 4:12 ESV).

Pride in Possessions

If the people of God live for finding meaning and purpose in owning stuff (just like our culture), it will definitely divert the church from fulfilling its mission. It ought to be clear why. The finances needed to make disciples both here and around the world get diverted to owning things.

The subtle strategy of Satan is to lull us into lethargy by living in a culture of abundance, prestige, and the dream of ease. It is so easy to love pleasure rather than love God (2 Tim. 3:4). Or love money rather than love God (1 Tim. 6:10). I feel the pull. Do you?

For many years I have been convinced that if the apostle Paul were in America, he would be preaching Isaiah 55: "Why do you spend your money for that which is not bread, and your labor for that which does not satisfy? Listen diligently to me, and eat what is good, and delight yourselves in rich food. Incline your ear, and come to me; hear, that your soul may live" (Isa. 55:2–3 ESV). I'm a counselor so I have to ask,

What do you value? What are you passionate about? What do you look to for help in dealing with the pressures of life?

THE GLORY OF GOD AND CREATING WORSHIPERS

For our eyes to be less captivated with the world, we need a bigger vision to live for. We need something that has the ability to capture our attention. Well, the glory of God is about the biggest thing I can imagine! This leads to a perennial question: Is the church about evangelism or the glory of God? The debates have been long and vigorous, but the answer is that it's both. The biblical counseling movement desires to be captivated by the glory of God and the cause of God, which is creating more worshipers (others who are captivated by the glory of God). This really is the amazing mission. It has always been the mission. To see the earth filled with God-worshipers (see Gen. 1:26–28; Ps. 67:1–3). For this to happen, we need to turn from false worship to the worship of the true God, and this happens through the mediation of our Lord, Jesus Christ. Instead of being disciples of the world, we can become disciples of our Lord, who is the most God-glorifying person who has ever lived.

Paul was thrilled to hear this report about the church at Thessalonica: "For they themselves report concerning us the kind of reception we had among you, and how you turned to God from idols to serve the living and true God" (1 Thess. 1:9 ESV).

Competing Value Systems

Other authors have commented on this temptation the church has of giving in to competing value systems. John Piper has challenged the church for years to live with the Lord and His cause as our greatest delight. Piper wrote, "If we want to make people glad in God, our lives must look like God, not possessions, is our joy."[207] Most poignantly Paul David Tripp wrote:

An idol of the heart is *anything that rules me other than God.* As worshiping beings, human beings always worship someone or something. This is not a situation where some people worship and some don't. If God isn't ruling my heart, someone or something will. It is the way we were made.... To make matters worse, this idolatry is hidden. It is deceptive; it exists underground. We can make this great exchange without forsaking our confessional theology or even our observance of the external duties of the faith. So we hold onto our beliefs, tithe, remain faithful in church attendance, and occasionally participate in ministry activity. Yet at the level of what we are really living for, we have forsaken God for something else. This is the silent cancer that weakens the church, robs individuals of their spiritual vitality, and leads to all kinds of difficulty in relationships and situations.[208]

THE SOLUTION

So, what is the solution? Let's go back to Isaiah 55 and see his clear answer. In verses 6 and 7 he writes, "Seek the Lord while he may be found; call upon him while he is near; let the wicked forsake his way, and the unrighteous man his thoughts; let him return to the Lord, that he may have compassion on him, and to our God, for he will abundantly pardon." The solution is repentance. Repentance and a wartime mentality.

Repentance

If false worship of the values of the world is the problem, then true worship is the solution. Or, as Paul said, we must "put off ... the old man,... be renewed in the spirit of [our] mind[s]; And ... put on the new man" (Eph. 4:22–24 kjv). Or, in another place he wrote, "Do not be conformed to this world, but be transformed by the renewal of your mind (Rom. 12:2 esv). We need a church that stops worshiping the same things as the culture. This would mean that after some serious soul searching to see what is robbing you of passion for the cause, some radical decisions would need to be made and forgiveness asked of the Lord.

A Wartime Mentality

Having grown up with grandparents and parents who lived through and even fought during World War II, I heard the stories of sacrifice for the sake of the cause. My mother worked in a munitions plant while my father was away fighting in Europe. They had been married just a few weeks when my father "shipped out." All the while, the family back in Pennsylvania had ration books. I still have some of those ration books, which represent the sacrifice the citizens of the US went through for the sake of the war effort. Virtually everything was rationed so that the military had what it needed to win. Can you see it? The church does not have this mentality. This preaches well and this talk is expected, but where is the passion for actually doing it? There is little passion *because the passion is going to other causes.* If a pastor lives for comfort and relaxation, like the culture, he will not be willing to put in the long hours necessary to see his church structured to make disciples. If a believer is living for materialism, just like the culture, then there will not be the necessary wartime mentality to sacrifice time and possessions for the cause.

John Piper helps us with our focus:

> Over and over Jesus is relentless in his radical call to a wartime lifestyle and a hazardous liberality.... I need to hear this message again and again, because I drift into a peacetime mind-set as certainly as rain falls down and flames go up. I am wired by nature to love the same toys that the world loves. I start to fit in. I start to love what others love. I start to call earth "home." Before you know it, I am calling luxuries "needs" and using my money just the way unbelievers do. I begin to forget the war. I don't think much about people perishing. Missions and unreached peoples drop out of my mind. I stop dreaming about the triumphs of grace. I sink into a secular mind-set that looks first to what man can do, and not what God can do. It is a terrible sickness. And I thank God for those who have forced me again and again toward a wartime mind-set.[209]

You have heard here from servants of the church who yearn for the church to be *The Church*. Who dream of pastors/elders who fully embrace shepherding their flocks in the nitty-gritty of life (chs. 1–4). Pastors have written who have experienced, by God's grace, the church being more than a weekend Bible conference where we sing songs and hear the Bible taught but, in addition, where true one-anothering is regularly taking place as the body counsels the body (chs. 5–8). Biblical conciliators who yearn to see purity in the body, repentance, and reconciliation have told you of resources to see it happen (chs. 9 and 10). You've even been given tools for how to work out this vision in your church no matter the size or location around the world (chs. 11–17).

It is a vision to see radical followers of Christ. It is a passion to see the real-life power of the gospel transform lives through local churches that are Christ exalting, God glorifying, led by the Spirit, and living by the principles of Scripture. We desire and are seeing the power of the gospel unleashed,[210] the potential of the church and para-church unleashed, and the beautiful wisdom of Scripture unleashed. The desire is for followers of Jesus Christ to be made as we also interact with competing worldviews (chs. 18–22). This has been the history of the biblical counseling movement, and it is our passion for the future (ch. 23). It is a big and wonderful cause to be part of! It is the greatest mission in the history of the world. Will you join us?

CLOSING PRAYER

Father, hear our prayer. We yearn for Your church to be awakened and to regain its confidence in the power of the gospel and the principles of Scripture to radically change lives. We repent of the worship of the same things as our culture. We pray, Lord, for Your people to be awakened to the cause and to catch a vision for what each individual local church can be for Your glory. Help us, Lord, to live for big things, and thank You, Lord, for Your work through churches that are doing so. This we pray in our precious Savior's name. Amen.

The Biblical Counseling Coalition Confessional Statement

PREAMBLE: SPEAKING THE TRUTH IN LOVE — A VISION FOR THE ENTIRE CHURCH

We are a fellowship of Christians committed to promoting excellence and unity in biblical counseling. Our goal is to foster collaborative relationships and to provide robust, relevant biblical resources that equip the body of Christ to change lives with Christ's changeless truth. We desire to advance the biblical counseling movement in Christ-centered cooperation by relating in ways that are loving and wise, pursuing the unity of the Spirit in the bond of peace (Eph. 4:3).

We pursue this purpose by organizing our thinking around one central question: "What does it mean to counsel in the grace and truth of Christ?" All that we do flows from our calling to equip people to love God and others in Christ-centered ways (Matt. 22:35–40).

More than counseling, our vision is for the entire church to speak the truth in love (Eph. 4:11 – 16). We are dedicated to developing the theology and practice of the personal ministry of the Word, whether described as biblical counseling, pastoral counseling, personal discipleship, one-another ministry, small group ministry, cure of souls, soul care, spiritual friendship, or spiritual direction. We seek to promote the strengthening of these ministries in churches, para-church organizations, and educational institutions by ministering to people who offer care, people who are seeking care, and people who train caregivers.

INTRODUCTION: IN CHRIST ALONE

The goal of biblical counseling is spiritual, relational, and personal maturity as evidenced in desires, thoughts, motives, actions, and emotions that increasingly reflect Jesus (Eph. 4:17 – 5:2). We believe that such personal change must be centered on the Person of Christ. We are convinced that personal ministry centered on Christ and anchored in Scripture offers the only lasting hope and loving help to a fallen and broken world.

We confess that we have not arrived. We comfort and counsel others only as we continue to receive ongoing comfort and counsel from Christ and the body of Christ (2 Cor. 1:3 – 11). We admit that we struggle to apply consistently all that we believe. We who counsel live in process, just like those we counsel, so we want to learn and grow in the wisdom and mercies of Christ.

All Christian ministry arises from and is anchored in God's revelation — which is both the written Word (Scripture) and the living Word (Christ). This is true for the personal ministry of the Word (conversational and relational ministry which our culture calls "counseling") and for the various public ministries of the Word. In light of this core conviction about Christ-centered, Word-based ministry, we affirm the following central commitments as biblical counselors.

BIBLICAL COUNSELING MUST BE ANCHORED IN SCRIPTURE

We believe that God's Word is authoritative, sufficient, and relevant (Isa. 55:11; Matt. 4:4; Heb. 4:12–13). The inspired and inerrant Scriptures, rightly interpreted and carefully applied, offer us God's comprehensive wisdom. We learn to understand who God is, who we are, the problems we face, how people change, and God's provision for that change in the Gospel (John 8:31–32; 10:10; 17:17). No other source of knowledge thoroughly equips us to counsel in ways that transform the human heart (Ps. 19:7–14; 2 Tim. 3:16–17; 2 Peter 1:3). Other systems of counseling aim for other goals and assume a different dynamic of change. The wisdom given by God in His Word is distinctive and robust. He comprehensively addresses the sin and suffering of all people in all situations.

Wise counseling is an insightful application of God's all-embracing truth to our complex lives (Rom. 15:4; 1 Cor. 10:6; Phil. 1:9–11). It does not merely collect proof-texts from the Bible. Wise counseling requires ongoing practical theological labor in order to understand Scripture, people, and situations (2 Tim. 2:15). We must continually develop our personal character, case-wise understanding of people, and pastoral skills (Rom. 15:14; Col. 1:28–29).

When we say that Scripture is comprehensive in wisdom, we mean that the Bible makes sense of all things, not that it contains all the information people could ever know about all topics. God's common grace brings many good things to human life. However, common grace cannot save us from our struggles with sin or from the troubles that beset us. Common grace cannot sanctify or cure the soul of all that ails the human condition. We affirm that numerous sources (such as scientific research, organized observations about human behavior, those we counsel, reflection on our own life experience, literature, film, and history) can contribute to our knowledge of people, and many sources can contribute some relief for the troubles of life. However, none can constitute a comprehensive system of counseling principles and practices.

When systems of thought and practice claim to prescribe a cure for the human condition, they compete with Christ (Col. 2:1–15). Scripture alone teaches a perspective and way of looking at life by which we can think biblically about and critically evaluate information and actions from any source (Col. 2:2–10; 2 Tim. 3:16–17).

BIBLICAL COUNSELING MUST BE CENTERED ON CHRIST AND THE GOSPEL

We believe that wise counseling centers on Jesus Christ—His sinless life, death on the cross, burial, resurrection, present reign, and promised return. Through the Gospel, God reveals the depths of sin, the scope of suffering, and the breadth, length, height, and depth of grace. Wise counseling gets to the heart of personal and interpersonal problems by bringing to bear the truth, mercy, and power of Christ's grace (John 1:14). There is no true restoration of the soul and there are no truly God-honoring relationships without understanding the desperate condition we are in without Christ and apart from experiencing the joy of progressive deliverance from that condition through God's mercies.

We point people to a person, Jesus our Redeemer, and not to a program, theory, or experience. We place our trust in the transforming power of the Redeemer as the only hope to change people's hearts, not in any human system of change. People need a personal and dynamic relationship with Jesus, not a system of self-salvation, self-management, or self-actualization (John 14:6). Wise counselors seek to lead struggling, hurting, sinning, and confused people to the hope, resources, strength, and life that are available only in Christ.

BIBLICAL COUNSELING MUST BE GROUNDED IN SOUND THEOLOGY

We believe that biblical counseling is fundamentally a practical theological discipline because every aspect of life is related to God. God intends that we care for one another in ways that relate human struggles to His person, purposes, promises, and will. Wise counseling arises from a theological way of looking at life—a mindset, a worldview— that informs how we understand people, problems, and solutions. The best biblical counselors are wise, balanced, caring, experienced practical theologians (Phil. 1:9–11).

Biblical counselors relate the Scriptures relevantly to people's lives (Heb. 3:12–19). All wise counseling understands particular passages and a person's unique life experience within the context of the Bible's larger story line: God's creation, our fall into sin, His redemptive plan, and the consummation of all things. Thus we engage in person-specific conversations that flow naturally out of a comprehensive biblical theology of life.

BIBLICAL COUNSELING MUST BE DEPENDENT UPON THE HOLY SPIRIT AND PRAYER

We believe that both genuine change of heart and transformation of lifestyle depend upon the ministry of the Holy Spirit (John 14:15–16:16; 2 Cor. 3:17–18). Biblical counselors know that it is impossible to speak wisely and lovingly to bring about true and lasting change apart from the decisive, compassionate, and convicting work of the Spirit in the counselor and the counselee. We acknowledge the Holy Spirit as the One who illuminates our understanding of the Word and empowers its application in everyday life.

Wise counselors serve in the truth that God reveals and by the strength that God supplies. By the Spirit's work, God receives glory in all the good that takes place in people's lives. Biblical counselors affirm the absolute necessity of the work of the Holy Spirit to guide and empower the counselor, the counselee, and the counseling relationship. Dependent prayer is essential to the work of biblical counseling (Eph. 6:18–20). Wise counselors humbly request God's intervention and direction, praise God for His work in people's lives, and intercede for people that they would experience genuine life change to the glory of God (Phil. 4:6).

BIBLICAL COUNSELING MUST BE DIRECTED TOWARD SANCTIFICATION

We believe that wise counseling should be transformative, change-oriented, and grounded in the doctrine of sanctification (2 Cor. 3:16–18; Phil. 2:12–13). The lifelong change process begins at salvation (justification, regeneration, redemption, reconciliation) and continues until we see Jesus face-to-face (1 John 3:1–3). The aim of wise counseling is intentional and intensive discipleship. The fruit of wise counseling is spiritually mature people who increasingly reflect Christ (relationally, rationally, volitionally, and emotionally) by enjoying and exalting God and by loving others well and wisely (Gal. 5:22–6:10).

Wise counseling seeks to embrace the Bible's teaching regarding God's role and human responsibility in spiritual growth. God's strength and mercy call for our response of faith and obedience. A comprehensive theology of the spiritual life provides the basis for applying relevant biblical methods of spiritual growth. Biblical counseling helps believers to understand what it means to be in Christ (Rom. 6:3–14). It equips them to apply the principles of progressive sanctification through renewing their minds and actions based on Scripture with a motive of love for God and others (Rom. 12:1–2).

BIBLICAL COUNSELING MUST BE ROOTED IN THE LIFE OF THE CHURCH

We believe that we best reflect the Trinity as we live and grow in community (John 17; Ephesians 4). Sanctification is not a self-improvement project, but a process of learning to love and serve God and others. Wise counseling embeds personal change within God's community — the church—with all God's rich resources of corporate and interpersonal means of grace (1 Cor. 12:12–27). We believe that the church should be both the center and the sender of Gospel-centered counseling (Rom. 15:14).

By example and exhortation the New Testament commends the personal, face-to-face, one-another ministry of the Word—whether in one-to-one or small group relationships (Heb. 3:12–19; 10:19–25). God calls the church to mutual wise counseling just as He calls the church to public ministries of the Word in preaching, teaching, worship, and observing the ordinances of baptism and the Lord's Supper. God desires His people to love and serve each other by speaking His truth in love to one another (Eph. 4:15–16). The primary and fullest expression of counseling ministry is meant to occur in local church communities where pastors effectively shepherd souls while equipping and overseeing diverse forms of every-member ministry (Eph. 4:11–14). Other like-minded counseling institutions and organizations are beneficial insofar as they serve alongside the church, encourage Christians to counsel biblically, and purpose to impact the world for Christ.

BIBLICAL COUNSELING MUST BE FOUNDED IN LOVE

We believe that Christ's incarnation is not just the basis for care, but also the model for how we care (Heb. 4:14–16; John 13:34–35). We seek to enter into a person's story, listening well, expressing thoughtful love, and engaging the person with compassion (1 Thess. 2:8). The wise and loving personal ministry of the Word takes many appropriate forms, from caring comfort to loving rebuke, from careful listening to relevant scriptural exploration, all while building trusting, authentic relationships (1 Thess. 5:14–15; 1 John 4:7–21).

Wise counseling takes into account all that people experience (desires, thoughts, goals, actions, words, emotions, struggles, situational pressure, physical suffering, abuse, injustice, etc.). All of human experience is the context for understanding how God's Word relates to life. Such awareness not only shapes the content of counseling, but also shapes the way counselors interact so that everything said is constructive, according to the need of the moment, that it may give grace to the hearer (Eph. 4:29).

BIBLICAL COUNSELING MUST BE ATTENTIVE TO HEART ISSUES

We believe that human behavior is tied to thoughts, intentions, and affections of the heart. All our actions arise from hearts that are worshiping either God or something else; therefore we emphasize the importance of the heart and address the inner person. God fully understands and rightly weighs who we are, what we do, and why we do it. While we cannot completely understand a person's heart (even our own), God's Word reveals and penetrates the heart's core beliefs and intentions (Heb. 4:12 – 13).

Wise counseling seeks to address both the inward and outward aspects of human life to bring thorough and lasting change into the image of Christ. The Bible is clear that human behavior is not mechanical, but grows out of a heart that desires, longs, thinks, chooses, and feels in ways that are oriented either toward or against Christ. Wise counsel appropriately focuses on the vertical and the horizontal dimensions, on the inner and the outer person, on observable behavior and underlying issues of the heart (Matt. 23:23 – 28). Biblical counselors work to help struggling people to learn wisdom; to love God with heart, soul, mind, and strength; to love one's neighbor as oneself; and to endure suffering in hope.

BIBLICAL COUNSELING MUST BE COMPREHENSIVE IN UNDERSTANDING

We believe that biblical counseling should focus on the full range of human nature created in the image of God (Gen. 1:26 – 28). A comprehensive biblical understanding sees human beings as relational (spiritual and social), rational, volitional, emotional, and physical. Wise counseling takes the whole person seriously in his or her whole life context. It helps people to embrace all of life face-to-face with Christ so they become more like Christ in their relationships, thoughts, motivations, behaviors, and emotions.

We recognize the complexity of the relationship between the body and soul (Gen. 2:7). Because of this, we seek to remain sensitive to physical factors and organic issues that affect people's lives. In our desire to help people comprehensively, we seek to apply God's Word to people's lives amid bodily strengths and weaknesses. We encourage a thorough assessment and sound treatment for any suspected physical problems.

We recognize the complexity of the connection between people and their social environment. Thus we seek to remain sensitive to the impact of suffering and of the great variety of significant social-cultural factors (1 Peter 3:8–22). In our desire to help people comprehensively, we seek to apply God's Word to people's lives amid both positive and negative social experiences. We encourage people to seek appropriate practical aid when their problems have a component that involves education, work life, finances, legal matters, criminality (either as a victim or a perpetrator), and other social matters.

BIBLICAL COUNSELING MUST BE THOROUGH IN CARE

We believe that God's Word is profitable for dealing thoroughly with the evils we suffer as well as with the sins we commit. Since struggling people usually experience some combination of besetting sin and personal suffering, wise counselors seek to discern the differences and connections between sin and suffering, and to minister appropriately to both (1 Thess. 5:14).

Biblical counseling addresses suffering and engages sufferers in many compassionate ways. It offers God's encouragement, comfort, and hope for the hurting (Rom. 8:17–18; 2 Cor. 1:3–8). It encourages mercy ministry (Acts 6:1–7) and seeks to promote justice. Biblical counseling addresses sin and engages sinners in numerous caring ways. It offers God's confrontation of sins, encourages repentance of sins, presents God's gracious forgiveness in Christ, and shares God's powerful path for progressive victory over sin (1 John 1:8–2:2; 2 Cor. 2:5–11; Col. 3:1–17; 2 Tim. 2:24–26).

BIBLICAL COUNSELING MUST BE PRACTICAL AND RELEVANT

We believe that a commitment to the sufficiency of God's Word results in counseling that demonstrates the relevancy of God's Word. Biblical counseling offers a practical approach to daily life that is uniquely effective in the real world where people live and relate (1 John 3:11–24). By instruction and example, the Bible teaches foundational methodological principles for wise interaction and intervention (Acts 20:26–37; Gal. 6:1–5; Col. 1:24–2:1).

Within the Bible's overall guidelines for the personal ministry of the Word, there is room for a variety of practical methods of change, all anchored in applying scriptural truth to people's lives and relationships. The Bible calls us to use wise methods that minister in Christ-centered ways to the unique life situations of specific people (Prov. 15:23; 25:11). We are to speak what is helpful for building others up according to the need of the moment, that it may benefit those who listen (Eph. 4:29).

BIBLICAL COUNSELING MUST BE ORIENTED TOWARD OUTREACH

We believe that Christianity is missionary minded by its very nature. Biblical counseling should be a powerful evangelistic and apologetic force in our world. We want to bring the good news of Jesus and His Word to the world that only God can redeem. We seek to speak in relevant ways to Christians and non-Christians, to draw them to the Savior and the distinctive wisdom that comes only from His Word (Titus 2:10 – 15).

We want to present the claims, mercies, hope, and relevance of Christ in a positive, loving, Christlike spirit (1 Peter 3:15). We seek to engage the broad spectrum of counseling models and approaches. We want to affirm what is biblical and wise. Where we believe models and methods fall short of Christ's call, we want to critique clearly and charitably. When interacting with people with whom we differ, we want to communicate in ways that are respectful, firm, gracious, fair-minded, and clear. When we perceive error, we want to humbly point people forward toward the way of truth so that we all become truer, wiser, more loving counselors. We want to listen well to those who disagree with us and learn from their critiques. Our mission to spread the truth and fame of Jesus Christ includes a desire that all counselors appreciate and embrace the beauty of a Christ-centered and Word-based approach to people, problems, and solutions.

CONCLUSION: UNITY IN TRUTH AND LOVE

We are committed to generating a unified effort among God's people to glorify Christ and multiply disciples through the personal ministry of the Word (Matt. 28:18 – 20). We trust in Jesus Christ in whom grace and truth are perfectly joined (John 1:14). We cling to His Word, in which truth and love live in perfect union (Eph. 4:15; Phil. 1:9; 1 Thess. 2:8). We love His church — living and speaking the truth in love, growing up in Him who is the Head, and building itself up in love as each part does its work (Eph. 4:15 – 16).

We desire to encourage this unity in truth and love through a fresh vision for biblical counseling. When people ask, "What makes biblical counseling truly biblical?" we unite to affirm:

> Biblical counseling occurs whenever and wherever God's people engage in conversations that are anchored in Scripture, centered on Christ and the

Gospel, grounded in sound theology, dependent upon the Holy Spirit and prayer, directed toward sanctification, rooted in the life of the church, founded in love, attentive to heart issues, comprehensive in understanding, thorough in care, practical and relevant, and oriented toward outreach.

We invite you to join us on this journey of promoting excellence and unity in biblical counseling. Join us as we seek to equip one another to promote personal change, centered on the Person of Christ through the personal ministry of the Word.

THE BIBLICAL COUNSELING COALITION DOCTRINAL STATEMENT

The following statement summarizes the core doctrinal beliefs of the Biblical Counseling Coalition. It is not an exhaustive statement, but a theological framework concerning our core affirmations regarding the central doctrines of the Christian faith.

ABOUT THE BIBLE

We believe that God has given the Bible as His inspired, infallible, inerrant, and living revelatory Word. We affirm the verbal, plenary inspiration of the Bible and are therefore committed to the complete trustworthiness and primacy of Scripture. The Bible is God's relevant, profound, deeply personal communication to us that invites us to intimate fellowship with Him. The Scriptures consist of the sixty-six books of the Old and New Testaments. They are the totally sufficient, authoritative, and normative rule and guide of all Christian life, practice, and doctrine, and are profitable for glorifying God through growth in likeness to Christ, which is our life purpose.

The Bible is complete in its revelation of who God is, His person, character, promises, commandments, and will for the salvation of a people for His own possession. The Bible reveals who we are: created in God's image, accountable to God, fallen into sin against God, judged and justly condemned by God, redeemed by Jesus Christ, and transformed by the Holy Spirit. The Bible reveals the meaning of our total life situation in each and all its aspects—all the blessings of this life, the variety of sufferings and hardships, Satan, the influence of other human beings, etc. The Bible also reveals the nature of the Christian life and the ministries of the church, showing the content, the functions, and the goals that express the image of Christ.

ABOUT THE TRIUNE GOD

We believe in one God, eternally existing in three equally divine Persons: the Father, the Son, and the Holy Spirit, who know, love, and glorify one another. They are forever equal in nature, attributes, and perfection, yet forever distinct in Their relations to one another and distinct in Their particular relationships both to the creation and to the actions and processes of redemption. They are equally worthy of our worship, love, and obedience. This One true and living God is infinitely perfect both in His love and in His holiness. The triune God, in affectionate sovereignty, sustains and rules over all things, providentially bringing about His eternal good purpose to redeem a people for Himself—to the praise of the glory of His grace.

ABOUT GOD THE FATHER

We believe that God, as the Father, reigns over His entire universe with providential care, holy justice, and saving mercy, to His own glory. In

His holy love, the Father is all-powerful, all-loving, all-knowing, and all-wise. He is fatherly in attitude toward all, but Father, indeed, to those who have been made children of God through salvation in Christ.

ABOUT GOD THE SON, JESUS CHRIST

We believe in the deity of our Lord Jesus Christ, the eternal Son of God, who humbled Himself by taking on the form of a man by means of His virgin birth, becoming forever both fully human without ceasing to be fully God. We affirm that He lived a sinless life of active love and perfect wisdom. He died by crucifixion on the cross, by His shed blood and death making a vicarious, substitutionary atonement for our sins. After three days, He was resurrected bodily from the dead, unto an indestructible life. After appearing to His disciples and instructing them for forty days, He ascended to heaven. He is now seated at the right hand of the Father, interceding for believers, reigning as King over all creation, and working in and through His Church. He will personally return in power and glory to judge the living and the dead, and to raise to immortality those who eagerly await Him, perfecting them in His image.

ABOUT GOD THE HOLY SPIRIT

We believe that God the Holy Spirit, sent by the Father and the Son, has come into the world to reveal and glorify Christ, and to convict and draw sinners to Christ. From the moment of spiritual birth, He indwells believers, individually and corporately, as their Helper. By the Spirit's agency, believers are renewed, sanctified, and adopted into God's family. He imparts new life to believers, placing them into the body of Christ, transforming and empowering them for Christlike living, and sealing them until the day of redemption. He is the source of power for all acceptable worship and ministry as He imparts a diversity of enabling gifts that equip God's people for service. He provides the power to understand and apply God's truth in love.

ABOUT HUMANITY — CREATION

We believe that God created Adam and Eve in His image, male and female, and declared them "very good," granting them all the capacities of image bearers. God created them to reflect and to enjoy His glory. They were created material and immaterial, physical body and spiritual soul, these qualities united and inseparably interdependent. They were created with a conscience able to discern good and evil, with the capacity to relate, think, choose, and feel in all the fruitfulness of wisdom. They were designed and commissioned to love God and one another, living in holy and devoted fellowship with God and in loving, complementary relationship with each other. They were designed and commissioned to care for and govern His creation, working in and ruling over all creation as God's faithful servants and stewards.

ABOUT HUMANITY — FALL

We believe that because of voluntary sin against God, Adam and Eve fell from the actively good, sinless, and innocent state in which they were first created. They became self-willed, perverse, and transgressive against God and each other. Immediately they died spiritually and also began to die physically. Consequently, for them and all their progeny, the image of God was distorted and their nature depraved and corrupted in every aspect of their being (spiritually, socially, mentally, volitionally, and emotionally). While human beings are corrupted in every aspect of their being and functioning, because of God's common grace the image of God has not been totally eradicated, and evil is not given full reign. God preserves and enables many common goods. All people have true dignity, a conscience in which clarity coexists with distortion, and many powers of mind, action, and feeling. All humanity is separated and alienated from God and thus spiritually dead — until God's own gracious intervention. The supreme need of all human beings is to be reconciled to God; and the only hope of all human beings is to receive the undeserved grace of God in Christ. God alone can rescue us and restore sinners to Himself.

ABOUT SALVATION — REDEMPTION

We believe that salvation is the gift of God by grace alone and is received through faith alone in the Lord Jesus Christ. Salvation is wholly conceived, accomplished, and applied by God's sovereign grace. It is not, in whole or in part, conceived or accomplished by human will or works. We believe that salvation refers comprehensively to the entire work of God that redeems His people from the penalty, power, and eventual presence of sin while imputing to His people the righteousness of Jesus Christ and all the benefits of adoption into His family. This salvation overthrows the dominion of darkness and creates a new people who enter Christ's body of light, truth, and love.

We affirm that salvation is only through Christ, for there is no other name given under heaven by which we must be saved. Christ voluntarily took upon Himself the form of a man, was tempted in all points as we are, yet without sin in nature, word, or deed. He honored the Divine Law by His personal obedience, and by His death made a full and vicarious atonement for our sins. Jesus, having risen bodily from the dead, is now enthroned in heaven, serving as the suitable, compassionate, all-sufficient Savior and the Mediator for His believer-priests.

We believe that all the blessings of salvation are free gifts of God, and that each is a glorious facet of union with Christ. In Christ, persons once justly condemned are now forgiven and justified because Christ died bearing our sins, because He was raised for our justification, and because God imputes to His people the righteousness of Jesus Christ. In Christ, persons once dead in trespasses and sins are now made spiritually alive in the new birth, receive the Holy Spirit, and receive eternal life. In Christ, persons whose father and master was the devil are now adopted by God the Father into His family and become citizens and servants in God's kingdom. In Christ, persons who were estranged from God are now reconciled forever. God gives all these gifts, and more, by the Holy Spirit, and we receive all these gifts by faith.

We believe that by His incarnation, life, death, resurrection, and ascension, Jesus Christ acted as our representative and substitute. He did this so that in Him we might become the righteousness of God. On the cross He canceled sin, satisfied by His sacrifice the wrath of God, and, by bearing the full penalty of our sins, reconciled to God all who believe. We believe that by His resurrection, Christ Jesus was vindicated by His Father, broke the power of death, defeated Satan who once had power over it, and brought everlasting life to all His people. We believe that by His ascension, Jesus Christ has been forever exalted as Lord and has prepared a place for us to be with Him. We believe that at His return, Jesus Christ will wipe away all tears, will remove all sin and suffering, will establish forever His kingdom of love, joy, and peace, and will perfect His holy Bride. We believe that all whom God regenerates are made at once children of God, justified in His sight through faith alone in Christ's atoning work, and brought into His family. We believe that believers are kept by the power of God through faith in a state of grace and are eternally secure apart from any human works. We believe that we who are Christ's body will see Him face-to-face, and that we will live with Him and with one another forever.

ABOUT SANCTIFICATION

We believe that sanctification is the process by which believers, each one and all together — set apart from sin and united in Christ — are increasingly conformed to the image of Christ. Sanctification has past, present, and future aspects. First, believers are "chosen, holy and beloved" in Christ, set apart for God in union with Christ, and are actually made new by regeneration (positional or definitive sanctification). Second, believers begin to mature in their new life, set apart day-by-day through growth in grace into the likeness of Christ. This process (progressive sanctification) takes place by the power of the Holy

Spirit, through the Word of God, in the communion of the saints, by the continual use of God's appointed means of growth in grace, each member contributing to the growth of the whole unto maturity in Christ. Third, believers will be set apart from the very presence of sin when sanctification is completed (glorification) at the coming of Christ for the Church. Definitive sanctification in the past and glorification in the future provide anchors that sustain hope and bring encouragement amidst the failures and sufferings that make progressive sanctification a long and arduous pilgrimage.

ABOUT THE CHURCH

We believe that the Church, the Body of Christ, is composed of all persons living and dead who have been joined to Christ and one another by the power of the Holy Spirit. Every true believer is baptized by the Holy Spirit into the Body of Christ and thus united in Christ to one another in unity and love across social, economic, and ethnic lines. We affirm that the local church is God's primary instrument and context for His work today; that every believer should be an active member in a local assembly; and that the Christian community is the context where believers are mutually encouraged, equipped, and empowered to conform to the image of Christ through worship, fellowship, discipleship, stewardship, and ambassadorship (evangelism). The sanctification of an individual is not a personal self-improvement project, but is the formation of a constructive, fruitful member of the Body of Christ. We believe it is every believer's privilege and obligation to be an instrument in the Redeemer's hands. This requires an intentional involvement in the lives of others: learning to speak and to live the truth in love, learning humility, and learning to forgive and to give, so that we all grow in unity and maturity into Christ, who is the Head. The true mission of the Church is to bring God glory, as believers (individually and corporately) live consistent with the Great Commandment and the Great Commission. We believe that baptism and the Lord's Supper are ordained by the Lord Jesus Himself. They are our public vows of submission to the once crucified and now resurrected Christ, and our anticipation of His return and of the consummation of all things.

ABOUT THE ETERNAL STATE AND THE RESTORATION OF ALL THINGS

We believe in the personal, glorious, and bodily return of our Lord Jesus Christ when His kingdom will be consummated. We believe in the bodily resurrection of both the just and the unjust — the unjust to judgment and eternal conscious punishment in hell, and the just to eternal blessedness in the presence of Him who sits on the throne and of the Lamb, in the new heaven and the new earth, the eternal home of righteousness. On that day, the Church will be presented faultless before God by the obedience, suffering, and triumph of Christ; all sin will be purged and its wretched effects forever banished. God will be all in all, His people will be enthralled with Him, and everything will be done to the praise of His glorious grace.

BIBLIOGRAPHY

Adams, Jay E. *The Christian Counselor's Manual*. Grand Rapids, MI: Zondervan, 1973.

_____. *Competent to Counsel: Introduction to Nouthetic Counseling*. Grand Rapids, MI: Zondervan, 1970.

_____. *Handbook for Church Discipline*. Grand Rapids, MI: Zondervan, 1986.

_____. *Insight and Creativity in Christian Counseling*. Woodruff, SC: Timeless Texts, 1982.

_____. "Looking Back." *Journal of Biblical Counseling* 9, no. 3 (1988).

_____. *A Theology of Christian Counseling: More Than Redemption*. Grand Rapids, MI: Zondervan, 1979.

_____. "What Is 'Nouthetic' Counseling?" http://www.nouthetic. org/about-ins/what-is-nouthetic-counseling.

Aponte, Harry J. "Love, the Spiritual Wellspring of Forgiveness: An Example of Spirituality in Therapy." *Journal of Family Therapy* 20 (1998): 37–58.

Bain, Ken. *What the Best College Teachers Do*. Cambridge, MA: Harvard University, 2010.

Bargerhuff, Eric J. *Love That Rescues: God's Fatherly Love in the Practice of Church Discipline*. Eugene, OR: Wipf & Stock, 2010.

Baxter, Richard. *The Reformed Pastor*. Carlisle, PA: Banner of Truth Trust, 1979.

Beck, Melinda. "Getting Mental-Health Care at the Doctor's Office." *Wall Street Journal*, September 24, 2013. http://online.wsj.com/news/articles/SB10001424052702303983904579095123535328450. Accessed December 4, 2013.

Berkouwer, G. C. *Man: The Image of God*. Grand Rapids, MI: Eerdmans, 1962.

Bettler, John. "CCEF: The Beginning." *Journal of Biblical Counseling* 9, no. 3 (1988).

Biblical Counseling Coalition. "Mission Statement." http://biblicalcounselingcoalition.org/about/mission-statement/. Accessed May 13, 2014.

Bonhoeffer, Dietrich. *Life Together: The Classic Exploration of Christian Community*. Translated by John W. Doberstein. San Francisco: Harper & Row, 1954.

Bradley, Anthony B. *Aliens in the Promised Land: Why Minority Leadership Is Overlooked in White Christian Churches and Institutions*. Phillipsburg, NJ: P&R, 2013.

Braverman, Beth. "6 Ways Obamacare Is Changing Mental Health Coverage." *The Fiscal Times*, November 6, 2013. http://www.thefiscaltimes.com/Articles/2013/11/26/6-Ways- Obamacare-Changing-Mental-Health-Coverage. Accessed November 27, 2013.

Bridges, Jerry. *Crisis of Caring: Recovering the Meaning of True Fellowship*. Phillipsburg, NJ: P&R, 1987.

Calvin, John. *Calvin's Commentaries*. Vol. 22. Grand Rapids, MI: Baker, 1999.

Carson. D. A. *Christ & Culture: Revisited*. Grand Rapids, MI: Eerdmans, 2008.

———. *The Gospel according to John*. The Pillar New Testament Commentary. Grand Rapids, MI: Eerdmans, 1991.

Cheong, Robert K. *God Redeeming His Bride: A Handbook for Church Discipline*. Ross-shire, Scotland: Christian Focus, 2012.

Christensen, Jen. "Feds Boosting Mental Health Access." November

12, 2013. http://www.cnn.com/2013/11/08/health/hhs-mental-health/. Accessed November 27, 2013.

Clebsch, William A., and Charles R. Jaekle. *Pastoral Care in Historical Perspective*. Northvale, NJ: Aronson, 1994.

Clinebell, Howard. *Basic Types of Pastoral Counseling*. Nashville: Abingdon, 1966.

_____. *Understanding and Counseling the Alcoholic through Religion and Psychology*. Nashville: Abingdon, 1956.

Collins, Gary. "A Letter to Christian Counselors." *Journal of Psychology and Christianity* 9:1 (1990).

"Come Thou Fount of Every Blessing." Wikipedia. http://en.wikipedia.org/wiki/Come_Thou_Fount_of_Every_Blessing. Accessed June 26, 2014.

Cooper, Lamar. *Ezekiel*. The New American Commentary. Nashville, TN: Broadman & Holman, 1994.

Dempster, Stephen. "Knowledge for What? Recovering the Lost Soul of Higher Education in the West." *Faculty Dialogue* 18 (Fall 1992).

Dodson, Jonathan. *Gospel-Centered Discipleship*. Wheaton, IL: Crossway, 2012.

Dumbrell, William J. *The Search for Order: Biblical Eschatology in Focus*. Eugene, OR: Wipf and Stock, 2001.

Elmer, Duane. *Cross-Cultural Servanthood: Serving the World in Christlike Humility*. Downers Grove, IL: InterVarsity, 2006.

Emlet, Michael. *CrossTalk: Where Life and Scripture Meet*. Greensboro, NC: New Growth Press, 2009.

Erickson, Millard J. *Christian Theology*. 2nd ed. Grand Rapids, MI: Baker, 1998.

Forde, Gerhard O. *On Being a Theologian of the Cross: Reflections on Luther's Heidelberg Disputation, 1518*. Grand Rapids, MI: Eerdmans, 1997.

Forrester, Duncan B. "Violence and Non-violence in Conflict Resolution: Some Theological Reflections." *Studies in Christian Ethics* 16 (2003): 60–67.

Frame, John. *Systematic Theology.* Phillipsburg, NJ: P&R, 2013.

Ganz, Richard. *PsychoBabble.* http://richardganz.com/books/psycho-babble.php.

Grudem, Wayne. *1 Peter.* Tyndale New Testament Commentaries. Downers Grove, IL: InterVarsity, 2000.

Guelzo, Allen C. *Gettysburg: The Last Invasion.* New York: Knopf, 2013.

Gundmann, Walter. "*agathos.*" In *The Theological Dictionary of the New Testament.* Abridged ed. Edited by G. Bromiley. Grand Rapids, MI: Baker, 1992.

Ham, Ken, and Charles Ware. *One Race, One Blood.* Green Forest, AR: Master, 2010.

Hambrick, Brad. "The Competency of the Biblical Counselor." In *Scripture and Counseling: God's Word for Life in a Broken World.* Edited by Bob Kellemen and Jeffery Forrey. Grand Rapids, MI: Zondervan, 2014.

Henderson, John. *Equipped to Counsel: A Training Program in Biblical Counseling—Leader Notebook.* Mustang, OK: Dare 2 Dream, 2008.

Hendricks, Howard. *Teaching to Change Lives.* Sisters, OR: Multnomah, 1987.

Hendriksen, William. *Galatians and Ephesians.* Grand Rapids, MI: Baker, 1968.

Henry, Carl F. H. *God, Revelation, and Authority.* Vol. 1. Wheaton, IL: Crossway, 1999.

Hesselgrave, David J. *Communicating Christ Cross-Culturally: An Introduction to Missionary Communication.* Grand Rapids, MI: Zondervan, 1991.

Hiebert, Paul G. *Anthropological Insights for Missionaries.* Grand Rapids, MI: Baker, 1985.

Hull, Bill. *The Disciple-Making Pastor: The Key to Building Healthy Christians in Today's Church.* Tarrytown, NY: Revell, 1988.

Johnson, Eric L., and Stanton L. Jones, eds. *Psychology & Christianity: Four Views.* Downers Grove, IL: InterVarsity, 2000.

Jones, Robert D. *Pursuing Peace: A Christian Guide to Handling Our Conflicts*. Wheaton, IL: Crossway, 2012.

Jones, Stanton L. "A Constructive Relationship for Religion with the Science and Profession of Psychology: Perhaps the Boldest Model Yet." *American Psychologist* (March 1994).

Kellemen, Bob, and Jeffery Forrey, eds. *Scripture and Counseling: God's Word for Life in a Broken World*. Grand Rapids, MI: Zondervan, 2014.

Kellemen, Robert W. *Equipping Counselors for Your Church: The 4E Ministry Training Strategy*. Phillipsburg, NJ: P&R, 2011.

_____. *Gospel-Centered Counseling: How Christ Changes Lives*. Grand Rapids, MI: Zondervan, 2014.

_____. *Gospel Conversations: How to Care Like Christ*. Grand Rapids, MI: Zondervan, 2015.

_____. "Pastoral Counselor Preparation in Evangelical Seminary M.Div. Programs: Toward a Best Practice Statement of Purpose, Theology, Pedagogy, Curriculum, and Educator" (paper presented at annual meeting for the Evangelical Theological Society, Milwaukee, WI, November 14–16, 2012).

_____. "The Rich Relevance of God's Word." In *Scripture and Counseling: God's Word for Life in a Broken World*. Edited by Bob Kellemen and Jeffery Forrey. Grand Rapids, MI: Zondervan, 2014.

_____. *Sexual Abuse: Beauty for Ashes*. Phillipsburg, NJ: P&R, 2013.

_____. *Soul Physicians: A Theology of Soul Care and Spiritual Direction*. Winona Lake, IN: BMH, 2007.

_____. *Spiritual Friends: A Methodology of Soul Care and Spiritual Direction*. Winona Lake, IN: BMH, 2007.

Ladd, George E. *A Theology of the New Testament*. Grand Rapids, MI: Eerdmans, 1993.

Lambert, Heath. *The Biblical Counseling Movement after Adams*. Wheaton, IL: Crossway, 2012.

Lane, Tim, and Paul Tripp. *How People Change*. 2nd ed. Greensboro, NC: New Growth, 2008.

Laniak, Timothy. *Shepherds after My Own Heart: Pastoral Traditions and Leadership in the Bible.* New Studies in Biblical Theology. Downers Grove, IL: InterVarsity, 2006.

LaSor, William, David Hubbard, and Frederic Bush. *Old Testament Survey: The Message, Form, and Background of the Old Testament.* 2nd ed. Grand Rapids, MI: Eerdmans, 1996.

Lauterbach, Mark. *The Transforming Community: The Practise of the Gospel in Church Discipline.* Ross-shire, Scotland: Christian Focus, 2003.

Levicoff, Steve. *Christian Counseling and the Law.* Chicago: Moody Press, 1991.

Lewis, C. S. *Mere Christianity.* London: Collins, 1952.

_____. *The Problem of Pain.* New York: HarperCollins, 2001.

Lichtenstein, Marsha. "Creating Awareness of the Spiritual Dimensions of Conflict Resolution by Contemplating Organizational Culture." *Conflict Resolution Quarterly* 23, no. 2 (Winter, 2005): 5–20.

Luther, Martin. *Works of Martin Luther.* Vol. 3. Philadelphia: Holman, 1930.

MacArthur, John, editor. *Counseling: How to Counsel Biblically.* Nashville: Nelson, 2005.

MacDonald, James, Bob Kellemen, and Steve Viars, eds. *Christ-Centered Biblical Counseling: Changing Lives with God's Changeless Truth.* Eugene, OR: Harvest House, 2013.

Marsden, George M. *The Soul of the American University: From Protestant Establishment to Established Nonbelief.* New York: Oxford University Press, 1994.

Mayer, Bernard. *The Dynamics of Conflict: A Guide to Engagement and Intervention.* 2nd ed. San Francisco: Jossey-Bass, 2012.

McNeil, John T. *A History of the Cure of Souls.* New York: Harper & Brothers, 1951.

Miller, C. John. *Evangelism and Your Church.* Phillipsburg, NJ: P&R, 1980.

Nicewander, Sue. *Building a Church Counseling Ministry without Killing the Pastor*. Leominster, UK: Day One, 2012.

Ohlschlager, George, and Peter Mosgofian. *Law for the Christian Counselor: A Guidebook for Clinicians and Pastors*. Dallas: Word, 1992.

Osborne, Larry. *Sticky Church*. Grand Rapids, MI: Zondervan, 2008.

Pelikan, Jaroslav. *The Idea of the University: A Reexamination*. New Haven: Yale University Press, 1992.

Piper, John. *Brothers, We Are Not Professionals: A Plea to Pastors for Radical Ministry*. Nashville, TN: Broadman & Holman, 2002.

_____. *Don't Waste Your Life*. Wheaton, IL: Crossway, 2003.

_____. "Large Sails and Little Ballast." *Desiring God* blog (February 9, 2011). http://www.desiringgod.org/blog/posts/large-sails-and-little-ballast.

_____. *Let the Nations Be Glad: The Supremacy of God in Missions*. Grand Rapids, MI: Baker Academic, 2003.

Powlison, David. *The Biblical Counseling Movement: History and Context*. Greensboro, NC: New Growth, 2010.

_____. "Counseling *Is* the Church." *Journal of Biblical Counseling* 6 (Winter 2002).

_____. "Crucial Issues in Contemporary Biblical Counseling." *Journal of Biblical Counseling* 9, no. 3 (1988): 53–78.

_____. "Does the Shoe Fit?" *Journal of Biblical Counseling* (Spring 2002): 2–15.

_____. *Speaking Truth in Love: Counsel in Community*. Winston-Salem, NC: Punch Press, 2005.

_____. "The Sufficiency of Scripture to Diagnose and Cure Souls." *Journal of Biblical Counseling* (Spring 2005).

Pratt, Loni Collins, and Daniel Homan. *Radical Hospitality: Benedict's Way of Love*. Brewster, MA: Paraclete, 2002.

Quine, Jay. "Legal Issues for Christian Workers and the Church." Seminar notes presented at Lancaster Bible College, Lancaster, PA, 1998.

Robertson, C. K. "Courtroom Dramas: A Pauline Alternative for Conflict Management." *Anglican Theological Review* 89, no. 4 (Fall 2007).

Rupprecht, David, and Ruth Rupprecht. *Radical Hospitality*. Phillipsburg, NJ: P&R, 1983.

Sande, Ken. *The Peacemaker: A Biblical Guide to Resolving Personal Conflict*. 3rd ed. Grand Rapids, MI: Baker, 2004.

Sande, Ken, and Kevin Johnson. *Resolving Everyday Conflict*. Grand Rapids, MI: Baker, 2011.

Schreiner, Thomas. *1, 2 Peter, Jude*. The New American Commentary. Nashville, TN: Broadman & Holman, 2003.

Scott, Stuart, and Heath Lambert. *Counseling the Hard Cases: True Stories Illustrating the Sufficiency of God's Resources in Scripture*. Nashville: B&H Academic, 2012.

Shaw, Mark E. *Strength in Numbers: The Team Approach to Biblical Counseling*. Bemidji, MN: Focus, 2010.

Sigley, Thomas. "Evangelism Implosion: Reaching the Hearts of Non-Christian Counselees." *Journal of Biblical Counseling* 17, no. 1 (Fall 1998).

Stetzer, Ed. "Multisite Churches Are Here to Stay." *Christianity Today* (2014). http://www.christianitytoday.com/edstetzer/2014/february/multisite-churches-are-here-to-stay.html. Accessed June 15, 2014.

Stewart, George. *Pickett's Charge*. Boston: Houghton Mifflin, 1959, 170.

Storms, Sam. *One Thing: Developing a Passion for the Beauty of God*. Ross-shire, Scotland: Christian Focus, 2004.

Strauch, Alexander. *The Hospitality Commands: Building Loving Christian Community, Building Bridges to Friends and Neighbors*. Colorado Springs: Lewis & Roth, 1993.

Tasker, R. V. G. *John*. Tyndale New Testament Commentaries. Downers Grove, IL: InterVarsity, 2000.

Thune, Bob. *The Gospel-Centered Life*. Greensboro, NC: New Growth, 2011.

Tripp, Paul David. *Instruments in the Redeemer's Hands: People in Need of Change Helping People in Need of Change.* Phillipsburg, NJ: P&R, 2002.

Turlock, Alice Rains. *In the Hands of Providence: Joshua L. Chamberlain and the American Civil War.* Chapel Hill, NC: University of North Carolina Press, 2001.

Vernick, Leslie. *How to Live Right When Your Life Goes Wrong.* New York: Doubleday Religious, 2003.

Volf, Miroslav. *Exclusion and Embrace: A Theological Exploration of Identity, Otherness, and Reconciliation.* Nashville: Abingdon, 1996.

Ware, Charles. *Prejudice and the People of God: How Revelation and Redemption Lead to Reconciliation.* Grand Rapids, MI: Kregel, 2001.

Ware, Charles, and Rod Mays. "The Importance of Multiculturalism in Biblical Counseling." In *Christ-Centered Biblical Counseling: Changing Lives with God's Changeless Truth.* Edited by James MacDonald, Bob Kellemen, and Steve Viars. Eugene, OR: Harvest House, 2013.

Warfield, Benjamin. *The Religious Life of Theological Students.* Phillipsburg, NJ: P&R, n.d.

Watters, Ethan. *Crazy Like Us: The Globalization of the American Psyche.* New York: Free Press, 2011.

Welch, Edward T. *Addictions: A Banquet in the Grave.* Phillipsburg, NJ: P&R, 2001.

Whitaker, Robert. *Anatomy of an Epidemic: Magic Bullets, Psychiatric Drugs, and the Astonishing Rise of Mental Illness in America.* New York: Random House, 2010.

Wilkerson, Mike. *Redemption: Freed by Jesus from the Idols We Worship and the Wounds We Carry.* Wheaton, IL: Crossway, 2011.

Winter, Ralph D. "The Two Structures of God's Redemption Mission." *Missiology* 2, no. 1 (1973): 121–39.

Wright, Christopher. *The Message of Ezekiel.* Downers Grove, IL: InterVarsity, 2001.

———. *The Mission of God: Unlocking the Bible's Grand Narrative.* Downers Grove, IL: InterVarsity, 2006.

ABOUT THE
CONTRIBUTORS

Ron Allchin, DMin. Ron Allchin is the Founder and Associate Executive Director of the Biblical Counseling Center in Arlington Heights, Illinois. In January 2015, his son, Tim Allchin, assumed the position of Executive Director that Ron had held since 1989. Ron holds his DMin in Biblical Counseling from Westminster Theological Seminary and is a Fellow and Board member of the Association of Certified Biblical Counselors (ACBC). He and his wife, Sherry, enjoy traveling to various missions locations and have had the opportunity to teach counseling in many foreign countries. They have three married children and seven grandchildren.

Tim Allchin, MDiv. Tim Allchin is the Executive Director of the Biblical Counseling Center (BCC) in Arlington Heights, Illinois, and he counsels out of all three offices. He is also part of the BCC's Teaching Team, who teach and equip local churches in the areas of counseling. He holds an MDiv from Trinity Evangelical Seminary. Prior to coming to the Biblical Counseling Center, Tim pastored for twelve years in a local church in Naperville, Illinois, where he served in a variety of roles working with students, families, and adults. He also had direct responsibility in the areas of counseling and recovery ministries and was a frequent teacher in many different venues within the church.

Ernie Baker, DMin. Ernie Baker joined The Master's College in 2005 as a faculty member in the College's Biblical Counseling Department. He received his MDiv from Capital Bible Seminary and his DMin from Westminster Theological Seminary. Dr. Baker has been in ministry since 1980 with thirty-five years of experience as a pastor and in training and equipping pastors and laymen in the skills of discipleship counseling and conciliation. He is a Certified Conciliator with Peacemaker Ministries, teaching a number of conflict resolution courses and doing conciliation. He is also a fellow with the Association of Certified Biblical Counselors and a Council Board member of the Biblical Counseling Coalition. He is married to Rose, and they have three sons and three daughters (five of whom are married) and six grandchildren.

Brad Bigney, MDiv. Brad Bigney is an ordained minister with the Evangelical Free Church of America, and is a graduate of both Columbia Bible College and Columbia Biblical Seminary in South Carolina. He has a BS in Bible Teaching along with an MDiv degree. He's a certified biblical counselor with the Association of Certified Biblical Counselors and is involved in the counseling ministry of the church, as well as teaching in conferences and training centers across the nation. He's the author of *Gospel Treason: Betraying the Gospel with Hidden Idols.* Pastor Brad has been serving as the Senior Pastor of Grace Fellowship Church in Florence, Kentucky, since January 1996. He and his wife, Vicki, have five wonderful children that God's used to teach him so much.

Kevin Carson, MDiv, DMin. Kevin Carson serves as Pastor of Sonrise Baptist Church in Ozark, Missouri, and as Professor and Department Chair of Biblical Counseling at Baptist Bible College and Theological Seminary in Springfield, Missouri. Kevin earned his MDiv from Baptist Bible Graduate School, Springfield, Missouri, and his DMin from Westminster Theological Seminary. He is ACBC certified and travels with ACBC as a teacher/trainer. Kevin also serves as an adjunct faculty member at several institutions. Kevin and his wife, Kelly, have four children.

Robert Cheong, PhD. Robert Cheong is the Pastor of Care at Sojourn Community Church, Louisville, Kentucky. He has the global responsibilities for equipping ministry leaders at each of Sojourn's four campuses so they can shepherd God's people with the gospel through community. He authored *God Redeeming His Bride: A Handbook for Church Discipline* and serves as a Council Board member for the Biblical Counseling Coalition. He enjoys life with Karen, his wife of thirty-one years, along with their three grown children, son-in-law, and two grandsons.

Greg Cook, MABC, DMin. Greg Cook has served in full-time ministry at Christ Chapel Bible Church (CCBC) in Fort Worth, Texas, since 1995. Pastor Cook founded the Soul Care ministry in 2004, which offers biblical counseling care and equipping for both those in CCBC as well as in the surrounding area. Greg and his wife, Nancy, have three amazingly wonderful women as daughters.

Judy Dabler, MA, MAC. Judy Dabler works nationally and internationally as a Christian conciliator, trainer, educator, conference speaker, counselor, and consultant. Judy is the Founder of Creative Conciliation, an organization designed to advance the field of Christian conciliation and provide reconciliation ministry to couples, families, churches, and organizations in conflict and crisis. In 2007, Judy founded and continues to serve as an affiliate of Live at Peace Ministries. Judy holds an MA in Theological Studies and an MA in Counseling from Covenant Theological Seminary. She has ten years of experience teaching counseling-related courses at the seminary level and has completed forty-two hours of doctoral-level courses in education at Trinity Evangelical Divinity School. Judy is a Licensed Professional Counselor and a Certified Christian Conciliator.

Jack Delk, MDiv. Jack Delk is Pastor for Counseling at the North Campus of Bethlehem Baptist Church in Minneapolis, Minnesota. He graduated with his MDiv from Bethel Seminary in 2002. Jack and his wife, Mary, have two grown sons, Josh and Jacob, and two grandsons.

Nicolas Ellen, DMin. Nicolas Ellen earned his BBA from the University of Houston, his MACE from Dallas Theological Seminary, his MABC from The Master's College, and his DMin from Southern Baptist Theological Seminary (in Biblical Counseling). Dr. Ellen serves as Professor of Biblical Counseling at the College of Biblical Studies in Houston, Texas. He is also the Founder and Director of The Expository Counseling Center. Additionally, Pastor Ellen is the Senior Pastor of Community of Faith Bible Church in Houston.

Howard Eyrich, DMin. Howard Eyrich leads a staff and a team of lay counselors at Briarwood Presbyterian Church in Birmingham, Alabama. Each year he leads a two-semester seminary-level training program to populate the team and train counselors for other area churches. He directs the DMin Counseling program at Birmingham Theological Seminary. Howard serves on several boards and is an adjunct professor for several institutions. Howard mentors young pastors, supervises candidates for certification with ACBC (Association of Certified Biblical Counselors) and AABC (American Academy of Biblical Counselors), and often consults with pastors regarding counseling situations. He provides consultation to churches desiring to establish a biblical counseling ministry.

Rob Green, PhD. Rob Green is a pastor at Faith Church in Lafayette, Indiana, focusing on counseling and seminary ministries. He and his wife, Stephanie, are blessed with three children. Rob earned a BS in Engineering Physics (Ohio State), an MDiv (Baptist Bible Seminary), and a PhD in New Testament (Baptist Bible Seminary).

Garrett Higbee, PsyD. Garrett Higbee is the Executive Director of the Biblical Counseling Coalition and one of the BCC's founding Board members. He also serves as Executive Director of Biblical Soul Care Ministries at Harvest Bible Chapel and is former President and Cofounder of Twelve Stones Ministries located in Brown County, Indiana. Dr. Higbee was trained as a clinical psychologist with a specialty in marriage and family counseling, but had a radical conversion in 1992 that led him to trust in Christ and His Word for all things related to life and counseling. He has over twenty years of experience using the Scriptures to counsel couples, families, and youth and is dedicated to training those who lead and counsel others in biblical soul care. Garrett is a frequent conference speaker and a contributing author for several biblical counseling books. Additionally, he has created several Biblical Soul Care® training resources focused on small group discipleship. He and his wife, Tammy, have three children and live near the Harvest Bible Chapel campus in Elgin, Illinois.

Jonathan Holmes, MA. Jonathan Holmes serves at Parkside Church in Cleveland, Ohio, as the Pastor of Counseling, and is the author of *The Company We Keep: In Search of Biblical Friendship*. He graduated with degrees in Biblical Counseling and History from The Master's College and a Master's degree from Trinity Evangelical Divinity School. Jonathan and his wife, Jennifer, are parents of three beautiful daughters, Ava, Riley, and Ruby.

Robert Jones, DMin. Bob Jones is a biblical counseling professor at Southeastern Baptist Theological Seminary, having served previously for nineteen years as a lead pastor. He is also the pastor of biblical counseling at Open Door Church in Raleigh, North Carolina, and a visiting professor at several seminaries. Bob graduated from The King's College, Trinity Evangelical Divinity School (MDiv), and Westminster Theological Seminary (DMin, Pastoral Counseling). He is a certified Christian conciliator and a church reconciliation trainer with Peacemaker Ministries, a certified counselor with the Association of Certified Biblical Counselors (ACBC), and the author of *Pursuing Peace*, *Uprooting Anger* and numerous booklets, articles, and chapters. Bob and Lauren, his wife of thirty years, have two adult sons.

Bob Kellemen, ThM, PhD. Bob Kellemen is the Resource Director of the Biblical Counseling Coalition, the Vice President for Institutional Development and Chair of the Biblical Counseling Department at Crossroads Bible College, and the Founder and CEO of RPM Ministries. For seventeen years he served as the founding Chairman of and Professor in the MA in Christian Counseling and Discipleship department at Capital Bible Seminary in Lanham, Maryland. Bob has pastored three churches and equipped biblical counselors in each church. Bob and his wife, Shirley, have been married for thirty-four years; they have two adult children and two granddaughters. Dr. Kellemen is the author of thirteen books, including *Gospel-Centered Counseling* and *Gospel Conversations*.

Heath Lambert, PhD. Heath Lambert serves as Executive Director at the Association of Certified Biblical Counselors. He is also an Associate Professor of Biblical Counseling at The Southern Baptist Theological Seminary. Dr. Lambert has authored or edited several books including *The Biblical Counseling Movement after Adams, Counseling the Hard Cases,* and *Finally Free: Fighting for Purity with the Power of Grace.* Heath lives in Louisville, Kentucky, with his wife, Lauren, and their children, Carson, Chloe, and Connor.

Lee Lewis, MA. Lee Lewis is the Pastor of Biblical Soul Care for Harvest Muskoka in Muskoka, Ontario, Canada. He also serves in a directing/consulting role for a network of church plants in Ontario. Lee previously served as a pastor at The Village Church in Flower Mound, Texas, for nearly ten years. He is a member of the Association of Biblical Counselors and sits on the Council Board for the Biblical Counseling Coalition. Lee is married to Andrea, and they have four children, Luke, Abel, Leah, and Miriam.

Ken Long, MDiv. Ken Long has the privilege of serving as Executive Pastor with Grace Fellowship Church in Northern Kentucky. He is an ordained pastor with the Evangelical Free Church of America, EFCA. Before joining Grace in 2006, he served with two churches, one in

Kansas and the other in Indiana. He received an MDiv from Columbia Biblical Seminary. He is certified as a biblical counselor through the Association of Certified Biblical Counselors. He is also a Council Board member for the Biblical Counseling Coalition. Prior to entering vocational ministry, Ken worked almost twenty years as a structural engineer, having degrees from North Carolina State University and MIT. Ken is married to Beth, and their son, Mark, is married to Rachel.

Rod S. Mays, DMin. Rod Mays serves as the Executive Pastor of Mitchell Road Presbyterian Church in Greenville, South Carolina, and as an adjunct professor of practical theology at Reformed Theological Seminary in Charlotte, where he teaches counseling, pastoral theology, and campus ministry courses. He is the Director of The Greenville Fellows Program, a faith and work initiative. Rod has served as a guest lecturer at Covenant Theological Seminary and Westminster Seminary in California and serves on the Board of the Christian Counseling and Educational Foundation (CCEF). For sixteen years (1999 – 2015) he was the national coordinator for Reformed University Fellowship (RUF), the campus ministry of the Presbyterian Church in America. Rod has forty years of pastoral and counseling experience and is the coauthor of *Things That Cannot Be Shaken* (Crossway). He enjoys playing tennis and traveling with his wife, Debbe. They have been married forty years and have one daughter and a grandson.

Abe Meysenburg. Abe Meysenburg serves as a pastor/elder with Soma Tacoma in Tacoma, Washington, as well as serving the larger Soma family of churches. He oversees all of the shepherding ministries of Soma Tacoma and works to equip other leaders to shepherd as well. Abe is a graduate of Moody Bible Institute and has been married to Jennifer for sixteen years. They have four children, Abby, Julia, Luke, and Noah.

Jim Newheiser, DMin. Jim Newheiser is the Director of the Institute of Biblical Counseling and Discipleship, an ACBC Fellow, a pastor of Grace Bible Church in Escondido, California, and a founding member and Executive Board member of the Fellowship of Independent

Reformed Evangelicals. He is an international retreat and conference speaker, author, and has been practicing biblical counseling since 1982. Jim also serves as an adjunct professor at The Master's College. He and his wife have three sons. Jim earned his MA and DMin from Westminster Seminary, California.

Lilly Park, PhD. Lilly Park is an Assistant Professor of Biblical Counseling at Crossroads Bible College in Indianapolis, Indiana. She also serves in the counseling ministry at her church.

Randy Patten, MDiv. Randy Patten is the Director of Training and Advancement for the Association of Certified Biblical Counselors (ACBC). Previously he led the organization for sixteen years as the Executive Director when it was known as the National Association of Nouthetic Counselors (NANC). He also served as a senior pastor for twelve years, followed by twelve years as a pastor to pastors and consultant to churches. Randy was a trainer and counselor at Faith Biblical Counseling Ministries in Lafayette, Indiana, for over twenty-four years. Randy and Cindy have been married for forty-four years and have two married children and six grandchildren. They are longtime members of College Park Church in Indianapolis, Indiana. He is pleased to have been a founding Board member of the Biblical Counseling Coalition (BCC) and a contributor to each of the three books produced by the organization.

Jeremy Pierre, PhD. Jeremy Pierre serves as Dean of Students and Associate Professor of Biblical Counseling at the Southern Baptist Theological Seminary. He is a coauthor of *The Pastor and Counseling* (Crossway, 2015) and author of *The Dynamic Heart in Daily Life: Counseling from a Theology of Human Experience* (New Growth Press). He has contributed to *Christ-Centered Biblical Counseling* and *Scripture and Counseling* (Zondervan). He serves as a pastor at Clifton Baptist Church and speaks at various engagements in the US and overseas. He is also a Council Board member of the Biblical Counseling Coalition. He and his wife, Sarah, raise their five children in Louisville, Kentucky.

David Powlison, PhD. David Powlison serves as Executive Director of CCEF (Christian Counseling and Educational Foundation), as faculty member at CCEF, and as the Senior Editor of the *Journal of Biblical Counseling*. He holds a PhD from the University of Pennsylvania and an MDiv from Westminster Theological Seminary. He has written numerous articles on biblical counseling and on the relationship between faith and psychology. His books include *Speaking Truth in Love, Seeing with New Eyes, Power Encounters: Reclaiming Spiritual Warfare*, and *The Biblical Counseling Movement: History and Context*.

Deepak Reju, PhD. Deepak Reju serves as the Pastor of Biblical Counseling and Families at Capitol Hill Baptist Church in Washington, DC. He did his theological training at The Southern Baptist Theological Seminary (MDiv, PhD). Deepak and his wife, Sarah, have been married since 2001 and have five children, Zachariah, Lydia, Eden, Noelle, and Abraham. Deepak is the author of several books and articles, including *Great Kings of the Bible: How Jesus Is Greater than Saul, David, and Solomon* (Christian Focus), *On Guard: Preventing and Responding to Child Abuse at Church* (New Growth), and *The Pastor and Counseling: The Basics of Shepherding Members in Need* (Crossway). He serves as the President of the Board of Directors of the Biblical Counseling Coalition (*www.biblicalcounselingcoalition.org*).

Michael E. Snetzer. Michael Snetzer serves as Groups Pastor at The Village Church in Flower Mound, Texas. In addition to his pastoral responsibilities, he is in part-time private practice as a biblical counselor under the umbrella of North Texas Christian Counseling. Michael coauthored *Recovering Redemption* with Matt Chandler (Lead Teaching Pastor at The Village Church). Michael enjoys life with his wife, Sonia, and three children — McKenna Paige, Ava Micah, and Greyson Michael.

Paul Tautges, DMin. Paul Tautges is the Senior Pastor of Cornerstone Community Church in Mayfield Heights, Ohio. He previously served for twenty-two years as a pastor in Sheboygan, Wisconsin. He also serves as an adjunct professor of biblical counseling here in the States and overseas. Paul has authored eight books including *Counseling One Another*, *Brass Heavens*, and *Comfort the Grieving*. He is also the editor of the *LifeLine Mini-Book* series (Shepherd Press). Paul is an ACBC Fellow. He and his wife, Karen, are the parents of ten children. Paul blogs regularly at Counseling One Another.

Wayne A. Vanderwier, DMin. Wayne Vanderwier is the Executive Director of Overseas Instruction in Counseling, an international biblical counseling training ministry with both leadership training (modular) and graduate academic (degree) programs around the world. He is a Fellow of the Association of Certified Biblical Counselors and serves on the Council Board of the Biblical Counseling Coalition. He has been married to Susan for more than forty years. They have five adult children and thirteen (and counting!) grandchildren.

Steve Viars, DMin. Steve Viars is the Senior Pastor of Faith Church (Lafayette, Indiana). He is an ACBC (Association of Certified Biblical Counselors) Fellow and Board member, Biblical Counseling Coalition board Vice President, Vision of Hope Board member, instructor and counselor at Faith Biblical Counseling Ministries, and a conference speaker. Steve earned his BS in Bible from Baptist Bible College (Clarks Summit, Pennsylvania), his MDiv at Grace Theological Seminary, and his DMin in Biblical Counseling at Westminster Theological Seminary. He and his wife, Kris, came to Faith Church in 1987. They have three children and one grandchild.

Charles Ware, DD. Charles Ware is President of Crossroads Bible College in Indianapolis, Indiana, a conservative evangelical institution dedicated to training Christian leaders to reach a multiethnic urban world for Christ. He earned his BRE from Baptist Bible College (Clarks Summit, Pennsylvania), and his MDiv from Capital Bible Seminary (Lanham, Maryland), and an Honorary Doctorate from Baptist Bible Seminary. Dr. Ware is on the Board for ABWE (Association of Baptists for World Evangelism), ABHE (Association for Biblical Higher Education), Anchors Away, and the Biblical Counseling Coalition. Dr. Ware has authored, coauthored, and edited several books; among these are *One Race One Blood*, *Reuniting the Family of God*, and *Just Don't Marry One*. Dr. Ware and Sharon celebrated forty-one years of marriage in 2014. They have six children, two daughters-in-law, one son-in-law, and two grandchildren.

Ed Welch, MDiv, PhD. Ed Welch is a counselor and faculty member at CCEF (Christian Counseling and Education Foundation). He earned a PhD in counseling (neuropsychology) from the University of Utah and has an MDiv degree from Biblical Theological Seminary. Ed has been counseling for over thirty years and has written extensively on the topics of depression, fear, and addictions. His books include *When People Are Big and God Is Small*, *Addictions: A Banquet in the Grave*, *Blame It on the Brain*, *Depression—A Stubborn Darkness*, and *Running Scared*. His newest book is *Side by Side*.

Mike Wilkerson, BA. Mike Wilkerson is the Founder of The Redemption Group Network and previously served as a pastor for ten years. Mike is the author of *Redemption: Freed by Jesus from the Idols We Worship and the Wounds We Carry*, which serves as the curriculum for Redemption Groups. Mike and his wife, Trisha, have six children.

Sam R. Williams, PhD. Sam Williams is Professor of Counseling at Southeastern Baptist Theological Seminary in Wake Forest, North Carolina, where he has taught for the last fifteen years. He was in private practice for ten years as a licensed clinical psychologist and has been counseling for thirty-five years. He loves his wife, Mindy, his three sons and daughter, his church North Wake, and Brazil.

NOTES

1. Piper, *Brothers, We Are Not Professionals*, 1–2.
2. Ibid., 3.
3. Hull, *Disciple-Making Pastor*, 12.
4. Welch, *Addictions*, 155.
5. Storms, *One Thing*, 123, 140.
6. Vernick, *How to Live Right*, 18.
7. Piper, "Large Sails and Little Ballast."
8. Carson, *The Gospel According to John*, 386.
9. Schreiner, *1, 2 Peter, Jude*, 233.
10. "Therefore" (NASB) or "so" (ESV) (5:1) naturally follows the explanation of suffering Christians in 4:19. Peter says to the elders, "In light of these suffering Christians, shepherd God's flock."
11. Grudem, *1 Peter*, 190.
12. Schreiner, *1, 2 Peter, Jude*, 235.
13. Calvin, *Calvin's Commentaries*, 142.
14. Schreiner, *1, 2 Peter, Jude*, 236.
15. LaSor, Hubbard, Bush, *Old Testament Survey*, 356–57.
16. Cooper, *Ezekiel*, 298–301.
17. Wright, *Message of Ezekiel*, 274–79.
18. Tasker, *John*, 128.
19. Laniak, *Shepherds after My Own Heart*, 211–18.
20. Carson, 382–83.
21. Tasker, 131.
22. Carson, 386.
23. Ibid.
24. I am indebted to the work of several people who had taken upon themselves the great task of describing the history of the curing of souls in the church

over the centuries. Used for this chapter were Clebsch and Jaekle, *Pastoral Care in Historical Perspective*; Johnson and Jones, *Psychology & Christianity*; Lambert, *Biblical Counseling Movement after Adams*; McNeil, *History of the Cure of Souls*; and Powlison, *Biblical Counseling Movement*.

25. Cf. chapter 12 in Kellemen and Forrey, editors, *Scripture and Counseling*.

26. McNeil starts his book by describing the term "cure of souls," vii. Additionally, in our day it seems that "cure of souls" and "caring for souls" have essentially become synonymous with "counseling," even from a secular perspective, though the reasons for and philosophies underlying that cure or care are vastly different from the Christian perspective.

27. Clebsch and Jaekle in particular emphasize again and again Christian borrowing from and adaptation of "various theories of the human soul," 68–69, 76.

28. Cf. McNeil, *History*, 161–62, and Baxter, *Reformed Pastor*, on pastoral care duties like visitation.

29. See McNeil's *History*, especially chapters 8 through 12, as well as Johnson and Jones, the chapter on "A History of Christians in Psychology" in *Psychology & Christianity*.

30. Lambert, *Biblical Counseling Movement after Adams*, 33; Powlison, *Biblical Counseling Movement*, 7; Clebsch and Jaeckle, *Pastoral Care*, 30–31; Johnson and Jones, *Psychology*, 13–19; and McNeil, *History*, 319–30, all point out these radical changes from the domain of the church to the domain of secular psychology and medicine.

31. Lambert, *Biblical Counseling Movement after Adams*, 33.

32. Clebsch and Jaeckle, *Pastoral Care*, support the notions of needed experts, 74, and a growing polemic against traditionally "accepted theory that the immortal soul and its relations to God and to man were matters into which religion had the deepest insight and over which religion held ultimate control," 78.

33. Powlison, *Biblical Counseling Movement*, 259.

34. Lambert, *Biblical Counseling Movement after Adams*, 36.

35. Bridges, *Crisis of Caring*. His main assertion is that "we believers today do not know, either intellectually or experientially, the meaning of true fellowship as it was practiced in the early Church and passed on to us by the writers of the New Testament," 10; and he tries to help the reader understand what biblical fellowship is.

36. It should be noted that this statement is really true of evangelical Christianity only at that time because, as Powlison well describes in *Biblical Counseling Movement*, mainline pastoral counselors had already been adapting and/or adopting secular practices for some time. See Powlison, *Biblical Counseling Movement*, 24ff.

37. Lambert, *Biblical Counseling Movement after Adams*, 163.

38. Advocates are people who love the Lord Jesus Christ, who are mature in their walk, and who desire to come alongside people in need (whether in small group context or formal counseling). They pray for/with the person

receiving help, they do homework (as applicable), they can provide context/ background info for various issues as they know the counselee, and they build a bridge between counselee and counselor as well as between the counseling context and the community in which the counselee lives. Their specific role and responsibilities are typically explained and agreed on in the very first "session."

39. Cf. Pratt and Homan, *Radical Hospitality*, for principles of radical hospitality that can be seen as an important way of caring deeply for the distressed soul; cf. Rupprecht and Rupprecht, *Radical Hospitality*, for a practical view on hospitality in our own day (which has been influential on the author of this chapter regarding one specific application of caring for the hurting).

40. I would like to acknowledge here that our Biblical Soul Care Ministry is certainly not the only place where community as context, apprenticeships for equipping, or even advocacy in counseling is practiced. However, as the biblical counseling movement overall, and even more so as the church at large, we have room to grow in being more consistent in applying these biblical principles to our counseling philosophy.

41. To further explore the theme of "spiritual friendship," consult Robert W. Kellemen, *Spiritual Friends*.

42. Again, other churches are doing the same thing, we're not alone, and, of course, Jay Adams' writings as a whole have that very focus. Yet, if we're honest about where we are as a biblical counseling ministry, have we really arrived or is there more that we can do to move toward more authentic community, deeper assessments, and even better equipped church-based counseling ministries?

43. Many biblical counseling ministries would acknowledge the benefit of counseling in community. Additionally, the differences between the traditional BC and CIC models are mostly in the area of emphasis and practical application.

44. It should be acknowledged too that not everything that makes BC what it currently is stems from Jay Adams. Interestingly, Powlison highlights that even Jay Adams and John Bettler had different views about who should be in the counseling room and why as well as how long sessions should be, etc., 207–19. Additionally, what I am after is not creating more division or making blanket statements about every ministry involved in the BC movement, but rather to point out that a lot of what many churches are moving toward is not yet reflected in overall training and teaching and has not gained movement-wide acceptance.

45. McNeil, in particular, highlights how this was a very important piece of the care for souls, especially during the Reformation years and among the Puritans.

46. In my assessment, this is probably the greatest distinction. Very few churches have sought to incorporate both a philosophy and community structure for biblical counseling in the local church. While this isn't an indictment on the movement, I see it as a challenge for us to more thoroughly incorporate what

we believe about biblical counseling in the local church to more effectively care for those who are hurting.

47. Colossians 3 and 1 Corinthians 12 should be instructive here for both put off/put on (put off the old self and put on the new self in Christ) as well as the church using (and equipping) all the parts that make up the body of Christ.

48. You can find some such training resources on our website: www.harvestbiblechapel.org/bscresources.

49. Piper, *Brothers, We Are Not Professionals*, 1–2.

50. Osborne, *Sticky Church*, 71.

51. Lewis, *Problem of Pain*, 91.

52. "Redemption Groups" is a trademark and may be used only under a licensing agreement. The Redemption Group Network helps ministry sites develop and license Redemption Groups.

53. As of late 2014, we are in a process of making changes to improve the quality and consistency of Redemption Groups. This chapter represents a snapshot in time amidst the development of those refinements. Current information is available at redemptiongroups.com.

54. Dumbrell, *Search for Order*, 9 (emphasis added). While God's story extends beyond the creation and new creation bookends of the Bible, most of what has been revealed to us of God's story in the Bible is concerned with redemption.

55. Forde, *Theologian of the Cross*, 7–9.

56. Wright, *Mission of God*, 265.

57. While I (Mike) wrote the book in its final form, it was born out of collaboration with my colleagues at the time, especially James Noriega and Bill Clem.

58. In Redemption Groups, we have utilized some of the best practices that I (Mike) experienced in another group process, formerly called "Grace Groups," conducted by Open Hearts Ministries.

59. Tripp, *Instruments in the Redeemer's Hands*, 242–43.

60. "Come Thou Fount."

61. Normally, participants remain in their regular small group communities during the short time that they also participate in a Redemption Group. I (Abe) also encourage them to actively share with their small group communities what they're learning in their Redemption Groups.

62. Dodson, *Gospel-Centered Discipleship*; Thune, *Gospel-Centered Life*.

63. See chapter 3 of this book for diagrams on the continuum of counseling and discipleship, which can help clarify this paradigm shift.

64. Advocates are people who come alongside the person receiving care (counselee). These advocates love the Lord, know and love the counselee, and are mature in their faith. They desire to see the counselee growing and changing. You might call them Proverbs 17:17 or 18:24 kinds of friends. They will come to all the sessions (formal or informal) and will pray for and with the counselee. They will participate in the counseling by giving more background

information and by clarifying, praying, and doing the homework assigned. They are an invaluable part of counseling in the BSC model.

65. The reader may want to consult chapter 6 in this book by Abe Meysenburg and Mike Wilkerson, as they speak about Redemption Groups in a similar fashion.
66. See note 64 on advocates.
67. We are indebted also to Tim Lane and Paul Tripp and their chapter on community in *How People Change*.
68. For more informal meetings at the small group level, this means that leaders ask the people being cared for for their consent to share information. At the formal level, counselees fill out forms that outline our approach to what and when we might share. In either case, the goal is always to share only what is necessary for a solid care plan and only with people who can help execute that care plan for the benefit of the person being cared for.
69. Henderson, *Equipped to Counsel*.
70. Snetzer, *Recovering Redemption*.
71. Matthew 18:15–18; 1 Corinthians 5; 2 Thessalonians 3:6, 13–15; 1 Timothy 5:19–20; 2 Timothy 3:1–5; Titus 3:10–11; Romans 16:17.
72. For more details about the process of God's discipline through the church, see Cheong, *God Redeeming His Bride*; Lauterbach, *Transforming Community*; and Adams, *Handbook for Church Discipline*.
73. Bonhoeffer, *Life Together*, 107.
74. For a thorough scriptural defense of God's loving discipline, see Bargerhuff, *Love That Rescues*.
75. On personal peacemaking, see Jones, *Pursuing Peace*; Sande, *Peacemaker*; and Sande and Johnson, *Resolving Everyday Conflict*.
76. For the Biblical Counseling Coalition Confessional Statement, see http://biblicalcounselingcoalition.org/about/confessional-statement/.
77. Mayer, *Dynamics of Conflict*, 3–32.
78. Sande, *Peacemaker*, 287–88.
79. Powlison, *Seeing with New Eyes*, 3.
80. Forrester, "Violence and Non-violence in Conflict Resolution," 65.
81. Lichtenstein, "Creating Awareness of the Spiritual Dimensions of Conflict Resolution," 231.
82. Aponte, "Love, the Spiritual Wellspring of Forgiveness," 39.
83. Volf, *Exclusion and Embrace*, 118–19.
84. Robertson, "Pauline Alternative for Conflict Management," 602.
85. Ibid., 604.
86. I am currently collaborating on a textbook for future reconcilers hoping to embrace biblical peacemaking.
87. For a comprehensive development of the "4Es" of envisioning, enlisting, equipping, and empowering, see Kellemen, *Equipping Counselors for Your Church*.
88. Faith Church in Lafayette, Indiana, is a powerful example of using biblical counseling to reach out to a community. See http://www.faithlafayette.org/church.

89. Web addresses: ABC: http://christiancounseling.com; ACBC: www.biblicalcounseling.com; CCEF: http://www.ccef.org; Faith Church: http://www.faithlafayette.org/counseling; IABC: http://www.iABC.net; IBCD: http://www.IBCD.org; and BCC: www.BiblicalCounselingCenter.org.
90. See http://biblicalcc.org.
91. Kellemen, *Equipping Counselors for Your Church.*
92. Ibid.
93. Strauch, *Hospitality Commands,* 7.
94. See also chapter 17 of this book, Kellemen, "Ethical and Legal Issues in Biblical Counseling in the Church: Caring Like Christ."
95. For those who are licensed as professional counselors, you will want to clarify with them that they are serving as volunteers, and make that clear to those they counsel as well. If you charge for counseling, it may be harder to claim that only volunteers are involved.
96. Adapted from the *Blanchard Situational Leadership II Model,* chapter 12.
97. http://www.usachurches.org/church-sizes.htm. Accessed March 20, 2015.
98. For a detailed discussion of the biblical counseling approach and the integrative approach, see Kellemen and Forrey, editors, *Scripture and Counseling.*
99. Kellemen, *Equipping Counselors for Your Church.*
100. Stetzer, "Multisite Churches."
101. See also Paul's encouragement in Ephesians 4:12 and 2 Timothy 2:2.
102. Luther, *Works of Martin Luther,* 31.
103. The Association of Certified Biblical Counselors, www.biblicalcounseling.com.
104. The Institute for Biblical Counseling and Discipleship, www.IBCD.org.
105. Jay Adams calls our meetings with non-Christians "pre-counseling."
106. We have been threatened with lawsuits from time to time. Much to our surprise, our biggest problems have been with people with whom we were not directly involved in the counseling (e.g., an angry husband who didn't like the counsel we gave his wife threatened to sue us). So far, by God's grace, we have had no significant legal problems.
107. Some counseling centers are unwilling to counsel someone unless a church leader will come to the counseling with him/her.
108. When counselees come from a church that does not affirm the gospel, we make the gospel a focal point in the counseling and seek to help the counselees draw their own conclusion from Scripture about their need to find a new church.
109. "Help! I Need a Church" by Jim Newheiser is currently self-published by IBCD (Institute for Biblical Counseling and Discipleship), but is due to come out soon as a booklet published by Shepherd Press.
110. We often say that our counseling is like triage in an emergency room. We help with the crisis, but then we need to hand them over to someone in their own local church for ongoing care. This is why it is important to involve the local church early in the counseling. Counselees aren't ready to graduate until you are confident that they will be shepherded in their local church.

111. We are grieved at how often we see pastors from biblical churches sending their members to counselors whose approach is very unbiblical.
112. IBCD's Care and Discipleship program is designed for this purpose; see www.IBCD.org.
113. Usually the weekends are not consecutive, but every third or fourth weekend.
114. Powlison, "Sufficiency of Scripture," 3–14.
115. Tripp, *Instruments in the Redeemer's Hands*, 108–12.
116. I (Charles) address some of these issues in two books: *Prejudice and the People of God*, which I authored, and *One Race, One Blood*, which I coauthored with Ken Ham.
117. Adams, "What Is 'Nouthetic' Counseling?"
118. For launching and leading formal biblical counseling ministries in the local church, see Kellemen, *Equipping Counselors for Your Church*.
119. See Hambrick, "Competency of the Biblical Counselor."
120. See chapter 3, Kellemen, *Gospel Conversations*.
121. Hendriksen, *Galatians and Ephesians*, 224–25.
122. Gundmann, *Theological Dictionary*, 3–4.
123. See chapters 6–7, Kellemen, *Gospel-Centered Counseling*.
124. See Adams, *Competent to Counsel* and *Theology of Christian Counseling*.
125. Ohlschlager and Mosgofian, *Law for the Christian Counselor*, 154.
126. Kellemen, *Equipping Counselors for Your Church*, 405, with modifications.
127. Ohlschlager and Mosgofian, *Law*, 17.
128. Quine, *Legal Issues*, 2.
129. Levicoff, *Christian Counseling and the Law*, 84–85.
130. We should not assume that eliminating all mixed gender counseling removes all possibility of sexual temptation or inappropriate behavior. Same-sex counselor/counselee attraction and seduction also must be guarded against.
131. Levicoff, *Law*, 71–73.
132. Ibid., 105–15.
133. Ibid., 110.
134. Quine, *Legal Issues*, 5.
135. Levicoff, *Law*, 114.
136. Sigley, "Evangelism Implosion," 5–11, 7.
137. The main verb is an imperative (make disciples) and is modified by three circumstantial participles (going, baptizing, and teaching). All three participles carry with them an imperatival force; however, the main thrust of the verse is to make disciples.
138. This apologetic trilemma, a choice between three options, was popularized by Lewis, especially in *Mere Christianity*, 54–56. In all editions, this is bk. II, ch. 3, "The Shocking Alternative."
139. Collins, "Letter to Christian Counselors," 37–39.
140. These first-generation biblical counseling para-church ministries were the Christian Counseling & Educational Foundation (CCEF); the Biblical Counseling Foundation (BCF); the National Association of Nouthetic

Counselors (NANC, now the Association of Certified Biblical Counselors, ACBC); the *Journal of Pastoral Practice* (now the *Journal of Biblical Counseling*); and Presbyterian & Reformed Publishing.

141. Winter's "Two Structures of God's Redemptive Mission" was seminal in defining para-church missions as a crucial aspect of how the Spirit has worked in history in order to build churches.

142. Some of these books have included Adams, *Christian Counselor's Manual*; Wayne Mack's contributions to MacArthur, *Counseling*; Tripp, *Instruments in the Redeemer's Hands*; and Powlison, *Speaking Truth in Love.*

143. Several certifying organizations now exist: the Association of Certified Biblical Counselors, the International Association of Biblical Counselors, and the Association of Biblical Counselors.

144. These include the Statement of Faith drawn up by the Biblical Counseling Coalition (www.biblicalcc.org); the Standards of Conduct available from the Association of Certified Biblical Counselors (www.biblicalcounseling.com), and "Affirmations and Denials" by Powlison in *Speaking Truth in Love.*

145. Dempster, "Knowledge for What? Recovering the Lost Soul," 37–57.

146. Marsden, *Soul of the American University*, 37.

147. Dempster, "Knowledge for What? Recovering the Lost Soul," 46.

148. Ibid.

149. Carson helpfully observes that Christ is neither *against* culture nor *transforming* culture exclusively. He operates in both ways simultaneously. Thus, Christians "embrace the exclusive claims of Christ and *the uniqueness of the church as the locus of redeeming grace*" (emphasis mine), yet also "reflect on the ubiquitous commands not only to love God but also to love their neighbors as themselves." Carson, *Christ & Culture*, 227.

150. The church is not the kingdom itself, but the earthly steward and herald of this kingdom, as Ladd explains: "The church is the community of the kingdom but never the kingdom itself. Jesus' disciples belong to the kingdom as the kingdom belongs to them; but they are not the kingdom. The kingdom is the rule of God; the church is the society of man." Ladd, *Theology of the New Testament*, 111.

151. For an excellent historical survey of this trend, see part 1 of Marsden, *Soul of the American University*, 33–99.

152. For an excellent summary of theology as a science, see Erickson, *Christian Theology*, 36.

153. Pelikan, *Idea of the University*, 34.

154. Ibid.

155. Henry, *God, Revelation, and Authority*, 92.

156. "While others might be satisfied if students perform well on the examinations, the best teachers assume that learning has little meaning unless it produces a sustained and substantial influence on the way people think, act, and feel." Bain, *What the Best College Teachers Do*, 17.

157. Hendricks, *Teaching to Change Lives*, 53–64.

158. Ibid., 55.
159. Adams, *Insight and Creativity*, x.
160. Frame, *Systematic Theology*, 8.
161. Ibid., 6.
162. Adams, *Competent to Counsel*, 260.
163. For ideas on counseling training methods, see Kellemen, *Equipping Counselors for Your Church*, 251 – 75. The ideas are also applicable for academic settings.
164. Benjamin Warfield, *Religious Life of Theological Students*, 7.
165. Miller, *Evangelism and Your Church*, 14.
166. We will evaluate how biblical counseling is doing in this mission, based on the content that is found on the following websites: the Biblical Counseling Coalition (BCC), the Association of Certified Biblical Counseling (ACBC), the Christian Counseling and Educational Foundation (CCEF), and the Association of Biblical Counselors (ABC). *Biblical counseling* is not a trademarked name, so there are many individuals and some groups that are not included in these organizations, but these four offer a representative sample of the movement.
167. Berkouwer, *Man: The Image of God*, 195.
168. Read Watters, *Crazy Like Us: The Globalization of the American Psyche*.
169. Jones, "Constructive Relationship for Religion with the Science and Profession of Psychology," 182 – 86.
170. Paul Vitz, *Psychology as Religion: The Cult of Self-Worship* (Grand Rapids, MI: Eerdmans, 1995).
171. Bettler, "CCEF: The Beginning," 45 – 51.
172. Howard Clinebell was a prolific writer, working on more than twenty books, some of which he cowrote or edited. He was best known for two titles of his own, the first being *Understanding and Counseling the Alcoholic through Religion and Psychology*, published in 1956 and updated many times. He provided leadership in the religious community that led to the acceptance of the disease model of alcoholism. His most influential book was likely *Basic Types of Pastoral Counseling* (1966).
173. Powlison, *Biblical Counseling Movement*, 1 – 50.
174. Bettler, "CCEF," 48 – 50.
175. Ganz, *PsychoBabble*.
176. Ganz email interview February 14, 2014.
177. Adams, "Looking Back," 1 – 3.
178. Johnson and Jones, eds., *Psychology & Christianity*, recognized biblical counseling as one of the four main views of counseling alongside the levels-of-explanation model, integration model, and Christian psychology model.
179. Steve Viars at Association of Biblical Counselors Symposium, moderated by Jeremy Lelek and John Henderson, http://biblicalcounselingcoalition.org/resources/biblical-counseling-symposium-steve-viars.
180. Braverman, "6 Ways Obamacare Is Changing Mental Health Coverage."

While we may well question the criteria for use of "mental health" as the basis of these statistics, the reality is that more and more people are in need of counseling and therapy.

181. Ibid.
182. Ibid.
183. Christensen, "Feds Boosting Mental Health Access."
184. Beck, "Getting Mental-Health Care at the Doctor's Office."
185. Whitaker, *Anatomy of an Epidemic*, 3.
186. Beck, "Getting Mental-Health Care."
187. Powlison, "Counseling *Is* the Church," 6.
188. Biblical Counseling Coalition, "Mission Statement."
189. Bettler, "CCEF," 47.
190. Powlison, "Crucial Issues."
191. BCC Council members: Heath Lambert, Jeremy Pierre, Stuart Scott. http://www.sbts.edu/theology/degree-programs/ma/biblical-counseling/.
192. http://rts.edu/charlotte/newsevents/NewsDetails.aspx?id=1966.
193. BCC Council members: David Powlison, Ed Welch, Mike Emlet. http://www.wts.edu/academics/programs/biblicalcounseling_2.html.
194. BCC Council members: John Street, Ernie Baker, Bob Sommerville. Undergraduate: http://masters.edu/academics/undergraduate/biblicalstudies.aspx; Graduate: http://masters.edu/academics/graduate/mABC.aspx.
195. BCC Council members: Robert Jones, Sam Williams, Brad Hambrick. http://catalog.sebts.edu/preview_program.php?catoid=5&poid=530&returnto=117.
196. BCC Council member: Jeremy Lelek. http://redeemer.edu/academics/disciplines/.
197. BCC Council members: Rob Green, Bob Kellemen, Steve Viars, Kevin Carson, Stuart Scott, Robert Jones. http://www.faithlafayette.org/seminary.
198. BCC Council member: Kevin Carson. http://gobbc.edu/graduate/programs/biblical-counseling/ma-biblical-counseling-overview.
199. BCC Council members: Bob Kellemen, Lilly Park, Charles Ware. http://www.crossroads.edu/academics/programs/bachelorofscience/biblicalcounseling.php.
200. BCC Council member: Howard Eyrich. http://birminghamseminary.org/?page_id=426.
201. David Powlison notes in his article "Crucial Issues in Contemporary Biblical Counseling" that many outsiders viewed BC as "anti-intellectual and simpleminded," 71.
202. Ibid.
203. Bob Kellemen, "Pastoral Counselor Preparation in Evangelical Seminary MDiv Programs: Toward a Best Practice Statement of Purpose, Theology, Pedagogy, Curriculum, and Educator" (paper presented at the annual meeting for the Evangelical Theological Society, Milwaukee, Wisconsin, November 14–16, 2012).

204. Powlison, "Counseling *Is* the Church," 6. Powlison notes five areas in need of improvement: (1) We need to become wise in the face-to-face cure of souls. (2) We need creedal standards in cure of souls, or at least a widely recognized corpus of practical theological writing. (3) We need educational institutions committed to the Bible's distinctive model of understanding persons and change. (4) We need cure of souls to become part of the church's qualifying procedures that recognize trustworthy and skillful practitioners. (5) We need ecclesiastically grounded supervisory structures for cure of souls.

205. Some sample churches include The Summit Church, University Reformed Church, The Village Church, Parkside Church, Faith Church, Harvest Bible Chapel, Capitol Hill Baptist, Sojourn Community Church, Bethlehem Baptist Church, Briarwood Presbyterian, Covenant Life Church, and College Park Church.

206. Turlock, *In the Hands of Providence*, 154–55. Part of Chamberlain's speech at the dedication of the 20th Maine monument at Gettysburg.

207. Piper, *Don't Waste Your Life*, 111.

208. Tripp, *Instruments in the Redeemer's Hands*, 66–67.

209. Piper, *Don't Waste Your Life*, 110, 112.

210. See the Biblical Counseling Coalition website for archived testimonies of transformed lives using the principles of Scripture. http://biblicalcounseling-coalition.org/resources/testimonials/. And see Scott and Lambert, *Counseling the Hard Cases*, for examples of using biblical principles to deal with difficult counseling situations.

SCRIPTURE INDEX

SUBJECT INDEX

A

academic institutions
  biblical counseling programs at, 415
  partnerships with, 414–17
  practical knowledge, 370–73
  theoretical knowledge, 373–76
  transference of knowledge, 376–81
Adams, Jay, 56, 57, 63, 65, 213, 350, 404, 406, 410, 415
addictions groups, 142, 203, 387
advocates, 64, 69, 70
aids for counseling
  social media, 285–86
  teaching aids, 246–47, 287–88
Aliens in the Promised Land, 257
Allchin, Ron, 18, 190, 456
Allchin, Tim, 18, 190, 456
American Psychologist, 393
Anatomy of an Epidemic, 412
antechomai counseling, 300
Association of Biblical Counselors (ABC), 150, 200
Association of Certified Biblical Counselors (ACBC), 57, 200, 241, 272, 406

B

Baker, Ernie, 19, 419, 457
Beautiful Mind, A, 387

Beck, Melinda, 413
Berkouwer, G.C., 391
Bettler, Dr. John, 402, 404, 407, 410, 414
Bible as the Word, 439–40
biblical counseling. See also church; legalities; biblical counselor training
  academia and, 369–81, 414–17
  administration, 205, 303–4
  attitude to, 40
  challenges, 320–23, 396–97, 421–25
  Christ–like counseling, 297–98, 435–36
  church equipping and, 28, 68–69, 137–41, 425–26, 432–33
  in community, 52, 59–60, 62
  conferences, 245
  conflict resolution and, 172–78, 181–85
  contemporary, 51–52
  counselee homework, 324–27
  counselees, 132–33, 201–2, 249, 320
  counselor equipping, 26–27, 66–71, 119, 145–46, 195–98, 190–200, 201, 202, 207, 218, 236–37, 297, 299, 317, 397–98
  discipleship and, 65, 69, 71, 96, 123, 125, 128, 191–92, 317–18, 335–36
  disciplining, 157–67, 306–7
  ethics in, 204, 290–312, 330
  facilities, 204–5, 214

leadership training, 122–26, 128–29
need for, 219
observing as training, 246
pastor led, 245
preaching and, 358–60
reading as training, 246
redemption groups and, 116–20
screening before, 219–20
biblical soul care. See biblical counseling
biblical value system, 82
Bigney, Brad, 17, 22, 65, 90, 241, 457
Bonhoeffer, Dietrich, 162
Boswell, Andrew, 405
Bradley, Anthony B., 257
Bridges, Jerry, 56, 65

C

Calvin, John, 39, 54
Carson, Kevin, 15, 18, 72, 240, 241, 248,
   314, 457
certification of counselor, 247
Cheong, Robert, 154, 458
Christ. See Jesus
Christian conciliation. 176–78, 187–88
Christian Counseling and Educational
   Foundation (CCEF), 57, 200, 387, 402,
   405, 406
Christian Counselor's Casebook, 406
Christian Counselor's Manual, 406
Christian Legal Society, 177
Christianity, pursuit of knowledge and,
   370–71
church
   belief in, 445–46
   beliefs of, 445–46
   history, 351–53
   importance of, 21, 370–71
   serving, 32
church, large, 210–22
   definition, 240
church, mid-size, 223–33
   definition, 240
church, multicultural, 255–89
   differences, 287–88

issues, 258–60
partnership and, 280–84
training, 284–85
church, para, 349–67
   accountability, 361–62
   collaboration, 360–61
   counseling attributes, 363–67
   training counselors, 358–60
church, small, 240–54
   counseling-scripture for, 243–45
   definition, 240
   issues, 247–48.
Clinebell, Howard, 403
communication, Christ–honouring, 85–86
Competent to Counsel, 56, 404, 406
concilium, 181
CONNECT, 268–70
connectors. See biblical counseling, leaders
Cook, Earl, reminiscence of, 407–8
Cook, Greg, 18, 210, 458
counseling
   importance of, 15–16
   lack of training for, 34–35
   Paul and, 15–16
   Scripture and, 35. See also biblical
      counseling
Counseling and Discipleship Training
   Conference, 102
Counseling in Community (CIC). See
   biblical counseling, in community
Creation, 442
culture, 276–80
   definition of, 276–77

D

Dabler, Judy, 18, 171, 458
data gathering, 63, 329–30
demographic, importance of, 409
depression, 395–96
Dialectical Behavior Therapy (DBT), 392
discipleship, 65, 73, 74
   general, 243
   intensive, 74–75, 95, 243
Discipleship and Counseling Continuum, 59

Scripture and Counseling

God's Word for Life in a Broken World

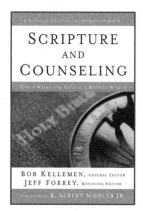

Bob Kellemen, General Editor; Jeff Forrey, Managing Editor

Today we face a tremendous weakening of confidence in the Bible. This is just as true for the pastor offering counsel in his office as it is for the person in the pew talking with a struggling friend at Starbucks or the small group leader who is unsure of what to say to a hurting group member. We need to regain our confidence in God's Word as sufficient to address the real life issues we face today. We need to understand how the Bible equips us to grow in counseling competence as we use it to tackle the complex issues of life.

Scripture and Counseling is divided into two sections of nine chapters each:

Part One helps readers to develop a robust biblical view of Scripture's sufficiency for "life and godliness" leading to increased confidence in God's Word.

Part Two assists readers in learning how to use Scripture in the counseling process. This section demonstrates how a firm grasp of the sufficiency of Scripture leads to increased competence in the ancient art of personally ministering God's Word to others.

Part of the Biblical Counseling Coalition series, *Scripture and Counseling* brings you the wisdom of twenty ministry leaders who write so you can have confidence that God's Word is sufficient, necessary, and relevant to equip God's people to address the complex issues of life in a broken world. It blends theological wisdom with practical expertise and is accessible to pastors, church leaders, counseling practitioners, and students, equipping them to minister the truth and power of God's word in the context of biblical counseling, soul care, spiritual direction, pastoral care, and small group facilitation.